Conversion of a Continent

Conversion of a Continent

Contemporary Religious Change in Latin America

EDITED BY

TIMOTHY J. STEIGENGA
AND EDWARD L. CLEARY

RUTGERS UNIVERSITY PRESS

NEW BRUNSWICK, NEW JERSEY, AND LONDON

LIBRARY OF CONGRESS CATALOGING-IN-PUBLICATION DATA

Conversion of a continent : contemporary religious change in Latin America /
edited by Timothy J. Steigenga and Edward L. Cleary.

    p.   cm.

Includes bibliographical references and index.

ISBN 978-0-8135-4201-0 (hardcover : alk. paper) -- ISBN 978-0-8135-4202-7
(pbk. : alk. paper)

    1. Latin America--Religion.   2. Conversion--Latin America.   I. Steigenga,
Timothy J., 1965–   II. Cleary, Edward L.

    BL2540.C67   2007

    204'.2--dc22   2007006032

                                             CIP

A British Cataloging-in-Publication record for this book is available
from the British Library.

This collection copyright © 2007 by Rutgers, The State University

Individual chapters copyright © 2007 in the names of their authors

Visit our Web site: http://rutgerspress.rutgers.edu

Manufactured in the United States of America

CONTENTS

PART TWO

Conversion to What?

PART THREE

The Implications of Conversion

ACKNOWLEDGMENTS

The editors would like to express our deepest thanks to our contributors and all those who read various drafts of this book. The impetus for this publishing project was provided by Andrew Walls and Lamin Sanneh through their mentorship of the Yale-Edinburgh Conference on World Christianity. Their framing of the issue of conversion for one of the annual conferences sparked serious reflection on the role of religious conversion in the context of Latin America. Many others, especially colleagues from the Latin American Studies Association, helped to refine the concepts presented in the book. Special thanks to Adi Hovav for her patience and guidance throughout the process of bringing this project to fruition. We would also like to thank Anna Peterson, who provided invaluable insights and direction through her comments. We owe a particular debt of gratitude to Johanna Sharp, David Smilde, Rachel Corr, and Henri Gooren, who all provided critical editorial input and technical assistance on many of the contributions to the volume. This book is dedicated to Mary and Emmet Cleary, John and Judy Steigenga, and Maria Graciela Argüelles.

PART ONE

Approaches to Conversion

1

Understanding Conversion in the Americas

TIMOTHY J. STEIGENGA AND EDWARD L. CLEARY

When two noted anthropologists canvassed colonization projects in Bolivia's lowlands, they reached the last house on the newly constructed dirt road. The owner heard them coming and ran out of the house yelling as they approached, "*Soy católico. Nunca van a convertirme*" (I'm Catholic. You're never going to convert me). As they soon discovered, he was the last Catholic left in the project.

Although this story represents the extreme case, it reflects a larger social reality in Latin America and the Caribbean. In a region that was nearly all Catholic just forty years ago, evangelical Protestants now represent approximately 15 percent of the population. In Guatemala estimates of the evangelical population are closer to 30 percent, with the vast majority belonging to Pentecostal or neo-Pentecostal churches.[1] The impact of these religious changes extends beyond the numbers, as many Catholics and Historical Protestants have also adopted some of the religious beliefs and practices of "pentecostalized" religion.[2]

These remarkable and largely unforeseen religious transformations extend to other religious groups as well. Indigenous religious movements and Afro-diasporan religions have also recently gained adherents in the region. Changes within traditional religious categories have accelerated as well. While many Catholics are becoming Pentecostal, many Mainstream Protestants and Classic Pentecostals are also converting to "health and wealth" neo-Pentecostal groups. At the same time, many Catholics have joined more Charismatic Catholic congregations. Among the indigenous groups of the region, millions of "officially" Catholic individuals now openly embrace some form of Mayan or Andean spirituality.

To a large degree, the process and meaning of conversion have been taken for granted in media coverage and many academic accounts of these recent religious changes. After all, if an individual in a survey reports being Catholic last year and a Protestant this year, that individual must have adopted a new set of beliefs along with a new associational participation somewhere in between. A central goal of this volume is to understand what happens in that area in between and to explore the implications for the convert and the surrounding society.

While researchers have made great strides in understanding the macro-level factors that set the context for religious conversion (such as major social and economic upheavals, changes within the Catholic Church, increased Protestant missionary activity, and changes in state policies on religious freedom), they have paid far less attention to questions of exactly who converts and under what circumstances, what the process of conversion entails, and how conversion impacts beliefs and actions. These are some of the key questions we seek to answer in this volume.

This book addresses these gaps in the literature on religious change in the Americas in four primary ways. First, we begin with a critical appraisal of the meaning of conversion. Understanding conversion requires a multi-dimensional and interdisciplinary approach. Rational actor theories, socio-logical analysis, anthropological perspectives, and psychological factors all provide insights, but should not be reified or treated as singular explana-tions for the conversion process. Instead, the authors in this volume adopt a conceptual model that allows us to examine different levels of conversion along a continuum, rather than treating conversion as a single event or static state. Such an approach places greater emphasis on the interactions between agents and contexts, rather than the more traditional "passive" interpretations of conversion. Drawing on empirical and qualitative case studies from Mexico, Brazil, Argentina, Ecuador, Bolivia, Guatemala, Nicara-gua, and the United States, we present an integrative perspective that can be used to guide research on conversion across different contexts and within multiple disciplines.

The second contribution follows from the first. If the definition and pro-cess of conversion are more problematic than has been previously suggested, the effects of conversion are as well. The political, economic, and social effects of conversion are multiple, complex, and even counterintuitive. From the indigenous Mexican woman who gains personal empowerment through her conversion and involvement with a local Pentecostal congregation to the Guatemalan presidential candidate who preaches the "health and wealth gospel" to a neo-Pentecostal congregation in Houston, conversion holds

different meanings to different individuals across contexts. Crude generalizations linking Pentecostalism to political authoritarianism and corporatism have not held up under empirical scrutiny. At the same time, overly
optimistic assessments linking Latin America's new religious pluralism to
democratization and upward social mobility have proven premature. This
volume makes a unique contribution, providing empirical case studies that
not only document the political complexities of recent religious changes,
but also point toward a new and more fruitful research agenda for understanding those changes. As Jeffrey Rubin has recently argued, we may gain
a better understanding of the effects of social and religious movements in
Latin America if we investigate the manner in which they introduce alternative rationalities, discourses, and narratives into public spaces, rather than
forcing our "square peg" research subject into the "round hole" of classic
sociological, anthropological, and political conceptions of "resistance" versus "accommodation."[3]

Third, this book addresses religious changes in Latin America beyond
the shift from Catholic to Protestant. By comparing conversion between
the various religious groups in Latin America's expanding religious market,
we provide a more accurate picture of the religious choices being made by
converts. From the "pentecostalization" of many Catholic and Mainstream
Protestant congregations to the growth of Afro-Brazilian and indigenous
religious movements, we can trace the movement of single individuals in
their conversion careers as well as compare the key variables involved in the
process of conversion across religious traditions.

Finally, this volume brings together insights from Latin American case
studies with existing literature and theory on conversion. By bringing Latin
American scholarship into dialogue with what has been primarily a Euro-
and North American–centric field of study, we can both refine our analytical
tools for studying conversion and gain new insights based on empirical and
qualitative case studies.

In order to provide the background necessary to address these issues,
we begin this chapter with a brief discussion of issues related to the definition and measurement of conversion. We then turn to an overview of the
changing Latin American religious landscape, again paying special attention to the key definitional issues that frequently cloud studies of religious
change and generate controversy over how religious adherents are counted
in the region. In the third part, we review some of the major approaches
to explaining religious change in Latin America, with a particular focus on
the implications for the study of conversion. The fourth section introduces
basic themes and guidelines for the study of conversion that arise from the
contributions to this volume and provides an overview of the organization
of the book.

Defining and Measuring Religious Conversion

One of the foremost scholars of conversion, Lewis R. Rambo, recently noted that "the definition of conversion remains a vexing problem" for academic studies.[4] In part, this is because the issues of defining and measuring conversion are thoroughly intertwined. Within the wide disciplinary range of European and North American scholars studying the theme, there has been a general consensus that conversion involves a process of radical personal change in beliefs, values, and, to some degree, personal identity and worldview.[5] However, questions about how to measure these changes (self-identification, degree of commitment, beliefs and convictions, demonstration events, and discourse or rhetorical indicators), which level of analysis to utilize (individual, societal, cultural, network location, or market analysis), and the role of personal agency versus external contextual factors remain matters of significant dispute and debate.[6] By bringing Latin American scholarship and empirical case studies into dialogue with this existing literature, we can begin to address these definitional and measurement issues.

A number of authors working in Latin America have argued that traditional Pauline (and, generally, North American) conceptions of conversion are challenged by evidence from the Brazilian case. In her widely cited work on cults of possession and Pentecostalism in Brazil, Patricia Birman introduces the concept of "passages" between and within religious traditions rather than clear-cut conversion.[7] Another Brazilian author, Clara Mafra, raises the notion of minimal conversions for understanding this phenomenon.[8] As some neo-Pentecostal churches move closer and closer to secular norms and society, they may reduce the tensions between the sacred and the secular sufficiently to make the process of conversion a less than drastic change. Yet another critique of classic concepts of conversion focuses on the syncretic nature of Brazilian culture and identity, arguing that because Brazilian culture is creolized and imbued with the sacred to a much higher degree than other places, transit between religious groups is a natural and non-dramatic occurrence for many converts. Taken together, these studies force us to take a closer look at what we mean by conversion in the Latin American context. If conversion is not always characterized by a dramatic change in religious beliefs and values, how can we define and utilize the concept in comparative study?

Distilling the insights from a vast literature on definitions of "conversion," we adopt what Henri Gooren calls a "conversion careers" approach, assessing levels of conversion as well as the movement in these levels over time. In contrast to previous models of conversion, the conversion career approach may be understood as "the member's passage, within his or her social and cultural context, through levels, types, and phases of church participation."[9] Gooren's model provides us with a five-level continuum for defining and measuring conversion (pre-affiliation, affiliation, conversion, confession, and disaffiliation). Adopting this continuum for measuring individual religious change allows us to bridge the gap between the Brazilian literature on passages and minimal conversions without discarding the traditional meaning of the term "conversion" altogether. Individuals may move in and out of various affiliations over time or even at the same time, with the categories of conversion and confession reserved for the elements of radical personal change in worldview, identity, participation, and discourse associated with classic definitions of conversion.

Thus, throughout this volume, we argue for a definition of conversion as a process rather than an isolated event. While the Pauline paradigm of conversion as a sudden, dramatic, and all-encompassing event certainly has a place within a continuum of conversion, uncritical acceptance of such a paradigm can cause us to miss important data and processes related to conversion. We argue that conversion takes place over time, interacts with institutional religious, network, and cultural contexts, and does not necessarily proceed in a linear or chronological fashion.

Sketching the Latin American Religious Field: Definitions, Meanings, and Numbers

The study of religious change in Latin America has long been plagued by the use of confusing terminology and questionable methods for counting adherents. In the interests of clarity and consistency, we present this brief outline of the major religious groups in Latin America as well as some of the issues raised in measuring changes between and within groups.[10]

Variations on the Growth of Protestantism

For the most part, scholars of Latin American religion and demographers have utilized the term *evangélicos* (evangelicals) to refer broadly to a wide range of Protestant groups. While the specific historical meaning of "evangelical" in the United States relates to its emphasis on conversion and the corresponding call to evangelize (as well as an emphasis on reading the Gospel), in Latin America the term is frequently used to include Classic Pentecostals, neo-Pentecostals, Historical (or Mainstream) Protestants, non-denominational Protestants, and, in some cases, Seventh-Day Adventists.[11] For the purposes of this volume, we will utilize the term "evangelical" in this broad sense, to refer to an entire range of Protestant groups.

Within the broad category of evangelicals, however, we explicitly distinguish the various historical and theological differences between Protestant denominations. Historical (or mainstream) denominations in Latin America, such as the Methodists, Presbyterians, Episcopalians, and Lutherans, have the longest history in the region and trace their Latin American roots both to immigrants and to early missionary movements of the nineteenth and twentieth centuries. Despite their long-term presence, both census and church-growth statistics suggest that most of the Historical Protestant denominations are primarily losing membership in Latin America.

Pentecostalism (or Classic Pentecostalism) was born in the North American "Holiness" movement of the early 1900s and made its way into Latin America through missionary movements and transnational religious networks throughout the century.[12] Pentecostal growth in the region increased most rapidly beginning in the 1960s, with intensified missionary movements from North America and increases in the number of Latin American pastors trained within Pentecostal churches. Latin American Pentecostal churches traditionally stress the importance of divine healing, empowerment through the Holy Spirit, speaking in tongues, asceticism, and a dramatic personal conversion. Examples of Pentecostal denominations prevalent in Latin America include the Assemblies of God, Four Square Gospel Church, the Church of God, and other independent churches characterized by a charismatic style of worship and evangelization. While the growth rates of Pentecostalism vary between countries and regions (and apostasy rates within the churches are high), there is a general consensus that Pentecostalism is continuing to gain shares in the Latin American religious marketplace.

Beginning in the late 1960s and early 1970s, a number of independent or semi-independent neo-Pentecostal (sometimes called neo-Charismatic) denominations and churches were formed in the United States and Latin America. While Pentecostal in origin, the defining features of these churches are that they are generally independent of strict North American leadership, tend to relax some of the strict requirements of Classic Pentecostalism (such as speaking in tongues and strict asceticism), and also preach some form of prosperity theology (otherwise known as the "health and wealth gospel"). Neo-Pentecostal churches are among the fastest-growing churches in Latin America. Examples include the Brazilian IURD (Igreja Universal do Reino de Deus, or Universal Church of the Kingdom of God) and other transnational churches such as Elím and El Verbo.

Another term frequently used to describe evangelicals in Latin America is "fundamentalist." Fundamentalism is not particularly useful as a categorical term in the Latin American context because various elements of fundamentalism pervade religious beliefs and practices across denominational lines in the region. At its most basic, fundamentalism implies attention to the religious fundamentals, doctrinal orthodoxy, and strict asceticism. Generally, groups who feel themselves to be "at risk" in society often return to certain sacred "fundamentals" as a method for both staving off the attacks of modernity and reclaiming their own place in a sacred history. Strict Christian fundamentalists may reject some of the charismatic "gifts of the Spirit" embraced by Pentecostalism, but many Pentecostals and some Charismatic Catholics embrace fundamentalist asceticism and doctrinal orthodoxy as part of the general package of beliefs and practices associated with their religion.

Other religious groups with a significant missionary presence in Latin America (sometimes referred to as neo-Christian groups) include the Mormons, Seventh-Day Adventists, and Jehovah's Witnesses. Though their total numbers are not as large as the combined numbers from Pentecostal and neo-Pentecostal churches, these groups have gained significant numbers of adherents throughout the region and now represent a permanent feature in the Latin American religious landscape.[13]

Diversity within the Catholic Church

While the growth of other religious groups in Latin America is commonly assumed to come at the expense of the Catholic Church, the reality is that Catholicism has also experienced a major internal revival during the same time period. Catholicism has certainly lost shares as a self-reported percentage of the population throughout the region, but many experts argue that the Catholic Church is more vibrant and healthy than ever before.[14] This apparent paradox can be explained by two factors. First, the major sector of Catholicism affected by this shift has been that of nominal, indifferent Catholics, who have supplied the majority of the converts to other religious groups.[15] This pool of nominal Catholics has historically been quite large. In 1960 probably two-thirds of the Catholic population seldom or never attended church. Second, religious competition and an ensuing process of diversification have spurred major changes within the Catholic Church. Today, it may be more accurate to speak of Catholicisms than a single tendency. Catholics committed to social justice, members of the Catholic Charismatic Renewal (CCR), acculturated indigenous Catholics, and traditional Catholics all occupy pews in the same church.

The evidence that Catholicism is also benefiting from Latin America's religious pluralism is significant. First, in a number of surveys over time, the Catholic Church has repeatedly received the highest level of confidence of any social institution.[16] Second, the church has acquired a substantial increase in its workforce. In the forty-year period between 1964 and 2004, the number of priests in the region increased by 70 percent. This stands in marked contrast to the well-publicized decline in clergy in the United States and Europe. In Mexico alone the number of priests more than doubled during this period. In Mexico, as in most of Latin America, the increases to the priesthood have come mainly from Latin Americans and not from the presence of foreign missionaries. At the same time, seminarians in college and graduate theological schools have increased 599 percent between 1972 and 2004. Religious sisters increased overall modestly and provide some 128,000 pastoral workers and contemplative prayer sources in the region.[17] Thus, faced with increasing competition from a diverse set of religious actors, the Catholic Church has responded with its own institutional resources and lay participation, leading to its own internal movement of religious revitalization and diversification.

Indigenous and African Diaspora Religious Movements

Among the approximately forty million indigenous persons living in Latin America, the majority practice some form of syncretism, mixing native religion mostly with Catholicism, but also with Protestantism, particularly in Guatemala, southern Mexico, and Paraguay. Recently there has also been a significant movement toward native (or neonative) spirituality among a number of indigenous groups and individuals in Latin America. From Andean spiritual leaders who seek to revive elements, practices, and symbols of their Inca heritage to Mayan religious practitioners who emphasize their pan-Mayan identity in Guatemala and Southern Mexico, there is a self-reflective process of cultural rescue and synthesis underway in the region. While it is too early to tell how "popular" these religious movements will become, there are clear signs that pre-Columbian symbols, practices, and beliefs are playing a greater role in the Latin American religious arena than they did fifteen or twenty years ago.

Finally, some of the fastest-growing religious groups in Latin America include African diasporan religions such as Brazilian Candomblé, Umbanda, and Haitian Vodou. Estimates are that some fifteen million people practice African-based religions, primarily in Brazil and Haiti, but these religions are spreading to other countries as well. As Andrew Chesnut has argued, it is difficult to measure the exact numbers of practitioners among these groups due to the historical stigma associated with membership.[18] Many practitioners simply self-identify as Catholics when asked by census takers.

The dilemma of how to count parishioners or adherents is not unique to the diasporan groups. Another major hurdle for measuring conversion in the context of Latin America is the issue of gaining accurate estimates for all religious affiliations. With the outlines of the major Latin American religious competitors drawn, we will now turn to a discussion of the figures used to measure religious change and movement between religious groups.

Numbers and Changes in the Religious Field

Statistics estimating the distribution of religious groups in Latin America are widely disputed, as they are collected by various governmental, academic, and religious organizations using different methods and different categories. Furthermore, the contributions to this volume suggest that there is frequent movement between and within religious groups, making the use of static figures even more problematic. The case of Guatemala provides a perfect example of this dilemma for social scientists seeking accurate statistics on religious affiliation. According to the *International Religious Freedom Report 2005*, released by the United States Bureau of Democracy, Human Rights, and Labor, estimates of the percentage of the Guatemalan population affiliated with Protestant and other non-Catholic groups (not including Jewish and Muslim Guatemalans) are approximately 40 percent.[19] According to Guatemala's 1994 census, however, the number of self-reported Protestants at that time was only 22 percent. Detailed 2005 statistics from the World Christian Database at the Center for the Study of Global Christianity at Gordon-Conwell Theological Seminary produce an even lower combined figure for membership in Protestant denominations of 1,945,100 (a little more than 15 percent) in a population of approximately 12.7 million.[20] However, the highly respected CID-Gallup polling organization estimated a population of 29.8 percent Protestant in their November 2001 poll conducted in Guatemala.[21]

What are we to make of these bewildering discrepancies? In each case we must consider the source. In many cases, religious institutions utilize weights and multipliers to enhance their statistics. In other cases, simple attendees are counted as adherents. Other new churches and nondenominational churches tend to be left out of denominational-based church-growth statistics. Furthermore, in some countries (such as Chile) the census includes detailed data on religious affiliation, while in other countries (such as Guatemala) it does not. Even in those countries that do collect census data on religious affiliation, the response categories frequently differ and include categories such as "Christian" which cannot be disaggregated into specific denominational groups.

Second, where reliable census data is available, we can make reasonably accurate estimates of the proportions of the population that self-report as belonging to the major religious groups. In Brazil, the 2000 census data produced a figure of 15 percent Protestants, the vast majority of whom are Pentecostals or neo-Pentecostals. Seventy-four percent of Brazilians self-identify as Catholics, but few report regularly attending Mass. While census takers found only 4 percent of the population who self-identified as practitioners of Afro-Brazilian religion, academics estimate that the actual figure remains significantly higher, with some estimates as high as 30 percent.[22] In the Chilean census of 1992 and 2002, the percentage of self-reported Protestants grew from 12.4 to 15.1 percent of the population, while self-reported Catholics dropped from 76.8 percent to 70.0 percent over the same period. In Mexico, generally considered one of the most Catholic countries in Latin

America, the 2000 census reported a Catholic population of 88 percent, with less than 5 percent self-reporting as Protestant. In the state of Chiapas, however, nearly 22 percent of respondents reported a Protestant identification. The estimates for other countries in the region fall between Guatemala on the high end, with reliable estimates for evangelicals reaching 30 percent, to countries such as Uruguay, Paraguay, Colombia, and Venezuela, with figures between 3 and 5 percent Protestant. The Central American region is the most heavily Protestant, with reliable estimates for Costa Rica, Honduras, El Salvador, Nicaragua, and Panama that range from 15 to 20 percent. In the Andean region, estimates for Bolivia, Ecuador, and Peru fall between 10 and 15 percent. Census information on religion is not collected in Argentina, but individual studies suggest a Protestant population of approximately 10 percent.[23]

As these figures make clear, counting religious adherents and measuring religious change in Latin America is no simple task. While census data and some academic studies produce reliable estimates, it is frequently only well after major shifts have taken place that the data become available to confirm these religious changes. The issue is further complicated by the fact that static counts and estimates cannot fully capture the dynamic nature of religious change. Recent data on disaffiliation and recidivism illustrate these complications, but also lead to important insights for the study of conversion.

Disaffiliation and Recidivism

A number of recent studies have suggested that relatively high levels of recidivism are slowing or even stopping the growth of Protestantism in the region. Kurt Bowen's study of Protestantism in Mexico found that a full 43 percent of those raised in Protestant churches were no longer Protestants as adults.[24] Bowen suggests that the sectarian zeal (demonstrated through asceticism and charismaticism) of Pentecostalism in Mexico is maintained precisely because of the high drop-out rate. He calculates that 68 percent of those baptized into Protestant churches in Mexico during the 1980s had left by 1990.[25]

Data from surveys conducted in Guatemala and Costa Rica in the early 1990s also help us to evaluate trends in conversion and recidivism. In a 1993 survey, 98 percent of the Catholics polled reported having always been Catholic. Among Protestants, 58 percent of Mainstream Protestants and 64 percent of Pentecostals claimed that these had always been their religion. Of those who had converted to their present religion, over 80 percent of Protestants were previously Catholic and nearly 12 percent were previously not affiliated with any religious group. Perhaps most surprising, 37 percent of the religiously non-affiliated reported that they had, at some point, experienced a religious conversion. These findings lead to four important insights for the study of conversion.[26]

First, a significant majority (over 60 percent) of Protestants in these polls were raised in the religion they now practice, challenging the conventional wisdom that evangelical churches are primarily filled with converts from other religions. At the same time, this does not mean that these individuals have not experienced a personal conversion. According to the same data set, close to 90 percent of all Protestants polled had experienced a personal conversion. In other words, the experience of a personal conversion is not limited to those who change religions. As the chapters that follow argue, this is strong evidence that the process of conversion must be viewed as more than a single moment of religious change implying a new religious affiliation.

Second, the growth in numbers of evangelicals in Central America (and Latin American in general) may have as much to do with the long-term presence of evangelical churches in certain regions as it does with new membership. In other words, many evangelical churches may have a majority of parishioners that are second- or third-generation Protestants. Because conversion is such an integral part of the evangelical experience in Latin America, even those who are raised in the church are likely to report a process of personal conversion. This fact must be taken into account in both macro-level studies of religious change (such as the religious economy approach) and individual studies of conversion careers.

Third, as noted above, of those Protestants who did report that they converted to their present religion from another, the vast majority (over 80 percent) were formerly Catholic. Only a little more than 10 percent were previously non-affiliated. This is not surprising, given the dominance of Catholicism in the region and the historically large pool of nominal Catholics present there.[27]

Finally, the high number of religiously non-affiliated (37 percent) who report a conversion experience provides evidence that many individuals pass in and out of religious affiliations over the course of their lives. When asked about their religious experience, 13 percent of the religiously non-affiliated reported that they had spoken in tongues. An amazing 57 percent reported the experience of a miraculous cure to some physical ailment or disease. These figures suggest that a significant number of those who self-report as religiously non-affiliated have participated in some form of charismatic religious practice. Again, by conceptualizing conversion on a scale we can capture the subtleties and degrees of religious participation and avoid some of the larger generalizations that have led researchers astray in the past.

An overview of the available data on growth rates, switching, and apostasy within and between Protestant and Catholic groups suggests that the

Latin American religious market remains in a high state of flux. High rates of both conversion and apostasy should serve as a clear sign to investigators that the process of conversion is much more than a one-time event. While certain religious groups continue to experience rapid growth in Latin America (Pentecostal and neo-Pentecostal churches, Mormons, Jehovah's Witnesses, and Afro-diasporan religions), growth rates are uneven and may have reached a relatively steady state in some contexts (such as Guatemala, where the percentage of Protestants has not increased sharply since the 1990s). Other regions, such as the greater Rio de Janeiro area in Brazil, continue to experience rapid growth rates.[28]

With the contours of the new Latin American religious landscape outlined, we can now examine the forces that have led to these major religious changes. What are the factors that have led to the major religious shifts in Latin America, and how do they help us to understand and contextualize the process of religious conversion?

Explaining Religious Change in Latin America

One way to organize the existing theories on religious change in Latin America is in terms of supply-side and demand-side explanations. On the supply side, some authors have focused on historical factors driving people to make new religious choices, including the most extreme versions, implying that conversion to Pentecostalism has been externally imposed by North American missionaries. More recently, a number of authors have interpreted the religious history of Latin America through the lens of religious markets, applying rational-actor assumptions, modeling religious institutions as firms and potential converts as preference-ordering religious consumers.[29]

On the demand side, numerous authors have pointed to the major processes of modernization, industrialization, and social change that have taken place across Latin America during the past forty years as precipitating factors for individual and group religious change. Depending on the context, these authors generally view the process of religious conversion as an individually adaptive, practical, or instrumental action for individual converts in the face of change or crisis. Such approaches include the anomie thesis and cultural perspectives, as well as explanations focusing on survival strategies, family relations, and healing. Some authors who focus on the demand side emphasize the specific religious preferences of a given population as well as the particular religious experiences offered to potential converts. Not surprisingly, demand-side approaches tend to focus more specifically on the act and process of individual conversions, while supply-side arguments generally address the broader macro-level of religious change. As might also be expected, the majority of this literature focuses on the biggest shift in the religious arena, the growth of evangelical Protestantism.

Supply-Side Factors and Religious Markets

The supply-side factors utilized to explain religious change in Latin America have to do with processes that are both external and internal to the region. Internally, one explanation for the high rates of conversion is associated with difficulties faced by the Catholic Church during the past forty years. The centralized nature of authority in the Catholic Church, shortages of national priests, and ongoing ecclesiastical tensions between lay workers, priests, and the hierarchy have served as push factors motivating some Catholics to make the switch to other religious groups.

From the religious market supply-side perspective, the difficulties faced by the Catholic Church have been revealed as Latin America's religious market has opened through guarantees of freedom of religion. Thus, depending on the unit of analysis (utility maximizing individuals, churches, or states), the religious market school emphasizes the production of religious goods in a model where the Catholic Church in Latin America is treated as analogous to a lazy monopolist. Anthony Gill has been the foremost advocate of this rational actor perspective in Latin America, applying it both to explain Pentecostal growth (correlated with market openings where states deregulated their religious markets) and to theorize and predict the actions of state authorities and the institutional Catholic Church.[30] Not surprisingly, the strict religious market approach has generated significant criticism from scholars in the field of religious studies for reducing the complex phenomenon of religious conversion to economic decision making; a point we will return to in the ensuing analysis.

Externally, we must look to the history of missionaries in Latin America to fully understand the supply side of the equation. First, the closing of Asia to missionaries and the battle with communism in the 1950s and 1960s brought Latin America to the attention of the North American religious and political leaders and led to a movement among many U.S. evangelicals to push religious missions as an alternative to communism in the region. While this was by no means the first wave of Protestant missionary activity in the region, it was the most vigorous and sustained up to that point. In many cases, divisions began to form between local church leaders and their North American counterparts. Many local leaders broke from their mother churches, abandoning the cultural barriers constructed around Protestantism by early North American missionaries. These new churches met with rapid success, as local Charismatic leaders made their services more culturally relevant and preached in the native languages of various indigenous groups. These changes combined with the "third wave" of Pentecostal (and

later neo-Pentecostal) Protestant missions to Latin America to produce a
new era of religious diversity.

Given the increasing supply of missionaries and their connections with
right-wing organizations in the United States, it is not surprising that much
of the early literature on conversion in Latin America was characterized
by the notion that religious conversion was externally imposed upon converts.[31] In crude terms, this perspective argued that Protestant missionaries
represented an invading force sent from the North to demobilize those who
might otherwise embrace liberation theology. There was some evidence to
support this interpretation of Protestant growth. Links between missionary organizations, right-wing evangelicals in the United States, and the U.S.
government have been well documented.[32] However, the notion that conversion can be primarily explained by the "external imposition" perspective has
been widely criticized for ignoring the popular and indigenous nature of the
movement, for denying the agency of individual converts, and for questioning the validity of individuals' religious experiences. The fact that the majority of Latin America's Protestant churches are now run by Latin Americans
adds empirical evidence to these critiques.

Demand-Side Explanations for Religious Change

Some of the most influential works on religious change in Latin America
assert that conversion represents an adaptive response to varying external structures and processes. Approaches within this school vary widely in
terms of the reasons for and the implications of conversion. Some influential
authors adopt versions of the "anomie" thesis. In this model, the drastic
changes associated with modernization (urbanization, changing land tenure
patterns, the loss of traditional community) cause a sense of moral uncertainty and a loss of security in terms of relationships and norms of behavior.[33] For other authors, religious conversion (to Pentecostal Protestantism
in particular) is posited as an attractive option either as a new set of norms
that has affinities with individualism and capitalist values,[34] or as a comfort-
ing replication of old norms and values such as corporatism, clientelism, and
authoritarianism.[35] Authors who embrace the first interpretation emphasize
the behavioral aspects of conversion related to pietism and egalitarianism.[36]
Authors from the second school frequently focus on the otherworldly and
millennialist elements of Pentecostal Protestantism.

More recently, a number of authors have stepped back from these broad
claims about the political and economic consequences of conversion and
focused instead on immediate and practical reasons for conversion. David
Stoll argues that conversion to Protestantism represented increased physical
security as well as economic security for potential converts in Guatemala's
Ixil Triangle during Guatemala's civil war. Studies by Cecilia Mariz and John

Burdick focus on religious choices in Brazil's diverse religious marketplace. Rejecting the anomie hypothesis, these authors conclude that conversion to Pentecostalism combines specific strategies for coping with poverty (based in a strict asceticism) with a policy of flexible admission (that allows for illiteracy, racial diversity, and a flexible schedule of religious worship).[37]

In her study of evangelicals in Colombia, Elizabeth Brusco examines the important practical motivations for women to join different congregations. According to Brusco, conversion to Protestantism may increase family cohesion, as Protestant women use religious authority to encourage more responsible behavior by their mates.[38] Cecilia Mariz makes a similar argument, noting that levels of family conflict may drop when women join Pentecostal churches.[39]

Andrew Chesnut's *Born Again in Brazil* also offers a very pragmatic explanation for conversion. According to Chesnut, converts are originally drawn to Pentecostalism when they reach the crisis stage of some form of poverty-related illness (physical, psychological, or social).[40] Chesnut found that after they had exhausted other potential healthcare options, poor Brazilians often turned to Pentecostal faith healers.

While these authors focus on pragmatic or instrumental explanations for conversion, others argue that it is primarily the spiritual, supernatural, experiential, and doctrinal elements of Latin America's new religious competitors that draw new converts. As anthropologist Daniel Míguez argues, motivation for conversion is "defined by people's needs to find answers to transcendental questions and what they feel are appropriate ways to relate to sacred beings and forces."[41] According to Míguez, the primary changes that come with conversion are not cultural, economic, or familial. Rather, it is religious change (in terms of doctrine, practice, rituals, and beliefs) converts seek and converts receive when they join Pentecostal congregations.[42]

Theologian Harvey Cox makes a similar argument. According to Cox, Pentecostal Protestantism is essentially a "restorationist" religious movement in that it helps people to restore "elemental spirituality" in the form of "primal speech" (speaking in tongues), "primal piety" (healing, trance, and other forms of religious expression), and "primal hope" (in the utopian and millennial eschatology of Pentecostalism).[43]

We should note that arguments such as Cox's have also drawn significant criticism for reifying cultural primitivism and/or ignoring critical differences in local culture.[44] In other words, the pneumatic elements of Pentecostalism may hold very different meanings for indigenous Pentecostals in Chiapas and black Brazilian Pentecostals in the slums of Rio de Janeiro. The fact that Pentecostalism is growing in both places requires a deeper explanation than a broad generalization about cultural affinity.

On the other hand, the anomie and practical explanations for conversion also raise legitimate criticisms. If we reify the instrumental nature of conversion as a path to resolving various life crises, we ultimately end up over-predicting the propensity for conversion. After all, many individuals throughout Latin America suffer similar life crises and not all of them change religions. Clearly there is more to conversion than short-term crisis management.

So where does this leave us in terms of conceptualizing and studying conversion in the context of Latin America? The supply-side and demand-side explanations we have outlined thus far provide a start, but they raise as many questions as they answer. How can we bridge supply-side and micro-economic explanations for religious change with demand-side explanations for individual conversion? How can we reconcile what appear to be purely instrumental explanations for conversion with the classic definition implying radical personal change in worldview, identity, participation, and discourse? Finally, how can we reconceptualize the effects of individual and group religious changes in a manner that avoids reifying them into traditional dichotomies of democratic or authoritarian? The chapters in this volume seek to answer these questions by providing a clear and measurable scale of conversion, explanations for conversion that link different levels of analysis (supply, demand, and networks), a critical treatment of the kind of data we utilize to understand conversion (such as conversion narratives), and an analysis of the specific connections between multiple religious and political variables.

Toward an Interdisciplinary Approach to Studying Conversion

Religious conversion has a rich history of study in the fields of theology, psychology, sociology, history, and anthropology.[45] The object of this volume is not to provide a comprehensive review of that literature, nor to directly engage in ongoing debates on the history of colonialism and conversion in the region.[46] Rather, the book is organized thematically into three parts, each corresponding to the major questions surrounding conversion in the Americas.

Defining and Measuring Conversion

Part I introduces the major approaches to defining and analyzing conversion in Latin America. In chapter 2, Alejandro Frigerio addresses Latin American challenges to the Pauline paradigm of conversion and introduces data from Brazil and Argentina to evaluate and compare the models of conversion that have emerged in these two countries. Frigerio concludes that the Brazilian literature advocating jettisoning the concept of conversion suffers from a methodological reliance on single interviews and statistics. He offers statistical evidence from Brazil and long-term ethnographic studies of conversion in Argentina as correctives to this tendency. Henri Gooren's chapter follows, laying out the conversion careers approach to understanding conversion based on an analysis of Pentecostal, Catholic, and Mormon conversion narratives. Gooren argues that personality, social, institutional, cultural, and contingency factors must all be taken into consideration for explaining conversion. Frigerio and Gooren place Latin America in the context of comparative literature on conversion, arguing for an understanding of conversion that is more of a continuum than a single event and providing a specific typology for comparing cases of conversion.

As these authors point out, tracking and measuring religious changes require a methodology that can capture the complex process of conversion. Qualitative interviews and survey data are both useful tools for understanding elements of conversion, but they have to be complemented with corroborating information through sustained participant observation to capture the unfolding of conversion careers. Furthermore, researchers must pay greater attention to who we interview when we study conversion. If we do not interview non-converts as well as converts, we are missing one-half of the story; a critical half for understanding the variables that interact to produce conversion. In order to understand who moves from affiliation to conversion and confession, we must take care to interview religious insiders and outsiders as well as individuals at all stages of the conversion career. Neglecting to include these control groups in the study of conversion has led some researchers to over-predict the causal nature of precipitant events, drug use, stress, and other emotional or psychological states in the conversion process.[47]

Markets and Networks in Conversion: Linking Levels of Analysis

The final two chapters in part I introduce market and network approaches to conversion in Latin America. In chapter 4 Andrew Chesnut outlines a modified religious market model of conversion to explain the growth of Pentecostal, Charismatic Catholic, and African diasporan religious groups in Latin America. As we noted earlier, the religious market approach has been vigorously criticized for over-emphasizing the role of competition and ignoring the role of individual agency in religious production.[48] Chesnut addresses these critiques by dropping one of the key assumptions underlying strict market approaches, the assumption that demand for religious goods is inelastic. Dropping this assumption allows him to evaluate how local context interacts with the new religious supply to increase the attractiveness of some new religious competitors to potential converts. What Chesnut calls his "heterodox" approach to the religious market calls for an evaluation of both the demand side and the supply side of the market, opening the way for an analysis of product specialization, marketing strategies, and the religious preferences of potential converts. Such an approach allows us to explore variations in religious demand and the multiple strategies religious groups may utilize to meet those demands, re-opening the interactions between agents, networks, and contexts as the locus of study.

The re-opening of the demand side of the market approach has four major benefits for the study of conversion. First, it contextualizes the role of religious economy as most useful for understanding and predicting major shifts in the religious field, rather than as a "stand-alone" theory that explains all levels of analysis in conversion. Second, it helps us to avoid two common pitfalls in the study of conversion: denying agency to converts and denying religious meaning to converts' decisions. Third, it helps us to understand how network, market, and religious-preference approaches can complement rather than contradict each other as explanations for conversion. Finally, it allows us to point out how strictly demand-driven explanations (anomie and crisis-based accounts) over predict conversion and are therefore likely to miss the influence of networks in the conversion process.

In the final chapter of part I, David Smilde takes on the issues of networks and agency in conversion. Based on his research in Caracas, Venezuela, Smilde argues that personal crises addressed by Pentecostalism are widespread among Venezuela's popular sectors and thus do not provide a sufficient explanation for conversion. Smilde discovered that those individuals who did convert either were not living with their family of origin or were living with an evangelical. In Latin America, even nominally Catholic families are a strongly conservative factor working against any type of religious innovation. Thus, those who have moved away from their family of origin are more likely to have the freedom to innovate. Furthermore, these individuals do not benefit from their family's social and cultural support when they confront problems and thus must find alternative solutions such as religious innovation. Those who live with an evangelical are exposed to evangelical meanings and practice. Frequently this leads to a desire to conform to the religious preferences of significant others. In other words, conformity due to network location is one explanation for conversion.

Adding to the strength of the pull to conformity in the case of Pentecostalism and neo-Pentecostalism are three basic advantages inherent in their discourse. First, Pentecostals have a discourse that predicts and explains the "pathologies of poverty" that afflict so many of Latin America's poor. Second, they are extremely persistent in repeating that discourse because it is part of their job as evangelicals to seek further converts. Third, in many cases, individual Pentecostals provide an example that proves attractive to those within their family or network sphere in terms of apparent upward social mobility, overcoming life struggles, and other factors.

Smilde cautions us, however, that some strict sociological network accounts of conversion view demand-side explanations as mere post-hoc rationalizations based on social conformity, thus diminishing the agency of converts.[49] Breaking with this approach, we are able to see that while conformity certainly plays a role in conversion, most individuals still engage in active processes of seeking meaning in an environment of networks that pull them both toward and away from conversion. When individuals find themselves in situations where their sense of personal identity (defined through family, religious, cultural, geographical, or other factors) is ruptured or otherwise strained, they become "structurally available" for joining a different religious or social group.[50] It is precisely at this juncture that we find the key intersection of demand and supply approaches. The broad historical and demand-side approaches provide us with the structural factors that may cause large numbers of people to reach such a point of structural availability (economic, political, and social processes that lead to the breakdown and reconfiguration of former identity ties). The market approach informs us how various religious suppliers may seek to meet this increased demand by offering religious goods that are in line with the preferences and needs of these structurally available individuals. A combination of conscious decisions about life change, exposure to alternative religious discourses and meanings, and location within social networks provides the most complete explanation for why particular individuals make specific religious choices. A narrow focus on only one of these levels of analysis is likely to lead researchers away from the fundamentally interactive nature of religious conversion.

Widening the Field and Analyzing Conversion Narratives: Continuity and Rupture

As Henri Gooren has pointed out, the vast majority of research on religious conversion has taken place in the United States and Europe, is concentrated on young people (generally under the age of thirty), and has tended to focus on sects (such as the Unification Church) rather than the fastest-growing religious movements (such as Pentecostalism) in Latin America, Africa, and Asia.[51] As an antidote to this shortcoming, this volume not only expands the focus of conversion studies to Latin America, but also carefully defines and extends the religious groups under study. Because the religious elements of conversion (doctrine, rituals, beliefs, and practices) are often downplayed in studies of conversion, it is critical to explain and define the differences between the major groups making up the religious field. Thus, part II of the volume provides an overview of some of the major competitors in the evolving Latin American religious market, paying special attention to the process of conversion and the role of narratives in that process.

In chapter 6, Patricia Birman, a leading anthropologist of religion from Rio de Janeiro, outlines some of the key factors driving conversion to neo-Pentecostalism in Brazil as well as some of the political/cultural effects of such conversion. María Julia Carozzi's ensuing chapter 7 analyzes the specific stages of conversion to Umbanda and Candomblé in the context of Argentina, a nontraditional site for these religious movements. As Carozzi's chapter underscores, the rapid growth of African diasporan religions is primarily made up of attendees or affiliates, while access to the "inner circle" of true converts and practitioners is significantly more restricted.

The chapters by Birman and Carozzi point to the key role of narratives for studying conversion. Conversion is defined, in part, by the new discourse repeated in the conversion narrative; pitting past against present and future, good against evil, and old against new as part of adopting a new identity (not only adopting it, but actively reshaping and re-embracing it in the retelling). The conversion narrative can thus make conversion appear purely tactical, precisely because the discourse is framed in terms of what was wrong and bad about the past. Conversion almost always has "instrumental" explanations: fighting addiction, bottoming out, facing a medical crisis, or other "pathologies of poverty." A common factor among conversionist religious groups is that converts must learn to interpret these factors in a manner consistent with the group's norms and discursive style.[52]

This is not to say that conversion narratives should be discounted as disingenuous or programmed, but rather that researchers must pay attention to the convert's stage in his or her conversion career (pre-affiliation, affiliation, conversion, confession, or disaffiliation), always remaining cognizant of the fact that narratives are socially constructed and retrospectively reinterpreted over time. In other words, conversion accounts may tell us as much about current identities, beliefs, and orientations as they do about the past.

Carozzi's chapter provides an excellent illustration of this point, as she follows the stages of conversion in an African diasporan religious group. By speaking with practitioners and analyzing their discourse at various stages of initiation into "the Religion," she informs us that converts are as much "chosen" by religious authorities as they are "choosers" in their conversion process.

Furthermore, the chapters by Carozzi and Birman provide critical insights into how Pentecostalism and Afro-Brazilian religions utilize both continuity and rupture with the dominant local culture in the process of conversion. In the case of Brazilian neo-Pentecostals, the spiritual forces of previous religious practice remain very much alive in the worldviews and narratives of converts, despite the fact that they are now demonized within the neo-Pentecostal dualist ontology. For those outside of the "inner circle" of Afro-Brazilian temples in Argentina, a syncretic blend of familiar religious practices and beliefs is offered on a regular basis. But for those deemed worthy of inclusion in the inner circle (based on willingness to participate in more demanding and different religious rituals), a radical break with the past and the adoption of "an understanding" which applies and reapplies the new religious worldview to all events and circumstances is a necessary precursor to full conversion. In each case, the new conversion discourse implies a radical break with the past, but one that allows a continuing location for past beliefs and practices. For Pentecostals, fighting against the "real" world of local spirits allows them, as Joel Robbins puts it, "to turn their new religion immediately to addressing local issues in locally comprehensible terms."[53] For practitioners of Afro-Brazilian religions, entry into the religious movement is mediated by the use of familiar images and practices, but once within the inner circle, the ontological break and corresponding new interpretive frame are equally radical changes, reflected in the new and all-encompassing discourse of converts.

Critically analyzing conversion narratives in light of each convert's location within a conversion career provides important insights for interpreting both the reasons for and the effects of conversion. The anomie thesis and the various instrumental explanations for conversion outlined earlier are generally interpreted through a convert's own discourse, a discourse that is informed and constructed within a particular religious and social context. It should thus come as no surprise that we find a certain degree of conformity among the set of practical crises converts describe as characterizing their pre-conversion life.

Thus, as researchers we are cautioned to approach conversion narratives as both an empirical indicator of conversion and a socially constructed account that is influenced by the particular religious institution/discourse/ritual context in which the individual is interviewed. Conversion narratives serve as both a resource for the convert and a window for the researcher into how the convert makes sense of the world. But if we do not approach the narrative with a careful eye to the past and the future of the conversion career, we can easily fall into an instrumental interpretation that may miss other critical variables, including the theological and ritual elements of religious conversion. Furthermore, we may lose sight of the fundamental tension in conversion discourses between the processes of choosing (individual agency) and being chosen (either by religious authorities or directly by a deity or spirit).

The final two chapters in part II focus on conversion within Catholicism and the recent growth of neonative religious practice. In chapter 8, Edward L. Cleary addresses the major shift within the Latin American Catholic Church toward Charismatic Catholicism and "pentecostalized" religious practices. Beginning in the 1970s the Catholic Charismatic movement sought to draw large numbers of laity into personal and institutional revitalization through conversion, emphasizing healing and other gifts of the Holy Spirit that would lead to dedication to God and service to the church and world. Cleary outlines this historical process and defines the critical institutional changes that led to the Charismatic Renewal in Latin America.

Finally, chapter 9 analyzes the recent growth of indigenous religious movements in South America, with a particular focus on the case of Ecuador. Rachel Corr explores both the growing return to pre-Columbian forms of religious practice and what this process means in terms of the loss of smaller and more local religious traditions that have evolved through syncretism with Catholicism.

Rethinking the Effects of Religious Change

While most of the chapters in this volume address the effects of conversion, part III is explicitly focused on the multiple and complex implications of religious conversion. In chapter 10, Christine Kovic analyzes conversion from traditional Catholicism to "Word of God" Catholicism in the state of Chiapas. Kovic argues that focusing on "lived religion" helps us to understand how the process of conversion cannot be separated from familial, community, or ethnic identity issues in this context. Stressing many of the same elements that have formerly been studied primarily in the context of Pentecostal conversion, Kovic points to the fact that conversion within Catholicism also has important long-term effects upon social and gender relations.

In chapter 11, Virginia Garrard-Burnett points to two critical and understudied aspects of conversion: reverse missionary movements and the role of spiritual capital. Examining the case of the Brazilian IURD church in an immigrant Houston community, Garrard-Burnett argues that the IURD may not provide material wealth to its adherents, but it does provide significant "spiritual capital" in the form of networks of support, beliefs, and practices that assist newly arrived immigrants.

Chapter 12, by Jill M. Wightman, on Bolivia focuses on the role of healing in Pentecostal conversion and argues that Pentecostal discourses on suffering and illness are not generally that of rewards in the afterlife, but rather focus on healing, both in a corporal sense and as a metaphor for how conversion modifies identity. Wightman also addresses the manner in which these discourses of healing and personal change lead to a critique of mainstream Bolivian (and global) society and a call for social change.

In chapter 13, Timothy J. Steigenga concludes the volume with an examination of the political implications of increasingly "pentecostalized" religious practices and beliefs in the Guatemalan context. Steigenga argues that religious affiliation is a less salient factor for understanding the political implications of religious change than religious beliefs. Rather, the increasingly pentecostalized religious beliefs that characterize both Protestants and Catholics in Guatemala are correlated with more conservative and quiescent political attitudes that have previously been attributed only to Protestants.

Taken together, the contributions to this volume point us in a new direction for studying the political, economic, and social effects of the large-scale religious changes underway in the Americas. After years of implementing the Washington Consensus (trade liberalization, privatization, deregulation, and tax reforms), the political arena in Latin America is now characterized by fractured parties, weakened states, mass-based ethnic and religious movements, and a recent upswing in populist politics. While political scientists, historians, and economists have couched the debate over the impact of religious change in broad terms of democracy and development or resistance and accommodation, the results of these studies have been largely inconclusive or contradictory.

To a significant degree, the lack of clear results is a function of asking the wrong questions. As the contributions by Birman, Kovic, Smilde, Steigenga, and Wightman demonstrate, the most important political effects of religious change in Latin America have to do with the manner in which new religiously held values enter the public sphere, inform public discourse, and combine to resolve or exacerbate local cultural, social, or familial tensions. This is not to say that such processes have no impact on development or democracy, but rather that they are not the primary factors driving political change among the traditional objects of political analysis: elites, parties, or state institutions.

So how should we reconceptualize the political effects of the ongoing process of religious change and conversion in the Americas? First, we must disaggregate and specifically define the religious variables we posit as having political effects. As Steigenga argues in the final chapter, religious affiliation is a poor predictor of political attitudes and activities. A more fruitful research agenda focuses on the specific religious beliefs and practices associated with the religious groups experiencing rapid growth in the region, and how those beliefs and practices interact with local and national contexts.

Second, we need to re-orient our focus on dependent variables away from sweeping generalizations about democracy and development. In a region where multiple powerful factors militate against significant progress on either of these fronts, we can hardly expect a series of individual religious choices to add up to a coherent, direct, and sweeping force for economic or political change. While religious change may provide a break with cultural hierarchy (as Birman argues in the case of Brazil), introduce a new discourse into the public sphere (as Wightman points out in Bolivia), or introduce new "publics" which open the possibility for new network connections and exchanges (as Smilde demonstrates in Venezuela), we must understand and evaluate the effects of these changes in the context of the political and economic realities of the region.

One way to accomplish this is to rethink the way marginalized groups participate in the public sphere. David Smilde argues that evangelical publics in Venezuela are purposely constructed relational contexts which extend network ties and introduce a "moralized" discourse into the public sphere. These publics are created and inhabited frequently by religious individuals who interact, exchange discourses, extend networks, and ultimately gain social influence in a manner that would otherwise be denied to them through the standard institutions of democratic states.[54]

In the case of Bolivia, Jill Wightman argues that evangelical publics also provide a forum for evangelicals to define their identity in opposition to "politics as usual," as hard-working, moral individuals seeking to heal Bolivian society one conversion at a time. Both Steigenga and Wightman also point out that the major exception to Pentecostal political "quietism" is evident when Pentecostals determine that a given political authority is illegitimate, corrupt, or immoral. In such instances, Pentecostals (and Catholics) can coalesce to make powerful political statements and even take to the streets to demonstrate their dissatisfaction.

In the context of Brazil, Patricia Birman's chapter provides another specific example of this process with the Neo-Pentecostal Universal Church of the Kingdom of God (IURD). Birman argues that the processes of exorcism and spiritual warfare within the IURD not only provide converts with the ability to break with their previously static position in the Brazilian social and racial hierarchy, but also introduce a new discourse into the public sphere. This new discourse allows converts to keep their previous religious forces (spirits) alive, while also relegating them (and their former political and social roles) to the world of evil.

Fourth, much of the political impact of religious change, particularly in terms of Pentecostalism, takes place at the nexus of the global and the local. As we have already noted, Pentecostalism preserves local religious ontologies in the process of simultaneously demonizing them. At the same time, the leaders and staff of most Pentecostal churches are locals, with social, political, and economic concerns that reflect those of their local community.[55] Thus, although Pentecostalism tends to "look the same" across the variant communities in which it has made significant inroads in Latin America, the political and social effects of Pentecostal growth interact with local contexts to produce very different political effects. Again, the same can be said for the pentecostalized Catholics of the CCR.

Finally, upward social mobility certainly plays some role in conversion, but whether or not it is perceptual or an empirical reality remains to be seen. Certainly, arguments that posit an upward swing in "development" on a national scale due to religious conversions should be discounted. At the same time, the stories of individuals and communities who have experienced upward social mobility along with conversion merit careful empirical analysis. As Virginia Garrard-Burnett argues, conversion may not make the convert financially rich, but it can provide a wealth of "spiritual capital" in the form of beliefs, networks, self-meanings, and affirmation that assists people in navigating the difficulties of everyday life.

In the broadest terms, the contributions to this volume offer a set of three clear guidelines for the study of conversion in Latin America and elsewhere. First, by conceptualizing conversion as a continuum, we warn researchers not to utilize a single form of measurement (self-identification, degree of commitment, beliefs and convictions, demonstration event, or discourse) to identify conversion. At one end of the spectrum, confession demands a fairly radical cultural and familial break with the past as well as a shift in personal identity. At the other end, our case studies and data suggest that there is a significant number of "seekers" who may nominally affiliate with different religious groups over time.

Second, our multiple-stage model of conversion serves as a cautionary factor, keeping us from uncritical acceptance of strictly demand-driven or supply-driven explanations for conversion. Clearly, social conformity, network location, life crises, and social support (or lack thereof) condition conversion, but they do not determine conversion. On the other hand, a purely instrumental approach may give too much credit to converts' "other" preferences (financial gain, personal safety, crisis management, or changes in gender relations). That which appears instrumental or purely preferences-based to the outside observer may actually have multiple contextual and network determinants that are not immediately evident. Keeping multiple levels of analysis (individual, societal, cultural, network location, market) in play helps us to overcome unnecessary contradictions while simultaneously nurturing healthy debate and generating new and testable hypotheses about the process and effects of conversion.

Finally, the complexities of measuring and explaining conversion should lead us to be skeptical of any study that posits simple political or social effects of conversion. The effects of religious conversion in Latin America are multiple and complex and are best examined through the lens of interactions with local contexts and structures of power. From Brazil to Guatemala, some of the most important effects of the recent religious changes in Latin America have more to do with alternative public (and private) discourses and new forms of identity politics than with elections or other traditional forms of political mobilization. By refocusing our analysis away from broad claims about democracy, development, accommodation, and resistance, we are much more likely to gain an accurate picture of most significant changes in the lived reality of Latin America's millions of recent religious converts.

NOTES

1. Estimate taken from a CID-Gallup poll conducted in Guatemala in 2001. See report findings listed at http://www.prolades.com/prolades1/cra/regions/cam/guate-cidp0112001.pdf. Also see Henri Gooren, "Reconsidering Protestant Growth in Guatemala, 1900–1995," in *Holy Saints and Fiery Preachers: The Anthropology of Protestantism in Mexico and Central America*, ed. James W. Dow and Alan R. Sandstrom (Westport, CT: Pearger, 2001), 169–203.

2. Pentecostalization refers to widespread religious beliefs across religious affiliations (such as belief in a dramatic personal conversion, millennialism, and, to some degree, biblical literalism) and the experience of particular pneumatic religious practices (such as speaking in tongues, divine healing, and other charismatic practices associated with Pentecostalism). See Timothy J. Steigenga, "Democracia y el crecimiento del protestantismo evangélico en Guatemala: entendiendo la complejidad política de la religión pentecostalizada," *América Latina Hoy* 41 (2005): 99–119; Andrew R. Chesnut, *Born Again in Brazil: The Pentecostal Boom and the Pathogens of Poverty* (New Brunswick, NJ: Rutgers University Press, 1997).

3. Jeffrey Rubin, "Meanings and Mobilizations: A Cultural Politics Approach to Social Movements and States," *Latin American Research Review* 39, no. 3 (2004): 106–142. Also see Jeffrey W. Rubin, "In the Streets or in the Institutions?" *LASA Forum* 37 (2006): 26–29. For an example of such a dialectical or oppositional approach, see Jean Comaroff and John Comaroff, *Of Revelation and Revolution: Christianity, Colonialism, and Consciousness in South Africa* (Chicago: University of Chicago Press, 1991).

4. Lewis R. Rambo, "Anthropology and the Study of Conversion," in *The Anthropology of Religious Conversion*, ed. Andrew Buckser and Stephen D. Glazier (Lanham: Rowman and Littlefield, 2003), 213.

5. David A. Snow and Richard Machalek, "The Sociology of Conversion," *Annual Review of Sociology* 10 (1984): 170.

6. Snow and Machalek, "The Sociology of Conversion," 168–174; Gooren, "Reconsidering Protestant Growth," 2006.

7. Patricia Birman, "Cultos de possessão e pentecostalismo no Brasil: Passagens," *Religião e Sociedade* 17 (1996): 90–109.

8. Clara Mafra, "Relatos compartilhados: experiências de conversão ao pentecostalismo entre brasileiros e portugueses," *Mana* 6 (2000): 57–85.

9. André Droogers, Henri Gooren, and Anton Houtepen, "Conversion Careers and Culture Politics in Pentecostalism: A Comparative Study in Four Continents," proposal submitted to the thematic program "The Future of the Religious Past" of the Netherlands Organization for Scientific Research (NWO), 2003.

10. There are significant historic communities of both Jews and Muslims in Latin America, though neither group represents more than 1 percent of the total population. Because these are not primarily religions of conversion, we do not devote

significant space to a discussion of their role in the changing Latin American religious landscape.

11. For a more complete discussion of the historical background, methods of classifying, and theological tenets of each of these groups, see Timothy Steigenga, *The Politics of the Spirit: The Political Implications of the Growth of Pentecostalized Religion in Central America* (Baltimore: Lexington Press, 2001). Also see Joel Robbins, "The Globalization of Charismatic and Pentecostal Christianity," *Annual Review of Anthropology* 33 (2004): 119–123.

12. We also should note that somewhat spontaneous Pentecostal religious events also took place early in the 1900s in the Southern Cone countries of Brazil and Chile.

13. In some countries these groups represent the largest of the specific non-Catholic denominations. For example, in Peru, Adventists are the largest non-Catholic denomination.

14. See Edward Cleary, "Shopping Around: Questions about Latin American Conversions," *International Bulletin of Missionary Research* 28, no. 2 (2004): 50–54. Also see Anthony Gill, "Protestant Problems, What Protestant Problems? The Coming of the Golden Age of Catholicism in Latin America," paper presented at the Workshop on Contemporary Challenges to Catholicism in Latin America, Notre Dame University, October 2–3, 2003.

15. Luis Corral Prieto, "Las iglesias evangélicas," *Estudios teológicos* 13 (January–June 1980): 1–199; Clifton L. Holland, interview with Edward Cleary, San Jose, Costa Rico, October 30, 1990. See also Guillermo Cook, "The Evangelical Groundswell in Latin America," *Christian Century*, December 12, 1990, 1175–1176.

16. The data is based on annual surveys conducted in various Latin American countries by Latinobarómetro, based in Santiago, Chile (http://www.latinobarometro.org/).

17. See Edward Cleary, "Shopping Around: Questions about Latin American Conversions," *International Bulletin of Missionary Research*, 28, no. 2 (2004): 50–54.

18. Andrew Chesnut, *Competitive Spirits: Latin America's New Religious Economy* (Oxford: Oxford University Press, 2003), 107.

19. See *International Religious Freedom Report 2005* released by the United States Bureau of Democracy, Human Rights, and Labor: http://www.state.gov/g/drl/rls/irf/2005/51641.htm.

20. See the *World Christian Database at the Center for the Study of Global Christianity:* http://worldchristiandatabase.org/wcd/.

21. Prolades, http://www.prolades.com/prolades1/cra/regions/cam/guate-cidp0112001.pdf.

22. See Chesnut, *Competitive Spirits*, 107.

23. Sources for these figures were compiled from the International Religious Freedom Report (http://www.state.gov/g/drl/rls/irf/2005/51641.htm); Prolades (http://www.prolades.com/prolades1/cra/regions/cam/guate-cidp0112001.pdf.), and the Latin American Network Information Center (http://lanic.utexas.edu/la/region/religion/).

24. Kurt Bowen, *Evangelism and Apostasy: The Evolution and Impact of Evangelicals in Modern Mexico* (Montreal: McGill-Queen's University Press, 1996), 218.

25. Ibid., 224.

26. Steigenga, *The Politics of the Spirit*.

27. Cleary, "Shopping Around."

28. See Ruben Cesar Fernandes et al., *Novo Nascimento: Os evangelicos em casa, na igreja e na politica* (Rio de Janeiro: Mauad, 1998), 27.

29. The "religious economy" perspective is most clearly developed in Roger Finke and Rodney Stark, *The Churching of America, 1776–1990* (New Brunswick, NJ: Rutgers University Press, 1992); and Rodney Stark and James C. McCann, "Market Forces and Catholic Commitment: Exploring the New Paradigm," *Journal for the Scientific Study of Religion* 32 (1993): 113.

30. See Anthony Gill, *Rendering unto Caesar* (Chicago: University of Chicago Press, 1998); Anthony Gill, "The Economics of Evangelization," in *Religious Freedom and Evangelization in Latin America: The Challenge of Religious Pluralism*, ed. Paul E. Sigmund (Maryknoll, NY: Orbis Books, 1999), 70–86.

31. For examples of this literature see Ruben Alves, *Protestantism and Political Repression: A Brazilian Case Study* (Maryknoll, NY: Orbis Books, 1985); Sarah Diamond, *Spiritual Warfare: The Politics of the Christian Right* (Boston: South End Press, 1989); Ana Maria Ezcurra, *The Neoconservative Offensive: U.S. Churches and Ideological Struggle for Latin America* (New York: New York Circus Publications, 1986); Collett Merrill, "The Cross and the Flag," *Progressive* (December 1987): 18–20; and Mary Westropp, "Christian Counterinsurgency," *Cultural Survival Quarterly* 7 (fall 1983): 28–31.

32. See Diamond, *Spiritual Warfare*. Also see Gerard Colby and Charlotte Dennett, *Thy Will Be Done: Conquest of the Amazon—Nelson Rockefeller and Evangelism in the Age of Oil* (New York: HarperCollins, 1995). Also see David Stoll, *Is Latin America Turning Protestant?* (Berkeley: University of California Press, 1990).

33. The classic text in this vein is Emilio Willems, *Followers of the New Faith: Culture Change and the Rise of Protestantism in Brazil and Chile* (Nashville, TN: Vanderbilt University Press, 1967).

34. For a text in this vein, see David Martin, *Tongues of Fire: The Explosion of Protestantism in Latin America* (Oxford: Basil Blackwell, 1990), 235, 289. Martin compares the spread of Pentecostal Protestantism in Latin America to the previous growth of Puritanism and Anglo-American Methodism in England and the United States, drawing out similarities in terms of social function. Also see Amy Sherman, *The Soul of Development: Biblical Christianity and Economic Transformation in Guatemala* (New York: Oxford University Press, 1997), 163–165; Sheldon Annis, *God and Production in a Guatemalan Town* (Austin: University of Texas Press, 1987).

35. Christian Lalive d'Epinay, *Haven of the Masses: A Study of the Pentecostal Movement in Chile* (London: Lutterworth, 1969); Jean-Pierre Bastian, "The Metamorphosis of Latin American Protestant Groups: A Sociohistorical Perspective," *Latin American Research Review* 28 (1993): 33–62.

36. While a correlation between conversion and the kind of upward social mobility posited by Sherman and others may be established, the cause of such a correlation remains an open question. See Carol Ann Drogus, "Religious Pluralism and Social Change: Coming to Terms with Complexity and Convergence," *Latin American Research Review* 35 (2000): 263–265.

37. David Stoll, *Between Two Armies in the Ixil Towns of Guatemala* (New York: Columbia University Press, 1993); John Burdick, *Looking for God in Brazil: The Progressive Catholic Church in Urban Brazil's Religious Arena* (Berkeley: University of California Press,

1993); Cecilia Mariz, *Coping with Poverty: Pentecostals and Christian Base Communities in Brazil* (Philadelphia: Temple University Press, 1994).

38. See Elizabeth Brusco, "The Reformation of Machismo: Asceticism and Masculinity among Colombian Evangelicals," in *Rethinking Protestantism in Latin America*, ed. Virginia Garrard-Burnett and David Stoll (Philadelphia: Temple University Press, 1993).

39. Mariz, *Coping with Poverty*, 97.

40. Chesnut, *Born Again in Brazil*. Also see David Smilde, *Reason to Believe: Cultural Agency in Latin American Evangelicalism* (Berkeley: University of California Press, 2007).

41. Daniel Míguez, "Exploring the Argentinian Case: Religious Motives in the Growth of Latin American Pentecostalism," in *Latin American Religion in Motion*, ed. Christian Smith and Joshua Prokopy (New York: Routledge, 1999), 222.

42. Míguez, "Exploring the Argentinian Case," 230.

43. Harvey Cox, *Fire from Heaven: The Rise of Pentecostal Spirituality and the Reshaping of Religion in the Twenty-First Century* (Reading, MA: Addison-Wesley Publishing Company, 1994), 81–83.

44. Robbins, "The Globalization of Charismatic and Pentecostal Christianity," 126.

45. For comprehensive reviews of this literature see David A. Snow and Richard Machalek, "The Sociology of Conversion," *Annual Review of Sociology* 10 (1984): 167–190; James Richardson, ed., *Conversion Careers: In and out of the New Religions* (Beverly Hills: Sage, 1978); Lewis R. Rambo, *Understanding Religious Conversion* (New Haven and London: Yale University Press, 1993); Henri Gooren, "Towards a New Model of Conversion Careers: The Impact of Personality and Situational Factors," *Exchange* 34 (2005): 149–166; Henri Gooren, "Towards a New Model of Religious Conversion Careers: The Impact of Social and Institutional Factors," in *Paradigms, Poetics, and Politics of Conversion*, ed. Wout J. van Bekkum, Jan N. Bremmer, and Arie Molendijk (Leuven: Peeters, 2006), 25–30.

46. For an excellent overview of these debates, see Peter van der Veer, ed., *Conversion to Modernities: The Globalization of Christianity* (New York and London: Routledge, 1996).

47. See Snow and Machalek, "The Sociology of Conversion," for examples of this research.

48. For an excellent example of these critiques see Manuel A. Vásquez's review of *Competitive Spirits: Latin America's New Religious Economy*, by Andrew Chesnut (Oxford University Press: 2003), in *Journal of the American Academy of Religion* 23, no. 2 (2005): 524–528.

49. Also see David Smilde, "Works of the Flesh, Fruit of the Spirit: Religious Action Frames and Meaning Networks in Venezuelan Evangelicalism" (PhD diss., University of Chicago, 2000), chapters 3 and 4.

50. See David A. Snow, Louis A. Zurcher Jr., and Sheldon Ekland-Olson, "Social Networks and Social Movements: A Microstructural Approach to Differential Recruitment," *American Sociological Review* 45, no. 5 (1980): 787–801; and Doug McAdam and Ronnelle Paulsen, "Specifying the Relationship between Social Ties and Activism," *American Journal of Sociology* 99 (1993): 640–667.

51. See Gooren, "Reconsidering Protestant Growth" and "Towards a New Model."

52. See Snow and Machalek, "The Sociology of Conversion," 175–178.

53. Joel Robbins, "The Globalization of Charismatic and Pentecostal Christianity," *Annual Review of Anthropology* 33 (2004): 129.

54. Religious television and radio programs throughout the region could also be conceptualized as publics. This discourse and political responses to it (such as Hugo Chavez's adoption of evangelical images and phrases or the ongoing political career of Rios Montt in Guatemala) make up a rich field for further study.

55. Robbins, "The Globalization of Charismatic and Pentecostal Christianity," 131.

2

Analyzing Conversion
in Latin America

Theoretical Questions, Methodological Dilemmas, and Comparative Data from Argentina and Brazil

ALEJANDRO FRIGERIO

Over the past decade, religious conversion has been the subject of significant debate in the Southern Cone of South America. In Brazil, where a long tradition of sociological and anthropological studies of religion has produced provocative theories and a rich body of data, scholars are somewhat skeptical about the utility of the concept of "conversion" and have preferred the use of the terms "passages" (*passagens*) or "multiple membership" (*pertença multíplice*) as more adequately explaining the religious dynamics in their country. In Argentina, where the term has been more thoughtfully evaluated by means of an integrated review of North American studies of conversion to new religious movements, the Brazilian concept has enjoyed a mixed reception. It has been fruitfully used to explain the expansion of Afro-Brazilian religions in the country but has suffered some criticism on the part of scholars studying Pentecostal growth. This chapter will review the arguments for and against the use of the concept of conversion in both countries as well as the most recent data that bear on the subject.

Brazilian Scholars on Conversion

Despite the presence in Brazil of a significant and long-standing tradition of the practice of Spiritism and of religions of African origin, it has been the more recent and impressive growth of Pentecostalism and neo-Pentecostalism that has forced the idea of the end of a Catholic monopoly upon scholars. Unlike the practitioners of Spiritism, Candomblé, or Umbanda, who usually do not vindicate a strong, visible social identity, preferring to identify themselves as "Catholic" in census data, Pentecostals forcefully and publicly assert their social religious identity. Thus they have become more visible, and their presence is especially evident in census figures or in polls.

The development of census figures shows that evangelicals in Brazil were 5.2 percent of the population in 1970, 6.6 percent in 1980, 9.0 percent in 1991, and 15.4 percent in 2000. Conversely, the percentage of Catholics diminished from 92 percent in 1970 to 89 percent in 1980 and 83 percent in 1991 to reach an all time low of 74 percent in 2000. Pentecostal growth became very visible during the 1980s, when they surpassed the Historical Protestant churches to constitute 65 percent of the Reformed Christian group in 1991 (up from 49 percent in 1980), and continued in the 1990s.[1] A survey carried out in Rio de Janeiro by the local Instituto de Estudos da Religião in the mid-1990s showed that "close to seventy percent of the Evangelicals in the Great Rio area were not born, nor raised, in Evangelical homes."[2]

Unlike in Argentina, where the growth of Pentecostalism and other new religious movements has focused scholarly attention on the process of conversion as one way of explaining this development, in Brazil the fact that, as sociologist Reginaldo Prandi notes, almost a quarter of the adult population has switched to a religion different from the one they were born into has, to the contrary, led to scholarly skepticism about the very existence of conversion.[3] Several articles by Brazilian anthropologists and sociologists have questioned the usefulness of this concept to describe the manner in which individuals pass from one religious group to another as well as the consequences this passage entails.[4]

The long-established practice by practitioners of Spiritism and Afro-Brazilian religions of identifying themselves as "Catholic" (a religious identity that may also include attending Sunday Masses and participating in other Catholic rituals) has led several researchers to consider "dual membership" a characteristic feature of the Brazilian religious experience. Also, the swift transit of individuals from Catholicism to the fast-growing Pentecostal churches and their later passages between them have convinced Brazilian scholars that contemporary religious affiliations and commitment are too light and fragile and not important enough in the lives of individuals to be considered conversion. Anthropologist Clara Mafra notes that "in order to account for the fluidity and syncretism present in these processes of (religious) change, some authors have chosen to reject the concept of conversion, which has functioned as a reifying and simplifying way to interpret these processes."[5]

Similarly, anthropologists Renato Almeida and Paula Montero, in their analysis of "religious transit" (*tránsito religioso*), argue, "The Weberian concept of conversion, that until recently explained the complex subjective process of adhesion to a new religion, does not seem capable now of explaining these fast coming and goings between these so apparently different religions: an inner process in which the religious conscience does not seem to register cognitive dissonances."[6] Working along the same lines, sociologist Lísias Nogueira Negrão describes a "Brazilian common religious denominator." In his words, "The common basis of beliefs (found among religious groups) belies the notion of religious conversion. Migration from one group to another does not require the individual's resocialization, and can be understood as a simple adhesion, motivated by specific events in the individual's life history."[7]

Although Brazilian scholars apparently share a skeptical view of the validity of the concept of conversion (when not an adamant denial of it), there is some diversity in the arguments that have been advanced to criticize this concept as well as in the terms they have proposed to replace it. As I will show, anthropologists and sociologists of religion have argued that the Brazilian religious experience is fraught with "passages" and "mediations." Conversions, therefore, are conceptualized as qualitatively shallow and conditioned by the particular syncretic character of Brazilian culture.

"Passages": Spaces of Interlocution between Religious Groups

In an often quoted article in the renowned Brazilian journal *Religião e Sociedade*, Patricia Birman, a leading anthropologist of religion from Rio de Janeiro, has advocated that social scientists

> explore the relationship between religious groups beyond the limits set by the notion of conversion. This concept, by favoring the idea of an individual trajectory—valorizing almost exclusively the subjective and interior elaboration of belief—gives little credit to the religious and social context that precedes the changes that take place. The individual movements of passage between groups include a constant space of interlocution where social and symbolic mediations (as well as mediators) are found that make conversion possible. This space of interlocution is necessarily fluid, syncretic. . . . It involves successive forms of appropriation and symbolic re-elaboration between the two religious systems that come into contact.[8]

This interlocution occurs at two levels: at the individual one, when persons redefine their place and religious identity and the way they think about themselves in relation to the supernatural sphere, and at the level of social relationships, where we find mediations that are constructed between the groups by their devotees.

Birman's analysis has gained favor among Brazilian anthropologists and has to some extent installed the idea that Brazil is a country of passages, rather than conversions. This is probably too strong a reading of her work. Even though she mentions criticisms of the concept of conversion that have been advanced in studies of religion in Africa, she does not explicitly disavow the notion of conversion, but rather suggests that one must go "beyond the limits set by (this) notion."[9] In her article, she states quite specifically that she will only be analyzing the passages of individuals who practiced Afro-Brazilian religions to the new Pentecostal groups (more precisely, to the Igreja Universal do Reino de Deus, IURD) and that other passages and symbolic mediations should be looked for if the converts to the IURD were previously of Catholic or Protestant background.[10] The IURD "establishes a group of ritual and symbolic activities that function as a bridge between both religious systems. . . . These activities facilitate passages between one group and the other," exorcism (of Afro-Brazilian religious spirits) being the basic form of mediation between both.[11]

Fragile Conversions: Religion as a Commodity and Minimal Conversions

In another often quoted paper by sociologist of religion Reginaldo Prandi, the author analyzes quantitative data on current and previous religious affiliation and notes that almost a quarter of the Brazilian adult population has experimented switching to a religious faith that is different from the one into which they were born.[12] He argues that because religion was slowly but continuously privatized, it was displaced to the domain of the individual and, from there, to that of consumption, where it is now obliged to follow the rules of the market. Thus, "religion is transformed into a commodity, and the devotee into a consumer," and, in his view, "religious consumption does not necessarily imply conversion."[13]

Working from Peter Berger's "sacred canopy" perspective, Prandi claims that "the old religion, source of transcendence for society, was shattered and the religion that took its place was a religion for specific causes. . . . Religious devotion is no longer eternal, and only lasts as long as the terms of interchange that are agreed to by both sides: the (religious) service providers, and the consumer." Prandi argues that "deceptions are followed by a new choice," since in this new religious situation "everything is sold and everything is bought."[14] In his view, entirely practical and individual reasons for conversion are nowadays widely accepted, and, therefore, "when confronted by a new problem, the convert will not hesitate in changing his religion again."[15] Prandi does not use the market perspective as an analytical model, but rather claims that religion actually became a commodity and therefore another item to be adopted and discarded according to its usefulness when dealing with specific problems of daily life. In his perspective, the strong commitment and change of worldview that should accompany conversion is not found when religion is paid for, just as any other commodity in the market.

A related but differently argued view of the fragile nature of religious conversion and commitment is proposed by Clara Mafra, an anthropologist from Rio de Janeiro who has studied the conversion process to the IURD in Brazil and Portugal. Central to her analysis is the observation that the fastest-growing Pentecostal groups are those that have reduced tension with the environment and have engaged more with secular culture, relaxing their requirements for membership and their ideological grip on their members. Adhesion to these groups, she argues, is more fragile and vulnerable, and membership is less exclusive and totalizing than was previously the case. Her main argument is that "Pentecostals are encouraging experimentation on the transformation of meanings produced by conversion. It is neither the preacher nor the congregation who teaches and closely guides the options available to the new convert, but he himself who goes adapting his new posture until, as they say, he feels good. Therefore, the field of the negotiation of meaning tends to respond to a dialogue between the personal trajectory and the Pentecostal cosmological imaginary."[16]

Mafra proposes the notion of "minimal conversion" (*conversões minimalistas*) to account for what she views as a new kind of conversion. In the case of maximal conversion, the control and cohesion of the group leads the convert to a "new world of beliefs and dispositions," whereas in minimal conversion the individual has more autonomy and responsibility in articulating Pentecostal beliefs, cosmology, and mythology to his previous trajectory. Unlike the dynamics of maximal conversion, in the minimal one there is less disciplining of the reception of the religious message, allowing for the possibility that different converts of the same denomination appropriate the religious message in multiple forms.[17]

Syncretic Nature of Brazilian Society and Culture

A third approach to the critique of conversion in Brazil is taken by scholars who argue that due to certain features of Brazilian society, religious identities are not distinct enough, and the passage from one to another is not sufficiently problematic to be considered conversion. The existence of a Brazilian syncretic *habitus* is believed to allow for "dual" or "multiple memberships" and "porous religious identities."

Anthropologist Pierre Sanchis is probably the scholar who has most forcefully argued for the peculiarities of Brazilian social structure and its incidence in the way religious identities are constructed. Although born in Belgium, Sanchis now works and lives in Brazil and has become a major reference in the social scientific study of religion, one of the most cited scholars in the field. Taking a diachronic perspective to account for the present characteristics of the Brazilian religious field, he argues that because the three ethnic groups that composed the Brazilian nationality (Portuguese, blacks, and Indians) were "uprooted from their homelands and were condemned, in an un-defined space, to re-define themselves constantly by reference to each other, a religious identity was developed that 'naturally' (albeit historically) tended to the incandescence of the syncretic process."[18] Thus a systematic plurality marks Brazilian sociogenesis, which was later translated into mutual porosities and contaminations giving origin to crossings, porosities, double membership, transit, mutual contamination, and borrowings. The peculiar features of Brazilian history have given birth, not only in the religious field, to "a structural predisposition for the porosity, albeit not the confusion, of identities. Brazil becomes a giant laboratory of cultural *creolization* and, when referring to religion, of syncretism, in a particular, pre-modern way."[19]

Sanchis's view of conversion is probably more nuanced than that of his colleagues. He believes that the spread of Pentecostalism has produced an important change in how social identities are constructed in Brazil: "Pentecostal identity delimits the fields and defines an exclusive adhesion. . . . [O]ne is not one thing and another at the same time anymore. In this sense and at this scale, conversion is a new phenomenon in Brazil."[20] The spread of neo-Pentecostalism, however, with its weaker membership and commitment requirements, makes him wonder if Brazilian culture has not prevailed once more and created its own, more syncretic and less exclusive, brand of this religion.[21]

Sociologist Lísias Nogueira Negrão, from São Paulo, has also stressed the peculiar "pre-modern" features of Brazilian society and culture that makes "double membership" (even "multiple membership") a common feature of the country's religious experience.[22] This "historical characteristic of Brazilian religiosity has nowadays been reinforced by the great diversification of alternatives found in the religious field" and has likewise allowed for the "easy religious mobility" between them.[23]

The widespread existence of a Brazilian popular religious culture (*cultura religiosa brasileira popular*) constitutes a "common religious denominator" present in the different groups that make up the religious field. Thus the belief in God and in a variety of intermediary spirits, the possibility of their interference in daily life, and their manipulation in the devotees' behalf, within a Christian moral context, are the minimal elements present in Brazilian religiosity. According to Negrão, these characteristics, common to most religions present in Brazil, favor their interpenetration and thus belie the notion of religious conversion. Migration from one group to another does not imply the re-socialization of the individual since it can be understood as a simple adhesion, motivated by specific circumstances in daily life. Thus, the specific historical formation of the Brazilian religious field, which is different from the European one that was the basis for the secularization model, deserves a different reading. The Brazilian religious field has, according to Negrão, logics and dynamics of its own that view double membership not as exceptional but as an adequate and coherent religious experience.[24]

Argentine Scholars on Conversion

Contrary to its unfavorable reception in Brazil, the idea of conversion has been more favorably accepted in Argentina. Early on, María Julia Carozzi argued for the need to understand the expansion of Pentecostalism, Afro-Brazilian religions, and other new religious movements (NRMs) not only in macro-sociological terms, as had mostly been the case, but as the result of individual decisions made by thousands of Argentines.[25] An understanding of the conversion processes involved, she argued, would confirm or question the macro-sociological interpretations which had up to then been advanced. In joint or single reviews, Carozzi and Alejandro Frigerio examined the North American literature on conversion to NRMs and emphasized the need for a perspective that stresses the processes involved in conversion and assigns a more active role to the individual convert.[26] They used such a perspective to analyze the conversion process to Afro-Brazilian religions in Argentina.[27] From a symbolic interactionist point of view, they defined conversion as a change in the conception that individuals have of themselves, of the world, and of God, that ultimately becomes interpreted in the terms provided by the new religion. Religious conversion implies a modification in the individual's personal identity and not merely in the social identities that one vindicates in different interactions.[28] It entails a process of redefinition of the personal identity through which individuals gradually come to consider themselves other, different beings. Conversion needs to be differentiated from recruitment to a religious group. When individuals are recruited, they formally belong to a group, adopting a new social identity without necessarily modifying their worldview or personal identity. The process of recruitment involves the social identities deployed by the individual vis-à-vis the religious group, while the process of conversion makes reference to the modifications in personal identity.

Subsequently, other Argentine scholars have used the concept of conversion to examine the growth of NRMs.[29] Caveats about the validity of the concept have come from academics researching the expansion of Pentecostalism. Daniel Miguez has been somewhat critical of the concept, arguing that many lower-class converts to Pentecostalism in the Greater Buenos Aires area do not adopt all tenets of their new religion's worldview and that they combine their new religious concepts with some of the old ideas they were supposed to have abandoned (e.g., they still resort to *curanderos*).[30] He considers these idiosyncratic combinations of new religious beliefs and survivals of old ones "popular uses of popular religions." These popular uses would belie the existence of a "strict" conversion. The same author, however, subsequently analyzed the successful identity changes accomplished by Pentecostals when dealing with minor delinquents (in contrast to the widespread failures of state-funded rehabilitation programs).[31] Therefore, if conversion is understood primarily in terms of identity changes, regardless of the survival of preexistent religious ideas, it seems that many individuals who become Pentecostals do indeed undergo conversion, successfully adopting a new personal identity.

The most forceful criticism on the appropriateness of the concept of conversion in Argentina was made by Pablo Semán in his PhD thesis on Pentecostalism and popular culture in a neighborhood of Buenos Aires.[32] Not unexpectedly, given the above review, his unfavorable evaluation of the concept, written for a Brazilian university, comes through the adoption of several insights developed by Brazilian scholars (Patricia Birman's concept of passages, Pierre Sanchis's definition of syncretism and the coexistence of pre-modern, modern, and post-modern logics in Brazilian society, as well as Luiz F. D. Duarte's view of the holistic and cosmological character of the religious experience of the popular sectors).[33]

Semán's criticism of the concept of conversion, grounded mostly on his perusal of Carozzi and Frigerio's review of the North American conversion literature, is based on the assumption of a radical discontinuity between the North American and the Latin American social contexts. In the former, he argues, religious pluralism is based on the existence of different religious denominations, whereas in the latter we find a popular mentality (*mentalidade popular*) that reduces this pluralism due to the (pre)existence of a holistic and enchanted logic. In the popular sectors, he argues, the religious world is not entirely separate from the secular one and the different religious alternatives are re-utilized within a wider and more comprehensive logic of the sacred that sees these groups as only partial moments of this totality. In his view, social scientists arguing for the existence of a situation of religious pluralism, comprised of different groups from which the individual chooses, are presupposing the existence of an entirely modern society in which the sacred is apart from the secular. To the contrary, the world of the popular working-class sectors of Argentina (in a manner similar to that of Brazil) does not separate the sacred from the secular since there is "a permanent presence of the divine and sacred" and "a dependence on the sacred."[34] In such a context, we find more (low-intensity) adhesions and passages through religious groups than conversions among different religious groups. These forms of transit are not traumatic since they do not presuppose exclusive membership, and, further, all individuals involved participate in the larger and more inclusive logic of an enchanted world containing the different religions only as specific expressions of this sacred cosmos.

Analyzing Competing Views on Conversion

From the review above, we can infer that most scholars in Brazil are working within a frame that does not favor the use of conversion as a suitable concept or perspective for the analysis of the expansion of new religious movements or for the understanding of transits from one group to another. They have advanced alternative explanations that stress the prevalence of passages between groups and the prevalence of dual membership or of minimal conversions. They have also argued that certain features of Brazilian society shape its religious field in such a way that "conversion" does not adequately explain its dynamics or its reality.

In Argentina the reverse seems to be true. Several scholars have argued for the usefulness of the concept of conversion and for its widespread occurrence in the light of the expansion of Pentecostalism, Afro-Brazilian, and other religions. In both countries, scholars who have been in favor of the use of the concept of conversion have had some access to the North American literature (or to the work of local scholars who review it) while most of its critics have not (with the exception of Semán, who has read the Argentine reviews of conversion as well as the Brazilian arguments against the term). Since most criticisms of the concept that have been advanced come from Brazilian scholars (or from academics who work or have been trained in that country), we can speak of a "Brazilian approach" to the topic.

There are at least three commonalities underlying Brazilian studies that allow us to understand their total or partial rejection of the concept of conversion. First, a "Pauline paradigm" implicitly underlies their understanding of conversion; second, they use mostly qualitative data drawn from interviews or quantitative data drawn from censuses or polls rather than participant observation in religious groups; and, third, they share a particular image of Brazilian society and culture.

Underlying "Pauline Paradigm" of Conversion

Despite the criticism the concept has received, few clear-cut definitions of conversion have been advanced or discussed in the Brazilian literature. It is assumed that the reader knows what has "generally" or "traditionally" been understood as conversion. Clara Mafra provides one of the few definitions of conversion to be found in the Brazilian literature and suggests that it is a radical and dramatic event. Mafra argues that, traditionally, the idea of conversion is associated with a process of radical change in the individual's trajectory, in which ego "accepts a belief system and behaviors strongly at odds with one's previous cognitive structure and actions or returns to a set of beliefs and commitments against which one has been strongly in rebellion."[35] This perspective informed most British and North American studies on religious conversion during the 1970s.[36]

Prandi suggests that conversion denotes religious switching that is long-lasting and that does not occur frequently in the life of an individual. As Prandi explains, "Perhaps one of the most shocking features of religion today is the easiness with which anyone can change from one to another without the world falling apart. The very notion of religious conversion is becoming a weak concept; there was a time when to convert to another religion meant breaking dramatically with one's biography, to change one's life in a radical way."[37]

These rare explicit references regarding the nature of conversion and the theoretical assumptions behind them show the prevailing nature of the traditional Pauline paradigm of conversion that assumes a passive subject. According to James Richardson's description, this paradigm considers the conversion experience to be sudden, dramatic, and emotional, thoroughly changing one's life in a relatively permanent way and in a manner that entails a total break with the past, causing a total negation of the old self and the implantation of a new one.[38] Within this view, conversion is generally interpreted in cognitive terms, since it is believed that a change in beliefs is followed by a change in behavior. Further, the individual undergoing conversion is considered mostly a passive subject, since that individual is thought to be either overcome by psychological strains or socially overdetermined. To this traditional, "Pauline," "passive convert" paradigm, Richardson has opposed an "active convert" paradigm that recognizes more self-determination in the process and visualizes a subject actively "working out" one's own conversion, or, in Machalek and Snow's phrasing, becoming a "self-determining agent," "author," and "negotiator" of one's conversion experience."[39]

The idea that there is no "real" conversion if individuals switch religions more than once (and especially if they do it because they try to solve specific problems in their daily lives) also reveals the implicit use of a Pauline paradigm. Richardson has suggested that it may be common that individuals undergo more than one conversion during their lifetime and therefore urges, instead, to study conversion careers:

> Conversion career is tied to the idea of serial alternatives by which is meant the sequential trying out of new beliefs and identities in an effort to resolve felt difficulties. Looking at the process of serial alternatives requires moving away from the focus on single-event conversions and toward a view that most contemporary conversions

are identity sequences that can often be viewed as cumulative. . . . Many people undergo multiple conversions or alternations within a relatively short period of time. . . . [W]e should focus on the conversion history, all conversion-related events that a person experiences. Such a history never really closes.[40]

Further, some of the ideas that have been proposed by Brazilian scholars as alternatives to conversion are, I believe, quite compatible with an "active convert" paradigm. This seems to be the case with Mafra's idea of "minimal conversion," in which "the individual has more autonomy and responsibility to articulate Pentecostal beliefs, cosmology, and mythology to his previous trajectory" and "it is neither the preacher nor the congregation who teach and closely guide the options available to the new convert, but himself who gradually adapts his new posture until, as they say, he feels good."[41] Likewise, Birman's notion of the "syncretic work" (of reinterpretation of beliefs) undertaken by individuals in their passage from one group to another certainly does not go against, but rather in the direction of, the idea of an active subject of conversion.

Finally, it is telling that sociologist Ricardo Mariano, probably the only Brazilian scholar to have reviewed skeptically his colleagues' approach to conversion (arguing for the need to distinguish between conversion and commitment and for the existence of different types of links between individuals and the Pentecostal churches they attend, ranging from the client to the convert), is one of the few academics who have quoted the Argentine reviews on conversion that stress the advantages of using an active convert paradigm.[42]

Methods for Studying Conversion: The Limits of Conversion Narratives

Besides the (often implicit) use of a theoretical paradigm that stresses the radical, imposed, singular nature of conversion, the kind of data that are collected and analyzed in many of the Brazilian studies also militate against the conceptualization of conversion as a process. The almost exclusive use of interviews, which oftentimes do not necessarily or exclusively focus on the topic of conversion, severely limits the scope of information researchers obtain about the circumstances surrounding the passage from one religious group to the other or the progression of events that make this transit possible. We are left with only the interviewee's understanding of this development and recollection of the events and surrounding circumstances. Further, the standardized nature of converts' accounts is seldom mentioned in the Brazilian analyses and almost never adequately problematized. As a result of the almost exclusive use of this technique, transits that may have actually taken weeks or months of doubts and coming and going between groups, that may have been very costly emotionally, and that may have involved the participation of various significant others may be retold, in an interview, in a very sketchy and uncritical manner, taking only a couple of minutes in the conversation and resulting in a few lines or paragraphs in the final transcription. Interviews guided by a Pauline paradigm will rarely yield an understanding of the conversion process that captures the entire progression of events the individual has undergone.

If the sole reliance on interviews greatly reduces the complexity of the conversion process, the use of quantitative data derived from censuses and polls almost completely hides it. Researchers, mostly sociologists, who interpret this data must then rely almost entirely on their theoretical perspectives to explain the shifts in group affiliation. Because of the peculiarities of the data gathered by these means, shifts from one group to another seem easy and unimportant, since the "identity work" involved (done both by groups and by individuals) is not revealed by these techniques.

Enduring participant observation, especially informed by an active convert paradigm, is necessary for a full appreciation of the difficulties and nuances of the conversion and de-conversion process that characterizes religious careers. The importance of the research techniques was stressed early on by Richardson, who noted that most of the scholars whose work he cited in support of the idea of an emergent new paradigm were carrying on sustained participant observation in their studies.[43]

Underlying Images of Brazilian Society and Culture

In a recent review of the anthropological study of religion, Paula Montero notes that "syncretism is the way in which (Brazilian) intellectuals formulate the representations of (their) nationality."[44] We have seen how Negrão and especially Sanchis see syncretism as a basic defining feature of Brazilian nationality. In her analysis of passages, Birman, following Sanchis, similarly stresses that syncretism is a relevant and habitual trait of Brazilian religiousness, marked by an accumulation of religious practices. All three scholars pinpoint the example of practitioners of Afro-Brazilian religions who identify as Catholic in order to prove the widespread existence of religious syncretism, double membership, or porous religious identities in the country.

Following Otavio Velho's lead that Brazilian anthropologists generally use a common and implicit meta-theory in their analyses, I have argued elsewhere that these presuppositions stem not from any social theory, but mainly from the image intellectuals have "of what makes brazil, Brazil" (*o que faz o brasil, Brasil*).[45] It has become customary to explain certain behaviors (and, certainly, religious ones) as deriving from specific *Brazilian ways of being* and *doing* that are, in turn, produced by the (postulated) unique characteristics of this society. These distinctive features are obtained by contrasting the local reality with a First World country, generally the United States or France, thus resulting in an image of Brazilian exceptionalism. Brazil is then visualized as a singular country that is religiously syncretic, culturally anthropophagic, and racially mixed, a country naturally characterized by mediations and mediators, religious, cultural, racial, and even social ones.[46] This image is clearly expressed by Da Matta when he states that:

> we are confronted with a social system founded on *relationships*, on the *intermediary* (*na relação, no elo, no intermediário*) that promotes social dynamics, creating zones of conversation between polar postures that may seem mutually exclusive from a practical or individualistic perspective. . . . Without considering relationship (*a relação*) as a structural element in Brazilian society . . . we cannot understand the profound basis of national identity. . . . Brazilian society is relational. A system where the basic, fundamental value is to relate, mix, put together, confuse, conciliate, . . . include (never exclude).[47]

The idea of the inexistence of conversion and, instead, of the prevalence of passages, syncretism, and double membership resonates strongly with this larger image of Brazilian society.

Assessing Recent Data on Religious Transit in Brazil

Recent data from studies of Brazil raises important questions about the "Brazilian school's" tendency to reject the concept of conversion. Furthermore, findings from these studies counter the idea of the ubiquitous prevalence of passages and syncretism and dual membership in the country. I believe the relevance of these new findings has gone largely unnoticed because of the theoretical and methodological blinders reviewed above. Especially interesting in this regard is Almeida and Montero's analysis of data on religious transit drawn from a 1998 quantitative research project called "Sexual Behavior of Brazilian Population and Perceptions of HIV" (featuring 3,600 individuals randomly drawn from urban areas of 169 micro-regions of Brazil).[48] Individuals were asked their current religion and the one into which they were born, so that each religion could be analyzed in two moments, as points of reception and of emission of devotees. The data they present show the following:

Historical Protestants who change their religion go mostly to the "without religion" category (79 percent). Some become Catholic (12 percent), few become Pentecostals (3 percent), and almost none convert to Afro-Brazilian religions or Spiritism. Likewise, Pentecostals who change their religion go mostly to the "without religion" category, albeit with a lower frequency (59 percent). A larger percentage become Catholic (37 percent), few become

Spiritists (only 2.5 percent), and almost none convert to Afro-Brazilian religions.

Spiritists who switch tend to become Catholic (63 percent) or go to the "without religion" category (30 percent). Few become Pentecostals (between 5 and 6 percent); almost none convert to Afro-Brazilian religions. Practitioners of Afro-Brazilian religions go mostly to the "without religion" category, albeit with a lower frequency (56 percent). Some of them become Catholic (24 percent) or Pentecostal (11 percent) or join Historical Protestant Churches (9 percent). Almost none convert to Spiritism.

Finally, Catholics who switch join mostly the ranks of Pentecostalism (46 percent), go to the "without religion" category (24 percent), or, to a lesser extent, become Historical Protestants (15 percent) or Spiritists (13 percent). Few convert to Afro-Brazilian religions (2 percent).

From this brief review of their data, it is evident that there are few, if any spaces of interlocution, mediations, or transits among religious groups that would be presumed by the Brazilian paradigm to be "close." Spiritists do not convert to Afro-Brazilian religions (less than 0.1 percent). Pentecostals do not convert to Afro-Brazilian religions. Few Spiritists become Pentecostals (less than 6 percent) and even fewer Pentecostals become Spiritists (less than 3 percent). Finally, even if Umbandistas sometimes become Pentecostals, the opposite is seldom true.

What these data, despite their limitations, show is that there are very definite trajectories of religious transit and that the starting point heavily conditions the arrival possibilities.[49] This strong conditioning of the range of transit possibilities belies the idea that passages are widespread and that spaces of interlocution among religious groups abound. They may be found, certainly, but to different degrees depending on the groups involved, and between some groups these data suggest that they are rare indeed. It also challenges the notion that the existence of a "common religious denominator" makes any kind of transition possible. If this were the case, the percentage of switching between certain groups (whose beliefs seem to be very close) would not be close to zero. Lastly, it likewise defies the idea that religious identities are porous and that they interpenetrate freely.

The majority of the Brazilian authors I have reviewed rejected the idea of conversion because of the supposed overabundance of syncretism, religious switching, and porous identities. These data seem to indicate that some kinds of conversions are indeed rare, but precisely for the opposite reasons: not due to the existence of many passages and mediations between groups, but instead because there seem to be important excluding forces at work that are not recognized or studied because they go against the prevailing image of a country characterized by syncretism, porous religious identities, and social mediations. While this does not necessarily disprove Brazilian interpretation of religious choices, it does suggest that the existence of passages and mediations has been overstated and that, because of theoretical, methodological, and factual reasons, it is premature to discard conversion altogether in favor of passages.

Re-assessing Conversion in Argentina through a Brazilian Lens

If Brazilians scholars may have overestimated the ubiquity of passages and mediations due to the prevalent image of their culture (and the implicit use of a passive convert paradigm), conversely, it may be argued that the ideal image of Argentine society as modern, rational, homogeneous, and Catholic has also contributed to the rather more supportive reception the concept of conversion has enjoyed in the country.[50] If Brazil is characterized by a culturally inclusive national image, Argentina is identified by an exclusive one. It is viewed as a nation and a culture that does not value mediations but separations and dichotomies.[51]

Perhaps Semán's (theoretically) "Brazilian" reading of the popular culture of the working-class sectors of the Great Buenos Aires as basically "pre-modern" is entirely accurate and individuals are not really choosing between groups, and their participation in one group or another does not imply a biographical reconstruction. The cultural distance of the beliefs proposed by the group may be, as he argues and as Carozzi and Frigerio have shown, important in the degree of identity and conversion work that need to be done in order for successful biographical reconstruction and socialization into the group's religious beliefs.[52] In Argentina, certainly, the symbols, concepts, and beliefs of Pentecostalism are less alien than those of Umbanda, for example.[53]

Social class is doubtlessly important also. The individuals studied by Semán in a southern neighborhood of the Great Buenos Aires are less educated and belong to a lower social stratum than most of those studied by Carozzi and Frigerio in their research on Umbanda in more lower-middle-class northern neighborhoods of the Great Buenos Aires. Because of their greater formal education, these individuals probably respond more to a modern logic stressing individuality and mutually exclusiveness and less to a pre-modern one (in Sanchis's terms) that allows for porous identities.

Conclusions

I have argued that the Brazilian approach to conversion is generally critical of the concept and stresses instead the existence of passages, mediations, double memberships, and porous identities. This approach is informed by a certain image of Brazilian culture and society, as well as by a "passive convert" idea of conversion. The heavy use of interviews and quantitative data rather than participant observations conspires against a processual view of conversion and also magnifies the unproblematic character of religious switching. Some of the data presented in Brazilian studies could be read from an "active convert" paradigm as evidence for, rather than against, conversion. Although dictating the death of conversion too hastily, the Brazilian approach may be useful to counter-ride an excessively "modern" reading of the Latin American religious field that sees an Anglo-Saxon situation of religious pluralism and modern individuals who choose among different religious options as commonplace (or also dominant) in the area (as Semán has contended).

It is probably unwise, however, to replace one approach with the other. If, as Sanchis has argued for Brazil, pre-modern, modern, and post-modern logics coexist and interact in the same situations, we are likely to witness passages, mediations, and conversions at the same time.[54] The exact nature of the religious transit or switching involved would depend on the groups studied, the social class to which devotees belong, and the stage of the religious career of an individual. Rather than opting for either passages or conversion, as seems to be the case in much of the Brazilian literature, it would be more productive to try to figure out the conditions or the contexts in which each happens. As Henri Gooren argues in the ensuing chapter, such an approach requires that we analyze the entire conversion career of individuals who move within and between religious groups.

NOTES

1. "Evangelicals" here is used as defined in chapter 1 (Historical Protestants, Pentecostals, and neo-Pentecostals). Census data are drawn from Ricardo Mariano, "Análise sociológica do crescimento pentecostal no Brasil" (Ph D thesis, Universidade de São Paulo, 2001), as well as from a personal communication from the author regarding the 2000 census.

2. Ruben Cesar Fernandes et al., *Novo Nascimento: Os evangelicos em casa, na igreja e na politica* (Rio de Janeiro: Mauad, 1998), 27.

3. Reginaldo Prandi, "Religião paga, conversão e serviço," in *A Realidade social das religiões no Brasil*, ed. Antonio F. Pierucci and Reginaldo Prandi (São Paulo: Hucitec, 1996), 257–273.

4. See, e.g., Patricia Birman, "Cultos de possessão e pentecostalismo no Brasil: Passagens," *Religião e Sociedade* 17 (1996): 90–109; Clara Mafra, "Relatos compartilhados: experiências de conversão ao pentecostalismo entre brasileiros e portugueses," *Mana* 6 (2000): 57–85; Lísias Nogueira Negrão, "Refazendo antigas e urdindo novas tramas: Trajetórias do sagrado," *Religião e Sociedade* 18 (1997): 63–74; Pierre Sanchis, "Para não dizer que não falei de sincretismo," *Comunicações do ISER* 45 (1994): 5–11; Pierre Sanchis, "O repto pentecostal à cultura católico-brasileira," in *Nem anjos nem demonios: interpretações sociológicas do pentecostalismo*, ed. Alberto Antoniazzi (Petrópolis: Vozes, 1994), 34–63; Pierre Sanchis, "Religiões, Religião . . .

Alguns problemas do sincretismo no campo religioso brasileiro," in *Fieis e cidadãos: Percursos de sincretismo no Brasil*, ed. Pierre Sanchis (Rio de Janeiro: EDUERJ, 2001), 23–25; Pierre Sanchis, "O campo religioso contemporâneo no Brasil," in *Religião e Globalização*, ed. Ari Oro and Carlos Steil (Petrópolis: Vozes, 1997), 103–115; Ronaldo Almeida and Paula Montero, "Trânsito religioso no Brasil," *São Paulo em Perspectiva* 15 (2001): 92–101; Prandi, "Religião paga, conversão e serviço," 257.

5. Mafra, "Relatos compartilhados," 58.

6. Almeida and Montero, "Trânsito religioso no Brasil," 92.

7. Negrão, "Refazendo antigas e urdindo novas tramas," 71.

8. Birman, "Cultos de possessão e pentecostalismo no Brasil," 91, 92.

9. Ibid., 94. See, e.g., Robin Horton, "African Conversion," *Africa* 61 (1971); John Comaroff and Jean Comaroff, *Of Revelation and Revolution: Christianity, Colonialism, and Consciousness in South Africa* (Chicago: University of Chicago Press, 1991); and R. Hefner, ed., *Conversion to Christianity* (Berkeley: University of California Press, 1993).

10. Birman, "Cultos de possessão e pentecostalismo no Brasil,"94.

11. Ibid., 93, 94.

12. Prandi, "Religião paga, conversão e serviço," 257.

13. Ibid., 260, 261.

14. Prandi, "Religião paga, conversão e serviço," 273.

15. Prandi, "Religião paga, conversão e serviço," 262.

16. Mafra, "Relatos compartilhados," 60.

17. Ibid., 73–74.

18. Sanchis, "Para não dizer," 10.

19. Sanchis, "Religiões, Religião," 25. In other articles he has referred to this structural predisposition as "a habitus, history made structure," e.g., Sanchis, "O campo religioso contemporâneo no Brasil," 112. For a fuller appreciation of Sanchis's work, see the dossier "Sincretismo, cultura e identidad: (Re) Leyendo a Pierre Sanchis desde Argentina y Brasil," *Ciencias Sociales y Religión/Ciências Sociais e Religião* 7 (2005): 187–237.

20. Sanchis, "O repto pentecostal," 47.

21. Ibid., 52. See also Pierre Sanchis, "Pentecostalismo e cultura brasileira," *Religião e Sociedade* 18 (1997): 123–126.

22. Negrão, "Refazendo antigas e urdindo novas tramas," 43–62.

23. Ibid., 64, 73.

24. Ibid., 72–73.

25. María Julia Carozzi, "Contribuciones del estudio de los nuevos movimientos religiosos a la sociología de la religión: Una evaluación crítica," in *Nuevos Movimientos Religiosos y Ciencias Sociales*, vol. 1, ed. Alejandro Frigerio (Buenos Aires: CEAL, 1993), 15–45; María Julia Carozzi, "Tendencias en el estudio de los nuevos movimientos religiosos en America: Los últimos veinte años," *Sociedad y Religión* 10/11 (1993): 3–23.

26. María J. Carozzi and Alejandro Frigerio, "Los estudios de la conversión a nuevos movimientos religiosos: Perspectivas, métodos y hallazgos," in *El estudio científico de la religión a fines del siglo XX*, ed. Alejandro Frigerio and María J. Carozzi (Buenos

Aires: CEAL, 1994), 17–53; Alejandro Frigerio, "Perspectivas Actuales sobre Conversión, Deconversión y 'Lavado de Cerebros,'" in *Nuevos Movimientos*, ed. Frigerio, 46–80.

27. María Julia Carozzi and Alejandro Frigerio, "Não se nasce batuqueiro: A conversão às religiões afro-brasileiras em Buenos Aires," *Religião e Sociedade* 30 (1997): 71–94.

28. By *personal identity* I mean the conceptualization persons make of their continuity as subjects and of the attributes that characterize them and make them different from other human beings. Personal identity is the product of reflexive action. It is the concept individuals have of themselves as physical, social, spiritual, and moral beings (see Carozzi and Frigerio, "Não se nasce batuqueiro," 73).

29. See Verónica G. Beliveau and Juan Esquivel, "Las creencias en los barrios, o un rastreo de las identidades religosas en los sectores populares urbanos del Gran Buenos Aires," *Sociedad y Religión* 14/15 (1996): 117–128; Silvia Citro, "La materialidad de la conversión religiosa: Del cuerpo propio a la economía política," *Revista de Ciencias Sociales* 10 (2000): 39–55.

30. Daniel Míguez, "*To Help You Find God": The Making of a Pentecostal Identity in a Buenos Aires Suburb* (PhD thesis, Vrije Universiteit, Amsterdam, Holland, 1997).

31. Daniel Míguez, "Conversiones religiosas, conversiones seculares. Comparando las estrategias de transformación de identidad en programas de minoridad e iglesias pentecostales," *Ciencias Sociales y Religión/Ciências Sociais e Religião* 2 (2000): 31–62.

32. Pablo Semán, "A 'Fragmentação do cosmos': Um estudo sobre as sensibilidades de fiéis pentecostais e católicos de um bairro da Grande Buenos Aires" (PhD thesis, Universidade Federal do Rio Grande do Sul, Porto Alegre, Brasil, 2000).

33. Birman, "Cultos de possessão e pentecostalismo no Brasil," 90; Sanchis, "Para não dizer," 7; Sanchis, "O campo religioso contemporâneo no Brasil," 104; Luiz F. D. Duarte, "Pluralidade religiosa nas sociedades complexas e 'religiosidade' das classes trabalhadoras urbanas," *Boletim do Museu Nacional/UFRJ* 41 (1983): 55–69.

34. Semán, "A 'Fragmentação do cosmos.'"

35. Here Mafra quotes Max Heirich in "A Change of Heart: A Test of Some Widely Held Theories about Religious Conversion," *American Journal of Sociology* 83 (1977): 653–680.

36. Mafra, "Relatos compartilhados," 58.

37. Prandi, "Religião paga, conversão e serviço," 260.

38. James T. Richardson, "The Active vs. Passive Convert: Paradigm Conflict in Conversion/Commitment Research," *Journal for the Scientific Study of Religion* 24 (1985): 163–179, 165.

39. Ibid., 172; Richard Machalek and David Snow, "Conversion to New Religious Movements," *Religion and the Social Order* 3B (1993): 54.

40. James Richardson, "Conversion Careers," *Society* 17 (1980): 49.

41. Mafra, "Relatos compartilhados," 73, 60.

42. Mariano, "Análise sociológica do crescimento Pentecostal no Brasil," 169–171.

43. Richardson, "The Active vs. Passive Convert," 175.

44. Paula Montero, "Religiões e dilemas da sociedade brasileira," in *O que ler na ciência social brasileira (1970–1995)*, vol. 1, ed. Sergio Miceli (Brasilia: Sumare/ANPOCS, 1999), 357.

45. Alejandro Frigerio, "Identidades porosas, estructuras sincréticas y narrativas dominantes: Miradas cruzadas entre Pierre Sanchis y la Argentina," *Ciencias Sociales y Religión/Ciências Sociais e Religião* 7 (2005): 223–237. *O que faz o brasil, Brazil* is the title of a popular book by noted anthropologist Roberto Da Matta (Rio de Janeiro: Rocco, 1998), whose interpretations of Brazilian society have been essential to the consolidation of a certain national image, together with those of other noted intellectuals of that country, like novelist Jorge Amado or writer Oswald de Andrade.

46. Roberto Da Matta, *Carnavais, malandros e heróis* (Rio de Janeiro: Zahar, 1981). Da Matta has argued that Brazil is "a semi-traditional society," characterized by "a social system divided and even balanced between two basic social units; the *individual* (subject of universal laws that modernize society) and the *person* (pessoa) (subject of social relationships), that points to the traditional pole of the system" (ibid., 96). This tension between the *individual* and the *person* reflects a more inclusive one between a modern egalitarian society and a traditional, hierarchical one. He has in several ways argued for the importance of mediations and mediators between the traditional and modern aspects of society (97), and for the existence of "zones of conflict and also *zones of passage between them (that are) critical for the understanding of certain Brazilian social processes*" (185, my emphasis).

47. Roberto Da Matta, *A casa e a rua* (Rio de Janeiro: Guanabara, 1987), 112, 114, 117.

48. Almeida and Montero, "Trânsito religioso no Brasil," 92–101.

49. The fact that Spiritism and Afro-Brazilian religions have the smallest number of devotees may influence the number of switching among them that appears in the tables provided by Almeida and Montero, "Trânsito religioso no Brasil." Given the closeness of their worldview however, the numbers should be more important and not non-existent. Despite their scarcity, the data do show, for example, that many more Umbandistas become Pentecostals (11 percent) than the opposite (almost none). This strongly suggests the existence of passages that are *only one-way*.

50. Alejandro Frigerio, "The Medicalization of New Religious Movements in Argentina: Cultural Themes and Deviance Designations," paper presented at the 58th Annual Meeting, Association for the Sociology of Religion, New York, August 15–17, 1996.

51. Nicholas Shumway, *La invención de la Argentina: Historia de una idea* (Buenos Aires: Emecé, 1993). This North American historian argues that the main ideological legacy of the intellectual fathers of modern Argentina was a *mythology of exclusion* that has become one of the main *orienting fictions* of the Argentine nation. These orienting fictions are rhetorical paradigms "necessary to provide individuals with a sense of nationhood, community, collective identity and the idea of a common national destiny" (ibid., 13). For an insightful comparison of the dissimilar national images of Argentina and Brazil, see Gustavo L. Ribeiro, "Tropicalismo e europeísmo: Modos de representar o Brasil e a Argentina," in *Argentinos e brasileiros: Encontros, imagens e estereótipos*, ed. Alejandro Frigerio and G. L. Ribeiro (Petrópolis: Vozes, 2002), 237–264.

52. Carozzi and Frigerio, "Não se nasce batuqueiro," 71–94.

53. However this argument cannot be extended too far, since at the same time the religious logic underlying Umbanda is quite similar to that of Folk Catholicism. See Carozzi and Frigerio, "Não se nasce batuqueiro," 76.

54. Sanchis, "O campo religioso contemporâneo no Brasil," 104–105.

3

Conversion Careers in Latin America

Entering and Leaving Church among Pentecostals, Catholics, and Mormons

HENRI GOOREN

This chapter applies the concept of the *conversion career* to Latin America by analyzing how people's involvement in churches is likely to evolve in the course of their lifetime.[1] The conversion career includes all episodes of higher or lower participation in one or more religious organizations during a person's life. The posited levels of religious participation include pre-affiliation, affiliation, conversion, confession, and disaffiliation. The central question framing the conversion career approach here is, What are the crucial factors that may cause people in Latin America to become religiously active at a certain stage of their lives?

During each individual's life, differing levels of religious participation are influenced by social, cultural, institutional, personality, and contingency factors. At the same time, careful attention must be paid to the five main phases of a person's life cycle: childhood, adolescence, marriage, midlife, and old age. This chapter attempts to provide a systematic schema for understanding the conversion narratives of Pentecostals, Catholics, and Mormons collected by multiple researchers in various Latin American countries. In particular, I focus on the varying levels of religious involvement of each of these individuals over time. Such an approach provides researchers with a systematic set of variables to take into consideration when studying conversion in variant contexts. I begin with a brief sketch of the contours of the conversion career approach. A subsequent section analyzes Pentecostal, Mormon, and Catholic conversion careers in the selected cases. The studies I quote from are almost all excellent ethnographies, mostly collected by anthropologists, featuring rich conversion stories from randomly selected informants. A final section comparing Catholic, Mormon, and Pentecostal disaffiliation addresses a major gap in the literature on conversion: the issue of backsliding or leaving a given affiliation. The conclusion weighs the importance of the types of factors mentioned above by relating the case studies to the different levels of the conversion career: pre-affiliation, affiliation, conversion, confession, and disaffiliation.

Conversion Careers: A New Approach to Religious Activity

The conversion career is defined as "the member's passage, within his or her social and cultural context, through levels, types and phases of church participation."[2] My use of conversion career is different from James Richardson's, who coined the term.[3] Here, it represents a systematic attempt to analyze shifts in levels of individual religious participation. Four important elements of this approach are the conceptualization of individual dissatisfaction with a former religion (or lack thereof), a five-level typology of religious activity, the need for a life-cycle approach, and the many factors influencing changes in individual religious activity.

An essential part of the conversion career approach is to develop a typology of religious activity that includes more dimensions than just disaffiliation and conversion. A review of the existing literature from psychology, social and cultural anthropology, sociology, and religious studies allows us to distill five primary levels of individual religious participation:[4]

Pre-affiliation is the term used here to describe the worldview and social context of potential members of a religious group in their first contacts to assess whether they would like to affiliate themselves on a more formal basis.

Affiliation refers to being a formal member of a religious group. However, group membership does not necessarily form a central aspect of one's life or identity.

Conversion, used here in the limited sense, refers to a (radical) personal change of worldview and identity. It is based both on self-report and on attribution by others. These others can be people from the same religious group, but also outsiders.

Confession is a theological term for a core member identity, describing a high level of participation inside the new religious group and a strong "missionary attitude" toward non-members outside of the group.

Disaffiliation refers to a lack of involvement in an organized religious group. This category may include various relationships with institutionalized religion. It can refer to an idiosyncratic personal religiosity, e.g., New Age. But it can also stand for an un-churched religious identity: either an apostate rejecting a former membership or an inactive member who still self-identifies as a believer. In the last case, the difference between affiliation and disaffiliation can be very small.

Since changes in the level of religious activity may occur throughout the entire lifespan, a life-cycle approach to conversion obviously becomes necessary. However, most of the literature on religious change (probably 90 percent or more) deals with conversion during adolescence.[5] Hence it is imperative that a more systematic approach should distinguish the various levels of religious activity during the various phases of people's lives. At the very least, the different aspects and dynamics of five phases of the life cycle should be differentiated: childhood, adolescence, marriage, midlife, and old age. These phases are operationalized both in terms of age and life phase (e.g., a teenaged couple with children would be in the marriage stage).

Finally, the factors influencing religious change should be identified, operationalized, weighed, and analyzed. I identify five main groups of factors influencing changes in the individual level of religious participation. First, personality factors, relating to the self and personality traits, influence conversion. Second, social factors, such as the influence of social networks of relatives, friends, or acquaintances, impact changes in religious activity. Another example of such a social factor would be the influence of other church members through socialization and role teaching. This factor is stressed especially in various conversion models by sociologists of religion, together with institutional factors. Third, institutional factors deal with dissatisfaction with the current religious group and the impact of the new group. How does it compete with other groups in a religious market by using its attractive elements (e.g., beliefs, doctrine, rules, and organization)? What are the group's recruitment methods? How does it socialize and discipline its new members? Fourth, cultural factors influencing conversion involve the influence on changes in individual religious activity of culture in a broad sense (including political and economic factors). Social/cultural anthropologists have obviously given special attention to these factors.

Finally, contingency factors are the situational events, random meetings with representatives of a certain religious group, acutely felt crises, stressful situations, and other contingencies that bring individuals into the orbit of various religious groups. I will now turn to an overview of some of the Pentecostal conversion careers that have been collected by researchers in Latin America, in order to evaluate these factors and the various stages of the conversion process.

Pentecostal Conversion Careers in Latin America

Based on an analysis of many of the conversion stories contained in the literature on Latin America and my own fieldwork in Nicaragua, I argue that many informants did not convert to a Pentecostal church, they only joined the church for a while (i.e., affiliation). Making this distinction between conversion and affiliation makes it easier to analyze the significant desertion rates in Pentecostal churches all over Latin America. It also helps explain the high mobility of some believers, who move easily from one church to another.

Few authors actually write out the conversion stories of their informants.[6] Others report they collected conversion stories, but they do not actually write them out or they use only tiny fragments of them.[7] This is regrettable if one wants to identify degrees of religious participation—in short, the person's conversion career.

The first book on Pentecostalism in Latin America contains excerpts from thirty-four conversion stories from Brazil and Chile.[8] Emilio Willems skillfully combined secondary materials, ethnographic methods (participant observation and interviews), and surveys in three states of Brazil and three provinces of Chile. He interviewed many leaders and collected thirty-four life histories from random members in many different churches. In all cases, the informant's initials, age, occupation, marital status, and religious background are mentioned.[9] The only missing information is the age at which the actual conversion took place. Almost forty years later, this material is still very rich and the parallels with conversion stories that have been collected decades later are very strong. In fact, many of the stories—right down to the phrasings—are identical to the more recent conversion accounts.

Take, for instance, the conversion story of E.C.G., an eighteen-year-old single woman:

> Grandmother used to take me to a Pentecostal temple, but I had no energy to resist temptations. Afterwards I returned to church to repent but I always fell back into sin. One day I heard the voice of the Lord who told me that all my sins had been forgiven. My heart filled with *gozo* and I was seized by the Holy Spirit. I danced and heard soft voices singing exquisite melodies. I felt carried away to another place of wondrous beauty. When I recovered I found myself kneeling and praying in front of the altar. Immediately all temptations and anxieties ceased. I gave up painting my lips and curling my hair. . . . When I was fourteen years old I had ear surgery and became almost deaf. After my conversion I took part in a *cadena de oración* (continuous prayer meeting of seven days). During one of these meetings an *hermano* laid hands on my head and gradually my hearing went back to normal.[10]

Willems already concludes in this early study that all who joined a Pentecostal church shared a strong desire to change their lives.[11] If a conversion took place, it was often connected to miraculous healings. This has proven to be a recurring theme in studies of Pentecostalism in Latin America.

Argentine anthropologist Daniel Míguez has also analyzed Pentecostal identity in a Buenos Aires suburb. He collected many rich conversion stories, like this one by Victor: "I was a true Catholic. . . . There were neighbors who were Evangelicals and [my grandmother] sent me there. . . . So I already had some respect for Evangelicals, a certain appreciation of them." Victor was already attracted to evangelical TV programs before his conversion, which happened after a dream:

> I was always looking for God, and . . . I had a very real dream. . . . I kept getting smaller. And I knew I was going to disappear, I felt I was disappearing. . . . The only thing I could think of . . . was to say: Lord, take care of me. . . . The desire to find God was so great that I read all the Bible. . . . Now the Church holds these house meetings. . . . Once there was a meeting near my home and a neighbour . . . invited me. . . . Seven years ago I went forward here at church and I made my vow of faith. . . . I received Christ in my heart, that's where all our life starts. . . . I studied, if there was a need to visit people I visited, then I was designated as leader. . . . First I was Visitor. . . . I traveled on my bicycle. . . . Then I was made Area Leader.[12]

Victor's conversion career can be sketched chronologically. As a child, he respected his evangelical neighbors. During his adolescence, he liked to watch evangelical TV programs because he was "always looking for God." This is the pre-affiliation stage. Then he had a supernatural experience in a dream, which seems to have confronted him with his mortality and insignificance. A neighbor invited him to a house meeting of a local Pentecostal church (a clear institutional factor), where he "received Christ in his heart." He became very active in the church, first as a visitor, then as an area leader. To utilize the terminology of the conversion career, he went from affiliation to conversion to confession in a relatively short time.

Míguez also describes the conversion experience of a married couple, Horacio and Elba García, who were around fifty. The Garcías converted in 1987 after experiencing economic hardships for some time. They were suffering from extreme anxiety and consequent family disruption. Their son Mario said, "We first went to a *curandero*. But the curandero offered us no solution. . . . Then some family problems started and we resorted to Umbanda. . . . I never believed in them [Catholic priests]." Elba, who was living separately from Horacio at that time, said, "Everything happened through television. . . . It was the program of pastor Gimenez, and through that message God touched my heart; things started to change. I had the desire to return home." After this experience, Elba and Horacio gradually became reunited. At a certain stage, about a month and a half after her conversion, Elba decided to "hand in all the medicines to the pastor" and to trust God for her cure: "It wasn't easy, it was not from one day to the other."[13] Shortly after they re-entered church life, Elba and Horacio were appointed as area leaders.

The conversion careers of Horacio and Elba are quite similar. In their pre-affiliation situation, they suffered economic hardship, anxiety, and a divorce (contingency factors). They experimented with a curandero (shaman healer), Umbanda, and a Catholic priest—showing they had a religious problem-solving perspective. Elba was touched by Christ through an evangelical TV program (institutional factor). She went to church and Horacio started going with her. Their conversions contributed to their reconciliation; religion turned out to be part of the solution. Their son Mario converted at a later age, after finding a job through a church member (social networks). He was less active for some time, but he became more involved in church life when he was made an area leader. The same happened with his parents. As with Victor, Horacio and Elba went quickly from affiliation to conversion to confession.

Spanish anthropologist Manuela Cantón notes that conversion stories are more or less standardized and fulfill three different functions. According to her, the conversion testimonies are socializing, didactic, and proselytizing at the same time. The narratives then form the basis of the informant's new spirituality.[14] It thus comes as no surprise that Cantón's book also contains rich and detailed conversion stories. The book also gives due attention to the time before conversion (pre-affiliation) in the five-tier typology described above. Cantón's informants mention the importance of their strong dissatisfaction with Catholicism, their extreme suffering, family and alcohol problems, illness, and a general dissatisfaction with their lives.[15] Over half of the informants report that the first contact with the church happened through a spouse, relative, friend, neighbor, or acquaintance.[16] Cantón's study thus confirms the importance of institutional, contingency, and social factors in recruitment.

The following conversion story is told by Carlos, who was forty-six at that time. He became an alcoholic at fourteen or fifteen and started using marijuana after he joined the army at eighteen. When he had no money to buy drugs, he engaged in armed robbery on the streets of Antigua and Guatemala City. He said he was in prison forty times and his resentment against society grew stronger each time he was there. He went to a Catholic church in Antigua Guatemala and said:

> Lord, I believe that you are the son of God; if you exist, change my life; take away this burden from my soul. Lord, I can't take it anymore! . . .

And you know what happened? Nothing happened, absolutely nothing happened! Witchcraft couldn't change my life; human science couldn't change my life; strong literature like Lenin and Marx couldn't change my life. Something was happening in my life; I didn't understand all of it. . . . For the first time I went to an evangelical congregation. . . . I went with long hair and a ring in my ear . . . but something stronger than myself touched my heart, it lifted me up and I walked to the platform. . . . I threw myself down on the floor and I started to cry. I started to see my life one by one, step by step, everything that was my earlier life (he is crying). And I told Him: "Lord, forgive me, if you are more powerful, if you are stronger than the drugs, change me please, take away what I'm feeling in my heart." . . . [N]obody could change my life, only His holy and powerful gospel.[17]

Carlos's dramatic conversion career went from adolescent alcoholism and drug use to crime and a long prison life, a contingency crisis brought on by a combination of social and personality factors. Carlos was violent and full of resentment against society. He looked for solutions in various places—not all religious. Ultimately, his conversion experience took place in a Pentecostal church, although we are unable to gauge his subsequent level of commitment because the author does not provide us with the data.

These studies show how most authors have focused on conversion among adolescents and married people in major urban centers of Latin America. The main factors reported in conversion were social (networks), institutional (evangelization methods), and chance events. Unfortunately, the authors do not provide an overview of the entire life history of their informants, making it impossible to trace their complete conversion careers.

During my recent Nicaraguan fieldwork, I collected full life histories from over forty random informants in seven churches in Managua and Rivas. In Managua, I got to know Ricardo well. Aged twenty-eight, he is one of the pastors of a very successful Nicaraguan mega-church. Ricardo joined the church twice and each time claimed a conversion experience. The first time he accepted Christ and his life changed; he stopped drinking. This is fairly standard. But he did not get involved in church life. They gave him an assignment, but his motivation wavered. He dropped out of church for a few months and then returned. With the alter call, he went forward and cried. He felt reconciled with Christ. After the meeting, a pastor asked if he wanted to lead a group of youngsters. He accepted and has had various church tasks. Ricardo said, "You need to commit time and money to the church. I gave up a well-paying job at an international enterprise for a job as a pastor in the church office. Without a real commitment, many brothers drop out within a few months. I've seen it happen often."[18]

The case of Ricardo shows how conversion is not necessarily a once-in-a-lifetime event. Tracking his conversion career, we see how conversion is followed by disaffiliation. After a second conversion experience, Ricardo is invited by a leader to become a leader himself. The confession level of our typology consolidates the conversion experience.

Catholic and Mormon Conversion Careers in Latin America

Focusing only on Pentecostal conversion careers in Latin America implies the risk that certain elements might be considered unique to Pentecostalism, whereas they may also be a part of conversion careers in other religious groups. By way of comparison, this section looks at Catholic and Mormon conversion careers, based on the available literature. Again, I should note that the literature is extremely scarce. Researchers rarely collect complete conversion narratives in general and hardly ever from Catholics or Mormons, even though the evidence suggests that the concept of conversion is also important in these religions.[19]

Dutch anthropologist Janneke Brouwer concludes, surprisingly, that there are many similarities between the conversion narratives she collected from Pentecostals and Charismatic Catholics in Masaya, Nicaragua.[20] For both of them, the conversion process was very emotional and happened at a crucial moment in their life. Both considered their "old" life to be meaningless, without purpose, empty, and often downright sinful. Both use the concept of "being reborn" to express the personal transformation they experienced. After conversion, life acquired a new meaning and a new purpose. Finally, both her Pentecostal and Charismatic Catholic informants said that they prayed often and have remained highly active in their respective churches by taking on various assignments. That is, her informants must be located at the confession level of the typology of religious activity.

According to Brouwer, the main difference between Pentecostal and Catholic converts in Nicaragua could be found in their conceptualization of the precise moment they converted.[21] For the Pentecostals, conversion happened the moment they accepted Jesus Christ as their personal savior, usually by coming forward toward the pulpit during a church service. This moment in time was later ritualized by their baptism and their acceptance as a full member in the Pentecostal church. For the Charismatic Catholics, the conversion moment is equated with the moment they became fully aware of God's love for them. Since they were already baptized as infants, no second baptism could be performed. However, they are very much aware that their life has to be transformed after dedicating themselves to Christ.

Another difference is that the Catholic informants in Nicaragua were converted to the Charismatic Renewal at a much later moment in their lives than the Pentecostals were. The average age for the Catholic converts was twenty-nine, against twenty for the Pentecostals.[22] Almost all of them were nominal Catholics who became active under the influence of certain events in their lives.

Miguel (thirty-six) was an ex-Sandinista fighter against the dictator Somoza; he became disillusioned and later joined the Contras to attack the Sandinista army in the 1980s. In combat, he started to drink heavily and use marijuana. He beat up his wife and his mother. This made him cry when he was sober again, and he wanted to go to church. There was a meeting of the Charismatic Renewal; he recognized the songs from afar and was greeted at the door by ex-friends from his Sandinista days. When the speaker invited people to accept Christ in their lives as the solution for their personal problems, he came forward. Miguel said, "Without realizing it, I had knelt down and I was crying. . . . Suddenly I longed for mass and the Eucharist. That week my happiness started." His drinking mates thought he would only last for a week without alcohol, but he never returned to his old ways. Church people took him to a prayer group to receive the Holy Spirit. He lost consciousness and had a vision of a man walking in the desert. "Everybody started praying and crying. Then I was embraced by everyone. We went home and testified to all people of what had happened." He soon became an active leader and a preacher at Charismatic Renewal meetings.[23]

The conversion stories of the spouses Isabel and José were very similar. Both had a conversion experience during a *retiro* (spiritual retreat) of the Catholic Church, but not at the same time. A close (lady) friend invited Isabel (forty) to come with her to the retreat. Isabel said, "That last Sunday the Holy Spirit descended upon me. . . . I felt how something filled me up, for I realized there was an emptiness inside me. . . . I felt loved by the people who were there." Isabel's husband, José (thirty-nine), said, "On the last day of the retreat, the Holy Spirit descended [upon me]. I told the Lord: 'If anything is going to happen here, I'm prepared to receive it. Lord, here I am.' When the Holy Spirit descended, the speaker gave indications of things we might experience. . . . I felt a warmth deep inside me. . . . As of that moment, I no longer was the same. I felt differently, I began to look at things differently, and I began to do things differently. I now read the Bible, I pray, I go to mass, something I never did before."[24]

All four Charismatic Catholics became very active in the church after their conversion experience. Two occasionally pray and sing in tongues. All four also report to have a very intense personal spiritual life, full of prayer and Bible study.

Brouwer concludes that the Charismatic Catholic informants tended to emphasize the practical changes in their social lives after conversion.[25] Most reported that they used to have an impatient character, easily provoked into anger. After conversion, they said they there were more calm and at peace with themselves and other people. Collecting extensive life histories, Brouwer shows similarities between the conversion experiences of Charismatic Catholics and Pentecostals in Masaya, Nicaragua. The link between conversion and confession is again confirmed. But since almost all of her informants are leaders, located at the confession level of our typology, her findings cannot simply be generalized to all of Latin America.

Mormon Conversion Careers

The detailed conversion stories of Mormon micro-entrepreneurs also shed light on the conversion careers in this particular offspring of Christianity.[26] The average age for conversion among my twelve Mormon key informants in La Florida (a typical low-income *barrio* of Guatemala City) was twenty-five, but almost all had gone through (long) periods of inactivity. I found three primary groups of informants who converted. First, there are adolescent religious seekers who visited various churches to see where they felt most comfortable (Mario, Patricio, and Ana). Second, I found informants who joined a new church or reactivated a prior church membership after going through a turning point in their lives such as facing up to their problems with alcohol or becoming parents (nine informants). Third, I interviewed informants who switched to another church under the influence of spouses or children (Raúl, Beatriz, and Miguel).[27] I will briefly analyze one conversion story for the seekers and the turning-point groups.

Almost all (male) Mormon informants reported having a turning-point experience in their lives connected to alcohol problems. When Guillermo (now twenty-nine) was only thirteen, his father kicked him out of the family home and he was forced to live on the street. In 1984, at eighteen, he first learned about the Mormon Church:[28] "I wanted to change my life, because I used a lot of alcohol, drugs; I hung out with youth gangs. . . . Some missionaries [Sisters] came here and talked to me about the gospel and I liked it. . . . They presented a Christ of love, someone who had mercy and that He could save my life. And at other times people had told me that I was a son of the devil, that I was possessed by Satan and that I'd go to hell with him. I got baptized, but I didn't have the strength—or the support, I think—to stay in church. After two months . . . I backslided. . . . I started drinking again . . . and I didn't have anything to do with the church for seven years."[29] Alcoholics Anonymous helped Guillermo to overcome his alcohol problem, but he still needed marijuana to make it through the day:

> I was fed up with the life I had and there were only two solutions for
> me: either I changed my life, or I would kill myself. That night I went
> to bed . . . and I awoke around five in the morning. . . . I saw all the

scenes from my life: the bad things I had done, what I was doing to my
body, the suffering and pain I was causing in my family. . . . I knelt on
the bed and asked God for forgiveness. And I said: God, if you really
exist, if you have a purpose for my life, manifest yourself. I put my life
into your hands and do what you want with me because *I* could never
do anything with it. Take me to a place where I will stop using drugs,
where I can change my life, where I can be happy and make my family happy. . . . So I got up, bathed myself, changed clothes and I didn't
know where I was going. . . . And when I noticed, I was again in the
church where I had been baptized seven years ago. Since that moment
my life began to change. . . . I did have a lot of support from all the
brothers of the church . . . [and] they took care of me like a baby and
taught me really how to live the gospel. After two months in church
they conferred the Aaronic priesthood on me. After three months in
church they conferred the Melchizedek priesthood on me . . . and so
they . . . called me as president of the young men of the ward.[30]

In the case of Guillermo, an even more troubled childhood of drugs and
alcohol is followed by a conversion at a young age (eighteen). The church
members cannot support him sufficiently, so he drops out of the Mormon
Church and is inactive for many years. Again, when the drug problem gets out
of hand and threatens to kill him, he appeals to God and has a supernatural
experience, after which God guides him back to the same Mormon congregation he visited before. Now, however, he does receive sufficient support from
the members and is also given an important calling soon. Again, the crisis is
caused by a combination of personality and social factors and resolved after
receiving the support from church members and becoming active in church.

The conversion careers described here among the Catholic Charismatics, Mormons, and Pentecostals are remarkably similar. In all cases, the
contingency factor of the crisis appears as the starting point. The informants
have a religious problem-solving perspective; some try to visit curanderos,
priests, and Umbanda leaders to find a solution. Charismatic Catholics in
Nicaragua stay in their church because they are happy with it. People who
are dissatisfied with Catholicism are reported to be more open to experiment
by visiting other churches, as noted in the studies on Argentina, Guatemala,
and Nicaragua. In the end, a contingency social factor, a chance meeting
with missionaries, or the influence of a friend or neighbor establishes the
first contact with their new church. If they receive support from members,
they will stay. But the support is often insufficient and the church demands
are high, which sometimes leads to (temporary) disaffiliation. I will return
to this theme in the conclusion.

Disaffiliation among Protestants, Mormons, and Catholics

The issue of disaffiliation is rarely treated in the literature on conversion in Latin America. Cantón's study in Guatemala provides no information on the informants' church commitment following their conversion. However, it is significant that all of the Pentecostal informants of Míguez's study in Buenos Aires were designated area leaders or visitors soon after their conversion and subsequent baptism into their church. The fact that these Pentecostals went from affiliation to conversion to confession in a relatively short time appears to have strengthened their church commitment, but Míguez provides no details to gauge how this process worked.

Protestant Disaffiliation

There are few comprehensive studies on religious disaffiliation in Latin America. In the previous chapter, Alejandro Frigerio quotes from a Brazilian study, which reports that no less than 59 percent of all Pentecostals who change their religion in Brazil end up in the "no religion" category. However, the corresponding figure from switchers from the Historical Protestant churches in Brazil is even higher, with 79 percent of those who leave reporting that they have no religion.

In 2000, a survey of over 2,400 Nicaraguans by the Dutch reverend Henk Minderhoud showed that the total Protestant church disaffiliation (or desertion) was 27 percent of all Protestants. Among these ex-Protestants, 8 percent said they had returned to the Catholic Church and 19 percent reported that they did not belong to any religion anymore.[31]

Jorge Gómez's study contains even more detailed information on disaffiliation in Costa Rica, based on three large surveys in 1989, 1991, and 1994. The total Protestant apostasy rate was 48 percent in 1989 and 53 percent in 1991. The 1989 survey showed that among these ex-Protestants, 62 percent had actually returned to the Catholic Church.[32] A full one-third had completely dropped out of any church and 6 percent had joined the Jehovah's Witnesses or the Mormon Church. Gómez reported that the Catholic desertion among those born into Catholicism was 12.5 percent.[33]

Gómez has a very interesting comparison of the main reasons for entering and leaving Protestant churches, based on the 1994 survey. The main reasons for the original conversion were "the desire to become a new creature in Christ" (50 percent), being born into an evangelical family (11 percent), church recruitment through a friend or relative (10 percent), the attraction of evangelical preaching (7 percent), and being healed (6 percent). The main reasons for dropping out were not being able to live up to the evangelical moral standards (29 percent), rejection of bad financial management in the

Pentecostal church (13 percent), bad conduct of other members (9 percent) or of the pastor (8 percent).[34]

The only complete monograph on religious disaffiliation is Kurt Bowen's study on Mexico. Bowen concluded that "conversion is often a process of encounter and retreat, which only after some time culminates in conversion. Altogether, fifty-four percent of converts identified one or another crisis in their lives that significantly affected their conversion decision."[35]

Typically, Bowen dedicated more attention to why Mexicans joined Pentecostalism than to why they left it behind. Consider this story by a woman, thirty-seven, who converted after seeing a leaflet advertising a Christian film during a campaign: "I like films of Christ. The first time I went, there was not a film. I felt deceived. . . . The pastor invited people to go forward to give themselves to Christ. I did not go. . . . After the film next time, he also made the call. I felt embarrassed, but my sister went up, so, with my children, we went up and delivered ourselves to Christ. I did not know anything of Christ. I did not know how to study the Bible. After the campaign we stopped attending, but some brothers came to visit us to teach us."[36] It is clear that some people may drift into a Pentecostal church after seeing a film or an evangelical TV program, but their continued commitment would seem to depend on finding a community, on receiving support from like-minded people, and above all on receiving attention by other members (for example, being visited by them).

Just like growth rates, the desertion rates were also very high in Mexican Pentecostal churches. According to Bowen, "sixty-eight percent of those baptized in Evangelical churches in the 1980s had dropped out by the end of the decade."[37] Based on Bowen's extensive surveys in over forty congregations, the total disaffiliation rate in Pentecostal churches was 43 percent, meaning that less than half of all those who once belonged to a Pentecostal church actually stayed in it.[38]

Mormon Disaffiliation

My own research on the conversion careers of Mormon entrepreneurs in Guatemala City also showed a rapid change from pre-affiliation to conversion to confession. Patricio and Guillermo both had a troubled childhood and adolescence, marked by alcohol and drug problems. Although they converted to the Mormon Church at a relatively young age, twenty-six and eighteen, respectively, both were inactive for a great many years. They felt that members showed no interest in them during this time. When their alcohol problems got out of hand, they prayed to God hoping for an intervention in their lives. Both had a supernatural experience, which they interpreted as support for the veracity of the Mormon Church. They subsequently returned to church, and this time they did receive the support from members and leaders.

An important element in my informants' Mormon socialization was, again, the fact that they soon received one or more important "callings" (church assignments). The callings seemed to reinforce and sustain their commitment: "In a calling, members are forced to learn new things, like teaching, that they are not used to and do not know how to do well. They would like to shirk their responsibilities, but they are afraid of losing God's blessing—God's favor—if they fail, so they go on."[39] However, there is a risk to giving the new members a calling too soon. When they feel too uncertain of themselves, some may become inactive, as happened with another Mormon informant, Miguel.[40]

Catholic Disaffiliation

There is surprisingly little literature on disaffiliation among Catholics, although most studies agree that nominal Catholics make up the bulk of all people identifying themselves as Catholic in surveys on religious affiliation (see also Steigenga and Cleary in chapter 1). In chapter 2, Alejandro Frigerio quotes from a Brazilian study which reports that 24 percent of all Catholics who switch in Brazil end up in the "no religion" category.

Based on a 1989 survey, Gómez reports that 13 percent of all reported Catholics in Costa Rica never go to church and 25 percent go only very rarely.[41] Pablo (forty-one, carpenter), an inactive Catholic who believed in being a Christian but not in going to church, told me, "In the Catholic Church they don't explain to you what it all means. . . . So you have to find a way to live well . . . To apply the law which our Lord Jesus Christ taught us, to be good, to give up vices."[42]

The Catholic Charismatic Renewal movement has become an important vehicle for Catholics to become active in church again, but in a very different way than before.[43] Although it usually occurred at a later time in their lives than with the Pentecostals and Mormons, Catholic Charismatics studied in Brazil and Nicaragua also had an encounter with Christ, which then affected their entire life. Like the Pentecostals, they usually called it a conversion. It often happened during a spiritual retreat and they received the Holy Spirit in a way similar to Pentecostals. Almost all the informants in Brouwer's study had been nominal Catholics who became active again in the Catholic Church under the influence of certain events in their lives. These events were alcohol problems or a feeling of meaninglessness, similar again to those described by Pentecostal informants. However, it is not clear why these informants had become nominal Catholics in the first place.

In sum, the remarkable similarities in the conversion careers of Pentecostals, Charismatic Catholics, and Mormons also extend to the dynamics behind the processes of (temporary) disaffiliation. I will now turn to a brief analysis of these conversion discourses, using the conversion career approach to shed more light on this phenomenon.

Analyzing Conversion Careers in Latin America

Sweeping generalizations explaining conversion in the context of Latin America should be met with skepticism. The available literature on conversion in Latin America remains limited, and the conversion stories presented in this chapter come from different churches in seven countries: Chile, Brazil, Argentina, Nicaragua, Guatemala, Mexico, and Costa Rica. Even in these testimonials, essential information on the conversion careers of informants was often missing. This is primarily due to the fact that conversion careers take place over time, include different levels of commitment, and frequently extend far beyond the particular time frame or interests of a given researcher. Most of the conversion narratives collected in Latin America, as in the North American literature on religious conversion, were collected among adolescents or people in their twenties and thirties.

Despite these limitations, we can draw some important insights from the literature on conversion that lead to a more comprehensive and interdisciplinary approach to explaining and comparing conversion. In this final section, I will follow the conversion career approach to analyze the conversion narratives presented in this chapter. The conversion career approach goes beyond the Pauline idea of conversion as a unique and once-in-a-lifetime experience, categorizing levels of conversion (pre-affiliation, affiliation, conversion, confession, and disaffiliation) and outlining the key factors that our approach identifies as essential in the conversion career (social, institutional, cultural, personality, and contingency factors).

The Role of Crisis in Conversion

First, during the pre-affiliation situation of the informants, the impetus most informants mention is a contingency factor: a crisis. This crisis can be of various sorts, although all of these touch upon the informant's personality. In the most extreme cases, the crisis involved drug or alcohol problems, often in combination with crime. These crises were related to the informant's social situation (poverty, child labor, absent fathers) or personality (machismo, insecurity). In other cases, the crisis was less extreme and related to illness, divorce, adultery, or poverty. Whatever its origin, the crisis always caused anxiety (Horacio and Elba), desperation (Carlos), and dissatisfaction with the current (religious) life style.

It is also important to note that most informants were at this time still adolescents or in their (early) twenties and that all informants couched the crisis—and its possible solutions—in religious terms. Most informants had a nominal Catholic background, as predicted by Steigenga and Cleary in chapter 1 of this volume. A few informants were active Catholics; some were seekers, always looking for God (e.g., Victor). When the crisis was at its worst, many experimented with different religious solutions: curanderos, Umbanda, Catholicism, doctors, or secular political philosophies such as Marxism. The vibrant religious markets all over Latin America, as Andrew Chesnut argues in chapter 4, allow lukewarm Catholics unprecedented opportunities for tuning into TV and radio stations and moving from one church to another. The pre-affiliation level makes visible the reservoir of potential converts, but for affiliation and an actual conversion, much more is needed.

Networks and Contingency Factors

Second, a combination of social and contingency factors is decisive in determining the particular church with which people will affiliate. It could be a chance meeting with Mormon missionaries or the influence of a spouse, friend, or neighbor which serves to establish the first contact with the new church. In some cases, the influence of evangelical TV programs is mentioned. In this volume and elsewhere, David Smilde outlines the crucial importance of social networks for understanding the process of conversion.[44]

Institutional factors also interact with networks. For example, the activities a religious group employs to recruit new members, either by sponsoring TV programs or by motivating their members to give their testimonies and bring their family and friends to the church, can make it more attractive. Not surprisingly, churches that put greater emphasis on this—like most Pentecostal churches and the Mormon Church—generally achieve higher growth.

Social factors are principally responsible for the question of whether or not the informant will decide to actually affiliate with a new church. Here, most informants mention the importance of receiving the support of the "brothers" (and sisters, who are grammatically included in the Spanish word *hermanos*). New members need a lot of attention, nurturing, and counseling; this is mentioned in the conversion career scheme under "incorporating, creating, and shaping activities."[45]

Confession and Crisis Resolution

The actual conversion usually follows when the new church is seen as (contributing to) the solution to the original crisis. This can take many forms: the healing of an illness, giving a new purpose and meaning to one's life, overcoming alcohol problems, giving people peace and tranquility. Even getting a job through another church member is often interpreted as a divine sign that conversion is the right choice.

Many of the informants from the literature fit in the highest level of the conversion career typology of religious activity: confession. In the conversion career approach, role learning is considered as the basis of church commitment.[46] A good way to strengthen church commitment is to give the novice a voluntary church assignment. In a great many cases, the informants remained active in church while accepting important leadership or teaching responsibilities. However, there is always the danger that the informants still feel insecure and may feel pressured into accepting a task they are not ready for yet. In that case, disaffiliation may follow. Maria Carozzi's chapter within this volume suggests that this process may well apply in the case of conversion to Afro-Brazilian religions as well.

Finally, disaffiliation also happens when the new members feel rejected or neglected by the other members of the church. Informants from the three groups mentioned that they remained active in church because "the brothers" visited them. However, because many congregations are big and leaders are overworked, one can safely assume that many people were not visited and hence dropped out after a while. This applied especially to people who converted very quickly, with only a rudimentary knowledge of the church's doctrine and rules of conduct. The fact that the consequences of conversion are rather limited in so many cases also suggests that many of these conversions are actually only a rather superficial form of affiliation and a temporary one at that.

In other cases, however, disaffiliation was caused exactly by the high demands—in discipline, morality, time, and money—of the church in question. This was noted particularly in the literature on Pentecostal churches. It means that the same factors which were originally responsible for the success of Pentecostalism in Latin America, in fact, also account for its high drop-out rates. Salvation sometimes proves to be less secure than people had originally hoped, the high levels of commitment and high standards of conduct are difficult to maintain, and the organization of many Pentecostal churches would seem to stimulate schism rather than control it.

During this process, religious seekers may join various churches. But researchers should be wary to simply equate affiliation with conversion. For researchers who wish to understand both the process and effects of conversion in the context of Latin America, the distinction between conversion and affiliation is critical. To a large degree, this distinction gives us greater insights into the high religious mobility of many individuals in Latin America.

In a context of growing religious competition in Latin America, it is all the more important that we (1) delineate the various levels of religious commitment we utilize in our studies of religion, (2) systematize the variables impacting both conversion and disaffiliation, and (3) endeavor to collect the most complete data possible in order to fill in the full model of the conversion career.

NOTES

This chapter has benefited greatly from critical comments and helpful suggestions made by Edward Cleary, André Droogers, Rijk van Dijk, Jan van Gelder, Linda van de Kamp, Miranda Klaver, Birgit Meyer, Azusa Miyashita, Elisabet Rasch, Regien Smit, Griet Steel, Timothy Steigenga, and Peter Versteeg.

1. For more details on the conversion careers approach, see André Droogers, Henri Gooren, and Anton Houtepen, "Conversion Careers and Culture Politics in Pentecostalism: A Comparative Study in Four Continents," proposal submitted to the thematic program "The Future of the Religious Past" of the Netherlands Organization for Scientific Research (NWO), 2003; see also Henri Gooren, "Towards a New Model of Conversion Careers: The Impact of Personality and Situational Factors," *Exchange* 34 (2005): 149–166; Henri Gooren, "Towards a New Model of Religious Conversion Careers: The Impact of Social and Institutional Factors," in *Paradigms, Poetics, and Politics of Conversion*, ed. Wout J. van Bekkum, Jan N. Bremmer, and Arie Molendijk (Leuven: Peeters, 2006), 25–40.

2. Droogers, Gooren, and Houtepen, "Conversion Careers," 5–6.

3. James T. Richardson, ed., *Conversion Careers: In and out of the New Religions* (Beverly Hills: SAGE, 1978). See also Alejandro Frigerio in this volume.

4. See Henri Gooren, "Towards a New Model of Religious Conversion Careers: The Impact of Social and Institutional Factors," in *Paradigms, Poetics, and Politics of Conversion*, ed. van Bekkum, Bremmer, and Molendijk, 25–40, for the review of conversion literature. Important inspirations for both the levels of religious activity and the factors in conversion were David G. Bromley and Anson D. Shupe, "Just a Few Years Seem like a Lifetime: A Role Theory Approach to Participation in Religious Movements," in *Research in Social Movements, Conflicts, and Change*, vol. 2, ed. Louis Kriesberg (Greenwich, CT: JAI Press, 1979), 159–185; Henri Gooren, "Reconsidering Protestant Growth in Guatemala, 1900–1995," in *Holy Saints and Fiery Preachers: The Anthropology of Protestantism in Mexico and Central America*, ed. James W. Dow and Alan R. Sandstrom (Westport, CT: Greenwood/Praeger Press, 2001), 169–203; Theodore E. Long and Jeffrey K. Hadden, "Religious Conversion and the Concept of Socialization: Integrating the Brainwashing and Drift Models," in *Journal for the Scientific Study of Religion* 22 (1983): 1–14; and especially Lewis R. Rambo, *Understanding Religious Conversion* (New Haven and London: Yale University Press, 1993).

5. Gooren, "Towards a New Model of Conversion Careers."

6. See, e.g., Janneke Brouwer, "Nieuwe scheppingen in Christus: Bekeringsverhalen van protestante evangélicos en katholieke carismáticos in Masaya, Nicaragua" (MA thesis, Utrecht University, 2000); John Burdick, *Looking for God in Brazil: The Progressive Catholic Church in Urban Brazil's Religious Arena* (Berkeley: University of California Press, 1993); Manuela Cantón Delgado, *Bautizados en fuego: Protestantes, discursos de conversión y política en Guatemala (1989–1993)* (Antigua, Guatemala/ South Woodstock, VT: CIRMA/Plumsock Mesoamerican Studies, 1998); Rowan Ireland, *Kingdoms Come: Religion and Politics in Brazil* (Pittsburgh: University of Pittsburgh Press, 1991); and Daniel Míguez, "'To Help You Find God': The Making

of a Pentecostal Identity in a Buenos Aires Suburb" (PhD diss., Vrije Universiteit, Amsterdam, 1997).

7. See, e.g., Elizabeth E. Brusco, *The Reformation of Machismo: Evangelical Conversion and Gender in Colombia* (Austin: University of Texas Press, 1995); Christian Lalive d'Epinay, *Haven of the Masses: A Study of the Pentecostal Movement in Chile* (London: Lutterworth, 1969); and Cecília Loreto Mariz, *Coping with Poverty: Pentecostal Churches and Christian Base Communities in Brazil* (Philadelphia: Temple University Press, 1994).

8. Emilio Willems, *Followers of the New Faith: Culture Change and the Rise of Protestantism in Brazil and Chile* (Nashville: Vanderbilt University Press, 1967), 125–131.

9. Ibid., 125–131.

10. E.C.G. quoted in Ibid., 127.

11. Willems, *Followers of the New Faith*, 130–131.

12. Victor quoted in Míguez, "To Help You Find God," 103–106. Míguez acknowledges the problems of "representivity and generalization" (ibid., 28) in ethnographic research. He randomly interviewed members and leaders in the Pentecostal Centro Cristiano in a typical suburb of Buenos Aires, Argentina.

13. Quoted in Míguez, "To Help You Find God," 107–109.

14. Cantón Delgado, *Bautizados en fuego*, 134.

15. Ibid., 148–160. Her twenty-three key informants, selected at random, come from seventeen different congregations in various Guatemalan towns and cities. Eight are Pentecostals; one is a Catholic Charismatic.

16. Cantón Delgado, *Bautizados en fuego*, 168.

17. Carlos quoted in ibid., 189–196; translation mine.

18. Ricardo is not his real name. Interviews in Managua, April 14 and 18, 2006.

19. Henri Gooren, *Rich among the Poor: Church, Firm, and Household among Small-Scale Entrepreneurs in Guatemala City* (Amsterdam: Thela, 1999); Brouwer, "Nieuwe scheppingen in Christus."

20. Brouwer, "Nieuwe scheppingen in Christus," 35.

21. Ibid., 36.

22. Ibid., 25–26. Brouwer conducted a community study in a Charismatic parish and an independent Pentecostal church in the provincial town Masaya.

23. Brouwer, *Nieuwe scheppingen in Christus*, 28; translation mine.

24. Quoted in ibid., 30–31; translation mine.

25. Brouwer, *Nieuwe scheppingen in Christus*, 32.

26. Gooren, *Rich among the Poor*. On the peculiarities of Mormonism, see, e.g., Douglas J. Davies, *An Introduction to Mormonism* (Cambridge: Cambridge University Press, 2003). On Mormonism in Latin America, see Gooren, *Rich among the Poor*, 63–68; or Henri Gooren, "Analyzing LDS Growth in Guatemala: Report from a *Barrio*," *Dialogue* 33 (2000): 97–115.

27. Gooren, *Rich among the Poor*, 153–154.

28. Ibid., 155–156, 163.

29. Guillermo quoted in ibid., 155.

30. Gooren, *Rich among the Poor*, 155, 163.

31. Interview with the Rev. Henk Minderhoud, director of INDEF, in Managua, June 15, 2005.

32. Jorge I. Gómez, *El crecimiento y la deserción en la iglesia evangélica costarricense* (San José, Costa Rica: IINDEF, 1996), 30. Gómez uses statistical materials from various censuses and from three CID/Gallup polls, which are based on over 1,200 randomly interviewed people from all over Costa Rica. In addition, Gómez selected a sample of fifty churches from sixteen different denominations, where he conducted survey research. In these sample churches, he also conducted over five hundred interviews with leaders and members.

33. Gómez, *El crecimiento y la deserción*, 42.

34. Ibid., 58–59, 75.

35. Kurt Bowen, *Evangelism and Apostasy: The Evolution and Impact of Evangelicals in Mexico* (Montreal: McGill-Queen's University Press, 1996), 95.

36. Ibid., 99. Bowen conducted three extensive surveys and interviews of members and leaders in the forty-three congregations he studied. This extensive statistical material was compared to secondary materials and census data and complemented with participant observation. The samples are not random, but they are representative of the population.

37. Bowen, *Evangelism and Apostasy*, 225.

38. Ibid., 70–71, 218–219.

39. Gooren, *Rich among the Poor*, 169.

40. Ibid., 170.

41. Gómez, *El crecimiento y la deserción*, 32.

42. Pablo quoted in Gooren, *Rich among the Poor*, 152.

43. Brouwer, "Nieuwe scheppingen in Christus"; Andrew R. Chesnut, *Competitive Spirits: Latin America's New Religious Economy* (New York: Oxford University Press, 2003); see also Chesnut in this volume.

44. David Smilde, *Reason to Believe: Cultural Agency in Latin American Evangelicalism* (Berkeley: University of California Press, 2007); see also Smilde in this volume.

45. Long and Hadden, "Religious Conversion and the Concept of Socialization."

46. Cf. Bromley and Shupe, "Just a Few Years Seem like a Lifetime."

4

Specialized Spirits

Conversion and the Products of Pneumacentric Religion in Latin America's Free Market of Faith

ANDREW CHESNUT

This chapter employs the theoretical tool of religious economy to explain the recent growth of Pentecostalism, Charismatic Catholicism, and African diasporan religions in Latin America. While these three religious traditions are united by their common products of faith healing and pneumacentrism, they each produce and offer specialized goods and services that allow for differentiation in the increasingly crowded Latin American market of faith. Conversion is Pentecostalism's premier specialized product and holds great appeal to tens of millions of Latin Americans seeking to change their lives for the better. The role of the Virgin in Charismatic Catholicism and the amorality of African diasporan groups now compete with Pentecostal conversion as specialized products in a highly competitive religious marketplace.

One of the key assumptions of a religious economy approach to religion in Latin America is that the region has undergone a major transformation from a monopolistic religious economy to an unregulated one in which faith-based organizations, like commercial firms, compete for religious consumers.[1] In this relatively new free market of faith, Latin Americans can now select from among a dizzying array of religious options that range from the African-Brazilian religion of Umbanda to the New Age group known as the Vegetable Union (*União do Vegetal* in Portuguese). Not surprisingly, the market share (in terms of percentages of adherents among the population) for the institutional Catholic Church has registered a corresponding drop. As Roger Finke and Rodney Stark have argued, the "invisible hand" of the free religious market may be as unforgiving with religious firms as it is with their commercial counterparts.[2]

Thus, a religious economy approach predicts that if religious consumers demonstrate a strong taste for more participatory types of faith (as they actually have), those religions that restrict lay participation will either have to modify their products or face marginalization. To extend this argument, if Pentecostalism, Charismatic Catholicism, and African diasporan religions are thriving at the beginning of the century, it is because they have learned to compete effectively in a pluralistic environment. On the other hand, if Catholic Base Christian Communities (CEBs) and mainline Protestantism are stagnating, it is primarily because they lack competitive products of mass appeal and are not skilled marketers.

The purpose of this chapter is to both situate this religious economy perspective within the literature on religious conversion and outline the specific religious products that have propelled the recent growth of Pentecostalism, Charismatic Christianity, and African diasporan groups in Latin America. In terms of the first goal, I argue that religious economy provides us with an excellent tool for understanding the common factors (religious preferences, goods, and marketing) that characterize the fastest-growing religious groups in Latin America. While such an approach cannot tell us exactly who will convert, which factors were most influential in their conversion, or what their degree of commitment may be, it does provide us with useful predictions, hypotheses, and explanations for macro-level changes in religious affiliation. Unlike strict rational-actor approaches that assume an inelastic demand for religious goods and/or an assumed and set order of religious preferences, the approach I present pays attention both to the individual preferences of those who convert and how the religious market responds to their preferences. The first half of the chapter lays out the basic assumptions of micro-economic approaches to religion and applies them in the context of Latin America. The second half of the chapter addresses which goods and services (beyond their immensely popular standard religious products of faith healing and the centrality of the spirit or spirits) differentiate the three most successful spiritual organizations in Latin America today.[3]

Spirited Success

Two Christian groups, one Protestant and the other Catholic, and the religions of the African diaspora have proven to be the most skilled competitors in the unregulated religious economy that has developed over the last half-century. Pentecostalism, the Catholic Charismatic Renewal (CCR), and African diasporan religions such as Brazilian Candomblé and Haitian Vodou have emerged as some of the most rapidly growing religious movements in the region. The great majority of believers from the popular classes who practice their faith in an institutional setting do so in the temples and *terreiros* of these three religious groups.[4]

While the focus here is on the distinct doctrines and practices that separate the three faiths, it should be noted that the common denominators of pneumacentrism and faith healing unite them in their success in the free market of faith. Deriving from the Greek word for soul or spirit, pneumatics is the branch of Christian theology concerned with matters of the Holy Spirit. Expanding the definition beyond its traditional Christian boundaries, this study considers pneumatic religion to be any faith-based organization that puts direct communication with the spirit or spirits at the center of its belief system. Thus both Pentecostalism and the CCR are pneumacentric in that their emphasis on the role of the third person of the Trinity distinguishes them from non-Charismatic Christian denominations.

Similarly, the African diasporan religions, which are often denominated "possession cults," place the relationship between human believers and divine spirits at the core of their practice. In fact, the ritual dances in which spirits such as the Cabocla Mariana possess believers and lead them into a trance-like state are the sine qua non of diasporan religion in Latin America.[5] Therefore, despite the fact that both the CCR and Pentecostals consider diasporan religions to be demonic and have even launched a minor holy war against them in parts of Brazil, the primacy of the pneuma unites the three in their mass appeal to Latin American religious consumers. A strong preference for pneumacentric religion on the part of popular religious consumers has greatly boosted the stock of these three competing groups.

These three pneumacentric groups also happen to be organizations that put faith healing, in its myriad manifestations, at the center of their theologies and praxis. Indeed, in my previous study of Pentecostalism in Brazil, I argued that the Assembly of God and others have proliferated on the basis of faith healing and its dialectical relation to poverty-related illness (the pathogens of poverty). Charismatic Catholics and practitioners of African diasporan religions share the Pentecostal emphasis on healing believers of their earthly afflictions through divine intervention. Given the greater incidence of all types of physical, psychological, and spiritual afflictions among the Latin American popular classes, the mass appeal of the standard product of *cura divina* should surprise few.

Microeconomic Theory, Rational Choice, and Religious Markets

Some readers who are not familiar with the application of micro-economic theory to the study of conversion may be surprised or even disconcerted by the description and analysis of religious phenomena in economic terms.

Indeed, the application of micro-economic theory to religious activity is a fairly recent development in the sociology of religion. North American sociologist Peter Berger pioneered the practice in the early 1960s by applying micro-economic principles to his analysis of ecumenism. A few years later in his classic book, *The Sacred Canopy*, Berger illuminated the dynamics of both monopolistic religious economies and free market ones through the employment of micro-economic theory. Berger's dynamic model demonstrated, for example, that in a pluralistic religious environment the faith that was once imposed as the product of a monopoly now must be marketed and sold to customers who are free to purchase the religious goods that most appeal to them.[6]

While Berger's subsequent work veered off in a different direction, another North American sociologist of religion, Rodney Stark, began to analyze the vibrant U.S. religious economy by employing the theoretical tools of micro-economics. One of his greatest contributions to the field is the discovery that rates of participation in religious activities are greater in unregulated spiritual economies than in monopolistic ones.[7] Thus, historically, a higher percentage of North Americans than Latin Americans has attended religious services and engaged in ecclesial activities. The application of micro-economic theory to the sociological study of religion is now commonplace in research conducted in the United States and is increasing in scholarly work on religious activity beyond North American borders.

Debating Religious Economy in Latin America

In the Latin American context, religious economy is of a very recent vintage. Anthony Gill's pioneering study, *Rendering unto Caesar*, was published less than a decade ago. Gill's deft application of the market model to the political orientations of the Catholic episcopacies in Latin America argued that religious competition from surging Protestantism led bishops in such countries as Brazil and Chile to first adopt a preferential option for the poor and oppose military dictatorships. Conversely, Gill showed that where Protestant growth was much slower, as in Argentina, episcopacies not only failed to opt for the poor but often actively supported the generals in their authoritarian rule. Hence, Gill argues, the preferential option for the poor in nations with high levels of Protestant competition was essentially a member-retention strategy aimed at those segments of the Catholic community that were most likely to convert to Pentecostalism.[8]

While many scholars of Latin American religion acknowledge that faith-based organizations compete with each other in the new pluralist economy, Gill's strict rational-actor approach has been widely criticized for its alleged reduction of "trajectories through the religious arena" to "purely opportunistic efforts to solve concrete problems."[9] Furthermore, rational-choice approaches to religion, such as Gill's, have been accused of denying agency to religious consumers and ignoring forms of religious production and consumption that go on outside of formal religious institutions (such as syncretism and folk Catholicism). Both of these critiques merit engagement and offer useful directions for modifications to strict rational-actor approaches to religious conversion.

On the first point, it is worth noting that an economic approach to understanding religious choices does not claim purely financial or material motivations on the part of religious producers or religious consumers. Religious producers may have multiple other goals alongside and beyond member retention. Religious consumers, on the demand side of the equation, seek not only to find opportunities to solve personal problems, but also to find faith communities, spiritual meaning, and other goals when they make their religious choices. That believers seek a variety of such rewards, including the resolution of concrete problems, in no way makes them spiritual opportunists. As Virginia Garrard-Burnett points out in her chapter within this volume, members of the IURD (Igreja Universal do Reino de Deus) in Houston remain with the church despite the fact that they do not necessarily find the great promise of financial gain. She does not label these adherents "opportunistic" for believing that the church offers them spiritual benefits or even "spiritual capital."

The second critique points to specific empirical indicators (such as the continuity of folk Catholicism in the Latin American religious market) which lead us to question the strict dichotomy between religious consumers and producers posited in some economic models. Indeed, while Gill has broken academic ground in skillfully applying micro-economic theory to the analysis of episcopal politics, he does not sufficiently focus on issues related to religious production or the possibility of variance in religious demand. Since orthodox religious economists posit inelastic demand for religious goods and services, they tend to ignore the particulars of those in the business of supplying spiritual products. Thus, the very significant differences between religious groups, such as mainline Protestants and Pentecostals, on one hand, and CEBs and the CCR, on the other, are often overlooked or ignored by researchers adhering to the classic paradigm of religious economy.

In order to address these legitimate concerns, we must begin by allowing for the fact that religious demand can vary across time and space. For example, within contemporary Latin America, demand for religious goods and services is much higher in Guatemala than in Uruguay. Furthermore, there may be a dialectical relation between demand and production. In other words, innovative religious producers can create demand for their new products through marketing while consumer tastes and preferences often determine the development of new goods and services. Finally, by allowing for the fact that religious production goes on outside of the realm of institu-tionalized religion, we can better understand the ways that creative religious consumers may resist, transform, and hybridize religious products to meet their own spiritual or material needs.

Even with these important modifications, the limitations of a religious economy perspective are clear. The model is best suited for explaining macro-levels of religious competition, growth, and decline. For understand-ing the micro-level of who converts, what contexts promote conversion, or how religious commitment changes over time, religious market analysis must be combined with life-cycle information, network analysis, and the other approaches to conversion outlined in this volume.

Understanding the Effects of Religious Monopoly

In order to understand the nature of the new free market economy in faith it is imperative to first comprehend the fundamental principles of a monopo-listic religious economy. Ibero-America, after all, has experienced only half a century of robust religious pluralism while it lived four and a half centu-ries of de jure and de facto spiritual monopoly. Perhaps the most important principle of religious monopoly is that the monopolist frequently depends on state coercion to enforce its hegemony.[10] In Latin America, for example, Catholicism was first the established religion of the Iberian colonies and then continued to enjoy state-sanctioned monopolies under the indepen-dent Latin American nations until the latter half of the nineteenth century, even into the first decades of the twentieth in a few cases.[11] Without access to the legal, economic, and political resources of the state, aspiring religious monopolists are very rarely able to impose the faith on their own.

With a market guaranteed by the state, the religious monopolist, like its commercial counterpart, is under no pressure to supply a quality product. In a monopoly, the only choices religious consumers have are to consume the official product, innovate through mixing that product with indigenous religious practices and beliefs, or not to consume institutional religion at all.[12] Whatever the degree of coercion enforced by religious or political authorities, the fundamental principle is that religious monopolists are naturally lazy.[13] The absence of competition in a state-secured religious mar-ket provides no incentive for the monopolist to produce high quality goods that meet consumer demand. Consumer tastes and preferences are largely irrelevant in a regulated religious economy.

Since no single religious firm can satisfy the varied tastes of consum-ers who may differ in age, gender, ethnicity, or class, the logical result is a substantial degree of apathy and indifference among religious consumers. More precisely, monopolistic religious economies will produce large num-bers of nominal believers, or those who feel culturally connected to the hegemonic faith but do not regularly participate in official religious services or activities.[14] The religious economies of Ibero-America perfectly illustrate this basic sociological principle. Although Latin America is considered the world's most Catholic region, historically not more than 15 percent of the population have been active practitioners of the faith, attending mass and other ecclesial activities on a regular basis. While the figure seems astoundingly low, it is but the logical result of four centuries of no religious competition. Interestingly, in the United States and Canada, where Catholicism has always been a minority religion competing in a free market economy, there are proportionately ten times as many priests as in Latin America.[15] Moreover, whereas close to half of the priests serving in Ibero-America are foreign, the great majority in the United States and Canada are North American. Until very recently with the development of the CCR, Latin American men have shown little interest in the priestly vocation. In the same vein, recent surveys of religious activity in Latin America have revealed that active Catholics tend to be disproportionately concentrated in the middle and upper classes.[16] This, of course, is the natural result of the church having during four centuries focused on those with the largest amounts of capital, both religious and financial. Thus, in the history of a monopolistic religious economy in Latin America, nominal Catholics have far outnumbered active practitioners.

The final significant postulate of a monopolistic economy is that the religious hegemony's main strategy for exercising its influence is through political channels. Since its hegemony is guaranteed by the state, the monopolist must invest significant institutional capital in maintaining and cultivating good relations with representatives of the state. It follows then that the chief executive officers of a religious firm that enjoys a monopoly would devote much more of their time and energy to currying favor with politicians than designing attractive spiritual products and devising innovative ways to market them, for it is the representatives of the state and not religious consumers who hold the power to dissolve the firm's monopoly through disestablishment. Once again the history of the Catholic Church in Latin America offers convincing evidence of the validity of this principle. During the three-century colonial era, the clergy and episcopacy were essentially state bureaucrats whose salaries were paid by the Iberian crowns. Since it was the state that paid their bills, priests, and especially bishops, had every incentive to maintain harmonious relations with government officials. Thus bishops, whose appointment to office ultimately depended on the Spanish or Portuguese crown and not the pontiff, spent far more time in the company of colonial officials than ministering to the spiritual needs of their humble parishioners. Humble parishioners, with a few notable exceptions, do not appear on the episcopal radar until the middle of the twentieth century, when millions begin to withdraw what little religious capital they had in Catholic accounts to reinvest it in the rapidly rising stock of Pentecostalism.[17]

In short, monopolistic economies are characterized by large numbers of nominal believers, questionable religious products, and varying levels of state coercion. Reflecting dissatisfaction with the monopolistic product, most consumers simply choose not to consume the official religious goods or find informal ways to produce and consume their own religious products, embedded within elements of the religious monopolist's institutions. Therefore, the origin of Latin America's vast flock of nominal, syncretistic, and non-institutional Catholics is firmly rooted in four centuries of religious monopoly.

Free Market Faith

Having explored the type of religious economy that predominated in Latin America until five decades ago, it is now time to examine the new type, the free market in faith that has developed rapidly since the 1950s. Of course, the development of a pluralistic economy is dependent on legal and constitutional guarantees of religious liberty. While Stark argues that a free market religious economy is the "natural" type, the history of the West during the last millennium demonstrates pluralism to be the exception to the norm of spiritual monopoly. In any case, it is only in those societies in which the state does not favor any one religious organization over others and all enjoy the same legal rights that free market economies will develop.

In Latin America it was only during the period that spans the mid-nineteenth century to the first quarter of the twentieth that liberal constitutions disestablished the Catholic monopoly and declared freedom of worship. By the 1920s, from Chile to Mexico, Latin Americans enjoyed the legal right to affiliate with religions other than Catholicism. It should be noted that African diasporan groups generally did not benefit immediately from constitutional guarantees since the ruling elites considered such religions as Umbanda to be closer to witchcraft than to religion. Indeed, it was as late as the 1960s, ironically under military rule, when African-Brazilian religions were accorded full legal status and the persecution of their practitioners and desecration of their terreiros ceased.[18]

With the legal framework in place, a free market in faith will develop in which religious firms compete with each other for the loyalty of spiritual consumers. The will to compete in a free market is predicated on the premise of member maximization. That is, religious firms, especially those belonging to proselytizing faiths such as Islam and Christianity, prefer more followers than less. A larger membership base means more souls saved and greater resources for the spiritual organization, which must depend on tithes and donations from believers in the absence of state subsidies.[19] Non-proselytizing religions such as the African diasporan groups do not possess the same will to compete as Christian denominations, but the prestige and livelihood of the *maes-de-santo* (priestesses) of Umbanda and Candomblé largely depend on the number of ritual clients and the amount of their payments or donations for services rendered.

In turn, competition for religious market share introduces the crucial element of consumer tastes and preferences.[20] Religious monopolists naturally need not concern themselves with producing and marketing attractive products. In a free market, however, religious firms ignore consumer preferences at their own peril. If Pentecostals, Charismatic Catholics and African diasporan groups have prospered in the new Latin American religious market, it is because they have developed religious products in accord with popular consumer preferences. Father Edward Dougherty, one of the North American founders of the CCR in Brazil, even conducts market surveys to "determine what the customers want."[21] Those groups without appealing products will either be driven to the margins of the market where they might survive by supplying a small niche of consumers or be altogether forced out of the business of religious production.

In addition to consumer preferences, the free market introduces the rationalization of religious enterprises.[22] Religious specialists must devise cost-effective ways to produce, market, and deliver the spiritual goods to the greatest number of consumers possible. And as in secular society, bureaucracy is the main expression of such organizational rationalization. A division of religious labor takes place in which bureaucratic officers specialize in different aspects of the spiritual enterprise, such as production and marketing. Having been conceived in the world's greatest unregulated religious economy during the era of industrial capitalism, Pentecostalism in Latin America has enjoyed a significant competitive advantage over its Catholic rival, which did not have to worry about rationalizing ecclesiastical structures until pneumacentric Protestantism forced it to do so.

Rationalization not only results in the division of labor within religious firms but also produces product specialization.[23] The one-size-fits-all approach of the religious monopolist gives way to a multiplicity of products that are designed to appeal to specific sectors of society. Nowhere is religious specialization as great as in the vast U.S. market, where religious organizations produce a vertiginous array of products for the world's most heterogeneous society of religious consumers.

In the emerging market of Latin America, neo-Pentecostal churches exemplify the degree of specialization that characterizes the region's new religious economy. Whereas Classic Pentecostalism, best represented by the Assembly of God, offered a rather generic form of faith healing, neo-Pentecostal churches, led by the Universal Church of the Kingdom of God (IURD), have tended to specialize in exorcism, a specific type of faith healing.[24] Moreover neo-Pentecostalism introduced prosperity theology to the Protestant market. Now Pentecostals who believe they are entitled to material as well as spiritual blessings can attend services that focus on financial prosperity. In a free religious market where hundreds if not thousands of spiritual firms compete for consumers, the logic of unfettered competition leads to a situation in which organizations must develop specialized products that consumers can distinguish from those of the competition. As Virginia Garrard-Burnett points out in her discussion of the IURD in chapter 11, the intense marketing of the IURD, its specialized logo, and its motto of "stop suffering" have made it one of the fastest-growing churches not only in Latin America, but in the United States as well.

Another major facet of the free market economy is the privatization of religion. Religion in monopolistic economies constructs a common Weltanschauung that binds society together and gives ultimate meaning to social life.[25] In marked contrast, religions of the competitive market provide meaning to and address the spiritual concerns not of society in general but of individuals. Thus religion operates predominantly in the private sphere, often far removed from its locus in the public arena of monopolistic economies. It follows then that the most successful firms in a free market economy will tailor their production and marketing of religious goods to the exigencies of private life.[26]

Again, the Latin American market offers a clear example of privatization. In addition to their common element of pneumacentrism, the prosperous Pentecostals, CCR, and African diasporan groups share a strong emphasis on faith that addresses matters, particularly afflictions, of private life. Almost in diametrical opposition, the Catholic Base Christian Communities (CEBs) have tended to give privilege of place to matters of public life, such as working to construct more just Latin American societies. As Burdick demonstrated in his study of CEBs on the outskirts of Rio de Janeiro, the small ecclesial groups often do not provide opportunities for members to discuss individual afflictions, such as alcohol abuse, domestic discord, and illness. Particularly in the popular Latin American religious marketplace, the relegation of such private concerns to the margins practically guarantees that an organization will fail to attract substantial numbers of adherents.

Their political importance aside, CEBs have not fared well in the new religious economy. A recent survey of religion in Brazil revealed that by the mid-1990s the Catholic Charismatic Renewal (CCR) had twice as many members as the CEBs.[27] Other studies show that in Brazil, where they found their most fertile soil in Latin America, approximately two-thirds of the CEBs that still exist operate in rural areas.[28] Given that 70 percent of Brazilians and

most Ibero-Americans are urbanites, the CEBs concentration in the countryside is further evidence of their lack of mass popular appeal.

The final salient characteristic of the unregulated religious economy
is its vibrancy. Challenging decades of accepted sociological theory, Stark
has convincingly demonstrated that pluralistic religious economies are
more dynamic than monopolistic ones. A comparison of Latin American
and North American religious economies confirms Stark's thesis. Until the
emergence of the free market in faith in the 1950s, Latin Americans regularly
participated in church life at one-third the rate that North Americans did. If
Latin America currently appears to be experiencing a religious renaissance,
it is because institutional religious participation has greatly increased across
the board. Of course there are still winners and losers in a competitive economy, but even the former religious monopolist has witnessed a recent surge
in participation, especially in its most popular movement, the CCR.[29]

Moving Beyond the Religious Products: Evangelism, Beliefs, Practices, and Structure

While this chapter focuses specifically on religious products, supernatural
goods and services are not the only determinant of a religious organization's
success or failure. In their groundbreaking study of the historical winners
and losers in the U.S. religious economy, Stark and Finke demonstrate that
the fate of religious organizations in a free market economy also depends on
their marketing, sales representatives, and organizational structure. Translating economic terminology into the ecclesiastical idiom, Stark and Finke
posit that the success or failure of religious groups in a pluralistic environment depends on evangelization techniques, clergy, polity, and doctrine.[30]
Their narrow pairing of the religious product with doctrine, however,
requires amplification. The religious product is not only an organization's
set of beliefs and principles, but also the practice of such beliefs in the form
of worship or liturgy. If, for example, the charismatic Masses of the CCR are
filling Catholic churches throughout Latin America, it is due in large measure to the appeal of its particular form of worship. Hence, incorporation of
worship into the definition of the religious product allows for a more complete understanding of the nature of spiritual goods.

Born Again

As the premier non-Catholic religion of Latin America, Pentecostalism has
been the primary religious architect and developer of the region's new free
market of faith. If the region's popular consumers are now free to choose
to consume the religious goods that best satisfy their spiritual and material
desires, it is largely due to the unparalleled growth of Pentecostal churches

since the 1950s. This charismatic branch of Protestantism single-handedly created religious and social space where Latin Americans from the popular classes are free not to be Catholic. Given Catholicism's historical role as one the constituent elements of Latin American national identities, Pentecostalism's construction of an alternative religious identity for those dissatisfied with their inherited faith is no minor achievement. For more than four centuries, to be Colombian or Mexican, for example, was to be Catholic. The tiny minorities who began to convert to Historic Protestant denominations, such as Methodism and Presbyterianism, in the latter half of the nineteenth century and then to the faith missions around the turn of the century risked social ostracism and sometimes even violence at the hands of Catholics who viewed Protestant converts as traitorous to the one true faith, if not the nation itself. Not surprisingly, Protestant converts during this period tended to be those Latin American men and women who had the least religious, social, political, and financial capital to lose in abandoning their native religion. Very rarely did members of the privileged classes shed their Catholic identities.

That not more than 1 percent of Latin Americans identified themselves as Protestant as late as 1940 is evidence of the failure of Historic Protestantism and the numerous faith missions to attract a critical mass of converts. Since Pentecostal churches currently account for approximately 75 percent of all Latin American Protestants after almost a century of evangelization, the obvious conclusion is that Pentecostalism's predecessors did not offer attractive religious goods and services to popular religious consumers. If the social cost of renouncing Catholicism had been the only factor impeding conversion to Protestantism, the historic churches and faith missions would be thriving at present, now that there is much less social stigma attached to shedding one's Catholic identity. However, the only historic churches able to effectively compete with the Pentecostals are those that have embraced spirit-filled worship and pentecostalized. In Brazil these schismatic churches generally maintain their denominational title but distinguish themselves from their non-Charismatic brethren by adding the term "renewed" (*renovada*) to their name.

If the standard product of faith healing, more than any other, induces religious consumers to join the Pentecostal enterprise, it is another specialized good that facilitates the recovery and maintenance of millions of believers' health over the long term. The doctrine of conversion in which joining a Pentecostal church is conceptualized as part of a process of spiritual rebirth allows the believer to be born again into a healthy new environment where the demons of poverty can be neutralized. Conceived of as a "positive transformation of the nature and value of a person," religious conversion appeals most to those individuals and groups who have been stigmatized or

negatively evaluated by society.[31] A conversionist religion then, which offers
the possibility of a new life far removed from the afflictions of the old, would
be understandably popular among those millions of Latin Americans seeking to turn away from family conflict, alcoholism, and illness.

The doctrine and experience of conversion provide the type of rupture
with secular society that many afflicted men and women seek.[32] In accepting
Jesus and receiving baptism by the Holy Spirit, neophytes are called upon
to abandon their worldly life for a holy one. What this implies on a practical level is a reorientation from the mundane pleasures and perils of the
street to the godliness of church and family life. The theological dualism
and asceticism of this conversionist religion present the street, on one hand,
and church and home, on the other, as polarities on a continuum of good
and evil. The street is the Devil's playground with its crime, prostitution,
gambling, and substance abuse. In stark contrast, God is manifest in the fra-
ternal worship of the church and harmonious family life. Converts thus learn
to demonize the street and its devilish temptations and thereby renounce
the very patterns of comportment that might have led them to convert to
Pentecostalism in the first place.

Of such importance is this element of conversion that two-thirds of
my male informants in Brazil mentioned the repudiation of "vice" as the
most important change in their life since conversion. And not surprisingly, they cited worldly temptations as their second greatest problem after
financial hardship.[33] Since the streets of Latin America, especially on the
urban margins, are still largely a male domain, it follows that the rupture
of conversion to Pentecostalism is greater for men. In short, the product of
conversion allows believers to reclaim and maintain their health through
their rebirth into a salutary new environment, largely devoid of the demons
of the street.[34]

The Role of the Virgin in the CCR

While Base Christian Communities (CEBs) struggle to maintain a presence
throughout Latin America, a contemporaneous Catholic movement easily
fills soccer stadiums in the major cities of the region with tens of thousands of fervent believers. At the beginning of the twenty-first century, the
Catholic Charismatic Renewal (CCR) stands as the largest and most dynamic
movement in the Latin American Catholic Church. Even leaders of the lib-
erationist wing of the Catholic Church, who often view Charismatics as alienated middle-class reactionaries, admit that no other ecclesial movement has
the CCR's power to congregate and mobilize the faithful. In Brazil the CCR's
popular appeal is not limited to the realm of the sacred. In 1999 the latest
CD of samba-inspired religious music sung by the young star of the Brazilian
CCR, Padre Marcelo Rossi, sold more copies than any other recording artist,

including Só Pra Contrariar (an immensely popular *pagode* band), in Latin America's largest country.[35]

For a movement rooted in Pentecostal spirituality, which has historically in Latin America been radically anti-Catholic, what better way to preserve the Catholic identity of the renewal than through emphasis on the element that most distinguishes the church from its Protestant competitors. Thus, the Virgin in her myriad national and local incarnations has over the past two decades developed into the premier specialized product and dividing line that separates Catholic Charismatics from Pentecostals. Episcopal emphasis on the importance of the Virgin of Guadalupe or Our Lady of the Immaculate Conception, among others, is a clear example of the marginal differentiation of a standardized religious product. That is, in the figure of the Virgin, the church's chief religious producers offer an appealing variant of the pneumatic spirituality shared by both Catholic Charismatics and Pentecostals. Without the Mother of God to differentiate their brand of charismatic spirituality from that of their Protestant rivals, only the pope is left to guard the bridge leading to Pentecostalism.

Thus, in their episcopal recognition of the Guatemalan CCR, the bishops attempt to place the Virgin at the center of the movement. Even before mentioning the positive and negative aspects of the renewal, the episcopacy devotes an entire section of the instruction to the Virgin's role in the movement. In their opening statement, the bishops remind Charismatics that Pope John Paul II wants Mary to be at the heart of the renewal since she is the one best equipped to guide and direct the movement.[36] This point is then reiterated in the section on pastoral recommendations in which the Virgin is presented as the "guarantee of orthodoxy . . . in face of the danger of the certain influence of non-Catholic currents."[37] Finally, the bishops conclude their pastoral instruction on the renewal by imploring the Mother of God to ensure faithfulness to the Holy Spirit and the church. "And may Mary, full of grace, help us all to be truly faithful to the Holy Spirit and to support her inspiration for a renewal of our church."[38] Even more explicitly than their Guatemalan homologues, the Honduran bishops in their approval of the CCR state, "Devotion to the Virgin and the saints should be an element that distinguishes the CCR from Protestants and that gives a certain guarantee of orthodoxy to the simple faithful."[39]

If both national episcopacies and individual bishops frequently exhort the renewal in Latin America to embrace the Virgin, it is also because during its first decade and a half, roughly until the mid-1980s, the CCR kept Mary at the margins of the movement. *Jesus Vive e é o Senhor* (Jesus lives and is Lord), one of the two main monthly journals of the Brazilian CCR, reflects the Virgin's early peripheral role. From the journal's founding by Father Cipriano Chagas in May of 1977 until 1983 there are no major articles on the

Mother of Jesus. Rather, the journal's primary focus during its first six years is faith healing, conversion testimonials, and the role of the Holy Spirit in believers' lives. However, starting in 1984 Mary began to command more attention, and within a couple years major articles on her role in the CCR became a regular feature of *Jesus Vive e é o Senhor*. And the Virgin currently has her own regular section, called "Our Mother" (Nossa Mãe), in the other major charismatic journal in Brazil, *Brasil Cristão* (Christian Brazil), which was launched in 1997 by one of the two North American fathers of the Brazilian CCR, Padre Edward Doughtery.

The Virgin's migration from the sidelines of the renewal to center stage is the result of episcopal pressure to ensure the Catholic identity of a movement that inherited its pneumacentrism from Pentecostalism and a response to the key role of the Virgin in popular Catholicism.[40] Mary played only a bit part during the first half of the renewal's three and a half decades in Ibero-America because of Protestant influences in the movement. But as the CCR rapidly expanded and sought episcopal approval, it increasingly became necessary to bolster the Catholic credentials of the movement. And, of course, the Virgin, particularly Guadalupe (the "Queen of Mexico"), is the most potent and visible symbol of Catholic identity in Latin America. Thus, by embracing her, the renewal has fortified its Catholic identity in the eyes of incredulous bishops and developed a specialized religious product that clearly distinguishes itself among spiritual consumers from its Pentecostal competitors.

Thus having embraced the Virgin and won widespread episcopal approval, the CCR began its third decade in Latin America as the largest and most vital Catholic lay movement in the region. Even in Brazil, where Catholic Base Christian Communities had found more fertile soil than in any other nation, CEB members in the early 1990s found themselves outnumbered by their charismatic coreligionists at a ratio of two to one.[41] Given the continuing expansion of the CCR and the declining stock of CEBs, the former probably claims four times as many members as the latter at the beginning of the new century.

Neither Black nor White

Joining Charismatic Catholicism and Pentecostalism in dominating Latin America's new spiritual marketplace is the region's third major pneumacentric religious tradition, the faiths of the African diaspora. Over the past half-century, the religions that African slaves brought over to the Americas as part of their cultural background have been thriving in Brazil and much of the Caribbean.[42] In Brazil, Umbanda and Candomblé, the two principal African-derived religions, successfully compete with pneumacentric Christianity for the loyalty of urban spiritual consumers. In the Caribbean, Vodou forms an integral part of the Haitian cultural fabric, much as Catholicism has historically in Ibero-America. Indeed, it was Vodou that inspired and sustained the slave revolt that culminated in Haitian independence and the world's first black republic in 1804. Santeria did not play the same revolutionary role in Cuba, but it has allowed African Cubans to maintain their African cultural roots and derive spiritual succor and power from West African *orishas* or spirits. Accompanying their human devotees, the orishas of Santeria have followed Cuban *santeros* to their diasporan communities in Miami and New York, among other U.S. cities.

Diasporan religions' most unique specialized product is the one that most differentiates them from their Christian competitors. While African-derived faiths are ones of inversion, they, in sharp contrast to Pentecostalism and the CCR (to a lesser extent), are definitely not primarily religions of *conversion*. Renouncing one's sinful past for a saintly new life is an alien concept to diasporan religion.[43] For example, there is no doctrinal reason that a prostitute would have to look for new work upon becoming an Umbandista. To the contrary, in Umbanda the streetwalker can find spiritual protection under Pomba Gira, patroness of prostitutes. Thus, the *garota de progama* (hooker) looking to leave her difficult trade would be more attracted to the Pentecostal or charismatic product, while the one simply seeking spiritual aid or protection would find Umbanda the more appropriate choice. As Patricia Birman explains in her chapter on conversion from Afro-Brazilian religions to neo-Pentecostalism, the former subject would find the opportunity to break with the social, religious, and cultural elements of her former worldview while the latter would not.

Relatively amoral diasporan doctrine provides spiritual assistance and protection for purposes and acts considered morally dubious at best and evil at worst by its Christian rivals and prevailing social mores. Hence, African-derived groups enjoy the competitive advantage of being the only major religious tradition in Latin America to offer an amoral product that can be used against personal rivals and enemies. Indeed, the act of calling upon a spirit to inflict injury upon one's nemesis has a name in diasporan religions. In Umbanda, the *coisa feita* involves offerings of food and drink to an *Exu* (a liminal trickster spirit) in exchange for its assistance in "tying up" (*amarrando*) or blocking the path (*trancando a rua*) of a rival or enemy. Among the more common coisas feitas in Brazil are those intended to harm romantic rivals. A married woman, for example, who suspects an acquaintance of having an affair with her husband might ask Pomba Gira to harm the other woman so that she is no longer the object of her husband's affection.

In extreme cases Umbanda clients have even contracted with an Exu, such as Seven Skulls (*Sete Caveiras*), to kill an enemy. Jim Wafer in his study

of Candomblé in Bahia tells of a medium who, possessed by the spirit Ze
Pilantra, sings a song about murdering his entire family.[44] Similarly, in
Belem, the Leacocks cite a prominent *pai-de-santo* who was said to have had
his wife murdered through a coisa feita so he could freely pursue another
woman.[45] Naturally, the great majority of diasporan mediums deny practicing sorcery or "black magic," but there is no question that many, if not
most, do, since to refuse work with the Exus would probably result in a loss
of clientele. This point is highlighted by Lisias Nogueira Negrão's study of
Umbanda in São Paulo, in which she found the Exus, including the female
variety of Pomba Gira, to be the most commonly manifested *guias* at the
sessions![46] There is obviously significant consumer demand for sorcery in
Brazil and the Caribbean, and diasporan religion's unique amoral product
gives it a distinct competitive advantage over Christian rivals who produce
no such goods.

More than any other element, it is the existence of the Exus or Eshus in
diasporan religions that allows for amoral practices and sorcery. As liminal
trickster spirits, Exus are not seen as intrinsically evil but as un-evolved
spiritual beings willing to work with clients for the right price. In effect,
they serve as amoral spiritual mercenaries ignorant of absolute standards of
good and evil and ready to work for the highest bidder. If they have become
associated with the Christian Devil and his minions in popular culture, it is
because the Catholic and Protestant churches alike have no room for amoral
figures and have demonized the Eshus. Interestingly, to a certain extent
practitioners of diasporan faith appear to be making the same association,
as several Exus of Candomblé and Umbanda are commonly represented as
statuettes of red devils, complete with horns and hooves. Thus, in a religious
marketplace in which supernatural healing and pneumacentrism are standard products among the prosperous spiritual firms, the amoral goods and
services of diasporan religions give them a unique product that has proven
popular among Caribbean and Brazilian consumers.

Conversion and Religious Economy

The primary contribution the religious economy approach makes to under-
standing conversion in Latin America takes place at the macro-level of trends.
By applying micro-economic principles to religious change, we can better
explain and predict major changes in the Latin American religious arena.
In this chapter, I have argued that Pentecostals, Catholic Charismatics, and
African diasporan groups are the most successful religious enterprises in the
Latin American market primarily because they possess appealing products.
As different as they are from each other in many regards, all three groups
share the standard products of pneumacentrism and faith healing.

Furthermore, product specialization allows each of these three religious groups to distinguish itself in the crowded religious marketplace. Pentecostal churches tend to specialize in conversion. The product of conversion appeals especially to impoverished and afflicted Latin Americans who seek rupture with their lowly positions in secular society. In contrast, the distinguishing product of the Catholic Charismatic Renewal provides both religious and secular continuity. The Virgin, in her myriad representations, is the premier symbol of Latin American Catholicism and in some instances, such as the Mexican Guadalupe, is even iconic of the nation. Across the Christian divide, the amorality of diasporan religion makes for a unique product that offers both supernatural healing and harm without conversion. Thus, Pentecostal conversion, the Virgin of the CCR, and the amorality of diasporan faiths are the leading specialized products that distinguish the three successful groups in a competitive religious economy in which pneumacentrism and faith healing are standard fare.

By dropping the assumption of inelastic demand for religious goods, adding the role of worship and liturgy to the religious products studied, and paying greater attention to the religious preferences of those who are converting in Latin America, I argue for a more heterodox version of religious economy, one that engages rather than dismisses the critiques of orthodox religious economy perspectives. This approach has multiple theoretical benefits. First, the inclusion of religious demand and preferences returns focus to the agency of the individuals who are making decisions about their religious affiliation. Thus, when combined with the approach to conversion outlined by Henri Gooren in chapter, 3, we can understand the fluidity in "conversion careers" over time as individuals respond and make choices in an increasingly differentiated religious market.

Second, we can generate specific and testable hypotheses about when, where, and how religious demand and supply may interact. For example, we might expect a relatively high demand for multiple religious options in some contexts (such as a war-torn indigenous Guatemalan village where Pentecostal churches, CEBs, and folk Catholicism are all active) while other contexts (perhaps a middle-class suburban neighborhood in Chile) generate lower demand and less diversity of religious offerings. On the supply side, we can predict/explain the recent resurgence within the Catholic Church, outlined by Edward Cleary in chapter 8. A market approach would hypothesize precisely the kind of upswing in missionaries, training, and adherents that has characterized the growth of the CCR in Latin America.

Third, a focus on demand and preferences forces us to come to terms with the agency of individuals who produce as well as consume religious products. In other words, rather than ignoring or marginalizing folk Catholicism or other forms of hybrid religious practice, our discussion of religious change now allows for an understanding of the kind of religious production that individuals have engaged in prior to, during, and after the shift from religious monopoly to free market in Latin America. While the focus of this chapter has been on the unique products that have propelled the growth of the CCR, Pentecostalism, and diasporan religions, we could also predict that the sea change in the Latin American market will reduce the demand for traditional forms of syncretism (like folk Catholicism) while new forms of hybrid religion will experience growth. This is not to say that folk Catholicism will disappear. Rather, as Rachel Corr argues in chapter 9, neo-native and other religious alternatives will increasingly compete with folk Catholicism for the hearts and minds of a new generation of indigenous young people.

Finally, relaxing the orthodox assumption of inelastic demand demonstrates that the contours of supply are directly connected to the nature of demand, i.e., consumer tastes and preferences. The rapid growth of pneumacentric religion in the Latin American free market of faith is due to high levels of consumer demand for worship and doctrine that put the spirit and spirits center stage. Likewise, if conversionist Protestantism has flourished over the past half-century, it is due to the preferences of millions of Latin Americans for religion that offers positive and often radical personal transformation. While the assumptions of the religious market model limit its utility for explaining individual conversions, conversion careers, or levels of commitment as individuals make their religious choices, the model does provide useful predictions and explanations for the major shifts within and between religious groups in Latin America during last fifty years.

NOTES

1. The conceptualization of laity as religious consumers does mean that they do not engage in spiritual production on their own, beyond the pale of specialized producers such as priests. Rather, the concept is meant to capture their primary role in organized religion as customers or clients who purchase spiritual goods from those who specialize in religious production. In religious economies, like commercial ones, the fundamental dichotomy is between producers and consumers.

2. Roger Finke and Rodney Stark, *The Churching of America, 1776–1990* (New Brunswick, NJ: Rutgers University Press, 1992), 17.

3. Sociologist of religion Peter Berger posits standardization and marginal differentiation as two major effects of consumer influence on religious production in unregulated religious markets. Berger points out that the similar religious "needs" of believers belonging to the same social strata will result in a standardized religious product, such as pneumatic spirituality in the Latin American case. Marginal differentiation arises from the need for religious producers to distinguish their standardized product from that of their competitors. Peter Berger, *The Sacred Canopy* (Garden City, NY: Anchor Books, 1969), 148–149.

4. The *terreiro* is the sacred space, often a believer's backyard, where the rites of African-Brazilian Umbanda and Candomblé are conducted.

5. The Cabocla Mariana (Half-breed Mary) is a ribald *guia* or spirit of Umbanda whose possession of female believers often leads them to dance suggestively and down liberal doses of distilled spirits. In many parts of Brazil she is especially popular among prostitutes.

6. Berger, *The Sacred Canopy*, 138.

7. Finke and Stark, *The Churching of America*, 18.

8. Anthony Gill, *Rendering unto Caesar* (Chicago: University of Chicago Press, 1998).

9. John Burdick, *Looking for God in Brazil* (Berkeley: University of California Press, 1993), 8.

10. Rodney Stark, *The Rise of Christianity* (Princeton: Princeton University Press, 1996), 194.

11. It should be noted that the wars of independence in Latin America left the Catholic Church in a significantly weaker position than it had been during the colonial era.

12. In the market analogy, we might consider such syncretic practices as a gray or black market phenomenon. The focus of this chapter is on institutional religious competition and thus does not explicitly address issues of syncretism.

13. Rodney Stark and James C. McCann, "Market Forces and Catholic Commitment: Exploring the New Paradigm," *Journal for the Scientific Study of Religion* 32 (1993): 113.

14. Ibid., 113.

15. Ibid., 114.

16. Rubem Cesar Fernándes, *Censo Institucional Evangelico* (Rio de Janeiro: ISER, 1992).

17. Religious capital is "accumulated symbolic labor" (Bourdieu), including the skills, experiences, and goods that religious consumers have acquired and that enable them both to consume and produce spiritual stock. Anthony Gill, *Rendering unto Caesar* (Chicago: University of Chicago Press, 1998), 198.

18. Diana Brown, *Umbanda: Religion and Politics in Urban Brazil* (Ann Arbor: UMI Research Press, 1986).

19. Gill, *Rendering unto Caesar*.

20. Berger, *The Sacred Canopy*, 145.

21. Edward Doughtery, personal interview, July 16, 1998.

22. Berger, *The Sacred Canopy*, 139.

23. Finke and Stark, *The Churching of America*, 20–21.

24. R. Andrew Chesnut, *Born Again in Brazil* (New Brunswick, NJ: Rutgers University Press, 1997).

25. Berger, *The Sacred Canopy*, 134.

26. Ibid., 147.

27. Reginaldo Prandi, *Um Sopro do Espirito* (São Paulo: Edusp, 1997), 14.

28. Madeleine C. Adriance, *Promised Land* (Albany, NY: State University of New York Press, 1995), 167.

29. As Edward Cleary points out in his chapter on the CCR, the Catholic Church has also benefited, in terms of vibrancy, from religious pluralism. The Catholic Church in

Latin America has made recent and unprecedented gains in terms of foreign missionaries, catechists, seminarians, and missionaries precisely because of growing competition and the internal responses within the Catholic Church.

30. Finke and Stark, *The Churching of America*, 17.

31. Rodney Stark and William Bainbridge, *A Theory of Religion* (New York: Peter Lang, 1987), 197.

32. And for those who prefer more continuity with secular society, the newer post-conversionist neo-Pentecostal denominations, such as the IURD, offer faith healing and other products without a strictly defined conversion.

33. Chesnut, *Born Again in Brazil*, 112.

34. As the preceding chapters by Alejandro Frigerio and Henri Gooren demonstrate, the definition, duration, and depth of conversion are all important questions as well—questions for which religious economy may not provide the best tools for analysis.

35. Pagode is an infectiously saccharine variant of samba popular among the urban popular classes.

36. Conferencia Episcopal de Guatemala (CEG), *Al Servicio de la Vida, la Justicia y la Paz: Documentos de CEG 1956–1997* (Ciudad de Guatemala: Ediciones San Pablo, 1997), 410.

37. Ibid., 418–419.

38. Ibid., 420.

39. Conferencia Episcopal de Honduras (CEH), *Exhortación pastoral de los obispos de Honduras sobre la renovación carismática* (Tegucigalpa: Central Impresora, 1984), 20.

40. It is said, often humorously, that Mexicans are 90 percent Catholic and 100 percent Guadelupano.

41. Prandi, *Um Sopro do Espirito*, 14.

42. Although data on the growth of diasporan religions are incomplete, sufficient research has been conducted, especially in Brazil, to show that they have experienced accelerated growth contemporaneously with the Pentecostal boom, which began in the 1950s.

43. This is not to say that there is not a process of conversion within Afro-Brazilian or other diasporan religions. As María Julia Carozzi aptly explains in chapter 7, the intensive interaction between potential adherents in an atmosphere that initially emphasizes resonance with pre-existing cognitive schemas plays an important role in engendering participation in Afro-Brazilian religious movements.

44. Jim Wafer, *The Taste of Blood: Spirit Possession in Brazilian Candomble* (Philadelphia: University of Pennsylvania Press, 1991), 43.

45. Seth Leacock and Ruth Leacock, *Spirits of the Deep* (Garden City, NY: Doubleday Natural History Press, 1972), 272.

46. Lisias Nogueira Negrão, *Entre a Cruz e a Encruzilhada: Formacão do Campo Umbandista em São Paulo* (São Paulo: Edusp, 1996), 204.

5

Relational Analysis of Religious Conversion and Social Change

Networks and Publics in Latin American Evangelicalism

DAVID SMILDE

Relational approaches to the study of religious practice and change can be thought of simply as micro-level versions of supply-side approaches, such as the rational-choice approach or "religious economy" (see Andrew Chesnut and Virginia Garrard-Burnett in this volume). Supply-side approaches hold religious interest or "demand" constant and do not, therefore, focus on the nature of religious products so much as the structural conditions facilitating or impeding growth as well as the range of competitors in a given "religious market." Network approaches do the same but at a more micro-social level. The most fundamental idea is simply that people convert to a religious group when they have more network ties pulling toward it than away from it. Demand-side approaches explain conversion by looking at a religious ideology and inferring what deprivations it addresses and then giving causal status to these deprivations.[1] From a relational, supply-side perspective, in contrast, "conversion is not about seeking or embracing an ideology; it is about bringing one's religious behavior into alignment with that of one's friends and family members."[2] In the strong version of this approach, networks are the "real" causes of conversion and any reported "deprivations" addressed by the religious beliefs and practices are better seen as emergent, ex post facto rationalizations or, at best, as general limiting conditions, not primary causes.[3]

Nevertheless, being more micro-level, relational approaches bring us down to the level of human actors and can point us beyond the strict assumptions of strong versions of the supply-side approach. In the first part of this chapter I will use network concepts of micro-social structure to help us understand the dynamics of conversion to new religious movements like evangelical Protestantism. But this examination will push at the limits of the network approach to the point that we will see some points where the differences between supply-side and demand-side approaches can be bridged.

Throughout this first part of the chapter, the micro-social effects of religious conversion will be touched on. In the second part of the chapter I will look more explicitly at the political effects of conversion. Here as well I will argue that the network concept, accompanied by its twin from relational sociology (the concept of "publics"), can help us understand the impact of new religious movements in Latin America. The study of social and political change in Latin America has been hampered by an overwhelming focus on political elites and core state institutions, on the one hand, and rigid concepts of the public sphere, on the other. As a result new religious movements, indeed, popular mobilizations of any kind, have usually been considered irrelevant and inconsequential. Concepts from relational sociology can help us catch up with history and understand how mobilization "in the streets" has impacted Latin American politics and how new religious movements have been a part of this.

Networks and Conversion to Evangelical
Protestantism in Venezuela

Networks are simply concrete social relationships that provide the basic units of social structure.[4] They are relevant to religious conversion simply because basic social relationships influence the way individuals act. The most basic view of the way such networks influence individuals comes from the theory of social psychological conformity. In this view, all humans have a fundamental need for social relationships and they cultivate and conserve them. Individuals adopt new cultural meanings and practices such as those provided by new religious movements, therefore, not because of any inherent characteristics of the latter, but rather to the degree that they reduce dissonance in these relationships.[5]

In my research on men and conversion to evangelicalism in Caracas, Venezuela, there were, indeed, many cases in which such straight-forward, direct network influence worked in the direction of conformity. In a number of cases of conversion, network influence clearly occurred in an asymmetric social context—a micro-social context in which the non-evangelical had less social power or status than the evangelical(s). Often this situation resulted from a move into a new household. For example, when Teodoro returned to his family from military service, he found that the majority of his family members had converted to evangelicalism and attended the evangelical church across the road from their home. He soon found out that they no longer were able to go to parties and social occasions with him. So when they invited him to attend a young adults program at their church, he gladly went and ended up converting as well. When Gregorio moved to Caracas after losing his job in the interior, he moved in with four evangelicals he had previously met. They brought him to church with them and his conversion process began. While specific aspects of evangelical meanings or practices may have been important in each of these cases, the asymmetric social context was probably more important.

Beyond Conformity

But many of my cases could not be explained through simple processes of conformity. In some cases evangelical networks influenced conversion processes through interactions in which conformity was irrelevant. Take the case of Ugeth. He converted as a result of a crack addiction that was undermining his relationship with his wife and children. During his problem period he lived in the same house with two brothers who had already converted a couple of years before because of a similar drug problem. However, so problematic was his sibling relationship with them that he said they never once tried to evangelize him. Nevertheless, when he actually did convert, his brothers' example was important for him. "They were an inspiration for me, seeing how the Lord had rescued them from the things they would do . . . and inspired, seeing everything that the Gospel was doing in the lives of those who were close to me, I realized that it was something supernatural, that it wasn't normal. And I said, 'Hey, I have to try this.'"[6] Interestingly, while his conversion did get Ugeth over his crack addiction, it seemed to have little effect on his distant relationship with his brothers. During the time I knew the three of them, I rarely found them together.

As Ugeth's case demonstrates, there are other mechanisms through which network influence can occur beyond social conformity. An evangelical's religious practice may change the ecological conditions to which the non-evangelical responds.[7] Wilkenman converted at age eighteen. Being a quiet, intellectual young man in one of the toughest, most violent neighborhoods in Caracas, he suffered severe problems of personal and social adjustment. When he was a boy, his mother separated from his father and began a new family. Because of frequent, acute conflict between his mother and stepfather, Wilkenman bounced between his "more-or-less" evangelical mother's house and his evangelical grandmother's house. In his description his mother was engrossed in her new family and small children and paid little attention to him. Wilkenman had no friends and would spend hours drawing or watching action movies on television. However his mother and grandmother would both put evangelical radio programs on at home. Once he started to listen, Wilkenman was hooked. He would spend hours listening and even calling in to radio talk shows until he finally decided that becoming evangelical would solve his problems. He went to church with his grandmother a few times and then started to go to evangelical concerts and events he heard about on the radio. In this case, Wilkenman reports no attempts at evangelization by his mother or grandmother—indeed, he eventually joined not his grandmother's church but the one he found with the most active youth program. Rather he worked through the possibility of religious innovation in engagement with his radio. He said, "I would listen to the church programs that were on at 9:00 p.m. and that talked about Venezuela's problems, people's problems, and Christ's solutions. . . . With the testimonies I heard, I found that Christ was the solution."

Having a social relationship with an evangelical clearly has an important causal impact on conversion. However, network influence should not be seen as simple conformity. Frequently, network contact has little to do with conformity and may even occur in the midst of antipathy. These mechanisms of observation or ecological influence reduce the reductionistic tendencies of network analysis by showing that networks function by channeling individual-level seeking and meaning-making.

Structural Availability

So far we have looked only at network influence leading to religious conversion. But networks toward conversion do not exist in isolation. Rather, they compete with networks leading away from participation in a particular religious group. Put differently, while participators pull non-participators toward conversion, other non-participators pull these same non-participators away from conversion. Rodney Stark says that recruitment to a new religious movement occurs when the potential recruit has more significant ties to members of the movement than to non-members. This is a variant of the "control theory" of deviant behavior, which says that because they have "stakes in conformity," people do not usually deviate. "Most of us conform in order to retain the good opinion of our friends and family. But some people lack such attachments. Their rates of deviance are much higher than are those of people with an abundance of attachments."[8] Social movements research addresses the absence of countervailing networks through the concept of "structural availability." In their seminal study David Snow, Louis Zurcher, and Sheldon Ekland-Olson argued that individuals who are structurally available "can follow their interests and/or engage in exploratory behavior to a greater extent than individuals who are bound to existing lines of action" by their network obligations.[9] This is the process behind the frequently replicated finding that immigrants and migrants are overrepresented among religious converts (see Virginia Garrard-Burnett in this volume), but it is not limited to these groups.

According to Doug McAdam and Ronnelle Paulsen, the most relevant network ties in studying social movement recruitment are those that individuals use to sustain their identity.[10] In Venezuela, these ties are most often family ties. Individuals are morally expected to support and defend their family of origin above and beyond any other social group or ideology, and they look to their families to provide identity, belonging, and a web of social support. Occasionally, a family will welcome an individual's religious conversion if he or she has experienced serious problems of personal or social adjustment. But more commonly, a family member's becoming evangelical may be considered an embarrassment, a rebuke, or simply a loss. For example, when Juan Betancourt returned to his hometown after converting in Caracas, his father broke down and cried because Juan would no longer drink with him. Such reactions are powerful reasons not to convert if there is valued and frequent rapport with non-evangelical family members. Thus, most of the converts in my sample whose families were not evangelical either converted after leaving home or because of long-standing inconformity with their family.

Willian is an example of one of those who lives apart from his family of origin for economic necessity. He moved from Venezuela's interior and became evangelical shortly thereafter. He explained to me that before he became evangelical, living with his family, he was "loaded with problems," and I asked him what type. He responded as follows: "I had personal afflictions, moments of loneliness. Those were tough times. Being here [in Caracas] without your family is tough. You tend to have economic problems. I also had problems with sickness, moments of loneliness. And sometimes you feel that there isn't anyone who can talk to you to raise your spirits. Because when you look at them [people you don't know very well], they have more problems than you do. So I couldn't trust them, their advice." What is interesting in Willian's case is not just that he experienced the normal problems of a young man living on his own for the first time, but the emphasis he put on not having anyone to talk to. In effect, Willian did not have trusted interlocutors who could, through dialogue, help him make meaning regarding the situations he was going through. When he came across some people he felt he could trust at an evangelical kiosk where he would eat lunch, he cultivated this network and started participating in an evangelical church.

But the character of non-conformity is most evident in those cases in which my respondents had been at odds with their family or for some reason felt the need to individuate away from its influence. Several of the men I interviewed became "structurally available" precisely because they did not conform to the dominant meanings embodied in their family of origin. Indeed, in several cases, their living apart from the family was part of an attempt to gain distance from them and be able to conduct their lives differently.

As an adolescent, Nelson suffered problems with depression that included a period of hospitalization. He has lived with depressive tendencies since and has largely experienced them through conflict with his family. He has a heavy, serious, and reflective manner combined with meticulous organizational skills. When he married and had kids, his concern for *fundamentos* (fundamentals) was expressed in a religious quest. Before becoming evangelical, he had studied the Jehovah's Witnesses and had taken a great interest in the heritage of the Jewish owners of the imitation-jewelry store he managed. When an evangelical started working for him at the store, he interestedly listened to his evangelization and ended up visiting an evangelical church. The next week he brought his wife and they ended up joining. Nelson said, "So on Sunday we went to church because if they showed me this part that I wanted to have in my life, then I wanted her to see it too. Because, basically we were looking for [something specific]. . . . I mean, it was for the girls [his two daughters]. I was very worried about the way things were going [in Venezuela]. The principles with which I had been raised and with which the majority of people are raised, were not solid." In Nelson's case, living apart from his family of origin and conversion to evangelicalism are each effects of inconformity with them. He was actively searching for alternative forms of meaning and practice that could give him the "fundamentals" he was looking for.

Pushing the Network Concept

As it works closer to the ground than the "religious economy" approach, some of the blind spots of supply-side approaches become evident when using a network approach to conversion; time and again we are confronted with the importance of religious meaning, problem-solving, and agency. Relational sociology does indeed seek to explain phenomena by focusing only on patterns of social relations, and thus usually regards attributes of individuals such as their problems, agency, and purposes as spuriously significant.[11] Nevertheless, in the rest of this section I will argue that if we look more closely we can see how networks function through meaning, how they channel people's problem solving, and how they themselves are the objects of agency.

Network Explanations Need Not Exclude Meaning

First, while network analysis has traditionally been seen as an alternative to analysis based on subjective meaning, network theory has itself undergone a "cultural turn." Network theorists like Harrison White now argue that we need to think of networks as stories.[12] If you think about it closely, relationships consist of stories. Two people have a network tie not because they are physically joined but because they have some history of interactions which they can narrate to themselves and others. The simple conformity model of network influence has been increasingly criticized by social scientists. Clearly, network influence happens. But we need more information to actually establish why it works in one direction rather than another.[13] Why would a network tie between a convert and a non-convert lead the later to conform instead of the former? Put differently, why would it lead the non-convert to religious participation rather than the convert to apostasy? One answer is to look at the character of the meanings in play. For example, in my sample, several men had converted to evangelicalism through a romantic interest. If the mechanism in play is simply social psychological conformity, we can ask why my respondent became evangelical rather than leading his partner away from her religious participation. In each of these five cases either the relationship was new or the couple was experiencing relationship problems. Given evangelicalism's strong association with fidelity, sobriety, and a household orientation,[14] participation likely added value to these new or troubled relationships.

There is another possibility for understanding how network influence occurs. Events and contingencies can revalue existing discourses and determine the direction they take and the symbolic elements that dominate.[15] When an evangelical and a non-evangelical share living space, there is a continual potential for "interanimation": the forced recognition of alternative, competing discourses.[16] In this situation, evangelicals who live with non-evangelicals tend to engage the latter in a low-intensity but persistent way by continually providing evangelical conceptualizations of the situations and dilemmas the non-evangelical confronts. This requires response from the non-evangelical, who develops a repertoire of ways to deflect the confrontation. The equilibrium is often broken when a misfortune arises that tips the interpretive balance of power toward the evangelizer, who inevitably provides an evangelical analysis of the non-evangelical's misfortune. The meaning system gains life for the evangelized and the non-evangelical assents to it.[17]

As both Henri Gooren and Christine Kovic argue elsewhere in this volume, this tip of the interpretive balance is the process that is behind the oft-noted tendency for conversion to happen during a moment of sickness or period of ill health. Consider the case of Darton and his wife, who converted while living with the latter's evangelical mother. Darton's mother-in-law continually tried to get them to convert to evangelicalism, and they would occasionally go to church with her. However, they never attended regularly until their child almost died from a respiratory problem. When he was revived after he stopped breathing, they viewed it as a miracle. And Darton's mother-in-law did not miss the opportunity to interpret the occurrence as a message from God.

INTERVIEWER: So after that happened, what did your mother-in-law say about it?

DARTON: She wasn't surprised because she knows that God truly is a God of miracles. But she recriminated us. [She said] it had happened to us because we were disobedient before God—because we knew. We would always go and ask for prayers when she was pregnant but we didn't serve him [afterwards]. So she said that God did that so that we would understand that he really is a living God and that we weren't serving him—that perhaps he was calling us through our child since we weren't going [to church] on our own accord. He started calling us through our child.

While theoretically such contingencies can work with any cultural practice or discourse, Venezuelan evangelicalism seems especially adept at building on them. Evangelicalism specializes in predicting precisely the types of misfortune lower-class Venezuelans are most likely to experience and this, combined with the relative inattention by the mass media and popular culture, means that when such a misfortune occurs, it constitutes prima facie evidence for the validity of evangelical discourse. Furthermore, while we know that actors frequently use highly general and ambiguous meanings to avoid an interanimation of competing or contradictory discourses that might undermine their network,[18] evangelicals often seem to use unambiguous terms that provoke interanimations, that generate confrontations that could lead to conversion.

Network Explanations Can Include Individual-Level Problem-Solving

We can also examine more closely the assumption that network explanations replace problem-based explanations. It is important here to realize that there is a difference between cause and explanation. Some causes are so widespread that they are not useful for explaining phenomena. However, that does not make them irrelevant or unimportant. For example, the biological need for food does not do very well in explaining why people in a given city go to one supermarket instead of another. Rather, explanations having to do with physical infrastructure and distances will likely be more robust. However, people clearly go to the supermarket because of the biological need for food. If there was no such need, they likely would not go grocery shopping anywhere.

In the same way, the fact that network location tends to provide the most robust explanations of religious conversion does not mean that people do not convert because religious meanings help them confront the existential problems of their lives—whether these have to do with the fulfillment of basic needs, social reproduction, or uncertainty regarding the afterlife. Rather, network location determines who addresses these needs through religious participation. Other individuals with similar needs may address them through other means or not address them at all—simply suffering their problems or explaining them away.

There are other ways that the experience of life problems can have an impact on networks. Explanations based on the idea of structural availability generally assume that this network situation is the product of happenstance, or at least the product of causes irrelevant to eventual religious conversion. So, for example, in their classic exploration of religious conversion and networks, Snow, Zurcher, and Ekland-Olson use the example of a twenty-five-year-old male whose luggage was lost on his flight to Los Angeles, and he wound up living on the streets. This contingent misfortune left him open and receptive to recruitment to a religious movement.[19] Indeed, in many of my cases, structural availability was caused by life-course characteristics or contingencies. However, it should come as no surprise that frequently structural availability is *itself* caused by a problem that is involved in the conversion project. Among the men I interviewed, for example, Alberto, Jhony, and Melvin all lived on the street as a result of their involvement in drugs and crime. In other cases, persistent problems had undermined the individual's place in the family of origin. Martín's mother forced him and his wife to leave because of their incessant fighting. Ernesto's mother threw him out of the house because of his consistent involvement with drugs and violence. In all, in fifteen of the fifty cases of converts who experienced problems while not living with their family of origin, it was the problem that would eventually lead to conversion that itself caused structural availability.

Network Explanations Can Include Agency

My research shows that we can question the notion that network explanations eliminate individual agency. Structural explanations based on networks assume that people do not usually know why they do what they do and do not fully understand the consequences their action will produce.[20] Structural approaches do not deny that people experience agency in what they do, nor that they can provide agentive stories regarding what they have done. Rather, they argue that these "vocabularies of motive" are not scientific explanations because they leave out the real causes that determine who acts in which way.[21]

First, in contemporary social theory, agency is not synonymous with purpose and intention. Anthony Giddens defines agency as "the stream of actual or contemplated causal interventions of corporeal beings in the ongoing

process of events-in-the-world," which is not confined to the intended consequences of an actors' action.[22] Defined in these terms, the majority of my
cases of conversion in which network location was causally effective demonstrate the respondents' agency in the construction of this network location.
In my sample, in the great majority of cases in which a respondent lived
away from family of origin, he moved away due to life-course considerations:
either he had gotten married and was able to move out or had moved from
the interior for employment reasons. In contrast, respondents who lived
with a spatially co-present evangelical did so not by choice but because that
was their family of origin or because the evangelical in question converted
after the respondent had joined the household. However, in ten cases, the
person intentionally moved into a household that had an evangelical in it.
Agency, thus defined, is quite compatible with the traditional network program. For networks to be key causal characteristics of social phenomena, it
is not necessary that they be uncaused, or even that they be uncaused by
the actors who eventually are constrained by them. Rather, the core claim
is that they have important effects that function beyond (even contrary to)
the conscious interests and intentions of actors. This would be like a person
who switches on the light to illuminate the room and unintentionally alerts
a prowler.[23]

A second, more direct challenge to the exclusion of agency in network
explanations comes from cases in which the respondent intentionally created the network location, as part of the same project of change that resulted
in conversion. In this case, network effects are no longer unintended. In
effect this is like a person who switches on the light to illuminate the room
in order to alert the prowler. In several cases I found evidence of such a process. Gregorio converted while living away from his family of origin and living with an evangelical. However, he actively sought these conditions as part
of a project of change. Two problems were affecting his life before his conversion. First, he had long suffered from bouts of depression, and, second, he
had just lost his job. While living at home with his family he became familiar
with evangelicalism through a revival and even had a religious experience.
Nevertheless, while he was interested, he did not participate in a church.
He did meet a number of evangelicals from Caracas, and they invited him to
stay with them if he ever came their way. Indeed, he was already considering
moving to the capital to launch a music career. When he did, he looked up
his evangelical friends, and they found him a place to stay with several other
evangelicals. He immediately began to attend their church with them. When
his music career sputtered, he put all of his energies into the evangelical
church he attended with his roommates.

In this case, moving away from family of origin to Caracas to live with
some evangelicals and pursue a music career was all part of a project of

change, a new start that eventually led to religious conversion. In this and other cases network location ends up looking like a mediating variable between individual motivations and conversion. It clearly has a causal impact, but the respondents themselves created that impact as part of a conscious project of change. The respondents did not necessarily see that a change in network location would lead to conversion in particular. But they did correctly perceive that, in more general terms, it would facilitate a project of change.

While these purposive constructions of network locations present a clear challenge to strong versions of the network project, the situation could hardly be otherwise. As people think about and imagine the social context in which they live, it would be surprising indeed if they never perceived the same causal sequences that social scientists do. Nevertheless, it should be underlined that this process is limited. Such purposive construction happened in less than 10 percent of conversions related to networks. In more than 90 percent of cases there was no purposive relationship between the respondent's stated intentions and network effects to which he was subject.

In sum, network analysis provides powerful tools for understanding individual-level conversion. Overall, my research on men in Caracas shows that it is not the experience of problems that explains exactly who converts to evangelicalism. Rather, location in social networks explains who addresses their problems through religious conversion. In my study of evangelical men in Caracas, family relationships constituted the most important kind of network. However, this may be a specific characteristic of the context of Caracas. In other times and places it might be quite different. In the case of Chiapas, for example, Christine Kovic (chapter 10) finds that the community was the relevant unit of analysis when looking at networks. While such network explanations reorient us away from individual-level attributes, they do not wipe cultural meaning, problems, and agency off the slate. Analysis of meaning can help us understand the way networks function. Individual-level problems and agency continue to have a role in the creation of network positions.

Networks and Publics in Social Change

The religious conversions of the evangelical men I studied in Caracas had far-reaching consequences for their own individual lives and as well as their families. However, one of the sustaining motivations of research on religious change in Latin America has been its implications for broader social and political change. As Steigenga, Wightman, and Kovic argue in part 3 of this volume, the political and social implications of conversion are multiple and complex. In the rest of this chapter I would like to suggest that concepts from relational sociology can also help us understand the implications of these new networks.

Research on social change in Latin America has long been dominated by a focus on elite political actors such as presidents, politicians, and party leaders as well as in the central institutions of political power such as the congress, the judiciary, and political parties. It was only natural, then, that social scientists seeking to understand the political implications of evangelical would look to assess whether evangelical movements could develop into viable political movements or parties that could realistically challenge power. In most cases these assessments were negative.[24] Another direction of thinking about the implications of evangelical growth in Latin America looked at the impact they might have on values conducive to democracy.[25] For the most part, the few studies actually based on empirical data were either methodologically flawed,[26] or revealed complex and more subtle effects.[27]

However, approaches to social change in Latin America have begun to broaden away from the search for coherent actors with deeply held values confronting central institutions of the state, in large part because of social scientists' almost complete failure to anticipate the wave of political change over the past five to ten years. On the one hand, from Mexico to Venezuela to Argentina, traditional political elites have been turned out in favor of populist candidates both left and right. On the other hand, the mobilizing power of traditional political parties and labor unions has been seriously challenged by ethnic, nationalist, and religious movements.[28]

There are a number of scholars who are looking to broaden the scope of our analysis of social change. Historian Jeffrey Rubin, for example, has closely argued how it is that peripheral, non-dominant social groups can impact core institutions not only by resisting or consenting to them, but by processes of resignification in which they change the terms of public discourse.[29] Following Rubin, we might be missing the mark if we simply ask whether evangelical groups can become a political force or whether they can directly influence elite actors and state institutions. Their larger impact might be better captured by poststructuralist concepts of decentered subjecthood, in which political change occurs when fragments and pieces of dominant discourses are reassembled through alternative rationalities and narratives.[30] In my view this is the direction that work on the politics of evangelical growth in Latin America needs to move, and I think relational sociology can facilitate this attempt.

Rethinking Liberal Conceptions of the Public Sphere

Increasingly, network scholars use the term "publics" as a counterpart to the idea of networks to create a more dynamic overall concept of social structure.[31] It also succeeds in rethinking the public sphere in ways that more adequately portray the involvement of non-dominant social groups. Classic liberal conceptions of the public sphere generally do not cast a favorable light on popular participation in developing regions of the world. In Jurgen Habermas's account, for example, a public sphere is a social space controlled neither by the state nor the economy, in which private citizens set aside their personal interests in order to deliberate on issues of common interest in terms of rational-critical debate.[32] From this perspective, the public participation of evangelical and other popular religious groups in Latin America looks deformed, pre-modern, or "proto-political" insofar as it directly brings in issues of personal well-being and communicates in idioms other than those of rational-critical debate.

Relational sociologists have attempted to unpack the concept of "public" and make it more versatile and sensitive to multiplicity. This work is inspired by the trend toward conceptualizing social networks as discourses or stories that tie actors together.[33] Publics, then, are relational contexts in which normally segmented social networks and their associated discourses come into contact in open-ended ways.[34] As such, publics are sites in which distinct networks are bridged, new understandings develop, and coalitions are formed. Rather than an absence of structure, publics usually exhibit stable features, involve existing social networks and discourses, and are shot through with power dynamics.[35] Thus, they are not liminal "free spaces" but structured relational contexts in which new articulations of structure can occur.[36] Publics can also be the objects of agency.[37] While their power comes from their open-endedness and resulting unpredictability, they are often planned by actors precisely to extend their networks and associated discourses. Social actors or networks of social actors create publics precisely to extend their networks or bridge particular networks.

Evangelical Publics in Caracas

The evangelicals I work with in Caracas provide good examples of publics in the numerous evangelistic events they hold in different forms. Virtually every plaza in Caracas has a Pentecostal service or pastor preaching at some point during any given day. These events range from a self-appointed individual preaching to a captive audience at a bus stop to well-organized initiatives, with sound equipment and municipal permits, that dominate a plaza for several hours daily. In general they simply consist of a normal church service held in public space. It begins with collective singing and announcements, a Bible reading, an offering, and then a sermon lasting twenty to thirty minutes. At the end there is a prayer and altar call. These public plaza services are an important means of recruiting converts. Compared to one-on-one evangelization, plaza services are non-threatening and permit a low-intensity engagement for those who are interested in "trying-on" the evangelical belief system.[38]

But these plaza services are not just about preaching. During the service a few Pentecostals work the crowd passing out Bible tracts with evangelistic messages on them. Others hand them to passers-by. Before and after the services or during and toward the periphery, the plaza is a place for Pentecostals to visit, exchange information relevant to economic opportunities, or meet up for an afternoon activity. In a context in which there is no functioning mail system and telephone communications can be difficult, such a recognized meeting place plays a vital function. The peripheries of the plaza service also serve as sites for counseling for both Pentecostals and non-Pentecostals. A non-Pentecostal who wanted to commit suicide because of his dependence on prescription drugs, a Pentecostal whose wife had left him with their children, and a young non-Pentecostal who feared he would lose his job were some of the cases I witnessed during my participant-observation. In all such cases the problem is given a Pentecostal interpretation as an earthly manifestation of the struggle between God and the Devil, and a prayer is raised asking God for help. If the person is non-Pentecostal, he or she is usually counseled to regularly attend a Pentecostal church. There are also occasionally transnational contacts made at the plaza services. The plaza services are frequently on the schedule of short mission trips from North America, where the services present dramas or puppet shows with translations depicting biblical stories. In these plaza services, networks are bridged and new relationships are formed between Pentecostals from different churches and between Pentecostals and non-Pentecostals.

In previous work I described an evangelical protest in downtown Caracas.[39] Organized by the Venezuelan Fraternity of Evangelical Pastors, the Clamor Por Venezuela sought to moralize the public sphere and bring God's blessings on Venezuela. The event lasted several hours and included public prayers, singing, several speakers, as well as children's programs. Such public events are not confined to downtown Caracas. At any given time the churches with which I worked held week-long campaigns in two to three dangerous, marginal barrios in Caracas. These could involve a provisional stage with lights and sound equipment. But more often than not, they amounted to little more than a handful of evangelicals with a microphone and amplifier or even simply a megaphone, holding an evangelical service in public space. One could add to this evangelical radio programs, door-to-door evangelization, and person-to-person witnessing. Occasionally, this contact is abstract and generic. But in many or most cases it is accommodated to the biographical realities of the person being evangelized—a problem with drugs, a spouse who has disappeared, or a sick child.[40]

These publics are purposefully constructed relational contexts in which non-elite individuals are able to collectively reflect on current social realities and alternative futures in their own terms. Through these publics they seek to extend their networks and the influence of their discourses, and thereby gain the social influence they do not have in the central institutions of the democratic state. As Garrard-Burnett argues in chapter 11, this is one of the keys to the emphasis put on telecommunications among evangelical churches throughout the Americas. As they generally do not have influence or access to the central institutions of democratic states and societies, buying airtime or radio stations is a way that they can get their message out.

With an exclusive focus on discrete actors with deeply held political values, the impact of evangelicals in places like Venezuela would be hard to see. The total number of evangelicals is still less than 10 percent; they do not constitute a coherent political movement; nor do they vote together as a block.[41] However, their public efforts have contributed, for better or for worse, to a moralization of public discourse in Venezuela.[42] Since the time he was a candidate, Hugo Chavez has used evangelical phrases and images—to the point that many have (erroneously) claimed that he is an evangelical convert. More broadly, openly moralistic, teleological, and often intolerant discourse has become widespread in Venezuelan politics in a way it was not only ten years ago. A direct path between evangelicals and this change would be hard to trace. But it is clear that evangelicals are one of a number of other new social movements that rely on cultural identities and alternative rationalities to contribute to public discussion of collective life.

Conclusion

Latin America is currently experiencing a dramatic period of change in its associational life that we are only beginning to understand. From a society characterized by strongly centralized states, parties, and an official religion, it is moving toward one in which diverse cultural identities form the basis of associational and political cleavage—from ethnic to nationalist to new religious movements.[43] Two of the main tasks in developing our understanding are understanding mobilization and social impact. In this chapter, I have argued that relational concepts of social structure can facilitate this understanding.

Network concepts have long provided much more successful explanations of religious conversion than those based on individual attributes, problems, or complaints. Nevertheless, social scientists frequently shy away from them because of their apparently reductionistic tendency to exclude meaning and individual-level problems and agency. Here I have argued that this reductionism is unnecessary and that meaning, problems, and agency are compatible with and can even improve network understandings of conversion. The perspective that emerges is one in which social structure consists of multiple articulations of concrete social relationships which not only enforce conformity, but provide conduits for information and spaces for discussion and conflict.

Relational concepts also point us in the direction we need to go in understanding the subtle, de-centered impact of religious change in Latin American politics. They can supplement our traditional actor- and institution-centered analysis with images of concrete relationships and spaces of interaction. New social movements and articulations, religious or otherwise, especially those occurring among marginalized social classes, are often ephemeral, with continual changes of participants and identities. Judged as nascent civic movements or proto-political parties, they are likely to be unimpressive. However, when seen through relational concepts, we find them creating new relational contexts in which networks and understandings are bridged and discourses are altered.

Using relational concepts can also help us step back from the quick normative judgments endemic to our current vocabulary. As scholars, our first goal should be to understand the impact of currently existing popular mobilizations and articulations on their own terms, and only later ask whether they fit with our preexisting normative notions of "public sphere," "civil society," "civic engagement," "social capital," "quality of democracy," or "democratic deepening." Starting out with normative concepts leads to truncated analyses that easily miss social change in the works. Speaking in terms of networks and publics does not require us to decide ahead of time whether they are civil or civic or whether they deepen and improve the quality of democracy or contribute to the power and autonomy of individuals. These concepts thereby give us the space to analyze the social impact of religious change without (or simply before) taking a normative attitude toward it.

NOTES

1. See Rodney Stark and Roger Finke, *Acts of Faith: Explaining the Human Side of Religion* (Berkeley: University of California Press, 2000).

2. Rodney Stark, *The Rise of Christianity: How the Obscure, Marginal Jesus Movement Became the Dominant Religious Force in the Western World in a Few Centuries* (Princeton: Princeton University Press, 1996), 16–17.

3. See Stark and Finke, *Acts of Faith*.

4. Parts of this section were previously published in David Smilde, *Reason to Believe: Cultural Agency in Latin American Evangelicalism* (Berkeley: University of California Press, 2007); and David Smilde, "A Qualitative Comparative Analysis of Conversion to Venezuelan Evangelicalism: How Networks Matter," *American Journal of Sociology* III, no. 3 (November 2005).

5. See Peter V. Marsden and Noah E. Friedkin, "Network Studies of Social Influence," in *Advances in Social Network Analysis: Research in the Social and Behavioral Sciences*, ed. S Wasserman and J. Galaskiewicz (Thousand Oaks: Sage Publications, 1994), 3–25; and Leon Festinger, *A Theory of Cognitive Dissonance* (Stanford: Stanford University Press, 1962).

6. All interviews were conducted by David Smilde in Caracas, Venezuela.

7. Marsden and Friedkin, "Network Studies of Social Influence."

8. Stark and Finke, *Acts of Faith*, 117–18.

9. David A. Snow, Louis A. Zurcher Jr., and Sheldon Ekland-Olson, "Social Networks and Social Movements: A Microstructural Approach to Differential Recruitment," *American Sociological Review* 45 (1980): 794.

10. See Doug McAdam and Ronnelle Paulsen, "Specifying the Relationship between Social Ties and Activism," *American Journal of Sociology* 99 (1993): 640–667.

11. See Mustafa Emirbayer and Jeff Goodwin, "Network Analysis, Culture, and the Problem of Agency," *American Journal of Sociology* 99, no. 6 (1994).

12. See Harrison White, *Identity and Control: A Structural Theory of Action* (Princeton: Princeton University Press, 1992).

13. Roger V. Gould, "Why Do Networks Matter? Rationalist and Structuralist Interpretations," in *Social Movement Networks: Relational Approaches to Collective Action*, ed. Mario Diani and Doug McAdam (New York: Oxford University Press, 2003), 233–257.

14. See Elizabeth Brusco, *The Reformation of Machismo* (Austin: University of Texas Press, 1995); and David Smilde, "The Fundamental Unity of the Conservative and Revolutionary Tendencies in Venezuelan Evangelicalism: The Case of Conjugal Relations," *Religion* 27 (1997): 343–359.

15. See Steve Ellingson, "Understanding the Dialectic of Discourse and Collective Action: Public Debate and Rioting in Antebellum Cincinnati," *American Journal of Sociology* 101 (1995): 100–144; Marshall Sahlins, *Islands of History* (Chicago: University of Chicago Press, 1985).

16. Ann Mische and Harrison White, "Between Conversation and Situation: Public Switching Dynamics across Network Domains," *Social Research* 65 (1998): 295–342; and Mikhail Bakhtin, *The Dialogic Imagination: Four Essays*, ed. Michael Holquist (Austin: University of Texas Press, 1981).

17. See Brusco, *The Reformation of Machismo*.

18. Ann Mische, "Cross-Talk in Movements: Reconceiving the Culture-Network Link," in *Social Movement Networks: Relational Approaches to Collective Action*, ed. Mario Diani and Doug McAdam (New York: Oxford University Press, 2003); and John F. Padgett and Christopher K. Ansell, "Robust Action and the Rise of the Medici, 1400–1434," *American Journal of Sociology* 89 (1993): 1259–1319.

19. Snow, Zurcher, and Ekland-Olson, "Social Networks and Social Movements."

20. See Anthony Giddens, *Central Problems in Social Theory: Action, Structure, and Contradiction in Social Analysis* (Berkeley: University of California Press, 1979), 59.

21. See Emirbayer and Goodwin, "Network Analysis."

22. Anthony Giddens, *New Rules of Sociological Method: A Positive Critique of Interpretative Sociologies* (New York: Basic Books, 1976), 77; see also William H. Sewell Jr., "A Theory of Structure: Duality, Agency, and Transformation," *American Journal*

of Sociology 98 (1992): 1–29; also Mustafa Emirbayer and Ann Mische, "What Is Agency?" *American Journal of Sociology* 103 (1998): 962–1023.

23. See Giddens, *New Rules of Sociological Method,* 77.

24. Jean Pierre Bastian, *Protestantismos y modernidad latinoamericana: Historia de unas minorías religiosas activas en América Latina* (México: Fondo de Cultura Económica, 1994); Andrew R. Chesnut, *Born Again in Brazil: The Pentecostal Boom and the Pathogens of Poverty* (New Brunswick, NJ: Rutgers University Press, 1997); Newton Gaskill, "Rethinking Protestantism and Democratic Consolidation in Latin America," *Sociology of Religion* 58 (1997): 69–91; Paul Freston, *Evangelicals and Politics in Asia, Africa, and Latin America* (New York: Cambridge University Press, 2001); and Paul Freston, *Protestant Political Parties: A Global Survey* (Burlington: Ashgate, 2004).

25. David Martin, *Tongues of Fire: The Explosion of Protestantism in Latin America* (Oxford: Basil Blackwell, 1990); Christian Smith, "The Spirit and Democracy: Base Communities, Protestantism, and Democratization in Latin America," *Sociology of Religion* 55 (1994): 119–142; Amy Sherman, *The Soul of Development: Biblical Christianity and Economic Transformation in Guatemala* (Oxford: Oxford University Press, 1997).

26. For an example of such flawed methodology see Sherman, *The Soul of Development.*

27. Timothy Steigenga, *The Politics of the Spirit: The Political Implications of the Growth of Pentecostalized Religion in Central America* (Baltimore: Lexington Press, 2001); Timothy Steigenga, this volume; and David Smilde, "Contradiction without Paradox: Evangelical Political Culture in the 1998 Venezuelan Elections," *Latin American Politics and Society* 46 (2004): 75–102.

28. Amalia Pallares, *From Peasant Struggles to Indian Resistance: The Ecuadorian Andes in the Late Twentieth Century* (Norman: University of Oklahoma Press, 2003); Deborah Yashar, *Contesting Citizenship in Latin America: The Rise of Indigenous Movements and the Postliberal Challenge* (New York: Cambridge University Press, 2005); David Smilde, "Los Evangélicos y la Polarización: La Moralización de la Política y la Politización de la Religión," *Revista Venezolana de Economia y Ciencias Sociales* 10 (2004): 163–179; Margarita Lopez Maya, *Del Viernes Negro al Referndo Revocatorio* (Caracas, Venezuela: Alfadil Ediciones, 2005).

29. Jeff Rubin, *Decentering the Regime: Ethnicity, Radicalism, and Democracy in Juchitan, Mexico* (Durham: Duke University Press, 1997); see also Jeff Rubin, "Meanings and Mobilizations: A Cultural Politics Approach to Social Movements and States," *Latin American Research Review* 39, no. 3 (2004): 106–142; and David Smilde, "Popular Publics: Street Protest and Plaza Preachers in Caracas," *International Review of Social History* 49, Supplement (2004): 179–195; Manuel A. Vasquez, "Toward a New Agenda for the Study of Religion in the Americas," *Journal of Interamerican Studies and World Affairs* 41, Special Issue: Religion in America: Churches, Globalization, and Democratization (1999):1–20.

30. Jeffrey W. Rubin, "In the Streets or in the Institutions?" *LASA Forum* 37 (2006): 26–29; Rubin, "Meanings and Mobilizations."

31. Parts of this and the following sections appeared in Smilde, "Popular Publics."

32. Jurgen Habermas, *The Structural Transformation of the Public Sphere,* trans. Thomas Berger (1962; repr., Cambridge: Cambridge University Press, 1989).

33. The seminal contribution in this trend is Harrison White, *Identity and Control: A Structural Theory of Action* (Princeton: Princeton University Press, 1992).

34. Mustafa Emirbayer and Miriam Sheller, "Publics in History," *Theory and Society* 28 (1999): 145–197; Eiko Ikegami, "A Sociological Theory of Publics: Identity and Culture as Emergent Properties in Networks," *Social Research* 67 (2000): 989–1029; Ann Mishe and Philippa Pattison, "Composing a Civic Arena: Publics, Projects, and Social Settings," *Poetics* 27 (2000): 163–194.

35. Francesca Polletta, "'Free Spaces' in Collective Action," *Theory and Society* 28 (1999): 1–38; Emirbayer and Sheller, "Publics in History."

36. Javier Auyero, "Relational Riot: Austerity and Corruption Protest in the Neoliberal Era," *Social Movement Studies* 2 (2003): 117–145.

37. Ikegami, "A Sociological Theory of Publics"; Taeku Lee, *Mobilizing Public Opinion: Black Insurgency and Racial Attitudes in the Civil Rights Era* (Chicago: University of Chicago Press, 2002); Mische, "Cross-Talk in Movements."

38. Smilde, *"Works of the Flesh, Fruit of the Spirit."*

39. See David Smilde, "El Clamor por Venezuela: Latin American Evangelicalism as a Collective Action Frame," in *Latin American Religion in Motion*, ed. Christian Smith and Joshua Prokopy (New York: Routledge, 1999).

40. David Smilde, "Skirting the Instrumental Paradox: Intentional Belief through Narrative in Latin American Pentecostalism," *Qualitative Sociology* 26 (2003): 313–329.

41. Smilde, "Contradiction without Paradox."

42. Smilde, "Los Evangélicos y la Polarización."

43. On this point, Phillip Berryman argues that one of the reasons for the success of Pentecostal groups is precisely their network form of organization in contrast to traditional, centralized, "fordist" religious organizations like the Catholic Church or mainstream Protestantism; see Phillip Berryman, "Churches as Winners and Losers in the Network Society," *Journal of Interamerican Studies and World Affairs* 41, Special Issue: Religion in America: Churches, Globalization, and Democratization (1999): 21–34.

PART TWO

Conversion to What?

6

Conversion from Afro-Brazilian Religions to Neo-Pentecostalism

Opening New Horizons of the Possible

PATRICIA BIRMAN

Over the last fifteen years, a broad swathe of people in Brazil has converted to Pentecostal and neo-Pentecostal churches. Their unprecedented rate of expansion has meant these groups have rapidly become a religious movement of undeniable importance in the country, displaying a significant presence in culture, politics, and the media. In this chapter, my aim is to show that the phenomenal growth of these churches is due in large part to changes within Pentecostalism itself, caused by the emergence of the neo-Pentecostal Universal Church of the Kingdom of God (IURD) and its theological and ritual innovations.[1] The IURD has reinterpreted Pentecostal theology by allocating a central role to exorcism. As a practice, exorcism looks to "expel" former spiritual entities derived from Afro-Brazilian cults (now considered diabolical) from the bodies of the individuals involved. Through this ritual, the IURD propagates a critical view of the Catholic and Afro-Brazilian religious practices that have dominated the country's religious scene. Conversion via exorcism provides individuals with the possibility of questioning the social and religious place attributed to them as erstwhile practitioners of magic and witchcraft. In this way, I suggest that exorcism, by enabling the mass conversion of Catholics and Afro-Brazilians to Pentecostalism, offers its converts the chance, previously difficult to contemplate, of breaking with the cultural, social, and religious principles that shape the popular image of the Brazilian Catholic worldview.

The advent of the IURD imposed an immediately perceptible change on the religious scene. A church emerged with a proselytism strongly rooted in a violent attack on Afro-Brazilian religious groups, accused of making pacts with the devil. Its incitement to invade cult houses, destroy images and sacred objects, principally those belonging to Afro-Brazilian cults, along with the verbal aggressiveness consistently used by the IURD in the pulpit and the media against the latter, began to make headlines in the popular newspapers. Its aggressive action against the Afro-Brazilian "devils" in this combat, described by the press as a "holy war," made the IURD the center of numerous polemics that filled newspapers pages and television airtime. The attacks on these targets by the church were all clearly made in the name of Jesus.[2] From the viewpoint of the IURD, it seemed indispensable to defeat the Catholics and Afro-Brazilians who had dominated the religious sphere since Brazil's foundation as a nation.

One of the most pronounced features of Brazilian neo-Pentecostalism is the sociological status of most of its church members. These churches have, in fact, proven much more successful among the subaltern sections of the population. But while conversion has clearly proven attractive to people living in precarious socioeconomic conditions, it is much less easy to understand what this conversion means for the individuals involved. I shall try to avoid a reductionism by looking at the conversion of individuals in terms of their claims and the meanings they attribute to conversion. Frequently conceived to be a decisive gesture, conversion may often take place in opposition to the person's friends and family, radically altering the direction of his or her life. Hence, we can ask, how is the social setting of the future convert related to his or her religious choices?

In other words, my aim is to comprehend the scope attributed to religion by the followers of neo-Pentecostalism as well as the basic connections made by them between their living conditions and the procedures through which they cultivate their links to the divine and the supernatural. The nature of the relationship between the two domains, the world and the supernatural, when interpreted according to the teachings of the IURD, provides these religious converts with the key to a new way of living this relationship both "in the world" and "with God." This, in turn, has notable effects on the resolution of the daily adversities they are forced to confront. I shall therefore privilege an analytic perspective that highlights the choices made by individuals and the ways through which they relate these choices to the supernatural interventions in their lives.

In the case in question, the conversion to neo-Pentecostalism steers individuals toward valorizing increased access to public space from which they had historically been blocked. Today, is it among the neo-Pentecostals that we see the inclusion of a large section of the Brazilian poor as actors in the public sphere who declare themselves to be "men of God" in a wide variety of domains: in politics, football, the arts, at work, in the streets and squares, as well as, in intensive fashion, in the media. As David Smilde argues in the previous chapter, the neo-Pentecostal religious discourse creates new modalities of interlocution with other social actors.

I do not doubt assertions that describe Pentecostalism and neo-Pentecostalism as forms of resistance of the poor populations of Africa and Latin America to the precariousness of their living conditions, the violence to which they are exposed, and the disdain and neglect of their governments in relation to their demands for respect and citizenship. But my question arises from the following observation: if Pentecostalism has indeed succeeded in attracting those individuals clamoring against the dysfunctional nature of current social situations, it does so in a manner that implies a new comprehension of the forms of social exclusion, along with the ways of dealing with them. The relations of meaning acquired by the Pentecostal reading of the world are, then, the key to this question. We have to valorize how Pentecostal discourse says things and induces the practices that are perceived and lived as better, more effective, and more harmonious with what a wide contingent of people think and feel to be necessary in order to live and prosper in the world. Hence, my proposal here is to explore the way in which people acquire new bearings via the life horizons opened up by conversion.

I shall specifically discuss conversion to neo-Pentecostalism on the basis of my research experience among a group of members of the Universal Church of the Kingdom of God, in Rio de Janeiro in 1996 and 1997; all converts from Afro-Brazilian cults. Other references are derived from my monitoring of Pentecostalism in the press and television. The presence of Pentecostalism in Rio de Janeiro's public spaces, therefore, also makes up part of my field of observations on the topic.[3]

I begin with a brief background on the history of Pentecostalism in Brazil and then turn to the manner in which the neo-Pentecostal IURD has changed the role of Pentecostalism and challenged the dominant paradigm of Brazilian hybrid culture. The next two sections explain the role of Afro-Brazilian testimonies in the IURD's discourse on exorcism and spiritual warfare, outlining the continuities and discontinuities involved with converts' previous religious culture and experiences. In the final section, I attempt to show how neo-Pentecostalism promotes an anti-hierarchical rupture in Brazilian society, precisely because it both valorizes and wages warfare on the spirits of the past.

"Believers" as a Minority Group

As I mentioned above, until the 1990s Pentecostalism had a relatively modest standing among the religious options existing in Brazil.[4] Its followers, few in number, adherents of a minority religion and proud to be so, appeared primarily in public spaces, emphasizing the moral difference separating them from other collectivities. Living in isolation, removed from the world, and sporting the signs of this cultivated difference, they made up part of a project at once individual and collective. Conversion enabled them to be closer to God and share the grace of the Holy Spirit in their rituals, where they spoke in tongues and confirmed their belonging to a community which did not mix with worldly others.

Belonging to Pentecostal communities therefore constituted an option for many who saw in the life "separate from the world" a powerful instrument for constructing ways of subjectively and objectively confronting social and moral difficulties.[5] However, these communities of believers, mostly gathered in small Assembly of God churches, deliberately distanced themselves in many aspects from the majority of the Brazilian population. For these Pentecostals, religious membership closely follows the self-reflection that develops into a progressive demand from the believer for respect and dignity. Bodily habits that reveal another ethic, displayed in public, assert a clear determination to refuse current forms of cultural consumption, such as alcohol, smoking, and dancing, along with all the manifestations of a pervasive "Catholicness" in Brazilian society, which works to contrast the believers as different from others.

The asceticism of Brazilian Pentecostalism offered, and in part continues to offer, the image of the good worker and the good family father, in contrast to the stereotypical images of the idle working classes, whose ideal type fed the national literature and cinema between the 1950s and 1970s (an image of religious links marked by a festive amorality).[6] This construction of a Pentecostal identity therefore contains a prominent feature: a searing critique of an unruly lifestyle claimed to dominate Brazilian society, whose values seduce rich and poor alike. The practice of a certain asceticism allowed followers in a variety of different circumstances to abandon alcoholism, adhere to a work ethic, revalorize the roles of family authority, and participate in various associations campaigning for rights and citizenship. Only the Pentecostals, poor but dignified, represented through their exemplary and critical posture the refusal of some of the prominent values associated with the popular image of "Brazilianness."

Sadly, though, the endless hours of prayer and exemplary lifestyle seemed almost innocuous to the distracted and inattentive ears of the many people they met on their way, Pentecostalism's pace of growth remained at low levels for decades. In other words, Pentecostalism, present in Brazilian society since 1910, remained relatively ghettoized in the popular sectors where the Catholic majority cultivated a close relationship with the latter church's saints while many simultaneously frequented Afro-Brazilian cult houses.[7] The question that surfaces, then, is: What transformed

Pentecostalism into an increasingly attractive religious option which both represents a serious threat to Catholic hegemony and drains membership from Afro-Brazilian cults?

Considering this sudden success would be impossible without referring both to the sea change occurring within Pentecostalism and to the equally important changes taking place in the lives of the poorer sectors in Brazil. Here I think we can risk a generalization. In the face of globalization and neoliberalism, the situations of social exclusion in Brazil have increased relentlessly.[8] At the same time, conversion to neo-Pentecostalism manifestly presents a different way of comprehending and surviving this situation for many poor Brazilians.

The Neo-Pentecostal IURD as a Challenge to Brazilian Catholic Culture

As many have observed, in Brazil so-called Catholic religious practices have always been a long way off the European model exported to the county since its "discovery" by the Portuguese in 1500. Gilberto Freyre, describing the cultural and religious habits existing since the colony was implanted, highlights what he believes to have been the main component in terms of the nation's religious values. According to Freyre, "Afro-Indigenous-Catholic" syncretism was the connecting principle between the racially conceived different groups inhabiting the new country.[9] The Brazilian racial mixture was transformed, Freyre argues, into a simultaneously descriptive and normative ethnic principle: it supplied a positive view of miscegenation among racially distinct groups as well as making this principle the cultural foundation of nationality. For Freyre, Brazil has been distinguished from other nations due to its hierarchical integration of its populations, each bringing specific contributions to the conjunction "headed" by whites of European extraction. There was, he argued, a clear link between this mixture at the racial level and the cultural level, given that each of the racial groups had elements of its own specific culture, providing the basis for the miscegenation with the others.[10]

The notion of *syncretic Catholicism*, as well as a nation that harmonized and hierarchized the legacy from each of its founding ethnic groups, made up part of the national image. To one degree or another, this concept of syncretism has dominated a large portion of the studies about religions in Brazil. Much of this research focused on understanding the form in which the associations and interconnections between the different faiths were experienced by their followers as belonging to specific ethnic groups. A certain consensus was established concerning the nature of the Catholic religion within the Brazilian nation: Catholicism was seen to be permeated by religious practices from a variety of origins that engendered equally porous, hierarchized, and non-excluding religious identities. A relational mode of constructing individual and group identities (one that privileged a hierarchical and totalizing principle of group rather than individual identities) was held not only to shape the Catholic religious tradition in the country, but also to comprise the most significant feature of Brazilianness.[11]

The Challenge of the Neo-Pentecostal IURD

In the 1990s, the IURD presented itself as a religious alternative in the country, displaying its radical disagreement with the dominant perception of Brazilianness described above. This hybrid identity, the IURD argued, excluded from the national community those who failed to share the hierarchical principles of syncretic Brazilian Catholicism. The attack made by the IURD on the syncretism of Catholicism with Afro-Brazilian religions succeeded in attracting large contingents from Afro-Brazilian religious groups into the new church. Luiz Eduardo Soares analyzed the deeper meaning of this rupture as an egalitarian challenge to the hierarchical logic that had dominated the conflicts between churches in the country previously.[12] We can therefore hypothesize that the IURD has defied the principle of articulation between religious groups or, more broadly, between the supposed ethnic blocks making up the Brazilian nation. Instead of accepting the place structurally established for members of Afro-Brazilian cults, with their activities confined to the fringes and margins of Catholicism, it convoked them to a church that, by demonizing the peripheral locations, offered them means of establishing direct contact with the divine. This placed them on an equal footing, we should note, with the Catholic priests who wished to retain the relationship with God as an exclusive power of the church.

The Afro-Brazilian Testimony and Its Neo-Pentecostal Version

An example of exorcism in the media is described for us by Alejandro Frigério and Pedro Ari Oro in the form of a television broadcast in which the IURD minister draws the attention of the viewers through interviews with multiple "ex-saint-mothers." These are witnesses who, for the listeners and the IURD ministers, are the most qualified to explain how the devils from Afro-Brazilian cults act.

> Salvador de Bahia, Brazil, February 2004. Television broadcast "Point of Light" (Ponto de Luz), retransmitted by the Rede Record channel across the whole of Brazil. A televiewer calls and says that he has found on the doorstep of his house a small sack containing earth and a chicken foot. Worried by this find, he asks what it means. The minister presenting the show speaks to someone placed behind a screen.

A backlight enables part of her silhouette to be seen: her torso and the profile of her face. The features able to be seen, as well as her voice, suggest she is a black woman. He asks this "ex-mother of bad spirits" whether she can explain what purpose this spiritual "work" ("trabalho") serves. She replies that this "work" is very dangerous, made with cemetery earth, in order to provoke the death of the person on its receiving end. When asked by the minister-presenter whether she used to make this kind of "work" herself, she replies that she made them regularly and that they were extremely effective. The minister then invites the person who called, as well as other televiewers with similar problems to come to the temple the day after, where twenty "ex-mothers of bad spirits" will welcome those who believe they may be victims of witchcraft and give them advice on the path to follow in combating it. In Brazil, practically everyone knows that the expression "ex-mãe-de-encosto" refers to an "ex-mãe-de-santo" (saint-mother) who, now they have converted to the Universal Church of the Kingdom of God, can help to undo the evil that she (the saint-mother) caused previously.[13]

Exorcism has been transformed into a mass ritual, repeated in all the branches of the IURD and expanded via the evangelical media, without mentioning the enormous gatherings which the IURD has also started to hold in stadiums such as the Maracanã, "the world's largest football stadium," in Rio de Janeiro. The centrality of exorcism has been maintained in the expansion activities of this church in Latin America and Africa.[14] These activities as a whole provoked a strong reaction from the lay and Catholic social sectors of Brazilian society. As a result of this increasing visibility, neo-Pentecostalism increasingly drew the attention of sociologists and anthropologists as an important phenomenon which merits new forms of understanding.[15]

We know that Pentecostal churches in Africa and other Latin American countries also attribute a special place to exorcism. However, what I wish to highlight is that, in the Brazilian context, exorcism was the key to opening the door to a new religious option for tens of thousands of new members following the emergence of the Universal Church of the Kingdom of God.

Exorcism as Spiritual Warfare

As the example described by Oro and Frigério clearly demonstrates, the neo-Pentecostal exorcism inaugurated by the IURD incorporates the speech and testimony of former Afro-Brazilian practitioners as *experts in witchcraft*, individuals better qualified to explain its effects than the ministers themselves.[16] The demonization of the divinities of Candomblé and Umbanda, as mentioned earlier, is found at the center of the exorcism activities of this church. The expulsion of these varied entities, reconfigured as devils in the church services, is undertaken daily, emphasizing the same aspects: these entities are held responsible for the problems of individuals and their expulsion from them offers converts the possibility of establishing a direct relationship with God. This relationship is frequently mentioned in a comparative context. The ex-saints, reconfigured as devils, are not only seen to block divine interventions, but themselves afflict harm on people, making these beings the true sources of the problems affecting them.

This argument is sometimes used by people who assert the relative incapacity of their former protective entities in comparison with the greater force of Jesus. Although not devils, they are inferior beings who need to be expelled from within people to allow space for divine intervention. The notion of a spiritual battle launched by the IURD makes this war on devils a form of ensuring future salvation on the cosmic level, establishing a permanent conflict with the malignant forces of evil.

Interestingly, the practice of exorcism obeys the logic of a "war of occupation." This makes the body, house, atmosphere, and territories into arenas where good and evil clash. Through this cosmic dualist order where good and evil oppose each other term by term, conversion prepares the individual to become better armed in what is, nonetheless, an unending war. Exorcism does not prevent diabolized beings from returning to the same bodies and places at a future date, renewing the disturbances they had caused earlier. The words used in the exorcism practiced by the IURD refer to the minister's victory over demons through the expression "it's bound up!" which indicates both the submission of the supernatural entities to the minister and the provisional nature of this conquest. Temporarily impeded from entering the body of their victim, demons are still able to do so again later, when the weakened body presents a new "opening." The ideal of a body and mind that are ultimately "closed" to invasions from outside, and therefore invulnerable to diabolical attacks, shapes the ritual practices of this church. The various flaws in the life of each person, in their smallest details, are interpreted by the IURD as attempts by demons to occupy their bodies and minds again, separating them from Jesus.

Situations in which they have seen demons acting through people occupied by them make up part of the reports related to the spiritual battle. In fact, the dualism presiding over this cosmology implies that the person is necessarily perceived as a continent occupied either by the forces of good or the forces of evil. As a result, divine intervention must be an object of daily attention, insofar as each individual in the world is an arena under dispute because of this antagonism. While the Christian divinity demands an enormous dedication to be contacted, his antagonists, the devils (sheltered in the Afro-Brazilian cults), are always ready to occupy the bodies of people and bring evil to their lives.

Interpreting the Meaning of Exorcism

Extrapolating from what I have been told by former members of Afro-Brazilian religions who have converted to the Universal Church of the Kingdom of God, the evil brought by their former saints is related to the inferior place of such spirits in their former social life. The refusal to accept this old hierarchy, combined with the adoption of a new and more egalitarian view of social life, allows converts to reinterpret both the spiritual beings and the hierarchy of their former life as evil and maladjusted. They judge these entities from the Afro-Brazilian cults in light of their new desires and new possibilities offered by the IURD.

In this sense, the judgment implied by conversion presents what amounts to the new expectations of the individuals in terms of their relationship to the supernatural. Discovering the diabolical nature of the Afro-Brazilian spiritual entities as well as the Catholic saints (in the form of a revelation) is inscribed in a judgment which corresponds to new demands on the individuals. The evil now attributed to the former religions derives from a change of expectation in relation to the benefits which they wish to attain through the direct link with Jesus.

The Spirits Are Still Alive: Continuities and Discontinuities with Brazilian Popular Religion

The conversion of large numbers of syncretic Catholics to neo-Pentecostalism implies a new religious posture which is exclusivist and combative. This stands in direct antagonism with the predominant forms of Catholicism previously practiced by the majority of Brazil's subaltern social groups. For many of Brazil's poor, it has long been normal practice to consider all religions to be beneficial. Each one with its specific know-how brings good to its followers. As a result, resorting to more than one religion is frequently seen as necessary and, in any case, morally correct.

But the neo-Pentecostal religious re-orientation toward exorcism and anti-syncretism challenges converts to reject such strongly naturalized cosmological principles, including the habitual ways of dealing with dramatic or life-threatening situations. The process of conversion involves a reconsideration of the nature of the supernatural ties that persons possess and the consequences that conversion will inevitably have on their current life. Most importantly, however, the former spirits and saints are not forgotten, but are rather incorporated into the neo-Pentecostal discourse and worldview as an enemy requiring due and on-going vigilance.

In some of the reports of conversion to which I had access, the authors presented, with a certain insistence, on the recognition from the spiritual entities themselves of their inferior status in comparison to Jesus. This is made clear in a small excerpt in which an ex-medium tells of how her former devils reacted to her conversion: "One night I was there and the *Boiadeiro*, an Umbanda spirit,[17] descended into me and I had a conversation with him. I spoke about my husband, who drank a lot, and when I was at the centre (cult house) nothing had really happened. So he then said that he couldn't help me because I was someone who believed only in what was on high and that I didn't believe in him."

What is important to note here is that her shift to neo-Pentecostalism made her reject these entities as a source of benefits, but she continued to perceive them as a source of information:

> The devil speaks. There's a woman here who lives near to the bakery; she manifested (incorporated the entity) at night. She arrived at the meeting on . . . Friday, and when she stepped foot in the church, she manifested. . . . The pastor came and placed his hand on her head and the demon spoke: "She (the converted woman in a state of pos-session) came here to the church to seek out this miserable God of yours. Because I'm going to kill her son." Between the next Wednesday and Thursday, he (the devil) killed her son. He said he wanted to kill her too, but then the pastor said: "Her, you're not going to kill, no, because she's in the hand of God, only if you're greater than God." He didn't kill her. But her son didn't even know about the church. He (the devil) also said that the boy was acting as a drug-gang lookout in the *favela*. She didn't know anything. But the devil manifested and told her everything. And the friend who was with her told her everything. The police went and killed the son. He (the devil) warned the mother, but her son didn't want anything to do with Jesus.

The speech of the devil within the IURD presents as his own work one of the most evident dimensions of the precariousness in which the populations of Rio de Janeiro's favelas live: the countless deaths provoked by the police in their neighborhoods, where drug traffickers vie with corrupt sections of the police in violently repressing the inhabitants. The woman continued:

> I asked him (the devil) why you did that (witchcraft) and he replied: "Because I was paid to do it." I (ex-saint-daughter) cried and he laughed. The saint-mother was with the *exu* Tranca Rua (a devil) and another was with the Senhor da Lama (also a devil) and another (devil) descended into me . . . and he (the third devil) began to ask the Lama *exu*, "Are you hers?" He replied: "No, I was paid to finish her

off, suck her blood and eat her flesh and leave just her bones." She addressed the *exu* Caveira (the third devil) and he said: "I'm hers," and she (the ex-saint-daughter) asked: "And do you do anything for her?" "No, I'm annoyed with her because she went to the house of God and abandoned me, but I didn't do anything."

The impossibility of "doing good," or merely the fact of recognizing their inferior and morally inadequate nature, makes up part of the ritual speech which the entities make in public when confronted by the IURD minister. Declarations and witnesses such as these form an integral part of religious television programs where the onstage combat between good and evil is transmitted to the entire country. Through the mediation of the IURD, the accusations of witchcraft gain a considerable impetus in the public space where the ex-followers of Afro-Brazilian cults provide testimony on the harm which the demonized entities cause. The ministers invite everyone to abandon their friendly conviviality with these malefic forces and to recognize the "primitive" and diabolical part of the cosmological order where the poor of spirit are found (who, in general, blend with the poor of the Earth). The combat against witchcraft merges, to a large degree, with the combat against the social and personal conditions of the poor through the links they possess with diabolical forces.

Bishop Marcelo Crivela, from the Universal Church, in his religious discourses promotes an equivalence between Africa, from where all these malefic entities are supposed to have come, and the ignorance and primitivism which affect a sizeable portion of the population of Brazil and South America, where the IURD, in fact, has implanted a strong presence.[18] In his biography, published in a Universal Church magazine, he tells his readers:

> When the Universal Church's work began in Africa, seven years ago, the then minister Marcelo Crivela was sent there with his wife, Silvia Jane and their three children. Africa is made up of countries with tribal customs, where the countries legally sell their daughters and men can have various wives. . . . And it was in this adverse environment, full of preconceptions, wars and poverty, that Bishop Marcelo lived preaching equality between men, opening up the church to blacks, taking the word of God to places where whites wouldn't venture, such as the Soweto district, in Johannesburg, South Africa. . . . The Universal Church grew and spread across the entire African continent, setting up hundreds of help centres for the needy, providing meals, medical and hygiene services, as well as spiritual guidance. Today there are around 700 IURD's in twenty-three countries.[19]

The continuity we can observe between the past religious perceptions and the new ones relates, therefore, firstly, to the fact that for the new converts the possibility of "extra-terrestrial" intervention in their lives remains unaltered. In other words, the reality of the world in this fundamental aspect continues to include supernatural mediators who vie with each other and provoke changes in the course of events at both an individual and collective level. Secondly, there is a certain continuity in the recognition of a celestial hierarchy: God was never confused with any of the beings belonging to lower spheres, although former practitioners believed that such spirits could help them. It was through the IURD discourse and preaching that they discovered that these forces act against each other. As Peter Fry astutely observed a few years ago, for Afro-Brazilians, the Christian God existed but was an "idle" God.[20] By introducing God as a new figure comprising the exclusive source of good in the relations between its followers and extra-terrestrial spheres, neo-Pentecostalism reinterpreted the archaic entities as a source of primitivism and backwardness. In this sense, it also looked to disqualify the work of intervention performed at a day-to-day level by subalterns, the members of these cults.

Everybody Believes in Witchcraft

In a study on the belief in witchcraft in Brazil, Yvonne Maggie develops the argument that, far from lessening society's belief in the power of witches, the attempts to combat witchcraft in the country have created social, political, and religious mechanisms that give them a place in the hierarchy of practices focused on extra-terrestrial spheres.[21] In other words, the battle against witchcraft has helped to create important social and juridical mechanisms for regulating social conflicts involving this type of accusation.

Among the Pentecostal and neo-Pentecostal churches, the Universal Church of the Kingdom of God is without a shadow of doubt the one which has undertaken an unprecedented fight, in both nature and extent, against witchcraft. It turns this ritual combat into a therapeutic instrument and, at the same time, an instrument for theatrically and spectacularly occupying the communication networks. From another angle, it also turns the attack on witchcraft into an instrument for dislocating an immense population that, from the religious and social viewpoint, was situated on the outer fringes of society and that was responsible for the visibility of the relations with the occult in Brazilian society. The largest appeal from the IURD has been directed at their followers, inciting them to abandon a subordinate and peripheral magic, whose powers are small, malignant, and, to a large extent, conceived as occult. They are called to utilize new forms of intervention based on another type of supernatural power, recognized as legitimate by society: the state and the church to which they now belong.

In fact, for the practitioners of Catholicism and Afro-Brazilian cults, what is habitually attributed to entities in terms of supernatural intervention in their lives is not experienced by them as an extraordinary event; it does not affect the *conventions of existence*.[22] The field of action of witchcraft seems more restricted; their masters may intervene in life as it is, that is, on well-defined and precise targets such as amorous relations, the lack of jobs, or problems with family and neighbors. In other words, these are forms of intervention which people wish to be effective in relation to obstacles and contingencies that affect their lives and protect them sporadically from large and small misfortunes. What the IURD offers as a novelty and break with the past is the possibility of its believers obtaining divine intervention without appealing directly to real but now "inferior" power of the former witches. As Joel Robbins has argued, by identifying the order of the world with evil, the rupture with this former order through divine intervention establishes itself as a new horizon of the possible for converts.[23]

Divine Protagonism

Put otherwise, the divine protagonism postulated by the IURD allows the convert to position himself/herself as someone who does not restrict his/her horizon of action to the field conventionally associated with magic activities in Brazilian society. Neo-Pentecostal actors can now perform miracles whose meanings imply a redefinition of conventions, or, in other words, a redefinition of what until then was socially perceived as impossible. One of the miracles frequently "performed" by the IURD (which has caused significant scandal) is the miracle of prosperity.[24] The capacity of agency of the neo-Pentecostal actor is, in this sense, seen to be infinitely greater than that perceived and claimed by Catholic and Afro-Brazilian actors. The miracle they promise and to which they provide witness is based on the idea that for Jesus there are no limits to be obeyed. Acting in his name is something that challenges the order of the world and the diabolical forces that take hold of it. The divine action guided by neo-Pentecostals does not abandon the small mishaps of daily life, but does offer, beyond these, something more, unthinkable until then within the bounds of syncretic Catholicism.

Elites, Subaltern Religion, and the
Neo-Pentecostal Rupture with Hierarchy

Although practitioners of syncretic and Afro-Brazilian Catholicism have always shared a perception of politics and other social domains to be subject to supernatural injunctions, the space of action that they had was basically limited to the margins. In other words, these forces simultaneously occupied a private space and exercised a subaltern sociability. Politics and society were subject to the intervention of "minor" saints and spirits at the fringes, sporadically and deliberately kept in the shadow of power relations.

Elites and the Allocation of Religious and Political Space

The effectiveness of powerful witches, healers, and saint-mothers has long been recognized in the discourse of Brazilian elites. This process has been mentioned (sometimes in accusatory fashion) by intellectuals, medics, and jurists as an evil to be combated and, above all, to be maintained as a marginal power, with an inferior status to be controlled and suppressed by the state.[25] As Yvonne Maggie points out, in this way the Brazilian state, through the establishment of its experts and its judicial mechanisms, was an important actor in the institution of witchcraft in Brazil. However, this reality took place through a set of devices that established a hierarchy among churches and cults in terms of their possibilities of intervention. Among the identifying marks attributed to Afro-Brazilian cults, the most important was the social and political allocation of these cults in peripheral spaces. This allocation reiterated a particular relation to the occult through its actual nature and social affirmation. It is not difficult to suppose that the relationship with the occult is historically constitutive of Afro-Brazilian cults and the place that has been attributed to them in social life. João do Rio drew attention to the duplicity in the behavior of Rio de Janeiro elites who frequented witches in the same way as they frequented the "tolerance houses" and their prostitutes. This double morality, the subject of many stories and critiques of customs, helped make these fringes of power and sexuality into a domain associated with magic and witchcraft.[26]

In fact, the provision of magic and occult services, frequently considered as witchcraft, was focused in certain subaltern social segments, and the use of these services spread indifferently throughout the entire society. Yvonne Maggie argues that the vast majority of Brazilian society took part in the belief in witchcraft and that the juridical and political mechanisms created during the Republic, far from abolishing its practice, were essential in engendering hierarchies in which it had a place.

In my view, what this argument missed is that the belief in witchcraft was constituted through a division of roles: broadly speaking, "production" for some and "consumption" for others. These places of production and consumption constantly mix, of course. However, there are situations in which this division of roles proves crucial and becomes mutually excluding. In fact, Afro-Brazilian cult houses, in general, look to possess recognized people or celebrities as members of their body of *sacerdotes* since they increase the appeal of their festivals as well as valorize the magical services they offer to more wealthy social groups. The more rich and wealthy people a house is able to attract, the greater its recognition will be. This process may even allow individuals to transcend their previous social environments, as has been the case with famous saint-fathers whose fame derives from catering to rich and powerful people. The orientation that seems to govern these relations makes the socially subaltern those who offer the religious services, while the more wealthy and powerful are ideally those who consume them.[27]

For those belonging to Brazil's social elite, the consumption of magic work is not an isolated phenomenon. It is not rare for more well-off individuals to mention the close relationship they cultivate with saint-mothers as something which is beneficial to them, despite the social and cultural differences that separate them from these religious figures. The country's social elite, whose formation historically bears traces of Catholicism, has created a unique inter-weaving between religious practices accused of witchcraft and the secular perspectives that developed during the history of the Republic. At the same time as, after the founding of the Republic, an attempt was made to adapt to the modern rule of secular behavior in the public sphere, important sectors of the national elite cultivated links with religious actors who provided them with magic services, in the context of a brand of Catholicism that approxi-mated this church to the nation's official religion. As a result, we find religious and political behaviors that associate social subalternity, magical efficacy, and amorality as identifying marks of the syncretic Afro-Catholic believers, among whom a large part of the Brazilian population would be located.[28]

The Neo-Pentecostal Rupture

Thus, what seems currently out of place in Brazilian society, as an outcome of this process of neo-Pentecostal growth, is what we could call an immense movement of enthroning Jesus as a protagonist in the public sphere and an increasing number of followers who abandon the demonized links with religious subalternity and claim the right to speak under equal conditions, "in the name of Jesus." The ex-Afro-Brazilian religious practitioners have thereby broken the convention of silence in the public sphere that has been historically reserved for them as actors at a political level. There is, then, a widening of the field of the possible as well as a multiplication of actors constructing this new religious protagonism.

It would be difficult, if not impossible, to separate the meaning of con-version from the meaning neo-Pentecostalism has come to acquire in Brazil-ian society. The transformation within neo-Pentecostalism occurs through the valorization of magic and witchcraft in Brazilian society, at once rework-ing them and discarding them as a form of supernatural intervention favor-able to the people involved. In the process, hierarchical images are broken or re-ordered, and neo-Pentecostal actors find a new role as participants in their own discourse in the public sphere.

The anti-hierarchical rupture found at the base of these processes of conversion can be discerned in other movements that seem to act in the same direction, namely, a progressive distancing from the national imaginary of Brazilianness. As Livio Sansone observed, the black movement in Bahia also currently makes use of images dissociated from the myth of Brazilian identity and its Catholic inscription.[29] Today, being "black" sends the individual more easily in search of Afro-American identifying signs than cultural movements such as samba and the Candomblé terreiros associated with Brazilian nationality.

In this sense, neo-Pentecostalism also makes up part of an era of globalization in which the transnational flow of ideas, beliefs, and identities strengthens other modalities of belonging within national spaces.[30] Rather than being abandoned, "African primitivism" (a formerly minor component of Brazilian Catholicism) became exposed and valorized as the major sign of what should be changed in the country and the world. In this view, God is offering his chosen people the means to construct forms of individual and collective equality (at least in principle) with those whom they formerly sought to serve and please through providing the services of the so-called devils of African primitivism.

NOTES

1. For a more complete history of the IURD and its missionary endeavors, see chapter II of this volume by Virginia Garrard-Burnett.

2. See, for example, the controversies provoked by the episode that became known as the "kick on the saint," in which a Pentecostal minister kicked an image of Our Lady of Aparecida, the patron saint of Brazil, in a television program. Emerson Giumbelli, *O fim da religião: Dilemas da liberdade religiosa no Brasil e na França* (São Paulo: Attar Editorial, 2002); Emerson Giumbelli, "O 'chute na santa': Blasfêmia e pluralismo religioso no Brasil," in *Religião e Espaço público*, ed. Patricia Birman (São Paulo: Attar editorial, 2003), 169–199; Patricia Birman and David Lehmann, "Religion and the Media in a Battle for Ideological Hegemony: The Universal Church of God and TV Globo in Brazil," *Bulletin of Latin American Research* 18, no. 2 (1999): 145–164; and the analysis by Cecília Mariz on the bibliography relating to the "Spiritual Battle" theology: Cecilia Mariz, "A teologia da batalha espiritual: Uma revisão da bibliografia," *Revista brasileira de Informação bibliográfica em Ciências Sociais* (Rio de Janeiro) 47 (1999).

3. Patrica Birman, "Feminine Mediation and Pentecostal Identities," *Cambridge Anthropology* 20, no. 3 (1998); Patrica Birman, "*Milagre e Poder* na esfera pública: O abandono de antigos paradigmas para melhor compreender a emergência dos pentecostais na política," paper presented at the thirteenth Jornadas da Associação de Cientistas Sociais da Religião do Mercosul, Porto Alegre, September 2005.

4. *Crentes* (believers) is the term most frequently used to refer to Pentecostals in Brazil. Their churches, though, increasingly use the term "evangelicals" instead of "believers," since this connotation is relatively stigmatizing.

5. Regina Novaes, "Os Escolhidos de Deus. Pentecostais, Trabalhadores e Cidadania," *Cadernos do Iser* 19 (1985); Cecília Mariz, *Coping with Poverty: Pentecostals and*

Christian Base Communities in Brazil (Philadelphia: Temple University, 1994); Maria das Dores Machado, *Carismáticos e Pentecostais: Adesão Religiosa na Esfera Familiar* (São Paulo, Campinas: Anpocs e Editores Associados, 1996); and Clara Mafra, *Na posse da palavra: Religião, conversão e liberdade pessoal em dois contextos nacionais* (Lisbon: ICS, 2002); among others, point to the forms through which this subjective and objective mode of constructing the presence in the world has been realized among Pentecostal groups.

6. See, among others, the works of Roberto da Matta, *Carnavais, malandros e heróis* (Rio de Janeiro: Zahar,1979); and Peter Fry, *Para Inglês ver* (Rio de Janeiro: Zahar, 1982), who analyze this polarity between "idlers" and "workers" in a variety of cultural settings.

7. Paul Freston, "Popular Protestants in Brazilian Politics: A Novel Turn in Sect-State Relationships," *Social Compass* 41, no. 4 (1994): 537–570.

8. Tereza Caldeira, *Cidade de Muros: Crime, segregação e cidadania em São Paulo* (São Paulo: Editora 34/Edusp, 2002).

9. Gilberto Freyre, *The Masters and the Slaves: Casa Grande Culture of Modern Brazil* (New York: Knopf, 1933).

10. Ibid.

11. Roberto Da Matta, *Carnavais, malandros e heróis* (Rio de Janeiro: Zahar, 1979), develops Gilberto Freyre's (*The Masters and the Slaves*) analysis in the construction of this model, valorizing the oppositions between hierarchic and individualist systems produced by Louis Dumont. A number of other authors have commented on Freyre's work, which has become a classic in studies of identity and nation in Brazil.

12. Luiz Eduardo Soares, "Dimensões democráticas do conflito religioso no Brasil: A guerra dos pentecostais contra o afro-brasileiro," in *Os dois corpos do presidente e outros ensaios*, by Soares (Rio: Relume dumará/ISER, 1993).

13. Alejandro Frigerio and Pedro Ari Oro, "Guerre sainte dans le cône sud latino-américain: Pentecôtistes versus umbandistes," *Journal de la Société des Américanistes* 91, no. 2 (2005): 185–218. The authors also explain that *encosto* is the name given to the spirit of a dead person; it "sticks" to a person to disturb him or her and cause harm. Saint-mother is the name given to the religious leader of a temple of one of the Afro-Brazilian religions. Hence, they add, "by defining the saint-mothers as 'encostos,' the ministers of the Universal Church of the Kingdom of God appropriate concepts derived from Afro-Brazilian religions, known to everyone, and use them against these religions" (ibid., 199).

14. Frigério and Oro, "Guerre sainte dans le cône sud latino-américain," 185–218; André Corten, Jean Pierre Dozon, and Ari Pedro Oro, eds., *Les nouveaux conquérants de la foi. L'Eglise Universelle du Royame de Dieu* (Paris: Karthala, 2003). Also see Virginia Garrard-Burnett, chapter 11 of this volume.

15. Corten, Dozon, and Oro, *Les nouveaux conquérants de la foi*; Soares, "Dimensões democráticas do conflito religioso no Brasil"; Giumbelli, "O 'chute na santa,'" 169–199; Birman and Lehmann, *Religion and the Media in a Battle*; Ricardo Mariano, "Os neo-Pentecostais e a teologia da prosperidade," *Novos Estudos Cebrap* (São Paulo) 44 (1996): 24–44.

16. Birman, "Feminine Mediation and Pentecostal Identities."

17. Umbanda is the name given to one of the versions of Afro-Brazilian cults.

18. Birman, "*Milagre e Poder* na esfera pública"; and the interesting ethnographic description produced by Martin Oosterban of the iconography of evil in the Rio de Janeiro media: Martin Oosterban, "Divine Mediations; Pentecostalism, Politics, and Mass Media in a Favela in Rio de Janeiro" (doctoral thesis, University of Amsterdam, 2006).

19. Marcelo Crivela, cited in Birman, "*Milagre e Poder* na esfera pública," 65.

20. Fry, *Para Inglês ver.*

21. Yvonne Maggie, *Medo de feitiço* (Rio de Janeiro: Arquivo Nacional, 1992).

22. For an analysis of such conventions see Joel Robbins, "The Globalization of Charismatic and Pentecostal Christianity," *Annual Review of Anthropology* 33 (2004): 117–130.

23. Ibid.

24. We can note that the theme of prosperity clashes with the hegemonic Catholic culture in which the figure of poverty is usually identified with that of saintliness as well as a harmonious hierarchic relation between the rich and poor as the social ideal. Here, by evoking prosperity as a possible effect of "magico-religious" ritual activities, obtained through a contribution in cash, the church was the repeated target of accusations of charlatanism. There is no doubt that the constant requests for money that accompany the promises of prosperity have contributed to arousing such accusations, yet I think that the latter arise from the fact that the promised miracles clash with the culturally established expectations concerning the desires of prosperity of the subaltern population. In a way, what is being proposed is the apparently impossible. Cf. Birman, "*Milagre e Poder* na esfera pública."

25. Maggie, *Medo de feitiço*, on the belief in magic and witchcraft.

26. In other words, the great witches mentioned in the literature, as well as the practitioners of these cults mentioned in the processes analyzed by Yvonne Maggie (*Medo de feitiço*), were mostly poor individuals—the majority blacks—in the nineteenth century, while during the twentieth century white individuals were also included in this category, "deracializing" to a certain extent the criteria of belonging to Afro-Brazilian cults. As is a consensus in the literature on religion in Brazil, the double belonging of religious people to Catholicism and Afro-Brazilian cults predominated in the religious practices of all the country's social segments until the Pentecostal "wave" in which apparently both the double belonging and the number of Catholics in Brazilian society diminished.

27. Peter Fry (*Para Inglês ver*) describes the circuit of exchanges of religious services and diverse goods involving the cult houses and social groups belonging to distinct spheres of the same society.

28. Fry, *Para Inglês ver.*

29. Livio Sansone, *Blackness without Ethnicity: Constructing Race in Brazil*, (Palgrave: Macmillan, 2003).

30. Arjun Appadurai, *Après le colonialisme: Les conséquences culturelles de la globalisation* (Paris: Payot, 2001).

7

Conversion to Afro-Brazilian Religions in Buenos Aires

Convincing Interactions

MARÍA JULIA CAROZZI

A number of studies carried out in diverse settings and denominations around the world have established a positive correlation between the development and maintenance of conversion, on the one hand, and the frequency of participation in a religious group, on the other. In this chapter I will analyze conversion processes in a particularly successful temple of Afro-Brazilian religions in Buenos Aires in order to determine the characteristics of group interaction that facilitate this process. The group does not perform overt proselytizing activities but offers magical services to the general population.

This research attempts to make a contribution to two bodies of literature on religious conversion. First, following an article by Patricia Birman, a significant number of investigators of recently introduced religions in Latin America have argued against the possibility of conversion, claiming that members of the lower classes in the subcontinent merely add new spirits and specialists in the supernatural to an already abundant population of religious beings and, therefore, never really convert.[1] Instead, this argument goes, they give origin to a space of fluid and syncretic interlocution and symbolic re-elaboration between new and preexisting religious systems coming into contact.[2] In this chapter, I argue that although religious fluidity and syncretism are pervasive and the study of syncretic processes is indubitably productive, these facts do not necessarily imply that the large body of literature on conversion processes elaborated by social scientists worldwide is irrelevant in Latin American contexts.[3] On the contrary, the studies of conversion processes, on the one hand, and the studies of mediations, on the other, constitute two distinct and complementary approaches. While the study of mediations and syncretic re-elaborations focuses our attention on relations between different systems of knowledge and their persistence in time, the conversion approach makes visible the relation that links group interaction and cognitive and identity transformation processes, something that the mediations paradigm does not take into account.

Second, this chapter seeks to contribute to the international literature on conversion processes, pinpointing the characteristics of interaction within religious groups that make these transformations possible. With few exceptions, studies of conversion have found that intense interaction with members of a group is a necessary requisite of conversion. Further, some comprehensive reviews of these studies have concluded that intensive interaction is the most important factor behind conversion processes once the potential convert has come into contact with a religious movement organization.[4] This literature also allows us to single out the key characteristics of interactions fueling conversion in other religious groups and in other geographical areas. Some authors have pointed out that before converting, individuals already held cognitive orientations that made them prone to accept the ideology of the new religious group.[5] This finding suggests that, at least in the first stages of contact with the group, interaction facilitating conversion should emphasize the resonance between potential converts' previous cognitive schemas and beliefs shared by the group, a condition also stressed by the literature on micro-mobilization processes in social and religious movements.[6]

Most studies of conversion suggest that interaction should promote the creation or re-actualization of affective links between members of the group and the potential converts to allow for their conversion.[7] Further, the literature indicates that interactional contexts offered by the group prompting the emergence of extraordinary experiences may provide adequate contexts for conversion to occur. Max Heirich has suggested that when people are confronted with experiences they cannot include in their previous cognitive schemas—nor ignore—they then question the knowledge that they previously considered real.[8] A number of studies seem to empirically support this hypothesis.[9]

In spite of the impressive body of literature on the subject, conversion has not been univocally defined and conceptualized. As the editors point out in chapter I, while the idea of a radical personal transformation is assumed in most studies, specification of the amount of change necessary to constitute conversion remains a debated issue. In this chapter I will define conversion as a modification of the vision that a person entertains about himself/herself and the world, which then comes to be interpreted in most situations in terms derived from practices and discourses interchanged within a given religious organization. To constitute conversion this change must be concurrent with a transformation of the individual's personal identity together with a fracture in his/her sense of self-continuity. The personal identity is constituted by both a subjective selection of some of the social identities that the person considers as central and some traits that the individual considers characteristic of his or her behavior across social situations (as, for example, joy, loyalty, timidity, spontaneity, emotionality, sincerity).[10] Consequently, I will consider that the modification of the concept that a person has of himself/herself as a "physical, social and spiritual or moral being" is a characteristic of the conversion process.[11] To constitute conversion, this personal identity change must involve a fracture in the sense of subjective continuity, not only the mere addition of new social identities.

Thus, conversion will be here distinguished from mere recruitment to or affiliation with a religious organization. When a person has been recruited she or he becomes affiliated to a new religious group without necessarily experiencing a sense of self-discontinuity or a radical change of worldview. As Henri Gooren argues in chapter 3, if we do not distinguish between these very different levels of individual's "conversion careers," we risk losing the utility of the concept of conversion.

Distinguishing conversion from mere affiliation also allows researchers to better understand the high religious mobility of many individuals in Latin America. To a significant degree, the characteristics of interaction allowing for high rates of attendance and affiliation in Afro-diasporan religious groups in Argentina promote mediations and syncretic re-elaborations of new and previously held religious concepts rather than strictly defined conversions. The experience of conversion is restricted mostly to a smaller group of people participating in semi-secret and secret religious activities. Interactions in these latter contexts do not favor syncretism, but promote, instead, radical identity transformations and the pervasive application of interpretations derived from a unique worldview (the stages that Gooren calls conversion and, eventually, confession).

Methodologically, I assume that the subtleties of the relationship linking group interaction, on the one hand, and identity and cognitive transformations, on the other, are more precisely revealed through a combination of participant observation and interviews with people in different stages of their relation with the religious group than through conversion narratives.[12] Consequently, data for this study were collected through four years of participant observation in an Umbanda and Candomblé temple in a popular neighborhood of Buenos Aires. During that period, interviews were conducted with consultants/clients, mediums, inner-circle members, and the temple leader; and conversion processes of newcomers were followed by frequent informal interviewing during participation in temple activities.

The Temple

To understand the process of conversion that I will describe, we should consider that in the temple under study, as in most Argentinean *terreiros*, two variants of Afro-Brazilian religions are practiced.[13] One of them, Umbanda, is a syncretic version developed in urban settings of Brazil around 1930. The other one, Candomblé, is more orthodox in relation to its African origin. In Argentina, the practice of Umbanda together with that of a more orthodox variant—mainly Batuque, from Porto Alegre, and, more rarely, Candomblé— is called *la Religión* (the religion) by practitioners.[14] Umbanda is seen by religious leaders as an introductory stage that allows individuals to be socialized in "the religion" and to be prepared for ulterior initiations in Candomblé (or Batuque). The latter is considered the core of the religious practice.[15]

The head of the temple where I practiced participant observation was a very charismatic young *mãe de santo*, Graciela, who, after quarreling with the *pai de santo* of the temple where she was introduced to the religion in Argentina, sought initiation in Candomblé in a Rio de Janeiro temple.[16] Back in Buenos Aires she opened her own Umbanda and Candomblé terreiro, which was consecrated by her new Brazilian *pai*. Following in the temple hierarchy was the *pai pequeno*, a cousin of Graciela who was in charge of its administration. Next came the *mãe pequena*, an old friend and former schoolmate.[17] In addition, both Graciela's brother and a former neighbor were part of the inner circle of the temple: a small group of ten young disciples with direct access to the mãe de santo, who exerted some measure of influence in her decisions and transmitted her orders to the rest of the recruited personnel. This inner circle grew during the time of my research at a rate of approximately one person per year.

At the time of my fieldwork the temple had 120 recruited members, while approximately 200 people attended consultations and public ceremonies regularly. In addition to these regular consultants around 200 new consultants attended the temple every week. The majority of recruited members and regular consultants were married to twenty- to forty-year-old women who had attended but not completed high school and worked as either housewives or employees.

In my analysis of the conversion process I will employ the categories used by temple inner-circle members. Regular consultants and recently recruited members distinguished only two categories of attendants: "the people" or "the public" (*la gente* or *la gente del público*) and "the people in white" (*la gente de blanco*).[18] As members progressed in the temple hierarchy, they learned a subtly growing repertoire of seniority distinctions that were related to the various degrees of initiation. As only those individuals having already undergone an initiation ritual had access to that same ritual when performed for the benefit of other members of the temple, the perceived subtleties of the classificatory system based on degrees of initiations only gradually unfolded through the years.

Inner-circle members were the recruited personnel with the largest number of initiation ceremonies performed on their behalf, with the sole exception of temple authorities. For them, the category "the people" included those persons occasionally attending the temple in order to consult with the mãe de santo or the mãe pequena about their personal problems and to ask for magical help to solve them. The people included a large number of individuals who attended the temple only once or twice in their lifetime as well as people who attended only when they went through a major crisis: sometimes once a year or once every two years. A very small part of the total consisted of people who attended the temple regularly: from once or twice a week to once or twice a month. These people were called "the people who always come" (la gente que viene siempre) by members of the inner circle surrounding Graciela.

Eventually, some of these regular consultants were diagnosed as mediums, and those who accepted the categorization became people in white. When Graciela made this diagnosis, she defined mediums as people who had the ability to receive and transmit spiritual energy. Once this condition was diagnosed, people were told about their need to develop this ability (desarrollar su mediumnidad), dress in white when they went to the temple, and cease to be consultants in order to help others through the performance of rituals.

The average frequency of initiation ceremonies that mediums underwent was once a year. But this frequency varied according to the enthusiasm they showed in attending the temple and the value the mãe de santo assigned to their participation. The more necessary their presence became for the intense ritual activity the temple displayed, the more frequently mediums would undergo initiatory rituals. The first among these initiatory rituals was generally the Obi. This ritual did not involve animal sacrifices and blood but only water and the application of an African nut on the crown of the head and selected parts of the body of the initiate. Inner-circle members and the authorities of the temple believed that it created a fragile commitment with the religion on the part of the initiate. If the medium continued to attend the temple regularly, she or he would eventually go through the Bori ritual. This ritual included the sacrifice of an animal and the pouring of its blood on the head of the initiate. It was believed to create a stronger compromise of the medium with the religion, but not to establish a permanent link with the temple. Mediums going through the Bori were called "sons and daughters of the religion" (*hijos e hijas de religión*).

The ensuing initiatory ritual would be Seating the Saint (*el Asiento de Santo*), which was believed to establish an everlasting personal bond with the Orixá, or African deity that "owned the head of the person," with the practice of the religion, with the mãe de santo performing the ritual, and with the temple where the initiation was performed (although other pais and mães de santo in Buenos Aires could eventually perform rituals to untie the initiate from these last two commitments). Those sons and daughters of the religion who went through the ritual became "sons and daughters of saints" (*hijos de santo*). If they continued attending the temple regularly, they eventually underwent two other similar rituals. These involved the seating of the Orixá that had been established by divinatory means as accompanying their main one and their personal Exu—the Orixá who acted as a messenger between people and other deities.

Graciela diagnosed some sons and daughters of saints as having the destiny of becoming temple leaders in the future, and they went through more "seating" ceremonies, eventually receiving all twelve Orixás worshipped in the temple. At the time of my research none of the sons and daughters of saints who were diagnosed as having this type of destiny had yet undergone the ceremony that would allow them to open their own temples and initiate others. As the conversion-career approach would predict, these people with future leadership responsibilities were the most committed, showing high levels of participation in temple activities.

The temple provided a more or less fixed sequence of contexts of interaction where people in each one of these categories could participate. Such contexts provided opportunities to experience transformations both in cognitive schemas and in definitions of personal identities. In the next part of the chapter I will analyze the relationship between the interactional contexts the temple provided for each one of these sequenced stages and the most common transformations people experienced in their interpretive schemas and self-definitions.

"The People": Point of Departure

According to semi-structured interviews conducted with ninety-six consultants, they first resorted to the temple as one of the several strategies for the solution of economic (35 percent), family and conjugal (33 percent), health (27 percent), or love (22 percent) problems.[19] Almost all of them went to the temple following the recommendation of a friend, neighbor, or family member. As David Smilde argues in chapter 5, networks channel people's problem-solving strategies. As in Venezuela, family ties are central to sustaining individuals' identities, but for some Buenos Aires dwellers, neighbors and friends fulfill identical functions. Consequently, they are also important in explaining religious movement recruitment.

For consultants, resorting to religious means to solve a problem was not an extraordinary measure implying a deep crisis. On the contrary, most of them (80 percent), at different moments in their lives, had consulted a vast array of specialists in the supernatural (including folk healers, diviners, and parapsychologists) or had directly prayed for the intervention of Catholic and folk saints. Seeking the help of a specialist in the supernatural for the solution of a problem was an ordinary practice for most consultants, and, likewise, hoping that the spiritual world would provide solutions to everyday problems was a familiar expectation.

In the temple my informants were first offered a consultation (*consulta*) with the mãe de santo and a ritual of spiritual help (*una ayuda espiritual*) immediately after that. During this first consultation Graciela generally determined the cause of the problem that brought them to her, divined some aspect of the life of the consultant related to the affliction, and determined the type of spiritual help needed. Finally, she told the consultant that she or he need not worry, for "the saints" would surely help in the solution of their worries. According to data from interviews with newcomers, the consultation had the effect of building confidence in the magical powers of the mãe de santo. This confidence, together with the demonstration of interest in the problems of the consultant, the responsibility assumed by Graciela on behalf of the saints in their solution, and the guarantee that they would be resolved by the action of the temple, often had a tension-releasing effect, liberating the consultant from his or her worries. Mediums performing "spiritual aid" rituals often said that people left the consultation with "half the work done" (*la mitad del trabajo hecho*), meaning that the consultation had an effect of its own, even when the energy of the entities, saints, or Orixás had not yet been activated through the performance of ritual actions.

"Work" (*trabajo*) is the term people in white employed to refer to rituals performed on behalf of consultants. When talking to consultants, they would never employ the word, but would rather say "spiritual help." Members of the inner circle also rarely referred to the saints (*los santos*) when talking amongst themselves. On such occasions they would either mention "the entities" (*las entidades*), if referring to the Umbanda spirits, or "the Orixás" (*los Orixás*), to designate African deities, restricting the use of the saints to interaction with consultants and mediums. These distinct lexical selections show that when talking to consultants an effort was made to present the procedures of the temple as one variety of those with which they assumed consultants were familiar, stressing the resonance between their practices and their interpretive schemas. Likewise, the first "spiritual-aid" rituals to which the consultants were subjected never implied animal sacrifices or elaborate foods (as did subsequent, more restricted rituals), but only included chanting in a special room where figures of Catholic saints were displayed and the sole offerings to the saints were candles, water, and popcorn.

Predictably, interviews with newcomers showed that attending the temple as a consultant did not imply conversion. Consultants generally interpreted the mãe de santo and the people in white as specialists in the supernatural that they added to the vast array already present in their cognitive universe. They also understood the ritual actions performed in the temple as similar to those performed by folk healers, parapsychologists, and priests. Assuming the social identity of consultant was more often than not a transitory state to be abandoned as soon the problem was solved or trust in the magical power of the temple vanished. Only a minority of the consultants acquired enough confidence in the magical power of the temple to continue attending consultations and receiving spiritual aid on a regular basis. This occurred much more often when consultants had direct familiar or friendship ties with the temple's recruited personnel, thus supporting the hypothesis that affective ties play a central role in continuous attendance to the activities of a religious organization. In this case, it also suggests that such ties made people more prone to evaluate magical rites as effective for the solutions of their problems. Although affective ties were objectively related to the degree of confidence consultants had in the temple and individuals acknowledged that they trusted and liked the mãe de santo as well as some of the people in white performing spiritual-aid rituals, these ties were not stated by them as the reason they continued to attend consultations. Rather, they argued that the reason that made them continue attending the temple was that they experienced a growing sense of well-being or the solution of specific problems. Thus, affective ties with temple personnel cannot be posed as the sole rationale to explain this faith. Both a previously existing interpretive schema allowing for the intervention of spiritual beings in the solution of problems and the mãe de santo repeatedly interpreting any improvement on the consultant's situation as the effect of the action of the saints invoked during spiritual-aid rituals combined to explain continued attendance. In other words, networks combine with an active attempt by individuals to resolve specific problems in an atmosphere that accommodates rather than challenges popular religious culture.

In terms of the conversion-career paradigm outlined in this volume, continued consultation can be defined as successful pre-affiliation. It constitutes a necessary, although not a sufficient, condition of both recruitment and conversion. Since consultants assert that magical solutions to their problems explain the persistence of their continued attendance to the temple, such successful pre-affiliations should be explained by the combination of factors that allow for such a belief to be held. These factors include a culturally shared disposition to believe that religious interventions can solve problems and to search for such interventions when the need arises; the pre-affiliate experiencing a difficulty (although not necessarily a major life crisis); the reaffirmation or establishment of affective ties with temple affiliates and/or personnel; and the characteristics of interaction that the prospective affiliate participates in when attending the temple.

Such characteristics of interaction that promote faith in the temple's problem-solving capacities include religious personnel listening to the pre-affiliate's problem and finding a religious cause for it; assuring the consultant that the problem will be solved by religious intervention; framing this intervention in terms of religious beings whose ability to bring about the solution of human problems was already known by the consultant; translating any religious terms alien to the prospective affiliate to words already present in her or his religious vocabulary; and interpreting any improvement experienced by the pre-affiliate as the result of ritual actions performed in the temple.

"The People Who Always Come": Gradual Re-interpretations

People who regularly attended consultations for a long period of time often started to ask the mãe de santo about the meaning of the songs sung in Portuguese and the names of the saints invoked or displayed during spiritual-aid rituals. Eventually, after showing enough trust in the temple and establishing or deepening affective links with its personnel, they were invited by Graciela to a Friday session (*una sesión de los viernes*), a public ritual summoning Umbanda spiritual entities.

Here consultants witnessed some practices completely alien to their worldview. They would see some of the people in white in trance, acting and speaking in ways completely different to their habitual ones, frenetically twirling around to the beat of drums. For most Argentine consultants, as opposed to Brazilian ones, the possibility of more than one personal identity cohabiting the same body is completely new and constituted a shocking and memorable experience. At one time or another every recruited member of the temple acknowledged that the first time they went to a session they thought that "everybody was crazy." Also vividly present in their memories was the fact that the spiritual entities present in the bodies of mediums had divined some aspects of their lives or instantly cured them from some illness. They took such experiences as evidence of the fact that they were not confronting madness but some kind of extraordinary power.

In later consultations Graciela interpreted to newcomers this first experience with trance possession as the physical manifestation of "spiritual entities": *Caboclos* (courageous Indians), *Oguns* (brave warriors), and *Preto Velhos* (wise old slaves) who helped the saints in their charitable work. As benevolent possession lacked suitable parallels in Catholicism, Graciela had to resort to a spiritualist vocabulary derived directly from her personal experience with Umbanda. Once again, this was not the same interpretation that inner-circle members held and shared in their conversations. Both for temple authorities and inner-circle members, spiritual entities were diverse manifestations of the Orixá of the medium and not sacred creatures with an independent existence entering his or her body. But this Orixá-centered interpretation was not communicated to people who did not belong to this restricted circle.

Consultants who frequently attended Friday sessions were eventually invited to a Monday session, where animal sacrifices were publicly performed for Exu. Participating in Monday sessions involved witnessing new practices such as the performance of animal sacrifices. The latter are completely alien to cognitive schemas related to religion in Argentine culture and constitute the most stigmatizing trait of the religion in the country.

As a result of participation in these interactive situations, habitual consultants expanded their interpretive schemas involving spiritual beings and religious personnel in order to encompass new practices and experiences. A new ability became associated to religious personnel: that of housing in their bodies other spiritual creatures during rituals. New religious beings were added to a spiritual repertoire already including Catholic and folk saints and the spirits of the dead. Habitual consultants now also asked Caboclos, Oguns, and Pretos Velhos to help them resolve practical problems. Unlike Catholic and folk saints, however, these new spiritual forces could come alive in the bodies of people in white during ceremonies.

Although habitual consultation involved progressive exposure to practices alien to their interpretive schemas, it almost never implied conversion. Habitual consultants did not show in their discourse signs of discontinuities in their personal identities, nor did they employ schemas derived from interactions within the temple to interpret situations occurring elsewhere, except when during consultations the mãe de santo explicitly performed this task for them. They assimilated, instead, the new practices to the old ones. They amplified their faith in spiritual interventions, in general, and in those prompted by temple personnel, in particular. As one of them asserted during an interview, "I always believed that the saints helped me, but since I started coming to the temple I have more faith in them."

Besides this increase in their faith in the saints, transformations explicitly acknowledged by habitual consultants as a result of attending the temple included an increase in their faith in God, the establishment of a more direct relation with him, the adding of faith in the Umbanda spiritual entities to that previously held for the saints, and the experiencing of an enhanced religious emotion during rituals. All these acknowledged transformations implied quantitative rather than qualitative modifications: enlarging preexisting schemas of interpretation rather than changing them.

Such enlargements of interpretive schemes attest to the pertinence of the mediations paradigm when analyzing participation in recently introduced religions in Latin America. As an effect of continued participation, new religious beings are added to the old ones in the fulfillment of identical tasks, while the latter acquire new characteristics as they become involved in new ritual actions. Mediations and syncretic re-elaborations also attest to the perils of confounding frequent participation in the activities of a religious group and conversion (or confusing affiliates and converts) when analyzing factors favoring conversion. Particularly in a region of the world where a syncretic cultural disposition is widespread, frequent and long-lasting participation in the activities of a religious group does not necessarily amount to conversion. Moreover, when the religious practices and worldview held by a group are radically different from those of Catholicism and folk religion, the maintenance of high rates of continued attendance can call for interactive strategies on the part of religious personnel and authorities that stress the similarities of old and new beliefs and practices. Such strategies, while making new practices understandable to large audiences, do not favor the experience of radical cognitive or identity discontinuities. Rather than fueling conversions, they stimulate syncretic re-elaborations and mediations between old and new systems of religious beliefs.

Mediums: The Bifurcation of the Roads

Eventually, the spiritual entities possessing the mãe de santo during sessions diagnosed some habitual consultants as mediums. Generally, this verdict was made after the person had gone through the first stages of possession trance during public sessions. The observation of backstage interaction, especially within the inner circle, and of public rituals showed that spiritual entities helped to enter trance those habitual consultants that the mãe de santo considered suitable to play a role in the temple. Nevertheless, diagnoses of mediumship were officially considered as something the spiritual entities performed for purely spiritual instead of practical reasons and with complete independence from the will of Graciela.

Once the diagnosis was communicated to the consultant, Graciela would, in subsequent consultations, tell them that they had "the ability to receive and transmit energy" and that they therefore needed to "develop their mediumship" (desarrollar la mediumnidad) in order to feel better. In time, this entailed wearing white clothes and ceasing to receive spiritual help in order to start helping others. At this point some people left the temple, rejecting the role offered to them, but most accepted the diagnosis.[20] Those who did so generally started having trance experiences both at home and in the temple or underwent other kinds of altered states of consciousness and extraordinary happenings until they finally decided to become temple members. During this liminal phase they were generally subjected to the Obi ritual in order to "strengthen their heads."

During consultations potential recruits were told that their "guardian angel" (*ángel de la guarda*) wanted them to develop their mediumship and needed to be fed in order to become stronger. Thus, altered states of consciousness were interpreted as signs of the need to become recruited in order to satisfy the will of the guardian angel. Again, inner-circle members while talking amongst themselves never employed the expression "guardian angel" nor mentioned the need of developing mediumship. They said, instead, that it was the personal Orixá (or owner of the head) of the potential recruit who wanted to be fed and developed in order to increase his or her *axé* (spiritual energy). In the same way that when talking to consultants they called saints what they knew to be Orixás, the fact that they used the expression "guardian angels" when talking to potential recruits showed an effort on the part of the mãe de santo and inner-circle members to stress the similarities between their beliefs and those prevalent in folk Catholicism. Instead of using "energy," "developing mediumship," or "spiritual help rituals," (terms already current in Brazilian Umbanda which translate the African religious vocabulary into Spiritualist terms—Spiritualism being much more popular in Brazil than in Argentina) these terms were only employed whenever a concept was unavailable in folk Catholicism in order to explain new beliefs and practices.

Likewise, religious knowledge verbally transmitted to new mediums during public gatherings was mostly worded in Catholic or Spiritualist terms. These explanations assumed that the beliefs and practices of folk Catholicism were known to everyone and were thus suitable to explain Umbanda practices by making reference to their similarities or to their differences. This verbally transmitted knowledge only applied to public Umbanda rituals, since the information related to Candomblé practices was only available to mediums through participation in restricted activities.

The Obi ceremony inaugurated a process of restructuring of the body schema that was only achieved through participation in repeated initiatory rituals. This restructuring enthroned a point in the upper region of the head, the *ori*, as the ruling center of the self. All initiatory rituals had this point as the main object of ritual actions. Besides rituals, body restructuring was achieved through prohibitions: recruited personnel could only let the mãe de santo touch their heads, they were told to always bathe starting with the head and moving downwards, and women were not allowed to either cut or dye their hair. Repeated initiatory and avoidance rituals undergone by sons and daughters of saints would create a sense of continuous relation with their personal Orixás that were thought to reside on that part of the body. But this process occurred only under certain conditions and restrictions within the temple.

New initiates could choose the frequency with which they attended temple activities. Some of them only did so when it was mandatory: for Monday and Friday sessions and when public festivities for one of the Orixàs were performed. Others also went once or twice during weekdays to perform spiritual aids for consultants. Only a few were present when public rituals were not performed, later in the night and during weekends. In these occasions they helped with the more restricted Candomblé rituals, at a distance, since they had not undergone the necessary initiations to fully participate in them.

Mediums attending the temple only when public rituals and rituals for the benefit of consultants were performed generally developed a strong faith in Umbanda spirit entities. They believed especially that the charismatic spirits possessing the mãe de santo and the entities that they themselves received during sessions had a direct influence in the solution of their problems. Although these entities—Oguns, Preto Velhos, and Caboclos—were conceived as somewhat different from folk Catholic saints (which do not possess mediums), they were granted a role similar to that formerly attributed to such saints. They were believed to chastise the medium when a problem arose and to have helped when a problem was solved. Furthermore, mediums undergoing full possession trance during Umbanda sessions sometimes experienced trance and believed they became possessed by their entities when facing difficult situations in their homes. Thus, they were possessed by their Oguns when they needed to deal with a fight or quarrel with someone, by their Caboclos when they needed to solve a situation with courage, and by their Preto Velhos when the situation called for wise advice. Once the matter was considered settled the entities departed.

For people attending the temple mainly for public Umbanda sessions, this faith in Umbanda entities persisted unaltered even when they underwent several Candomblé initiation rituals after many years in the temple. For this faith to be replaced by other beliefs, radically different from those of folk Catholicism, it was necessary for the mediums to attend the temple regularly when restricted Candomblé ceremonies were performed. Attending these ceremonies implied frequent and direct interaction with inner-circle members.

Peter Berger and Thomas Luckmann have asserted that religious conversion entails the problem of dismantling beliefs once taken for granted as

characterizing the real world.[21] In the temple under study this process of dismantling took the form of a gradual reinterpretation. Well-known religious
concepts and terms were progressively redefined through participation in
activities that put their referents in new relationships. Thus, guardian angels
had to be strengthened; saints were offered food and eventually entered
the body of the mediums; and some spiritual-aid rituals (such as those performed for Exu) involved animal sacrifices.

For recruited personnel both public and initiatory rituals played a central role in paving the road for conversion. They provided contexts that facilitated the emergence of non-ordinary experiences such as possession trance.
These experiences defied initiate's preexistent schemas of interpretation
and their body schemas. But for such experiences to become interpreted in
the same terms that the authorities of the temple and inner-circle members
held, intensive interaction in contexts where they alone were present was
required. Thus, a more radical transformation of cognitive schemas and
identities was restricted to the few mediums who chose to attend the temple
when all the public had left or had not yet arrived. Then, the Orixás received
their offerings and people in white were subjected to initiations.

Sons and Daughters of Saints:
The Conditions That Allow for "Understanding"

Sooner or later, every medium who continued to attend the temple underwent the Bori ritual, feeding his or her head with the blood of an animal
corresponding to his or her personal Orixá, and, later on, through the
Asiento, the ritual allowing his or her Orixá to be "seated" (asentado). This
was a necessary course, for the mãe the santo and inner-circle members
believed that mediums could not provide ritual help to others without
constantly renewing their axé (sacred energy). These initiatory rituals were
the only way to develop and restore this energy for one "having been born
to serve one´s Orixá" (que han nacido para servir a su Orixá), the inner-circle
conceptualization of people in white. These reasons were irrelevant, if not
altogether unknown, to the majority of the people in white, even for those
who had undergone the first initiatory rituals but only participated regularly
in public Umbanda ceremonies.

The decision leading mediums to actively help in restricted rituals was
not altogether their own, but the result of a co-construction: those mediums
who arrived at the temple by recommendation of inner-circle members
as well as those who during their attendance established close links with
them were more likely to habitually participate in such rituals. Because of
these relationships, they were better informed about when restricted rituals
took place and felt more comfortable attending the temple on semi-secret

occasions. Furthermore, the mãe de santo herself invited those mediums with whom she felt affectively closer to attend the temple when these events took place.

Prospective sons and daughters of saints who attended restricted ceremonies first participated at a distance, chanting in the surrounding patios of the buildings where rituals were performed, preparing food and drinks for those performing the ceremonies during breaks, and cleaning and ironing ritual objects and clothes. On these occasions they could hear inner-circle members talk among themselves and started to become familiarized with their pervasive use of the vocabulary of the Orixás and the renewal of axé.

For mediums who frequently interacted with inner-circle members, the Bori ritual made possible a substantial transformation of their subjective personal identity. The performance of this initiatory ritual involved the confirmation of which of the twelve Orixás acknowledged in the temple "owned the head" of the initiate: which of these various deities ruled her or his life and, therefore, determined her or his character, appearance, and destiny. Having undergone the ritual, the son or daughter of religion could start to define himself or herself as son or daughter of a specific Orixá. If he or she continued to participate frequently in the restricted activities of the temple, this identity was reconfirmed by inner-circle members, who oftentimes greeted the sons and daughters of religion with the name and ritual salutation corresponding to their Orixá. Further, they interpreted their acts, life circumstances, illnesses, problems, inclinations, desires, elections, and physical traits as a result of their being a son or daughter of a specific Orixá.

For these sons and daughters of the religion who frequently attended Candomblé rituals, the new identity became central: they progressively interpreted most events in their lives past and present as byproducts of it. The Asiento ritual, or seating, of their personal Orixá, that implied the creation of an object condensing its spiritual energy, confirmed and ritualized the centrality of this identity. Having undergone the Asiento also allowed the sons and daughters of saints who frequently attended the temple when restricted activities were performed to enter restricted areas of the temple and directly participate both in rituals performed for the Orixás of the temple and in rituals performed for the benefit of other temple members. On these occasions, they learned to chant in Yoruba, clean sacrificed animals, and prepare the foods corresponding to each one of the Orixás of the terreiro.

For sons and daughters of saints, frequent interaction with inner-circle members also involved participating in their interpretations of the activities, inclinations, desires, elections, and physical traits of other temple members in terms of their personal Orixás. In time, these interpretations resulted in the acquisition of a full repertoire of personal traits associated with each one of these divinities. Eventually, events and places of both the natural (such as rains, storms, winds, fire, air, plants, and animals) and the cultural world (laws, weapons, wars, cars, machines, jewelry, etc.) became increasingly associated to different Orixás through repeated participation in Candomblé ritual actions establishing these relationships. Thus, conversion not only required participation in rituals allowing for the emergence of experiences that defied preexistent schemas of interpretation and self-definitions, but also intensive interaction within a selected group of people who consistently applied the same schema of interpretation to every situation and constantly reconfirmed for each member her or his religiously defined identity.

The correct application to every situation of an interpretive frame that basically classified people, life circumstances, and the natural and cultural world according to the Orixás controlling them was interpreted by inner-circle members and the mãe de santo as "understanding." When they listened to a new son or daughter of an Orixá correctly applying such interpretations, they made comments like this: "Until recently, Lucy did not understand anything, but now she understands everything."

It is worth noting that this "conversion" remained hidden to the view of most people with whom sons and daughters of saints interacted outside the temple, creating a good deal of subjective distance separating them. In "Social Cocoons: Encapsulation and Identity Transformation Organizations," Arthur Greil and David Rudy asserted that encapsulation is an important structural feature of "identity transformation organizations," since it is necessary to avoid situations in which the identities and beliefs held by the group may be disconfirmed by those who do not share them. Inner-circle members of the terreiro experienced social encapsulation, similar to that reported by the authors who studied Scientology and found that Scientologists also do not reveal their beliefs while in company of non-Scientologists. In effect, while interacting outside the temple with colleagues and friends who did not know of their involvement in the religion, converts secretly interpreted both their identities and those of people in their presence in terms of the Orixás they supposed owned their heads. When wanting to achieve something, they took into account these Orixá-related identities in order to understand, convince, seduce, comfort, or appease others. A basic premise of social interaction was thus broken: the assumption that other people interpret our actions in the same way that we ourselves do while interacting with them. The only people with whom this assumption held true for the converts were other members of the inner circle. Thus, if converts rarely become objectively isolated from the world outside, conversion did entail some sort of subjective isolation. They interacted with others holding the conviction that they understood whatever was said and done in a way different from other participants.

The illusion of communication with those who did not share their world of meaning was broken. Concurrently, affective ties established with other inner-circle members acquired an importance proportional to the subjective distance separating them from the outside world. People in the inner circle were the only people who shared a similar worldview and the only people who were believed to "understand" the true identities of each of its members. Thus, for converts, contacts with other converts were the sole truly intimate ones where their true identities were revealed.[22]

Conclusions

Utilizing a methodology of long-term participant observation among practitioners of "the religion" in Buenos Aires allows us to better understand the relationships linking modes of interaction and the transformation of cognitive schemas and identities among converts and affiliates. Most studies of conversion processes around the world have found that intense interaction with members of a group is a necessary requisite of conversion. The present exploration of conversion processes in a particularly successful temple of Afro-Brazilian religions in Buenos Aires shows that not just any kind of intensive interaction with a religious group favors conversion. Conversion remains useful as a conceptual category, particularly when broken down into meaningful definitional stages (such as affiliation versus conversion and confession). In the temple under study, the dynamics of interaction favored conversion for a limited number of recruits who actively participated in restricted activities. Amongst many recruits, they were singled out on the basis of both their willingness to participate in secret rituals and the affective ties linking them to temple authorities and to inner-circle members surrounding them.

Outside this somewhat restricted circle of people, translations, mediations, and creative combinations of new and old practices and beliefs were the most common occurrence. Such creative combinations were not only spontaneously produced by the enlargement of old schemas of interpretation, but also actively encouraged by the translating efforts of the authorities and the converts themselves. When interacting with the public and recruits outside the inner circle, both the members of the latter and temple authorities employed a language derived from folk religion, Catholicism, and spiritualism, thus favoring mediations between their beliefs and those already held by other participants. In so doing, they allowed for people to continue attending the temple and understanding its public ceremonies in their own terms, thus not favoring conversions. Thus, the Brazilian literature on mediations and passages helps to inform our analysis of these individuals' "stage of conversion," without throwing out the concept all together.

Temple authorities and converts believed that "understanding" (their own term to designate conversion) was not for everybody, nor even for every initiate, but only for a selected group of people.[23] This fact, combined with a religious disposition on the part of temple attendants that inclined them to add spiritual entities to an ever-growing repertoire, made conversions a somewhat rare occurrence in the temple. Conversions, however, did occur. What factors can be singled out as favoring it?

In the temple under study both public and initiatory rituals played a central role in paving the road for conversion. They provided contexts that facilitated the emergence of non-ordinary experiences such as possession trance. These experiences defied preexistent schemas of interpretation for participants and audiences as well as their own body schemas for those undergoing them. But for such experiences to become interpreted in the same terms that the authorities of the temple and inner-circle members held, intensive interaction in contexts where they alone were present was required.

In these contexts the basic tenets of the religious worldview held by the temple authorities were applied to the interpretation of almost every natural and social situation that was commented on, from rains, storms, and floods to car accidents and robberies. Further, the actions, personality, physical characteristics, and life histories of the prospective or actual converts were constantly explained as a result of the diverse religiously defined identities ritually attributed to them. These religiously defined identities were also attributed to non-initiates known to the members of the group, and their actions were explained as a result of them. Thus, conversion was made possible by a combination of rituals allowing for the emergence of experiences that defied preexistent schemas of interpretation and self-definitions, on the one hand, and by intensive interaction within a selected group of people who consistently applied the same schema of interpretation to every situation and constantly reconfirmed for each member his or her religiously defined identity, on the other hand. We can conclude that conversion in Latin America is not made possible by just any kind of intensive interaction with a religious group, but by one that involves the consistent and constant application of the same religiously derived interpretive frame to both the situations that are commented and acted upon and the personal identities of its participants.

NOTES

I am grateful to Timothy Steigenga and Alejandro Frigerio for their insightful comments and editorial assistance.

1. Patricia Birman, "Cultos de Possessão e Pentecostalismo no Brasil: Passagens," *Religião e Sociedade* 17 (1996): 90–109.

2. See, for example, Clara Mafra, "Relatos Compartilhados: Experiências de Conversão ao Pentecostalismo entre Brasileiros e Portugueses," *Mana* 6 (2000): 57–85; Ronaldo Almeida and Paula Montero, "Trânsito Religioso no Brasil," *São Paulo en Perspectiva* 15 (2001): 92–102; and Pablo Seman, "A 'Fragmentação do Cosmos': Um Estudo sobre as Sensibilidades de Fiéis Pentecostais e Católicos dum Bairro da Grande Buenos Aires" (Tesis de doutorado, Programa de Pos-Graduação em Antropología Social, Universidade Federal do Rio Grande do Sul, Porto Alegre, Brasil, 2000).

3. María Julia Carozzi and Alejandro Frigerio, "Mamãe Oxum y la Madre María: Santos, Curanderos y Religiones Afro-Brasileñas en Buenos Aires," *Afro-Asia* 15 (1992): 71–85; M. Carozzi and A. Frigerio, "Não se Nasce Batuqueiro: A Conversão das Religiões Afro-Brasileiras em Buenos Aires," *Religião e Sociedade* 30 (1997): 71–94.

4. See, for example, David Snow and Cynthia Phillips, "The Lofland-Stark Conversion Model: A Critical Reassessment," *Social Problems* 27 (1980): 430–447; Arthur Greil and David Rudy, "What Have We Learned from Process Models of Conversion? An Examination of Ten Studies," *Sociological Focus* 17 (1984): 306–323.

5. Robert Balch and David Taylor, "Seekers and Saucers: The Role of the Cultic Milieu in Joining an UFO Cult," *American Behavioral Scientist* 20 (1977): 839–860.

6. According to Claudia Strauss and Naomi Quinn, schemas are "the generic versions of experience that remain in memory." They are prototypes with an expectational force. Whenever a present experience has missing or ambiguous information, we fill in the blanks or gray areas with information provided by the schema it evokes. C. Strauss and N. Quinn, "A Cognitive/Cultural Anthropology," in *Assessing Cultural Anthropology*, ed. Robert Borofsky (New York: Mc Graw-Hill, 1994), 285. On the relevance of resonance for the construction of mobilizing frames in social and religious movements, see David Snow and Robert Benford, "Ideology, Frame Resonance, and Participant Mobilization," *International Social Movement Research* 1 (1988): 197–217; and Alejandro Frigerio, "Estabelecendo Pontes: Articulação de Significados e Acomodação Social em Movimentos Religiosos no Cono Sul," in *Religião e Globalização*, ed. Ari Oro and Carlos Steil (Petrópolis: Vozes, 1997), 153–178.

7. John Lofland and Rodney Stark, "Becoming a World-Saver," *American Sociological Review* 30 (1965): 862–874; Greil and Rudy, "What Have We Learned from Process Models of Conversion?" 306–323; David Snow and Richard Machalek, "The Sociology of Conversion," *Annual Review of Sociology* 10 (1984): 167–190.

8. Max Heirich, "A Change of Heart: A Test of Some Widely Held Theories about Religious Conversion," *American Journal of Sociology* 83 (1977): 653–680.

9. Gregory Johnson, "The Hare Krishna in San Francisco," in *The New Religious Consciousness*, ed. Charles Block and Robert Bellah (Berkeley, Calif.: University of California Press, 1976), 31–51; David Stone, "The Human Potential Movement," in *The New Religious Consciousness*, ed. Block and Bellah, 93–115; and David Preston, "Becoming a Zen Practitioner," *Sociological Analysis* 42 (1981): 47–55.

10. Peter Burke, "The Self: Measurement Requirement from an Interactionist Perspective," *Social Psychology Quarterly* 43 (1980): 18–29.

11. I take the phrase "physical, social and spiritual or moral being" from Viktor Gecas, who employs it in reference to the self-concept. V. Gecas, "The Self Concept," *Annual Review of Sociology* 8 (1982): 3.

12. As Timothy Steigenga argues in chapter 1, conversion narratives are important pieces of evidence for understanding conversion, but they are also socially

constructed, retrospective in character, and interact with the convert's current institutional stage of conversion, perhaps telling us more about the convert's present status than their past.

13. *Terreiros* are temples where Afro-Brazilian religions are practiced.

14. Alejandro Frigerio, "Por Nuestros Derechos Ahora o Nunca! Construyendo una Identidad Colectiva Umbandista en Argentina," *Civitas: Revista de Ciencias Sociais* 3 (2003): 35–68.

15. For a comprehensive rendering of the history of Afro-Brazilian religions in Buenos Aires see Alejandro Frigerio, "El Rol de la 'Escuela Uruguaya' en la Expansión de las Religiones Afrobrasileñas en Argentina," in *Los cultos de posesión en Uruguay: Antropología e Historia*, ed. Renzo Pi Hugarte (Montevideo: Facultad de Humanidades and Ediciones Banda Oriental, 1988), 75–98.

16. *Mãe de santo* is the term employed to designate the head of an Afro-Brazilian religious temple when she is a woman, *pai de santo* when he is a man. These terms could be translated as "mother of saints" and "father of saints," respectively, since they are believed to give birth to the personal deities, or Orixás, of religious personnel.

17. *Pai pequeno* is the term employed to designate the second person in authority in an Afro-Brazilian religious temple when he is a man, *mãe pequena* when she is a woman. The terreiro under study had both a pai pequeno and a mãe pequena sharing this position.

18. So called because of the white clothes members of the temple wear while performing their religious activities.

19. Some people arrived for the solution of more than one type of problem; this explains why the total sum of the percentages is more than one hundred.

20. Again, note the similarities in the conversion process among those individuals Henri Gooren interviewed who converted to Mormon, Pentecostal, or Charismatic Catholicism.

21. Peter Berger and Thomas Luckmann, *The Social Construction of Reality: A Treatise in the Sociology of Knowledge* (New York: Doubleday and Company, 1967).

22. A. Greil and D. Rudy, "Social Cocoons: Encapsulation and Identity Transformation Organizations," *Sociological Inquiry* 54 (1984): 260–278.

23. Perhaps because of this fact conversions were rarer than in other terreiros of Buenos Aires where Frigerio and I analyzed similar processes. See Carozzi and Frigerio, "Não se Nasce Batuqueiro."

8

The Catholic Charismatic Renewal

Revitalization Movements and Conversion

EDWARD L. CLEARY

When Nicholas D'Antonio, the bishop of Olancho, Honduras, was thinking of joining the Catholic Charismatic movement, he wondered if he was betraying his commitment to change in the Catholic Church. He had painfully reshaped his own views on the church and society during the 1960s era of Vatican Council II and its Latin American follow-up, the Medellin Conference. During this period, he changed his view of the church from being hierarchical to participatory, from concentrating on devotions and rituals to encouraging activity to make better the world in which the people of Olancho lived. For Bishop D'Antonio to be drawn into a social justice orientation meant a conversion, a commitment that was demanding and would cost him considerable sacrifice, even possibly threats to his life.[1] The later step of becoming Charismatic in the 1980s also involved a conversion, in this case, a deepening of a commitment to living a life in the spirit.

The Catholic Charismatic movement (CCR, Renovación Carismática Católica) has become widespread in Latin America. Conversions and intensified religious practices among Charismatics have played a role in the reinvigoration of religion within the Catholic Church. This consists of a deepening spiritual life, a greater sense of responsibility for one's own actions, a greater attachment to the church, and often an increased concern for one's neighbors. Charismatics are having an effect on Latin American culture as well through music, lively religious rituals, and contra-cultural lifestyles.

The first section of this chapter addresses the role of conversion in the Charismatic movement, outlining theoretical and theological debates. The

second section locates the role of the CCR within renewal movements in
the Catholic Church. Section three provides a specific historical outline of
origins of the movement, emphasizing the missionary roots and spontaneous nature of the CCR. Section four details the struggle of the movement for
Catholic acceptance in a church with competing pastoral strategies, with
emphasis on Brazil, where the movement has unusual vitality amid strong
competition from other churches and religions. In the final section, I address
what conversion means within the CCR and its possible melding with social
justice movements within the Catholic Church.[2]

Conversion among Catholic Charismatics

Conversion lies at the center of understanding the Catholic Charismatic
movement. Conversion, as envisaged by movement leaders, is a lifelong process. Thus, as Henri Gooren argues in chapter 3, the notion of a conversion
career as a life lived through advances and declines and changes derived
from developmental stages in life fits well with the narratives many Charismatics provide of their conversions.

From its beginning as a movement forty years ago conversion has occupied a central space in the Catholic Charismatic Renewal. In many places,
people interested in the movement were invited to a Life in the Spirit retreat
as the initial step. They were advised to go to confession or in some other
way acknowledge their sins, resolve to improve their lives, and dispose
themselves for the indwelling of the Holy Spirit. In the Life in the Spirit
retreat many participants then experienced a coming of the spirit as joyful
awareness of God's presence within them. This conversion is experienced as
illumination, many say, which makes the bonding with God stronger and the
moral path to the future clearer; that is, decisions are made that amount to
a moral conversion.

In brief, conversion for Catholic Charismatics means a new way of life,
a commitment with new elements (such as healing) which are referred to
as the gifts of the spirit. This depiction of a way of life accords with Henri
Gooren's characterization of conversion career and his five-level topology
of religious activity. Thus, for the most part, Charismatics are at the third
and fourth level of religious activity. They have gone through the ritual of
affiliation/initiation, baptism, at an early age. But beyond mere affiliation,
group membership now forms a central aspect of their life and, indeed, of
their identity. More, they report that they experienced a radical change, in
the sense of a deepening of worldview and identity. They have advanced
from indifferent or lukewarm affiliation. As Gooren has depicted in his
fourth level as confession, in the sense of proclamation, Charismatics tend
to practice a high level of participation inside their religious group and

have a strong "missionary attitude" toward non-members outside their group.

The Charismatic movement also appears to be an excellent exemplification of what David Smilde explains in chapter 5 on network and publics. This is not a movement or activity that started from above. At its inception, the Catholic Church hierarchy neither mandated the movement nor initially sponsored the movement. Quite the contrary, the bishops typically delayed granting approval. Rather, the renewal began from the mid-level workforce and from the grassroots. Priests, sisters, and lay persons working in Latin America picked up the core ideas and practices in the United States or Canada and communicated what they knew to small groups in Latin America whose members in turn recruited others. Or Charismatic personalities communicated through television or live performances the main ideas and practices to adherents who in turn recruited friends, relatives, and associates.

The movement in Latin America has not developed much reflective thought (theology) on conversion but relies on a very long tradition and twentieth-century interpretations of thought about conversion. Through centuries of Christian theology from medieval theology on, Catholic writers commonly spoke of first and second conversions. First conversion was said to occur at baptism, in which one was dedicated to a life in God. This initial dedication to God was reinforced typically in adolescence by the sacrament of confirmation. Many persons did live good lives without evidence of further conversion. But a second conversion also occurred in many lives. Persons, as Teresa of Avila, lived mediocre lives until some further event occurred. In Teresa's case an image of Jesus appeared to her and triggered a mystical experience. This event produced a deeper insight or sense of God and an enthusiastic response in the form of a commitment to live a deeper spiritual life. "What this [Charismatic] movement seeks to do," said noted theologian Yves Congar, "is to ask the Lord to actualize what the Christian people have already received."[3]

Theologians have been drawn into theoretical debates about conversion within CCR, with practical implications. These discussions about the understandings of conversion illuminate key differences between Catholics and Protestants, that is, between Charismatics and Pentecostals. Among Catholics generally, conversion is a process that takes place over time; conversion can be "lost" or diminished. Among many Latin American Protestants, conversion is a once-and-for-all-time event, as it is for some North American Evangelicals. The idea that a person such as North American televangelist Billy Graham was converted in the 1940s and later "saved" as person with many years to live is foreign to many Catholics.

Theological disputes show clearly the wide pluralism of the movement in which there has not been a unified view of conversion. Nor, say some theologians and practitioners, should there be a single understanding. Theologian Donald Gelpi, who has observed the Charismatic Renewal for years, believes that there are at least four different types of conversion and that the interplay of these types helps to explain personal growth. Within the conversion process, one may then speak not only of religious conversion but of affective, intellectual, and moral conversion as well.[4] Nonetheless, the main thread of understanding of conversion is clear: it is the conscious decision to turn to a life faithful to God and to turn from evil. Conversion is thus defined here as a change of mentality and also a lifelong process. In "Church in America" in John Paul II's fullest statement about the church in the Western Hemisphere, he repeats the common understanding of conversion as a process that is never finished, a continual challenge, and always under threat of being lost.[5]

One should note, too, that there has been an evolution in some regions away from initial Protestant emphases to those that are more distinctly Catholic. While Pentecostal and Catholics groups hold much in common, forty years of history has shown a growing Catholic recognition of their distinctive identity.[6] First, Catholics became more fully aware of their mystical and spiritual theological traditions. This was aided by research into their tradition of previous manifestations of the spirit through the centuries.[7] A wide renascence of interest in mysticism occurred in Spain, Germany, and Britain in the 1960s, centered in the study of spiritual masters such as John of the Cross, Meister Eckhardt, and Juliana of Norwich. Second, spirit baptism has been seen as fitting within traditional sacramental theology, especially the sacraments of baptism and confirmation; that is, spirit baptism does not take the place of other sacraments, but it does represent a decisively new work of grace in a believer's life. Third, most Catholics tend not to see speaking in tongues as evidence of spirit baptism, as do Pentecostals. Catholics also argue for a wider range of spiritual gifts beyond those typically cited by Protestants. Fourth, the Eucharist and the Mass are central practices in which the divine presence in the Eucharist is acknowledged, and charisma, including healing, is often received during the Mass. Lastly, devotion to Mary, the Mother of God, is an integral part of many Catholic's spiritual life. This is especially evident among the numerous adherents to the movement in Mexico.

Healing is central to many in the Charismatic movement, so the link between healing and conversion is crucial to the discussion here. Healing which is born of faith takes several forms. The first is conversion itself that induces healing. The unconverted individual is diminished as a person by a disordered relationship with God and with other persons. Conversion is believed to bring about the reordering of social and religious attitudes in line with what God wishes. Theologian Donald Gelpi believes this reordering heals the human heart in its deepest center.[8]

Given the Catholic view of the precarious quality of conversion, the community assumes a responsibility to nurture the newly initiated. They do this through mentorship in prayer and in helping new members assume roles in the church and through strong emotional support and example. For their part, new members are expected to attend community meetings frequently, to have docility to spiritual masters, and, eventually, to bring in new members, once one has gained some experience in living as a Charismatic. The main thrust of life after the initial intense religious experience, called here a second conversion, is *revisión de vida*, a "change of life," avoiding what is considered evil and the occasions that will lead to slips and falls and attempting to be active and generous in relations with others.

This program is morally demanding and time consuming. Some drop out. The numbers of those who do is unknown. Interviews with Charismatic leaders through forty years lead to a tentative conclusion that most dropouts remain Catholic and continue to attend church with a bit more fervor and a greatly enhanced musical repertoire. Many dropouts from Pentecostalism fall into the category of "no religion," a growing pool of persons in Latin America.[9] This does not seem to be the case with Pentecostal Catholics.

In sum, the Charismatic conversion experience is characterized by an initial intense experience of God, with the gifts of the Holy Spirit being received by many persons as healing and speaking in tongues. This is followed by dedication to personal renewal and an ongoing growth in a life of holiness. After the Life in the Spirit retreat, participants typically join small prayer groups. The groups serve to instruct, encourage, and challenge members to greater spiritual growth. The groups are better called communities and resemble extended families. Members help one another to grow in holiness and to build stronger relationships. Social justice activism is not generally emphasized, although CCR groups in some Spanish-speaking countries, as Colombia, have stressed working against the drug trade or joining in emergency service after disasters.

The few researchers who have looked into the Catholic Charismatic Renewal have stressed problem-solving as a central motivation for persons to join the movement. Illnesses, addiction, suffering in many forms—this is an almost universal condition among the poor or alienated in Latin America—draw some into the movement. Andrew Chesnut, in an earlier work, describes this universal condition as the "pathogens of poverty," the rotting food, dirty water, tattered clothing, frequent illnesses, and lack of schools, police, and clinics. Janneke Brouwer found that in Nicaragua almost all her informants became members of the Charismatic movement under the influence of certain needs, as recognition of addiction or feelings of alienation, in their lives.[10] In chapter 5, David Smilde argues that network location provides the most robust explanation of who addresses these needs through religious participation. Other persons with similar needs find other means to address problems, continue suffering, or in some cases simply explain them away.

Smilde also suggests that seeking solutions is situated in sites where networks are bridged, new understandings develop, and coalitions develop. For Pentecostals and Charismatics these sites include both services in churches and interactions in the streets. In other words, gathering together is done not only in churches but on the streets or, more accurately, in the numerous small plazas of Latin America. While reaching out to bring in new converts is central, it is far from the only event. Charismatics also frequently gather in public and private spaces to engage in study circles, exchange information, receive counseling, or simply engage in song or other forms of worship. Here the Charismatic movement clearly overflows traditional church structures into sites that are public and serve as the grounds for network activity.

To integrate the models of explanation offered by both Gooren and Smilde, one may note that crisis, often in the form of suffering that needs a solution, acts as a catalyst, moving some to the Charismatic movement and conversion because of the powerful attraction of a network. Others who suffer from the same problems but without influence of a network do not choose this religious solution. For individual persons, conversion and confession frequently occur as solutions to crisis. For the Catholic Church it means that Catholics become active in the church in an intense and participatory manner that revitalizes the institution.

Renewal Movements

As noted in the introduction, as Bishop D'Antonio was introduced to the Charismatic movement, he found himself deeply drawn into a movement that seemed to be the polar opposite of the progressive church, one that emphasized prayer and otherworldly praise of God. Like many other Catholics in Latin America, he was about to join the fastest growing movement in the Latin American church. Latin America leads the world in numbers and percentages of Catholic Charismatics. David Barrett and Todd Johnson, who attempt to track world Christian statistics, estimated for 2000 that more than seventy-three million Catholic Charismatics were present in Latin America, representing some 16 percent of Catholics in the region and more than half of the Charismatic Catholics in the world.[11]

With claims of a hundred million participants worldwide, the CCR has achieved an important place in the Catholic Church. However, the movement has diminished in the United States and some developed countries. But looking at the larger Catholic world, Donald Gelpi, a longtime observer, expresses a consensus view that the Catholic Charismatic Renewal "remains a significant movement of international proportions in Catholic lay prayer and spirituality."[12] While Catholic Charismatics have been called "Catholic Pentecostals" by some observers, this chapter argues that there are significant differences between the groups.

Catholicism's greatest challenger in Latin America is Pentecostalism and its various branches. Catholic Charismatics did not begin in Latin America as a conscious imitation of Pentecostalism. Rather, the movement began as a result of missionary activity from the United States and Canada. The aim of the missionaries was, as it had been for decades, the revitalization of the church in a region where Catholicism, as measured by workforce and orthodox practices, had fallen into deep decline. Before 1950, few priests served thousands in urban parishes, and rural areas had even fewer priests; many seminaries had few students, and lay participation in the church was passive or little more than a cultural practice without religious education. Many regions of Latin America virtually experienced a priestless church. Lay women and men carried on the practice of traditional peasant religion, based at home.

To revitalize the Catholic Church, beginning in the early twentieth century, a series of movements, most of them imported, was employed to help create an active and religiously educated laity. Some of these movements had a lasting effect on society as well as on the church.[13] Among a wide panoply of movements, Catholic Action stands out.

Using Brazil as an example, from the 1930s Catholic Action groups formed hundreds of thousands of lay leaders within cell-like structures. Catholic Action's greatest innovation was convincing lay people they had a role in the church and in society as members of the church. Members included the world-famous educator Paulo Freire and many others who influenced public spheres of Brazilian life. Other lay movements added their own character to the mix of lay renewal. These included the Better World Movement, Cursillos do Cristão, and many others. A later generation of movements included Opus Dei, Focolare, and Schoenstat. Earlier movements had strong political implications through ties to political parties, unions, or human rights advocacy groups. Later movements tended toward spiritual renewal, typically without an activist political orientation.

Catholic Action in Mexico, Latin America's other large country, likewise had hundreds of thousands of members and helped to lead sons of the movement to enter seminaries and daughters to enter convents in large numbers. Nonetheless, the movement was primarily a lay movement in which *militantes* were formed to fight against a godless state and against secularizing tendencies in society. Catholic Action and other initiatives brought the Mexican church a remarkable vitality in terms of church attendance (the second best in Latin America in the 1980s) and enough seminarians to send missionaries to Japan. The movement was also strong in Argentina and some other countries.

Catholic Action led to an equally important lay movement, Christian Base Communities (Comunidades Eclesias de Base, or CEBs). The progressive and centrist wings of the ranks of bishops frequently supported the movement. This was especially true in Brazil, where the bishops conference chose CEBs as the preferred contemporary policy for extending the church influence.[15]

The CEBs brought perhaps two million lay people into more intense church life through Bible study, prayer, and community action concentrated within small groups of twenty to forty adults. Many priest and lay CEB members were especially influenced by liberation theology, with its view of the church as being of service to society. It should be noted that the Brazilian bishops said the communities began from *"conversions that involve the whole church . . . in which the Spirit is at work"* (emphasis mine).[14] The bishops and others viewed commitment to social justice as a second conversion after baptism.

Bishop D'Antonio was caught up in the confluence of these renewal movements as both movements were in flux. Revitalization movements change, especially when new organizational leadership takes over. After his ascension to the papacy in 1978, Pope John Paul II began to make a heavy conservative imprint on the Latin American church. He did this by appointing conservative or centrist bishops and by indicating lack of approval for some activist stances. Many bishops ceased to support CEBs and sought alternatives. The shift in policy shows up in Latin America in the statements from three major Latin American bishops conferences: Medellín, Puebla, and Santo Domingo. Support for the CEBs began with affirmation in 1968, ascended to ringing approval in 1979, and descended to faint praise in 1992. As noted, many CEBs were carriers of the theology of the liberation that conservatives spurned. By contrast, movements that emphasized community and spirituality, as Opus Dei, were praised and achieved growth and prominence.

Beginnings of the Charismatic Movement in Latin America

The Charismatic movement is part of a second wave of Pentecostalism, a Christian religious movement centered on the gifts of the Holy Spirit. Church historians believe Pentecostalism had a beginning in Topeka, Kansas, in 1901 but typically cite the events at Azuza Street Baptist Church in Los Angeles from 1906 to 1913 as the starting point for Pentecostalism in the United States, beginning a stream of influence that spread to many countries.[15]

Charismatics are Pentecostals within mainline Protestant churches or the Catholic Church. They differ from Classical Pentecostals, as the

Assemblies of God, and from third-wave neo-Charismatics (the latter to be found especially between the independent and indigenous churches) in ways that will be shown later.[16] The Charismatic movement began in an Episcopal church in California and spread quickly through Methodists and Presbyterians to Catholics in a matter of a few years in the 1960s. Jack Hayford and David Moore describe what followed as part of the Charismatic century and show the enduring impact of the Azuza Street Revival.[17]

In the Catholic Charismatic case, almost all histories recount its beginning at Duquesne University in Pittsburgh in February 1967. This is misleading because a similar event was occurring in Bogotá, Colombia.[18] It is also misleading because a major figure in the United States and in initiating the movement in Latin America was Francis MacNutt, who was not drawn into the movement by ties with the Duquesne experience. At both Bogotá and Duquesne, participants said that they experienced baptism in the Holy Spirit and spoke in tongues. Baptism in the spirit and speaking in tongues were at the time considered the threshold experiences for entry into the Charismatic movement. Some have described this as a peak experience; that is, a detachment from pedestrian concerns and a time of wonder and awe.[19]

After MacNutt was ordained a Dominican priest, he went on to further studies in speech and communication at Northwestern University in order to teach preaching at a seminary. Catholic homiletics was then an underdeveloped professional area, so MacNutt joined and became executive director of the Christian Preaching Conference, a group of mostly Protestant seminary professors of preaching. As executive director, MacNutt attended the annual conference of the umbrella professional organization, the Speech Association of America. At a yearly conference of that association, MacNutt learned of Christian healing from a Protestant colleague. Later he was invited to a Protestant retreat in Tennessee in August 1967, where he received the baptism of the spirit.

MacNutt was thus somewhat apart from the central axis of the Catholic Charismatic movement, an axis that moved from Duquesne to Notre Dame, Indiana, and to Ann Arbor, Michigan. Nonetheless, he was one of the principal figures in introducing U.S. Catholics to the healing ministry. Thousands of persons attended his retreats or stadium rallies (as at Yankee Stadium). His book *Healing* (1974) sold hundreds of thousands of copies. He followed this with other religious bestsellers, including *The Power to Heal* (1977) and *The Prayer That Heals* (1981).

Another major force in starting the CCR in the west coast countries was Javier García Herreros of Colombia. He too received baptism in the spirit through Protestant colleagues and not through Catholic sources. One of these colleagues was Sam Ballesteros, of Mexican descent, from a Pentecostal Baptist church in Chula Vista, California. García Herreros's reception of the spirit in Colombia in 1972 ignited the movement that spread through a Catholic community that already existed, called Minuto de Dios.

When Francis MacNutt, the author's classmate, came to Bolivia in 1970, he was not coming primarily to visit the author but to light a spark that led to the beginnings of the Catholic Charismatic Renewal in the Andean countries of South America. As this movement grew, it was the author's destiny to watch it, from the sidelines, for forty years.

In Colombia, Costa Rica, and the Andean countries, partnership with Protestant Charismatics was important. At the time he came to Latin America, MacNutt worked with two highly regarded Methodist preachers (Tommy Tyson and Joe Petree) and with William Warnock (a United Methodist businessman). They conducted three Life in the Spirit retreats, first with a largely Protestant audience at the Pentecostal Holiness conference center near San Jose, Costa Rica. The audiences at the next two stops, Lima and Cochabamba, comprised a majority of young Catholic priests and sisters. Because the team from the United States preached in English, their audience included mostly English-speaking missionaries. Cochabamba was becoming a religious center where some 120 religious groups, Catholic and Protestant, maintained houses. This concentration made the spread of the movement easier. The retreat ignited a burst of enthusiasm that quickly spread from the retreat participants to their Spanish-speaking constituencies.

Within Bolivia, two U.S. Dominican priests, familiarly known as Padres Cris and Daniel, established a Charismatic community known as La Mansión at Santa Cruz.[20] Daniel Roach (another of my classmates) attended a Life in the Spirit retreat in 1971 at Cochabamba directed by MacNutt and associates. During the retreat he asked publicly for the gift of tongues. He began speaking in a language that no one understood, a sign that he and others understood to mean that he had been baptized in the spirit. By contrast, Chysostom Geraets, while on a visit home from Bolivia, spent a weekend praying with MacNutt in St. Louis, Missouri, in 1969. During prayer he received a deep inner sense of the presence of God. But a considerable time passed before he began to speak in tongues in 1971.

Cris and Dan began preaching, based on the Life in the Spirit retreat, to a handful of university students. The students experienced a greater sense of God, spoke in tongues, and acted as missionaries to family and friends. They formed the initial core of a network of persons who knew one another, a network that served as a medium leading others to a conversion experience. The enthusiastic recruiting by these first adherents in Santa Cruz led to the formation of a socially diverse congregation at La Mansión that grew to six thousand regularly attending members. In the 1970s Geraets spent years in biblical and theological study, joined at times by Roach, in an attempt to ensure a Catholic and biblical character for the sector of the movement under their care. They communicated these interpretations of the new movement in mimeographed "Experiences" and "Orientations." For them, the themes of the movement needed careful adaptation to a centuries-long Catholic tradition.

Both Geraets and Roach believed in delegating as many roles as possible. Within months a wide range of responsibilities were taken up by laity, including the teaching of prayer. Rituals of Mass and confession were central, but these sacraments were enshrouded with testimonies, spiritual counseling, singing, petitions, and healing ceremonies.

The main focuses of the Life in the Spirit retreat as practiced by MacNutt became conversion and physical and spiritual healing, not primarily speaking in tongues or other major emphases typical of classical Pentecostalism. However, speaking in tongues, at least at the beginning of the movement, was considered a sine qua non sign of entry. This issue and many theological and practical questions remained after the MacNutt-Tyson-Petree team departed. The team was urgently invited back to foster the somewhat fragile beginning. A second year of retreats in Peru and Bolivia was held, followed by third year in February 1972. This time the team extended their efforts to Chile, with a retreat for Catholic missionaries.

The first Spanish-speaking retreat was held in Lima in 1972 for a mostly Catholic audience. Some 250 Peruvians attended. This was followed by an English-language retreat for a lesser number. Two retreats followed in Bolivia. By this time, missionaries and Latin Americans were helping to lead the retreats and the movement was being adapted to the local cultures. Further north of Peru, Colombian priest Javier García Herreros transformed an existing center, Minuto de Dios, into a Charismatic locale. García Herreros was soon joined in his efforts by another Colombian priest, Diego Jaramillo, who became probably the best-known promoter of the movement in the South American west coast region.

These two streams of influence became more unified through the First Latin American Leadership Conference called by MacNutt and held in February 1973 in Bogotá, Colombia.[21] By then the movement had spread to the Dominican Republic, Mexico, Puerto Rico, and Venezuela, and those countries sent representatives. At the conclusion of the meeting, the participants created ECCLA (Encuentro Carismático Católico Latinoamericano), a major organizing force for Latin America.

Brazilian Catholics also began to become Charismatic through the international network that grew from the United States and Canada. However, the movement acquired a Brazilian imprint, was absorbed in taking care of the great growth of "converts" within Brazil, and continued on a somewhat separate path from ECCLA and the Spanish-speaking countries. Two priests from the Jesuit province of New Orleans, Edward Dougherty and Harold

Rahm, carried the movement to various parts of Brazil beginning in 1972. The character and growth of the movement are treated below.

In many ways the direction followed and the emphases placed for future efforts in the Spanish-speaking countries were consolidated at the Bogotá meeting. Reading through interviews and documents of forty years shows a remarkable consistency in vision carried into the future. Itinerant preachers would go on for many years to promote conversion and healing in other countries. The best-known Charismatic missionary traveled from his base in the Dominican Republic. Emiliano Tardif, a Canadian priest, went as a missionary for the movement to seventy-one countries. Tardif himself contracted tuberculosis in 1973, returned to Canada, where he was healed through Charismatic services, and returned to the Dominican Republic, from which he conducted a ministry of healing and spiritual growth. When he died in 1999, the president of the Dominican Republic declared a national day of mourning for the so-called apostle of healing.

Other groups also operated as itinerant preachers and prime movers in the movement. Ralph Rogawski and Helen Raycraft, with various team members, refined their approach as the Dominican Missionary Preaching Team, working first in Latin America and then through most of the United States. Carlos Talavera Ramírez, another of the participants in the Colombia meeting, went on to become bishop in the Vera Cruz region of Mexico and a major figure in Mexico's Charismatic Renewal.

Catholic Charismatic Renewal
and the Struggle for Church Acceptance

The Catholic Charismatic Renewal movement is a revitalization movement that offers a clear and popular alternative to Base Christian Communities. Its numbers match or exceed those of CEBs in a number of Latin American countries. This is a movement with definite demands made on new candidates, in contrast to other movements that do not have initiation criteria and tend toward inclusion rather than exclusion. At least in the early days of the movement, one had to speak in tongues and believe in healing. Once having been taken over by the Holy Spirit, once having spoken in tongues and believing in healing through prayer, converts could advance to a higher plane of Christian life.

When first faced with these "requirements" and the unusual emotional religious ceremonies the movement employs, bishops recoiled. As mainline Protestant churches before 1960 opposed speaking in tongues and Charismatic healing, the Catholic Church at first found these practices difficult to accept. In Latin America, leaders from the progressive wing, especially theologians and lay leaders, threw their weight against the Charismatic Renewal.

Theologians and lay leaders committed to the CEBs lobbied mightily with the bishop's conferences and with key bishops to keep the Charismatic movement at the margins of church influence.

One of the first to attack the movement was Leonardo Boff, the best-known Brazilian liberation theologian. The CCR had begun in Brazil in the early 1970s. By 1978, Boff was urging the Brazilian Bishops Conference to never officially approve the CCR in its present state.[22] Some progressive leaders saw the Charismatic movement as a European-Latin alliance against CEBs.

Progressive bishops and theologians succeeded in calling attention to serious flaws in the Charismatic Renewal. Belatedly in 1994, the Brazilian bishops approved a policy statement about the Charismatic movement. This was long after Rome, European countries, and the United States had done so. Some bishops continued to express their grave reservations about the movement after 1994. The bishop who was then head of the Nova Iguaçu diocese, Monsignor Adriano Hypolito, forbade praying in tongues and ceremonies that purported to lead to healing. He allowed worshipers to raise their arms in praise, but they could not jump.

Acceptance and Expansion

One of the first Latin American countries where the bishops approved the Charismatic movement was Guatemala, the country with the highest percentage (estimated 25 to 30 percent of national population) of Pentecostals. In 1986 the bishops issued "Guidelines for Charismatic Renewal," in which they noted the fruits of the action of the Holy Spirit in terms of deepened spiritual lives of lay persons and priests.[23] They repeated the commonly expressed fears that, without close watching on the part of authorized chaplains, "Charismatic groups easily go off tracks" into such practices as peculiar kinds of prayers, exclusive attitudes (non-Pentecostal forms of prayer were frowned upon), and overemphasis on emotions.

Back in Brazil, the battle against CCR was being lost. Talented Brazilian priests caught the Charismatic spirit. Padre Marcelo Rossi, Padre Zeca, and others interpreted the Charismatic movement in their own dramatic ways. Brazilians followed in droves. Bishops, too, took note that the Charismatics were fulfilling one of the Episcopal conference's goals, that of having a TV channel and satellite network, Redevida.

The unexpected innovation of the Brazilian Charismatic Renewal has been priest performers. None exceed Padre Marcelo Rossi.[24] He looks like an incarnation of an evangelical televangelist, only better. He has drawn two and a half million persons to a Charismatic celebration, needing a racetrack because a soccer stadium was not large enough. "He drew as many people as the John Paul II did when he came to Brazil," a middle-of-the-road Catholic priest said. He was not thinking of John Paul II as a performer, but many observers have seen the Pope's appeal as similar to that of a rock star. Whatever else he did, John Paul II showed (rather than merely told) another way to be a priest. When Pope John Paul spoke to young priests in Brazil about reaching out to young people in contemporary forms, Rossi and other priests listened and responded.

In Rossi's case, he incorporated singing and movement into both stadium events and daily Mass. He became a singing star. His CDs have risen to the top of the charts. He also dances, in the sense of moving to the music. These are the surface qualities that have attracted attention, but one cannot explain Rossi without his message. He believes he should lead his listeners, especially the younger ones, to commit themselves to God, allow the divine spirit to enter their lives, and live according to a Christian code of ethics. The message is one of personal conversion in an atmosphere of joy and hope.

In his first parish where he was an assistant pastor, Rossi's preaching and services soon attracted large audiences. Once bound to be parishioners within the territorial limits of parishes, contemporary Catholics tend to choose parishes by what they see as most congenial to themselves, a notable trend in religion. People began overflowing the church. Rossi was assigned before long to his own parish, and many people followed. As his church building proved quickly to be inadequate, Rossi moved Sunday services to a rented dance hall. Then the diocese provided him with rent money for an old glass factory. This hanger structure accommodated thirty thousand persons. Five days a week he celebrated Mass at Santuario Terza Vizentino. This Sanctuary of the Byzantine Rosary held more persons than capacity crowds at Madison Square Garden. Thirty thousand persons for a weekday parish Mass could find a place in a mythical Guinness book of religious records.

Marcelo Rossi is not alone among priests who perform before large audiences. Rossi gets the spotlight from the media in Brazil's megacities, while other young priests have drawn large crowds to ceremonies on Rio's beaches. Up the Atlantic coast in Recife, Padre Zezinho and Padre João Carlos have also become major draws.

Padre Marcelo is best described as an athletic event. He spins, twists, and speaks directly through a hand mike that looks like part of his large hand. His weightlessness makes it easy to believe that he and at least some of the other priest performers will blow away before long. Brazil has plenty of academic skeptics, as J. Reginaldo Prandi, who views Marcelo as trivializing religion.[25] They believe not only that Marcelo will pass away as a fad but also that he will damage religion's role as a carrier of needed values, as justice. They feel the same about the "beach priests."

Charismatics and Religious Changes

Pentecostalization has affected a wide swatch of Brazilian religions and culture. Evangelical churches that are not Pentecostal have nonetheless taken on many aspects of Pentecostalism in music, manners of praying, and conducting religious ceremonies. Rossi and others reflect Pentecostal influences in the Catholic Church, influences originating in North America and amplified in Brazil. Some further forces are at work here. Brazilian parishes are changing within themselves and in the way priesthood is expressed. Alberto Antoniazzi, a priest-researcher and adviser to the Brazilian Bishops Conference, has traced the evolving of parishes from the traditional dispenser of rituals, until the 1960s, to emphasizing community, in the 1970s and 1980s, to the prevalence of religious expression and personalized religion in some parishes in the following decades. Thus, in the 1990s some pastors changed from animators of community to "personalities" whose *performances* are judged by the value of the emotional expression they generate.[26] This does not mean other priests attempt to match Rossi, but it is no surprise when ordinary parish priests record CDs of music or spiritual messages for use at home while one vacuums or washes the car. The parish, Antoniazzi believes, is affected by what Brazilians see in the mass media, bringing the parishes toward emotional expression and experience to match in a general way what they receive from television. He believes that change may occur in that direction, but that only some parishes and priests have changed toward a performance style.

The solid place the CCR has in Brazil is indicated by its two television enterprises, Rede Brasil Cristão (Christian Brazil Network) and Redevida (Life Network). Behind Rede Brasil, the first of the Charismatic TV efforts, lies the strong personality of Padre Eduardo Dougherty, a New Orleans Province Jesuit. He represents a generation of Catholic Charismatics before Padre Marcelo. Dougherty went to Brazil in 1966 as a Jesuit student. He then went to Canada for further studies, heard about the Charismatic Renewal there, and had a Pentecostal experience in March 1969. He began giving priests retreats in Brazil in 1971. Harold Rahm, another New Orleans Jesuit, began slightly before Dougherty to introduce Catholic Charismatic Renewal to Brazil. Dougherty carried his initial efforts much further to become a major figure in Brazil. By 1983 he was producing a weekly Charismatic TV show called *We Announce Jesus*. Then he centered his efforts on Channel 53 and its satellite and UHF networks that extended in a limited way through much of Brazil. Century Twenty-one, his production studios in Valinhos, outside Campinas, began exporting TV programs to other countries.

One of the major concerns of Charismatics, especially families, is the maintenance of Christian values in secular society. These efforts in television and other media are aimed at helping people become more deeply Christian. Estimates of the amount of Charismatic programming on Redevida run from 60 to 80 percent. The primary target audience is the "Charismatic" type, middle-class, with no advertising for alcohol, tobacco, or other products not in line with Christian family life.

Life for many Charismatics is lived out in small communities. It is there, along with the larger parish church, that conversions are fostered, life-changing decisions are supported, pneumatic gifts are received, and God is praised. These communities are sometimes called prayer groups, but this description is too mild for the intense religious life experienced in the communities that, for many, have become extended homes. Without the communities, Charismatic Renewal would not exist. CCR, at heart, is not a mass following of Father Marcelo; it is life lived out in a neighborhood, with community and parish as its pillars of participation and support for weakness amid alienating stimuli (temptations). Conversion, conceived as a lifelong process of adhering to the precepts of God with increasing love and devotion, involves daily discipline and vigilance. For Catholics, participation in the sacraments, centered in the Mass, is a principal source of strength. The community itself is seen as a space through which the Holy Spirit acts. This is roughly similar to an American Quaker understanding of the action of God through a group.

Erosion of Opposition and Grassroots Synthesis

For some time liberation theologians and prominent religious journals in Latin America largely ignored the Catholic Charismatic Renewal, holding it as beneath the dignity of serious theological investigation. A change occurred in 2000 when Clovodis Boff (Leonardo Boff's brother), a major and highly respected Brazilian theologian, wrote with appreciation of the Charismatic movement.[27] With millions of Brazilian members and still growing, the movement had not only gained numerical importance but acceptance or tolerance from the majority of bishops. This represents an erosion of the caution the Brazilian Bishops Conference expressed in 1994 when it viewed the Charismatic movement with "serious reservations."[28]

One can thus better understand that when Padre Marcelo is seen performing at large public gatherings, his bishop is often present as a sign of approbation. The Charismatic Renewal now appears as the chosen instrument of a large number of conservative bishops to turn the Brazilian church away from what they view as excessive and damaging activism.

Even Leonardo Boff can picture the Charismatic Renewal becoming "a singular expression of Christianity in the Twenty-First Century."[29] However, many Catholic leaders remain adamantly opposed to the Charismatic movement, including what they regard as fostering immature psychological dependencies. While some, as ecumenist Jorge Atilio Silva Iulianetta, would like to see good on both sides, another religious intellectual, Pedro Ribeiro da Oliveira, views the conflict as a war of titans. As a thinker favoring dialectical analysis in appositional terms, Ribeiro sees CEBs and the Charismatic Renewal as dialectical *contradictions*. They will compete until one becomes dominant. He writes in the heavyweight *Revista Eclesiástica Brasileira:* "Probably they will coexist for some time until one of them shows greater plausibility, incorporates the other, and creates a new Catholic synthesis for the Twenty-First Century."[30]

The perceived opposition between CEBs and CCR is, in fact, being reduced in practice at the grassroots, at least in some places. Margo de Theije, an anthropologist, found in her Brazilian field studies that Catholic lay participation in the two movements overlapped and participation in one group informed the other.[31] Thus, for example, CEB members who became Charismatic considered themselves "more Catholic" than they were previously. Further, membership in the Catholic Church was integral to their identity, salvation, and loyalty.

CERIS, the respected Brazilian research organization, surveyed small communities in two major regions of Brazil and found that aspects of Theije's study were replicated, showing that the celebratory style of CCR was permeating the daily practices of CEBs through its music, fervor, and spirituality. Younger members especially were drawn to giving testimonies and prayers of adoration. This influence occurred in regions even where CCR had not established communities, presumably through television, word of mouth, and other means.

From the beginnings of the movement, at the founding of ECCLA, some participants came from CEBs and activist–social justice backgrounds and found that the CCR movement supplied for them and their collaborators a strong spiritual basis that they felt had been missing in their activism. In a word, transforming society demanded a new attitude (conversion) and a new mindset for the new structures of justice and equality to be effective. Personal renewal would help to bring societal renewal. The Dominican Missionary Team, mentioned above, carried both messages for thirty-five years with no sense of the contradiction alleged by Ribeiro da Oliveira.[32] For team members, the melding of CCR and CEBs seemed the next best step in the evolution of the Latin American church.

The growth of the CCR has had several effects. One has been a notable reinvigoration of religious practice at the grassroots. Second has been a remarkable increase in priests, seminarians, sisters, and, above all, in lay people dedicated to work in church ministries.[33] Some 1.1 million catechists served the church in 2004, a great increase over twenty years. These increases cannot be only attributed to CCR, but no one denies that CCR and other revitalization movements have had a positive impact on the Catholic Church's workforce. Third, CCR has reinforced Catholic identity and adherence to the church. Further, Charismatics typically respond to questioners by saying not only that they are Catholics but that they are happy in the church. Fourth, a distinctive feature of the Latin American church has been the high level of confidence in the church, shown in various polls, over time and across different countries. The church has the highest level of confidence of any institution in the region.[34] One could argue plausibly that satisfying spiritual needs and providing community, as CCR does, contributes to this confidence.

Fifth, Charismatics are re-creating aspects of popular culture. They, like Evangelicals, see themselves as *contra mundum* (while enjoying a middle-class and moderately consumeristic lifestyle). They de-emphasize drinking and life-in-the-streets machismo and support the rule of law and obedience to authority. Their songs and dance are infectious and have entered mainstream entertainment. They offer alternatives to promiscuous sexual behavior and the easy contracting of HIV-AIDs, and they offer support for youth persons who desire to remain celibate until marriage.[35] Sixth, Charismatics tend to be more generous than other Catholics in contributing economic support to the church. They may represent a turning point in the troublesome issue of under-funding of the Latin American church. Through centuries of custom, ordinary Latin Catholics have not been generous but have expected either the state or the rich to supply most of the capital for constructing and keeping up buildings and supporting the church's workforce. Without foreign aid in the past, as from Catholic sources in Europe and North America, the Catholic Church, at least in poorer countries, would be in dire straits.

Lastly, Charismatics are missionaries; they want to make converts. They go door to door to do that. This style differs from the majority of Catholics who do not go door to door to make converts and do not have a proselytizing edge. Charismatics use the best means they can afford, as television to reach millions, and excellent sound systems for street preaching. Thus, more than most other lay renewal movements, Charismatic Catholics use aggressive tactics to meet the challengers from other religions. They also become foreign missionaries themselves; perhaps some five thousand lay people, priests, and sisters have left Latin America as missionaries to other countries. This may be the crowning touch of the movement.

Conclusion

The Catholic Charismatic Renewal has become a major sector within the movements dedicated to the renewal of the Catholic Church in Latin

America. It contributes to revitalization by emphasizing a deeper spiritual life and a greater bonding among Catholics through small communities. It has also fostered this-worldly safeguards of more dedicated moral and spiritual life through the intentional communities, service within the church, and concern for the welfare of neighborhoods. Charismatic Catholics have stressed personal conversion as the door to entry into the movement, encouraged openness to the gifts of the Holy Spirit, and offered life within a community.

What emerges from a careful review of the history of the CCR is that the movement displays a largely spontaneous process, driven by the conversion experiences of key missionaries and other individuals. Furthermore, the movement has taken varying periods of time to be accepted and incorporated into the institutional church, depending on the local context and church politics. This history shows not only the complexity of conversion, but also the weakness of views that treat churches strictly as if they were economic firms, with top-down policies directing growth and innovation. Indeed, the institutional church generally frowned upon the CCR for quite some time despite its rapid growth in popularity. The growth of the movement was less of an innovation by a monopolistic institutional religious supplier than a spontaneous reaction on the part of key individuals and missionaries to events and practices that were simultaneously sparking the growth of Pentecostalism.

Finally, much like Pentecostalism, the effects of the growth of the CCR are not easily characterized into traditional political categories. As the movement increasingly gains acceptance among the episcopate, is it simultaneously permeating religious practice within traditionally activist CEBs. Furthermore, many of the changes in discourse, lifestyle, and local participation outlined by Timothy Steigenga (chapter 13), Jill Wightman (chapter 12), and Christine Kovic (chapter 10) among Pentecostals and the pentecostalized are also prevalent within the Charismatic movement. The most critical long-term effects of the movement both within the Catholic Church and across society are still underway, taking place in individual lives and small communities across the Americas.

NOTES

1. In neighboring El Salvador, Archbishop Oscar Romero had been gunned down for his commitment to human rights.

2. The following historical account is based on numerous interviews and observations in South and Central America and Mexico from 1969 to the present.

3. Yves Congar, *I Believe in the Holy Spirit* (New York: Seabury, 1983), 198, quoting Kevin Ranaghan and Dorothy Ranaghan, *Catholic Pentecostals* (New York: Paulist, 1969), 148ff.

4. Donald Gelpi, *dialog: Journal of Theology* 41, no. 1 (spring 2002): 32.

5. John Paul II, *Ecclesia in America* (Vatican City, online at www.vatican.va), chap. 3, "Caminos de Conversión," no. 28.

6. The five distinctive features given are an expansion of T. Paul Thigpen's "Catholic Charismatic Renewal," in *International Dictionary of Pentecostal and Charismatic Movements*, rev. ed., ed. Stanley Burgess (Grand Rapids, MI: Zondervan, 2003), 465–466.

7. See, for example, Congar, *I Believe in the Holy Spirit*, vol. 2.

8. Donald Gelpi, *Charism and Sacrament* (New York: Paulist, 1976), 90.

9. Henri Gooren, chapter 3 in this volume.

10. See chapter 3, by Henri Gooren, for a more complete explanation of Brouwer's findings.

11. Statistics posted by *International Center for Catholic Charismatic Renewal* at www.iccrs.org.

12. Gelpi, *Charism and Sacrament*, 32.

13. The author has published historical accounts of church renewal, especially in *Crisis and Change: The Church in Latin America Today* (Maryknoll, NY: Orbis, 1985).

14. Brazilian Bishops Conference, "Basic Christian Communities (1982)," in *The Path from Puebla: Significant Documents of the Latin American Bishops since 1979*, ed. Edward L. Cleary (Washington, DC: National Conference of Catholic Bishops, 1988), 44.

15. The account here follows Burgess, *International Dictionary of Pentecostal and Charismatic Movements*, 955 and passim. However, one should note that many authors cite the pneuma (speaking in tongues, baptism in the spirit) events at Azuza Street Church in Los Angeles from 1906 to 1913 as the beginning of the Pentecostal movement in North America.

16. See Stanley Burgess in *International Dictionary*, ed. Burgess, 928.

17. Jack Hayford and David Moore, *The Charismatic Century: The Enduring Impact of the Azuza Street Revival* (New York: Warner, 2006).

18. Thigpen, "Catholic Charismatic Renewal."

19. See Gelpi, *Charism and Sacrament*, 150–151.

20. Their conversion histories are recounted in Daniel Roach and Gugui Roda da Sauto, *Cris y Daniel: Principios de La Mansión* (Santa Cruz, Bolivia: n.p., 2003).

21. Notes from the meeting supplied by Francis MacNutt.

22. Clovodis Boff, "Carismáticos e libertadores na Igreja," *Revista Eclesiástica Brasileira* 60, no. 237 (March 2000): 36–53.

23. English version in Cleary, *The Path from Puebla*, 67–71.

24. The closest counterpart in the United States is John Michael Talbot, a lay Franciscan whose concerts and CDs are widely popular.

25. Bruno Weis, "O bem o a banal," *IstoE*, January 5, 2000, no. 1579.

26. Albert Antoniazzi, "As transformaões e o futuro da paroquia," *Jornal de Opináo*, March 19–25, 2001, 6–7.

27. C. Boff, "Carismáticos," 36–53.

28. National Conference of Brazilian Bishops, *Orientações Pastorais sobre o CCR* (Brasilia: Conferencia Nacional dos Bispos do Brasil, 1994).

29. Note also his profound reservations in Leonardo Boff, *Etica da vida* (Brasilia: Letra-viva, 1999), 168–169 and 184–189.

30. Pedro A. Ribeiro de Oliveira, "O Catolicismo: De CEBs à Renovação Carismática," *Revista Brasileira Eclesiástica* 59 (December 1999): 823–835.

31. Margo de Theije, "CEBs and Catholic Charismatics in Brazil," in *Latin American Religion in Motion*, ed. Christian Smith and Joshua Prokopy (New York: Routledge, 1999), 111–124.

32. See reflections in Ralph Rogawski, *History of Dominican Missionary Preaching Team* (Austin, TX: n.p., 2001).

33. Despite an overall increase in sisters in 2004, some countries had notable declines.

34. See yearly polls by Latinobarómetro, www.latinobarómetro.org.

35. This is in contrast to Lauren Winner's op-ed piece, "Saving Grace," which argues that communities in the United States failed to support teenagers' vows to remain celibate. *New York Times*, May 19, 2006.

9

Conversion to Native Spirituality in the Andes

From Corpus Christi to Inti Raymi

RACHEL CORR

In 1991 I was interviewing "Pablo," an indigenous man from highland Ecuador who had grown up poor and illiterate, took night classes with Catholic nuns to learn to read and write, had converted to Evangelical Christianity, and was now a father of two and sold traditional weavings and farmed. Pablo allowed me to record his life history; he taught me some Quichua and told me about how shamans cure people and how believing in God and not being fearful can protect one from the phantoms that lurk in abandoned places. In return I introduced Pablo to "Diego," a man from another region of Ecuador who was an advocate for indigenous cultural and political movements. Diego had purchased several weavings from Pablo, and, in a typical move to solidify social networks, Pablo used the *compadrazgo* system and asked Diego to become the godfather of one of his children. Diego replied that he did not believe in church baptisms, that he would do the baptism but it would have to be at a spring or waterfall or some sacred natural place. Pablo looked confused. He later told me how strange he found it that someone would do a baptism at such a place rather than in a church. Today, such a suggestion in an indigenous Andean town might not seem so strange.

Here we have an indigenous man relying on a traditional indigenous practice in order to ritualize his relationship with an outsider, and the outsider views the practice as a Christian imposition on indigenous religion. The system of forming "co-parenthood" bonds by selecting godparents developed around the Catholic sacrament of baptism, but anthropologists often argue that compadrazgo should not be considered a Spanish institution.

Indigenous people have made the compadrazgo system their own way of extending social networks with other indigenous people, with mestizos, and with foreigners. Furthermore, indigenous people choose godparents not only for Catholic sacraments, but for Andean rituals such as the first hair cutting or for cutting the baby's umbilical cord. The compadrazgo system serves as an example of how indigenous people appropriated and reworked colonial Catholic practices within their own traditions. No wonder, then, that Pablo was confused when he relied on this time-honored indigenous tradition to expand his relationship with his new friend. The idea of performing such a rite at a spring was unheard of to Pablo, but indicates an increasing trend toward practices that are perceived to represent autochthonous Andean spirituality.

In this chapter I present native Andean spirituality as one choice in the religious arena of alternatives to traditional Catholicism for indigenous people in the Andes. I analyze the discourse and organized religious activities of indigenous intellectuals who study and reflect on what it means to be indigenous in a globalized world. Neonative spirituality involves a self-conscious, reflexive discussion of indigenous cosmology based on intellectual exchanges with other native peoples and readings about pre-Columbian religion in the Andes. New theoretical approaches to conversion provide analytical tools for understanding religious transformations among Andean indigenous people. The approaches to conversion illustrated in the chapters in this volume and in the book *The Anthropology of Religious Conversion*, edited by Andrew Buckser and Stephen D. Glazier, focus on conversion as an ongoing process and show that converts often accept aspects of more than one church or sect rather than making a clean break from one religious affiliation for total immersion in another. A significant aspect of new approaches to conversion is the relationship between individual consciousness and social transformations. The social context in which I analyze conversion to native spirituality is one of increasing social movements and political organizations based on identity; one in which indigenous people proclaim pride in their unique cultural heritage, a heritage that connects them in time to a pre-Columbian (pre-Christian) past and in space to all native peoples of the Americas. The case of Andean neonative spirituality is best understood through new theoretical approaches to conversion in that (1) the process is one of continuous transformation rather than a sudden and definite break from an old religion and (2) there is not an organized religion to which people are converting, but rather a change in attitudes, discourse, and practice. As people move away from (but do not completely abandon) traditional, syncretic, colonial-style "folk" Catholicism, they are not only converting to Protestantism or new forms of Catholicism. Any study of what people are converting to must include the "passage" toward native spirituality.[1]

Background

Indigenous Latin Americans who are disillusioned with traditional Catholicism have a choice of churches and religious movements they can join if they find them spiritually fulfilling. Some convert to Protestantism. Others turn to Liberation Theology or Christian Base Communities.[2] Some others are turning to a spirituality based on indigenous identity. This spirituality, which emphasizes autochthonous rituals and practices, may be part of an organized, official effort, such as the Catholic Church's theology of inculturation. Alternatively, it may be an individual, self-motivated search for a connection with one's indigenous heritage. In this chapter I draw on examples from indigenous people in Ecuador (the Salasacans and Otavaleños) and Bolivia (the Aymara) to examine this new embrace of native Andean spirituality as a type of conversion and as one choice among several for those who want an alternative to colonial-style Catholicism. In addition to the transformation in religious discourse, I use three examples of ritual practice in the Andes that reflect changes in native spirituality. The first example is the appointment of festival sponsors that I witnessed in Salasaca, Ecuador, in 1998. The second is the pilgrimage to a sacred tree in Otavalo, Ecuador, as described by anthropologist Michelle Wibbelsman. The final example is a coca divination workshop led by an Aymara catechist in Bolivia, as described by Andrew Orta. I use these examples to show that changes in religious discourse can affect changes in religious practice; that is, indigenous people do not just espouse a pride in native Andean identity, but are implementing innovations in religious rituals to express that identity.

Admittedly, I deal with a very small sample of indigenous people in my discussion, and I borrow ethnographic data from anthropologists whose conclusions about native spirituality may be different from my own. Still, in a discussion of religious transformations it is important to emphasize that, as people move away from syncretic, colonial Catholicism, they are not only joining new Christian churches, but also taking up the study of the nature of Andean cosmovision and engaging in intellectual exchanges with other indigenous people. I do not wish to engage in a discussion of identity politics,[3] or to pick out invented, constructed traditions from "authentic" ones, but rather to (1) study which specific aspects of native spirituality are being highlighted and (2) examine how the discourse and practice of cultural revival differs from traditions of previous generations. The information in this chapter, like all ethnographic projects, is a snapshot in time. I cannot predict how much influence native intellectuals and political activists will have on the spirituality of indigenous people, but I can look at the changes in discourse I have witnessed in my own work in Salasaca, Ecuador, and compare my observations to the observations of other anthropologists working in the Andes.

During the past three decades indigenous people have made their voices heard as active agents in defining themselves rather than being defined by others. Social movements based on identity have superseded traditional class-based movements.[4] For indigenous people in Latin America, part of this process involves defining one's cultural identity against five hundred years of Western cultural imperialism. In many parts of the Andes, the process of cultural valorization was fostered by Catholic priests who promoted the study of native culture and spirituality. In his work on the Bolivian Aymara, Andrew Orta notes the conversion experienced by foreign priests, who began to sense a connection to native cultural practices.[5] In the post–Vatican II Andes, there were several members of the clergy who promoted the intellectual study of native culture and spirituality, and this led to the growth of native intellectuals and *teología india*.[6] While the process of self-reflexive study of indigenous spirituality started earlier in some parts of the Andes, the past twenty years have been a time of increasing intellectual discussion, on the part of indigenous peoples, of native Andean spirituality. This transformation is manifest in changes in discourse, the renaming of festivals, an increase in the number of native anthropologists and catechists, and the creation of educational institutions, cultural organizations, and organized rituals.

Some indigenous activists view Catholicism as a foreign imposition,[7] while others value the inclusion of Jesus Christ along with Incaic deities. Ironically, the emphasis on "tradition" sometimes excludes elements of folk Catholicism, even if these syncretic Catholic practices were part of the traditions of the elders. Leaders who embrace neonative spirituality try to emphasize what they feel are the authentic, autochthonous elements of native Andean religion, based partly on local tradition and lived experience and partly on what they have read about the Incas and other Andean indigenous societies. In other words, the "return" or "rescue" of the old religion is based on an invented collective memory taken from local practices and lived experience, books, and the popular imagination. Throughout this chapter I use the term "neonative spirituality," not because the beliefs and practices are entirely new, but because the consciousness and self-reflection that is taking place among indigenous intellectuals is part of recent social and political transformations that emphasize indigenous culture and contrast that culture against Western culture. It is important to note, however, that indigenous Ecuadorians have always incorporated outside elements into local cultural practices, so adoption of pan-Andean or Amazonian or North American symbols is not entirely new.[8] In fact, indigenous intellectuals emphasize the value of *intercultural* education and ritual performances; that is, they acknowledge that they combine local tradition with elements from various cultural practices.

Early Colonial Incaism and Resistance

Religious conversion is a personal, transformative experience, but it must be understood within a sociopolitical context. The idealization of the Incas that we are witnessing today in the Andes is not entirely new. Native Andeans began to idealize the Incas during the colonial period, when indigenous people "labored under the increasingly heavy demands and oppression of the Spanish, and the reign of the Inca came to be looked upon by more and more sectors of indigenous society with increasing sympathy and nostalgia. Negative memories of the Inca conquest faded and the reign of the Inca began to be seen as a period of benevolent and just rule."[9] Throughout the colonial period, this yearning for the return of idealized Inca rule was manifest through rebellions and religious movements based on millenarian beliefs. One of the most notable of these is the early colonial Taqui Onqoy movement, in which indigenous prophets declared that indigenous people should reject European food, clothing, and priests and return to worshipping the Andean sacred shrines called *huacas*.[10] Other anti-colonial religious movements emerged in different parts of Peru in the 1770s and 1780s. Such nativistic or revivalist movements are a common phenomenon during the early stages of foreign domination.

The romantic views of the Incas continued throughout the colonial and post-colonial periods as indigenous people suffered exploitation; they were marginalized from nationalist goals of "progress" and "modernity" and suffered from racist stereotypes. In Ecuador, for instance, the image of the Indian was one of a dirty, backwards, ignorant person who was holding up progress and keeping Ecuador from joining in the progressive modernity of (white) first-world nations.[11] Modern Ecuador could embrace its "indianness" only as a pocket of quaint folkloric performances or as the relic of a glorious but bygone era of the powerful Inca Empire.[12] Ecuadorians are proud of the Inca heritage, so it is no wonder that modern-day indigenous people, seen as impoverished and culturally corrupted, would not only embrace that glorious past, but also come to identify themselves as the direct inheritors of Incaic culture. The current "conversion" which I describe for the Andes involves identification with Inca religion and an appropriation of Incaic religious terms and symbols as part of a larger process of identity politics. One organization that uses symbols that refer to the Incas is the Confederation of Indigenous Nationalities of Ecuador (CONAIE). As Lynn Meisch notes, "It is ironic that CONAIE, the national indigenous federation composed of organizations representing indígenas from the Sierra, Oriente (Amazon basin) and coast, has adopted as its flag the rainbow banner of Tahuantinsuyu, the Inca

Empire. In the century before the Spanish conquest, Ecuador's aboriginal population suffered an invasion and conquest by the Incas of Cuzco (Peru). Resistance to the Incas in the north was so fierce that a lake near Ibarra in Imbabura Province bears the name Yaguar Cocha (Blood Lake) because its waters were stained red by the bodies of slain Ecuadorian warriors tossed in by the Incas."[13] We are witnessing the selective exclusion of the narrative of Incaic slaughter of native Ecuadorians in order to embrace a narrative of a unified, idealized Inca past, one that offers an alternative identity in a globalized world that is encompassed by Western cultural imperialism. It is not that CONAIE denies the native resistance to the invading Incas; rather, in the context of indigenous political movements, Incaic symbols serve to unify and mobilize people on the basis of cultural identity.

Anthony F. C. Wallace defined a revitalization movement as a "deliberate, organized and conscious effort by some members of a society to construct a more satisfying culture."[14] Revitalization movements are characterized by rapid, sudden changes in culture and often involve mass followings of charismatic leaders. While the neonative spirituality I describe here does not follow the classic pattern of a revitalization movement, it does share characteristics with revitalization movements and is definitely a deliberate and organized attempt "to construct a more satisfying culture." Among the different types of revitalization movements are nativistic movements, which involve a rejection of alien customs, and revivalist religious movements, which aim to revive past cultural and religious traditions. Many societies undergoing religious transformation show elements of both. The conversion to native spirituality in the Andes is not a conversion to any unified religious movement, but rather takes place individually or in small local groups or in inculturationist branches of the Catholic Church. Symbols of Native American spirituality, whether Andean, Amazonian, or North American, are the basis for the type of nativism and revivalism taking place in the Andes. As indigenous people strive to create a more satisfying society, they can draw on nativistic principles of harmony with nature and communal values in opposition to the individualism and materialism endemic to neoliberal policies and global capitalism. They can "revive" religious traditions that provide an alternative model of culture, instill a sense of pride in their ethnic identity, and offer an alternative to colonial Catholicism.

Colonial Catholicism

Native religious practices were never completely abandoned after the conquest. Instead, they were blended (or juxtaposed) in various local ways with colonial-style Catholicism. Writing of religion among the Bolivian Aymara, Orta describes colonial Catholicism as "characterized by rote knowledge of

Church doctrine, the 'superficial' performance of Catholic ritual, and the 'inauthentic' syncretic juxtaposition of indigenous and Christian practices."[15] I will use the term here (interchangeably with traditional Catholicism and syncretic Catholicism) to refer to characteristics such as petitioning saints, paying for masses for special intentions, celebrating fiestas, and beliefs in hell and purgatory. For example, a traditional practice in Salasacan Day of the Dead celebrations is to request that a Catholic priest sprinkle holy water on a list of names of deceased ancestors in order to "cool off" the hot, thirsty, souls.[16] This tradition reflects how much Andean cultural practices, such as commemorating deceased ancestors, are intertwined with powers associated with the Catholic Church.

It is precisely such notions as purgatory and hell that have caused some indigenous Ecuadorians to turn away from colonial Catholicism. Some indigenous people now interpret Catholic teachings about punishment as part of the legacy of colonial oppression. For example, Barry Lyons writes about Taita Aurelio, a catechist from Chimborazo Province, Ecuador, who was disillusioned with both colonial Catholicism and indigenous shamanism. Many indigenous people in Chimborazo have joined Evangelical churches, and others have followed Catholic liberation theology. In the traditional, colonial Catholicism of the region, the volcano Tungurahua was associated with purgatory and/or hell. In reference to beliefs in the volcano's powers, Lyons notes that Taita Aurelio "has looked for references to mountains (as animate beings) in the Bible but, having found none, said he does not believe in them. Likewise, his commitment as a catechist to liberation theology, with its notion of a loving God and its attack on what it depicts as a traditional religion of fear, has tended to undermine his belief in the fires of purgatory and hell (locally identified with Tungurahua)."[17]

Among the Quichua-speaking Napo Runa of Ecuador's eastern tropical forest, Protestants associated beliefs in purgatory with the Catholic Church's colonial exploitation of indigenous people. Michael Uzendoski describes one evangelical preacher who specifically mentioned the belief in purgatory as a way to extract money from indigenous people, who had to pay priests in order to get their deceased family members out of purgatory.[18] In both cases, the Quichua speakers of Chimborazo and Napo who were disillusioned with the colonial Catholicism of their grandparents turned to alternative Christian movements. Increasingly, though, more indigenous people are "converting" to native spirituality.

Salasacan Religiosity: Three Voices

Not all areas of the Andes are affected equally by liberation theology, inculturationist Catholicism, or Protestantism. Among the Quichua-speaking people of Salasaca in the Ecuadorian Andes, where I have been undertaking ethnographic research since 1991, syncretic Catholicism is a pervasive part of traditional cultural practices. There is an evangelical church with a small group of followers who strive to maintain their cultural traditions while not participating in activities that violate their beliefs, such as drinking and dancing at sacred places. To my knowledge, liberation theology has not been very influential. There is one Salasacan who was ordained as a priest, but he is not permanently assigned to the parish. There is one catechist, and his duties are mainly to give courses to prepare young people for the Catholic sacraments. In my experience, people do not attend Mass on a regular basis unless they are festival sponsors, in which case they are obligated to attend Mass every Sunday for the year of their sponsorship. The Salasacans I know attend Mass on festival days and for life-cycle rituals of Catholic sacraments, weddings, and funerals. However, it is important to emphasize the transient nature of participation in Catholic activities; when a priest was permanently assigned to the parish in the 1990s, he motivated the youth to actively participate in Mass, Catholic musical groups, and Easter performances. But priests get moved and reassigned, so such religious participation fluctuates.[19]

What I wish to emphasize here is the transformation in religious discourse from traditional, syncretic, colonial Catholicism to a more pan-Andean discourse that emphasizes native spirituality. Although it is only a small number of people who espouse pan-Andeanism, it is important to understand this as one type of spirituality among other alternatives to colonial Catholicism, such as Protestantism and liberation theology.

Salasacans often relate spiritual experiences to sacred places, such as mountains and crossroads, and these are connected to shamanic offerings and saints' day celebrations. Household rituals during fiestas, weddings, and funerals depend on ritual specialists who have memorized knowledge of Catholic prayers, specifically, the blessing of the Father, Son, and Holy Spirit, the Our Father, and the Hail Mary. Other rituals incorporate aspects of Catholic ritual and symbolism in unique ways. When I interviewed people about the sacred geography around them, they described the journey to the afterlife and details of the trials and punishments along the way. Descriptions of the afterlife reflect the influence of both colonial Catholic imagery and Andean sacred geographies.[20]

Pan-Andean spirituality, while not completely excluding Catholicism, focuses more on Mother Earth, Father Sun, shamanism, and the Incas. I present here the views of three different Salasacan sources on traditional religion. The first is based on my interview with an elder who is considered to be knowledgeable in local history and traditions and exemplifies the characteristics of colonial Catholicism syncretized with local sacred geography. The second is based on the writings of a political activist and exemplifies a nativistic approach. The third is from the Web site of a musical group and shows the direction that some young indigenous people are following.

Eduardo, an elder known for his knowledge of oral history, told me: "Those old people of the past, they remembered Dear Father God (Taita Dioshuadaga); they lived believing. God gave many grains, such as barley. There was a mountain they venerated; they held two fiestas on that mountain: the fiestas of Capitan and Caporales. . . . In the past, people worshipped San Buenaventura and they had lots of grains: potatoes, corn, and lentils. Those who believed put corn, or whatever grains they had, next to the saint, in order to have more grains. . . . People of the past had fiestas with all their faith in God, and they had many grains."

Another elder stated that the ancestors "had the custom of praising San Buenaventura and praying, and remembering that it is Taita Diositu (Dear Father God) who provides food for us." Both elders, who rely on oral memory rather than writing, link God (referred to using the Spanish word *Dios*) with native foods. Elder Salasacans often tell of the goodness of these natural, indigenous foods in the past and the superior strength of the old ones who ate these foods. Abundant, nutritious crops were gained by worshipping God and Catholic saints through the fiesta cycle. To this day, some Salasacans attend Mass at older churches with seeds tucked into their clothing, in order to make the seeds "hear Mass" (*misata oyachingabuj*), so that they will grow well when planted. Indigenous sponsors honor saints, God, and sacred places through the fiesta system, and they receive abundant crops and livestock in return.

In the 1990s, indigenous intellectuals in Ecuador collaborated on a project to write about the situation of indigenous people in contemporary Ecuador in their own voices. The result was a book titled *Identidades Indias en el Ecuador Contemporaneo*, and the author of the chapter on Salasaca is José Masaquiza. After telling a local legend from Salasaca, he writes: "When a family or the Salasacan community faces a calamity, the yachac (shamans) go to the wacas (sacred places) to leave their offerings and lift up their prayers to Pachacamac, the Almighty God, directing their gaze toward the South, to the camino real."[21] Later in the chapter, he describes Salasacan spirituality: "The Salasacas, like other ethnic groups, conceive of cosmic nature as the generator of life in general; that is to say that in nature is the Almighty (Dios). As such, nature and its phenomena are considered sacred, whether beneficent or malignant. Moreover, they deserve the celebration of rituals and sacrifice, which must be directed by the yachaccuna or 'shamans' of the community. These rites are celebrated at sites called wacas, which have been revealed to the anointed ones by nature and which have been preserved for millennia, from generation to generation. These sacred places constitute for indigenous people, cathedrals and temples, where one can meditate and perceive cosmic energy."[22]

While much of Masaquiza's chapter does describe very local, unique aspects of Salasacan culture, he has read widely about the history, culture, and religious beliefs of other Andean indigenous people, and he places Salasacan spirituality within the context of other Andean cultures. Therefore, he uses terms such as *yachac* (shaman), *ayllu* (family), and *waca* (sacred place), which are commonly used in the Andes, rather than the local Salasacan terms. Furthermore, he uses the term "Pachacamac" alternately with Almighty, rather than the Tayta Dios (Father God) specifically mentioned by the elders of Salasaca. For Masaquiza, the Catholic nuns who set up a mission in his community (in 1945), as well as the evangelical missionaries, are trying to impose a foreign, Western ideology on the people, and they have had little success. Thus his writings reflect a nativistic discourse. Of course, he also writes about the syncretic religious festivals, but his writing indicates that he is most interested in studying beliefs and practices that connect with pan-Andeanism.

A final voice in the descriptions of Salasacan spirituality comes from the Web site of a young group of indigenous musicians: "Until nowadays, the Catholic Church keeps forcing the native population to accept the catholic faith. The influence of the church though is presently going back in Ecuador as it does in many places of the world. At the same time it becomes clear that a substantial part of the pre-Columbian cosmovision lives on and keeps influencing the lives of the native population greatly."[23]

Notice the recognition of the process of native revivalism as the Web site states that the Catholic religion is losing influence, while pre-Columbian "cosmovision" is alive and well. One can view this revival as a similar but slow version of nativistic or revivalist movements that have occurred historically under conditions of foreign domination. Among the celebrations mentioned on the Web site is that of Inti Raymi, "a celebration in honor of the Inka sun god Inti."[24] Elder Salasacans refer to this festival (Corpus Christi) as *Corpus pishta*, but younger people are increasingly using the Inca name Inti Raymi to refer to this celebration, which is held around the time of the summer solstice. Inti Raymi was the Inca solstice celebration, and during the colonial period it coincided with the Catholic celebrations of Corpus Christi and the feast day of St. John. Celebrations from June through August refer to the fiestas of San Juan and San Pedro in northern Ecuador and the fiesta of Corpus Christi in the central and southern Ecuadorian Andes. The change in name from Corpus Christi (or San Juan) to Inti Raymi took place throughout highland Ecuador. In an article on the symbolic significance of indigenous political movements, Pablo Davolos discusses the reinvention of this celebration: "Before it was the festival of San Juan, Corpus Christi. Now, after the indigenous uprisings, after the new relationship of power between the 'Indians' and society has emerged, it is possible to speak with greater freedom. A new voice emerges which gives a precise name to the most important event in the life of the indigenous peoples, now it is Inti Raymi, the Festival of the Sun. A political appropriation of a symbolic event that shows the nature of this profound transformation that the indigenous movement has experienced in Ecuador."[25]

In this case, the conversion is from the Catholic feast days to the Incaic summer solstice. Michelle Wibbelsman, who has undertaken extensive ethnographic research in the Otavalo region of Ecuador, points to evidence of a regional, pre-Incaic tradition of observing the solstice. Therefore, although the term "Inti Raymi" is "knowingly borrowed from Peruvian and Bolivian sources," it still refers to a local tradition of honoring the sun.[26] But it is the younger generations who use the term "Inti Raymi" and emphasize the sun, whereas older generations and those in outlying areas of Otavalo still refer to the festival as San Juan.

Changes in Ritual Practice: Salasaca

The three views of Salasacan spirituality presented above and the change in name of the fiesta show a change in the discourse about Andean spirituality. To a lesser extent, cultural revivalists are transforming traditional practices. In 1996, indigenous leaders in Salasaca instituted a change in the process for selecting festival sponsors. The traditional method, which dates to the eighteenth century, was for the Catholic priest to appoint the sponsors for the year at Mass on New Year's Day.[27] In Salasaca, men would traditionally vie for positions by bringing a food gift to the priest (or the resident nuns, the Madres Lauritas). The priest and nuns would keep a list of names of men who brought offerings and wanted to be sponsors. In 1996 political leaders in Salasaca decided that the main festival sponsor would be selected based on a competition in which candidates were asked questions about Salasacan history and culture. Many of the questions were about local place deities, but candidates were also tested on their knowledge of Catholic prayers. As one leader explained to me, knowledge of Catholic prayers is necessary for the blessing of the ceremonial food table during weddings, funerals, and fiestas. These blessings are given by older men who are specialists in Quichua oratory, but the indigenous leaders wanted to ensure that there would be knowledgeable orators around in the future, so they made memorization of prayers a requirement for becoming lead festival sponsor.

In 1998 I observed the New Year's Day Mass in which the Catholic priest appointed the festival sponsors and gave them their staffs of office, which they received and kissed. One of the political leaders then described the new selection process to those in attendance at the Mass. He read some of the questions that the candidates were asked and spoke about the importance of *rescate cultural*. Although it was indigenous political leaders who instituted the change, in the name of cultural rescue, the priest and nuns supported their efforts. The change in the process of selecting festival sponsors reflects a change from colonial Catholicism, in which the priest selected sponsors based on gifts of food, to a self-reflexive discussion of native Andean spirituality (exemplified by place deities) and local tradition, such as the syncretic Catholicism of blessing the ceremonial table. Thus the Catholic Mass on New Year's Day became the forum for transforming a colonial Catholic institution into an opportunity for promoting cultural rescue. In this case, the emphasis was on local tradition and place deities rather than pan-Andean deities like Taita Inti (Father Sun). But knowledge about local tradition was now formally recognized as part of a unique cultural heritage.

Otavalo: A Tradition of Interculturality

Otavalo is famous for its indigenous market, which draws thousands of tourists each year, and indigenous Otavaleños are traveling merchants who have spent a considerable amount of time in North America and Europe. Many Otavaleños hold university degrees, and native anthropologists from Otavalo have long been engaged in the study of their own culture and history. Michelle Wibbelsman describes Otavalan rituals as creative, innovative, multivocal social practices that connect diverse individuals to their past. Indeed, many transnational Otavaleños return home for the Inti Raymi celebrations, and some festive rituals are even organized by migrant Otavaleños from abroad.[28] Indigenous Otavaleños themselves reflect on the ability of festive rituals to bring indigenous people—from local subsistence farmers to international commercial merchants—into a shared collectivity.

According to Wibbelsman, for many years now, the Association of Imbaburan Shamans has been organizing a pilgrimage to the sacred *lechero* tree located on a mountain that overlooks a sacred lake. In 2001, the pilgrimage was organized by the shamans' association, an indigenous Catholic organization, and other cultural and educational groups. The vestment of the shamans reveals the intercultural nature of the pilgrimage. As Wibbelsman describes, the shamans drew on native Andean, Amazonian, and North American elements in choosing their attire for the occasion: "Shamans, both male and female, dressed in multicolor beads, feathers, crosses and headbands, wearing T-shirts that advertised SHAMAN in big letters across the back, and carrying lances and staffs led the pilgrimage."[29] In Quichua healers are called *yachac* (one who knows) or *jambic* (one who heals), but they are increasingly employing the non-Quichua term "shaman" to refer to themselves. In my opinion, the increasing appropriation of the term "shaman" by Ecuadorian indigenous peoples is a conscious effort to connect themselves to worldwide traditions and spirituality of native peoples.

Before starting the procession, the shamans honored the Inca general Rumiñahui, then the grandfather sun, the earth mother, and Jesus Christ. Participants were instructed to approach the lechero tree barefoot, as a sign of respect. Upon reaching the tree, the head shaman greeted the mountains surrounding the area. The lechero tree has long been a significant part of life for Otavaleños, and people have prayed at this site for years. Wibbelsman provides extensive information on the significance of this sacred tree in everyday, lived experience. According to Wibbelsman, interculturality has always been a part of indigenous life, and Otavaleño festival organizers recognize the intercultural nature of their performances. I want to suggest, though, that the shaman-led pilgrimage exemplifies the type of organized, self-reflexive religious practice of native spirituality that contributes to the collective identity of Otavaleños. Appropriation of the nonnative term "shaman," self-designated as such through the wearing of T-shirts, and the incorporation of indigenous objects from outside the Otavalo region (such as lances), reveals a step in the move toward organized religious practices that embrace native spirituality. However, Wibbelsman cautions against judging the planned event as staged. According to her, "Ritual performances elicit curiosity and attention from a variety of audiences. They often become the object of tourist attractions, cultural education lessons, municipal events, and social scientific inquiry. This does not mean, however, that rituals are staged for those purposes. This event was not advertised publicly and was conducted as a rather intimate ceremony."[30]

I interpret this event as a planned, organized religious pilgrimage based on native spirituality with new, pan-indigenous elements added. As an intercultural event, sponsored in part by an indigenous Catholic organization, it honored Jesus Christ along with the historical figure of the Inca general Rumiñahui. Although rituals are always changing and incorporating new elements in innovative ways, I believe that incorporation of pan–Native American elements and the invocation of the famous Inca Rumiñahui, combined with the local traditions of approaching the lechero tree, are emblematic of the type of religious transformations promoted by native spiritualists. Anthropologist Barbara Butler notes: "In some respects, Otavaleños may be more 'andean' than they were a century ago,"[31] and "as Otavalans became more in touch with panandean movements and sources of symbolism, Indi has taken on a greater role in the religious symbolism of Huaycopungo."[32] By no means does this indicate that the rituals are staged; to the contrary, I believe that participants in the rituals truly feel moved by their participation and that those who embrace neonative spirituality fully believe in its power. Butler states, "However invented or reimagined, ritual by its nature penetrates and projects the consciousness of the participants."[33]

Indigenous intellectuals are also contributing to a new spiritual awareness through workshops and writings, through which they present a model of the cosmos based on the world above, this world, the world within, and the other world. This model is increasingly becoming a standard through which indigenous people define their own cosmology, and it lacks colonial Catholic mappings of hell and purgatory. One institution that promotes studies of indigenous cosmology is the new Universidad Intercultural de las Nacionalidades y Pueblos Indígenas Amawtay Wasi (House of Knowledge) in Ecuador. This university was co-founded in 1989 by the Scientific Institute of Indigenous Cultures and the Confederation of Indigenous Nationalities of Ecuador. The mission is "to contribute to the promotion of human talents that priorises a harmonious relationship between the Pachamama (Mother Nature) and the Runa (Human Being) based on 'Sumak kawsanamanta sumac yachay' (to learn in wisdom and good living) as the Foundation stone in the construction of the plurinational state and an intercultural society."[34]

The university is divided into four "knowledge centers," which are associated with the elements land, air, fire, and water. At the center of this model is wisdom. According to the university's Web site, "Andean wisdom is the ancestral science and encompasses the understanding of the elders through the following Knowledge Centres." One of those centers is called Munay-Yachay, and "its challenge is to tackle ancestral cosmovision, it will promote and develop research and actions in this line."[35] This university takes an innovative, intercultural approach to knowledge, which is based on communitarian values and respect for the elders. For example, upon completion of a project students must contribute in some way to a local community, and they will be evaluated not only by university authorities, but by members of the community. Amawtay Wasi is an example of the growing exploration of indigenous culture (along with science, technology, and other areas of study) by indigenous people, and the university's organization indicates that this exploration will include intellectual exchanges about indigenous cosmovision and spirituality.

Shamans associations constitute further evidence of the increasingly organized, self-reflexive nature of native spirituality. The pilgrimage to the sacred lechero tree that Wibbelsman observed was led by the shamans' association in Imbabura. In the Ecuadorian Amazonian province of Napo, there is another shamans' association that offers training courses and certificates in shamanism. Neonative teachings on shamanism differ from traditional shamanism not only in that the practice and training of shamans is now organized, but in the emphasis on shamans as benevolent wise people who help restore balance with the cosmos. In highland communities, many shamanic rituals *do* aim to restore a balance with nature, and shamanic rituals are therapeutic. I have seen people cured of drinking and "laziness"; the shamans serve as people who have contact with the spirits and who restore human social relations and human relationships with nature. But many of the rituals are to undo harm caused by witchcraft and envy. In some Amazonian contexts, this work is risky and dangerous, as shamans are believed to send evil back to the sorcerer, they become suspects for further sorcery.[36] Shamanic knowledge is secret, shamanic rituals are done at night and in private, and shamans themselves are viewed with awe and admiration as well as suspicion. The selective representation of shamanism is no doubt influenced in part by the Western fascination with shamanism and the desire to valorize indigenous spirituality.

Inculturationist Catholicism and Aymara Spirituality

In the discussion above I noted that while neonative spirituality aims to foster appreciation for ancestral traditions, the religious discourse of the elders often reflects colonial Catholicism. For example, if we compare the quotes from the three different Salasacan sources, it is the oldest man, who is considered knowledgeable in the traditions of his community, who speaks of God (Dius) and the local patron saint. Similarly, traditions throughout the Andes are bound with Catholic feast days and saints' day celebrations. These traditions require that blessings be given over the ceremonial table with traditional food and drink: maize beer, cane alcohol, and hominy. It is elder males who are charged with giving these blessings, and the most respected of these are the ones who recite the prayers from memory. Many of these elder males are illiterate, and the prayers are Catholic prayers spoken within a Quichua oratory that frames the prayers as ancestral knowledge.[37]

The prayer-makers always remind the others that these are the traditional words of the ancestors. Orta reports a similar value among the Aymara of Bolivia, where people value a "fluency with colonially derived doctrinal knowledge that many contemporary Aymara associate with the ancestors."[38] For the Aymara, it is the inculturationist influence of Catholic missionaries that encourages a move away from colonial Catholicism and an embrace of the "authentic" Aymara spiritual practices, such as divination with coca leaves. Inculturationism seeks to find Christian values within local cultural practices: "Simply put, inculturation strives to recuperate and revalorize indigenous culture."[39] Inculturationist practices incorporate local cultural practices into the Catholic Mass. For example, inculturationist Masses in Brazil incorporate African drumming and dancing and honor historical Afro-Brazilian martyrs, such as rebellious slaves.[40] In the Andes, Catholic priests brought the theology of inculturation to indigenous communities and trained indigenous catechists. This new theology of inculturation meant that native Aymara catechists, rather than criticizing traditional practices, now sought to embrace them. Orta describes this as an individual conversion on the part of Aymara catechists: "One of the results of this new pastoral posture was a conversion on the part of Alejandro, as he came to see his catechist identity as a basis for acquiring and enacting prototypical ethnographic knowledge about the Aymara."[41] Like others who seek to understand native Andean spirituality, this Aymara catechist sought knowledge from a book written about *yatiris* (Aymara ritual specialists). Another inculturationist catechist teaches parallels between the Bible and Aymara history and culture and leads organized ritual libations of alcohol and coca leaf divination workshops during sessions with his faith group.

The Aymara ritual practices described by Orta differ from the neonative spiritual practices I described in Ecuador in that these are part of the Catholic Church policy of inculturation, and the catechist used the Bible (along with coca leaves, alcohol, and cigarettes) in his classes. But there are some similarities. One is the use of a book about Aymara culture as a source of information. Another is the selective use of certain cultural practices and not others. For example, coca divination can be seen as a pan-Aymara practice, whereas certain local household rituals may be overlooked in this inculturationist embrace of indigenous culture. Related to both of these similarities is that, while organized neonative spiritual practices are framed as the continuation of tradition, they downplay some local practices and elements of colonial Catholicism that constitute the traditions of their parents and grandparents. Finally, in both Ecuador and Bolivia, neonative spiritual practices use symbols that are at once religious and political. That is, certain modern and historical figures (shamans, the Inca general Rumiñahui in Ecuador or Tupac Amaru in Bolivia), deities (the Sun god and the Earth Mother), and practices (coca divination in Bolivia) become emblematic of cultural and political resistance to Western hegemony. This Western hegemony spans from the Spanish conquest and attempted destruction of indigenous religion and culture to the current Free Trade negotiations taking place between the United States and Andean governments. As Orta states, "Prototypical exchange practices such as ayni, highly formalized ritual actions such as the waxt'a (burnt offerings to place deities), the local authority of yatiris, the use of coca and alcohol, and perhaps above all the socio-ritual solidarity of the ayllu are routinely deployed by pastoral workers as metonyms for an authentic shared Aymaraness. A number of these traits are already politically charged, having been taken up in recent decades by neotraditionalist political movements and as points of conflict in community-level religious disputes arising from both Protestant and neo-Catholic evangelization."[42]

The conversion in discourse is taking place among indigenous people throughout the Andes. Orin Starn writes about the case of Peru and what he calls "Andeanism," a term he uses to criticize Western anthropologists' romantic descriptions of indigenous people as isolated populations with a pre-Columbian mentality. Starn acknowledges that in Peru indigenous people themselves are appropriating such a romanticized discourse: "an idealized sense of Inca lineage, harmony with nature, and communal values has filtered across the mountains through schoolbooks, radio, TV, and political speeches." Starn argues that rural Andeans now appropriate such idealized concepts "to articulate political identities and answer contemporary needs."[43] The conversion to native spirituality in the Andes indicates that one of those contemporary needs is to hold religious beliefs that correspond to one's sense of ethnic identity.

Like all studies of conversion, neonative spirituality in the Andes must be understood within sociopolitical contexts. Certain symbols of indigenous culture are emblematic of a unique cultural heritage and an enduring indigenous identity that has not succumbed to the pressures of nationalist hegemony or Western cultural imperialism. The politically charged nature of the symbols and practices does not make them any less real to indigenous people; ritual and symbols "establish powerful, pervasive, and long-lasting moods and motivations" in people, as Clifford Geertz explained in his definition of religion.[44] They indicate the direction that some indigenous people are taking in terms of religious choices.

Conclusion

These examples indicate changes in discourse and some initial transformations of Andean practices as seen in the appointment of festival sponsors in Salasaca, the collective pilgrimage to the lechero tree in Otavalo, and the Aymara catechist's divination with coca leaves in Bolivia. There are also new organizations to promote the study of indigenous culture and spirituality; these include experimental schools in Salasaca, shamans' associations, and a new university in Ecuador.[45] These forums promote a particular construction of indigenous culture, including indigenous spirituality. But does participation in these forums qualify as a religious conversion? That depends on the experience of the individual and on how one defines conversion. For some, their experience is articulated in a conversion narrative in which the individual left an on old life, in which he or she was lost or blind, for a new life in which one is enlightened.[46] For example, the Aymara catechist who led the coca divination workshop, reflecting on his pre-inculturationist years, said, "I remember as a young catechist telling the awkis [elders] to stop with their costumbres, that the culture was ruining them. I don't know who

I was then."[47] Thus we have the old life/new life theme of conversion and an indication that this indigenous catechist has found his true identity.

For some, perhaps, it was a particular experience in the dominant religion that caused disillusionment and, therefore, a turn to an alternative based on their ancestors' traditions. José Masaquiza describes an experience he had at the age of nine. The Catholic nuns from his school held him in the school yard and, in front of all the students, cut his long hair, while saying disparaging remarks. Masaquiza describes this as a humiliating experience and sees it as an affront to indigenous culture. He once told me, "There is nothing in *our* culture that says that men shouldn't have long hair."[48] He could embrace his membership in indigenous culture as a proud heritage, a part of his identity. And religious rituals and beliefs are part of that heritage. But I don't believe that most neonative spiritualists have had such clean breaks in their pasts. Rather, the intellectual study and promotion of native Andean spirituality is part of identity formation in modern Andean societies, and those societies are part of a transnational world. Indigenous intellectuals have a genuine interest in indigenous Andean history and culture. New theoretical approaches to religious conversion that view it as a continuous process of movement between religious affiliations, rather than a clean, sudden break from older religious affiliations, facilitate our understanding of the current cultural practices we are witnessing in some parts of the Andes. These are not the colonial Catholic, syncretic rituals of the elders, but rather an intercultural blend of local tradition, Incaic symbols, and non-local native traditions from Amazonia and North America. Indigenous people who want an alternative to colonial Catholicism or Protestantism can seek out spiritual fulfillment and indigenous identity in neonative spirituality.

These rituals and discourse are not inauthentic, rather they are self-reflexive performances influenced by native intellectuals. Just as major world religions offer courses and workshops to discuss theological concepts of the faith, so native intellectuals are reflecting on the meanings of native Andean spirituality. These intellectuals base their writings on their own lived experience as well as books and articles. Still, such transformations are in a flux: the Salasacan organizers of the competition for festival sponsors promoted the discourse and practice of cultural rescue. However, when their terms of office ended, the new political leaders were not as interested in organizing the event, and the selection process has reverted back to the nuns.

Even if not many indigenous people participate in the organized neonative rituals, it is possible that more young people perceive these rituals as their true religion; and, consequently, some, such as the Salasacan folkloric musical group, will view Christian churches as a foreign ideology. Therefore, changes in native Andean spirituality must be considered in discussions of conversion in Latin America, not only because it is one alternative choice in the religious marketplace, but because it is highly compatible with social and political movements based on ethnic identity. Although many native spirituality movements are either part of the Catholic Church or acknowledge the importance of Christianity, the new emphasis puts pre-Columbian symbols at the forefront of indigenous cosmology.

The chapters in this volume offer new insights into the analysis of religious conversion in Latin America, from social network analysis (David Smilde) and life-cycle approaches (Henri Gooren) to market-oriented approaches (Andrew Chesnut). All acknowledge, though, that individual conversion must be understood within the wider social context in which it occurs. In the Andes, this social context is one of identity politics, or "decolonization," as indigenous people assert their cultural and political rights. Although this is not a religious movement in any unified sense, the discourse and practice of native spirituality seem to be increasing, independently, in different parts of the Andes. Proponents of some of these practices aim to "recuperate" the past and "rescue" indigenous culture. The exchange between Pablo and Diego that I described at the beginning of this chapter exemplifies the shift from colonial Catholic indigenous traditions to native spirituality. Pablo relied on a traditional method of ritualizing a social relationship through the sacrament of baptism; Diego attempted to move ritual out of the Catholic Church and into an Andean sacred place. The religious arm of identity politics does not focus on the colonial Catholic past of hell, purgatory, and offerings to saints, but on the glorified Incaic past embraced by national governments in the Andes. This is not the past of the grandparents or great grandparents of indigenous youth, but the past of a proud civilization that worshipped the sun and moon, or a past based on spiritual unity with other native peoples of the Americas. It is likely that, with increased study of indigenous spirituality through institutions such as Amawtay Wasi in Ecuador, indigenous intellectuals will increase their study of local rituals along with intercultural practices. As people move away from traditional Catholicism in Latin America, and as identity politics is increasingly becoming the basis for social movements, native spirituality is an attractive alternative for a new generation of Andean youth.

In our ongoing attempts to understand religious change in Latin America, we must acknowledge the study of native spirituality as a conscious choice for indigenous people seeking a more satisfying spiritual life. My intention in this chapter has been to examine which aspects of native Andean spirituality people are highlighting in order to understand religious transformation in the Andes; that is, in addition to conversion to Protestant religions or new Catholic movements, some Andeans are reflecting on the meanings of native Andean spirituality. While it is impossible to predict the future trajectory of the revival of native spirituality as a religious movement, I suggest that theological introspection on native religious concepts and practices will increase.

NOTES

I would like to thank Tim Steigenga and Father Edward Cleary for their assistance with this chapter. I also thank Jacqueline Fewkes and Michelle Wibbelsman for critical comments on an earlier draft.

1. For the concept of conversion as a "passage" see Alejandro Frigerio, this volume; and Diane Austin-Broos, "The Anthropology of Conversion: An Introduction" in *The Anthropology of Religious Conversion*, ed. Andrew Buckser and Stephen D. Glazier (Lanham: Rowman & Littlefield, 2003).

2. The Catholic Church has accepted several changes in practice since Vatican II, changes which have led to liberation theology, Christian Base Communities, inculturation, and indigenous theology. These recent Catholic movements have influenced indigenous participation in Catholic faith groups throughout Latin American indigenous communities. See Edward L. Cleary and Timothy Steigenga, "Resurgent Voices: Indians, Politics, and Religion in Latin America," in *Resurgent Voices in Latin America: Indigenous Peoples, Political Mobilization, and Religious Change*, ed. Cleary and Steigenga (New Brunswick: Rutgers University Press, 2004), 1–24.

3. For an in-depth discussion of the history and debates of academic theories on identity politics, see Charles Hale, "Cultural Politics of Identity in Latin America," *Annual Review of Anthropology* 26 (1997): 567–590.

4. See Hale, "Cultural Politics," for a general discussion of this history in Latin America. For a discussion of this history in Ecuador, see Melina H. Selverston, "The Politics of Culture: Indigenous Peoples and the State in Ecuador," *Indigenous Peoples and Democracy in Latin America*, ed. Donna Lee Van Cott (New York: St. Martin's Press, 1994), 131–152; Alison Brysk "From Civil Society to Collective Action: The Politics of Religion in Ecuador," in *Resurgent Voices*, ed. Cleary and Steigenga, 25–42.

5. Andrew Orta, *Catechizing Culture: Missionaries, Aymara, and the "New Evangelization,"* (New York: Columbia University Press, 2004).

6. See Edward Cleary, "New Voice in Religion and Politics in Bolivia and Peru," in *Resurgent Voices*, ed. Cleary and Steigenga, 43–64; Stephen P. Judd, "The Indigenous Theology Movement in Latin America: Encounters of Memory, Resistance, and Hope at the Crossroads," in *Resurgent Voices*, ed. Cleary and Steigenga, 210–230.

7. For an interesting comparison with Mayan spirituality movements, see Virginia Garrard-Burnett, "God Was Already Here When Columbus Arrived," in *Resurgent Voices*, ed. Cleary and Steigenga, 130. Garrard-Burnett states that the Peace Accords in Guatemala "opened a social space for Mayan spiritual leaders to break off their tie to Christianity and return to an autochthonous spirituality they believe has retained its pre-Christian essence" (ibid., 130).

8. I thank Michelle Wibbelsman for emphasizing this point to me.

9. Ward Stavig, "Túpac Amaru, the Body Politic, and the Embodiment of Hope: Inca Heritage and Social Justice in the Andes," in *Death, Dismemberment, and Memory:*

Body Politics in Latin America, ed. Lyman L. Johnson (Albuquerque: University of New Mexico Press, 2004), 35.

10. Sabine MacCormack, *Religion in the Andes* (Princeton: Princeton University Press, 1991); for information on eighteenth-century rebellious movements, see Steve J. Stern, ed., *Resistance, Rebellion, and Consciousness in the Andean Peasant World, 18th to 20th Centuries* (Madison: University of Wisconsin Press, 1987).

11. See Norman E. Whitten Jr., introduction to *Cultural Transformations and Ethnicity in Modern Ecuador*, ed. Whitten (Champagne: University of Illinois Press, 1981), 1–41; Ronald Stutzman, "El Mestizaje: An All-Inclusive Ideology of Exclusion," in *Cultural Transformations*, ed. Whitten, 45–94.

12. Rebecca Tolen, "Receiving the Authorities in Chimborazo, Ecuador: Ethnic Performance in an Evangelical Andean Community," *Journal of Latin American Anthropology* 3 (1998): 20–53.

13. Lynn Meisch, "We Will Not Dance on the Tomb of Our Grandparents: 500 Years of Indigenous Resistance in Ecuador," *Latin American Anthropology Review* 4 (1994): 55–74.

14. Anthony F. C. Wallace, "Revitalization Movements," *American Anthropologist* 58 (1956): 265.

15. Orta, *Catechizing Culture*,127

16. Peter Wogan, *Magical Writing in Salasaca* (Boulder: Westview Press, 2004).

17. Barry Lyons, "Taita Chimborazo, Mama Tungurahua: A Quichua Song, a Fieldwork Story," *Anthropology and Humanism* 24 (1998): 39.

18. Michael Uzendoski, "Purgatory, Protestantism, and Peonage: Napo Runa Evangelicals and the Domestication of Masculine Will," *Millennial Ecuador: Critical Essays on Cultural Transformations and Social Dynamics*, ed. Norman E. Whitten Jr. (Iowa City: University of Iowa Press, 2003), 129–153.

19. I do not know the circumstances under which the bishop chooses to assign and reassign priests; in the case of Salasaca, the resident priest was reassigned in 1998 after some Salasacans suspected he was embezzling funds. Different priests have been serving the community since then. The main church contact seems to be the local indigenous catechist, who is sought whenever a family needs to prepare a child for making one of the Catholic sacraments.

20. Rachel Corr, "The Catholic Church, Ritual, and Power in Salasaca," in *Millennial Ecuador*, ed. Whitten.

21. José Masaquiza, "Los Salasacas," in *Identidades Indias en el Ecuador Contemporaneo*, ed. José Almeida Vinueza (Quito, Ecuador: Abya Yala, 1995), 213–246.

22. Masaquiza, "Los Salasacas," 238.

23. See http://www.salaskamarka.com/E/salaskae.htm.

24. Masaquiza, "Los Salasacas," 2.

25. Pablo Davalos, "Festival and Power: The Rite of 'Occupation' in the Indigenous Movement," *Boletin ICCI-RIMAI* 23 (February 2001): 14 (http://icci.nativeweb.org/boletin/23/).

26. Michelle Wibbelsman, "Encuentros: Dances of the Inti Raymi in Cotacachi, Ecuador," *Latin American Music Review* 26 (fall/winter 2005): 222.

27. Elsie Clews Parons, *Peguche: A Study of Andean Indians* (Chicago: University of Chicago Press, 1945).

28. Michelle Wibbelsman, "Otavaleños at the Crossroads: Physical and Metaphysical Coordinates of an Indigenous World," *Journal of Latin American Anthropology* 10 (2005): 165.

29. Ibid., 168.

30. Ibid., 180, n.17.

31. Barbara Butler, *Holy Intoxication to Drunken Dissipation: Alcohol among Quichua Speakers in Otavalo, Ecuador* (Albuquerque: University of New Mexico Press, 2006), 374.

32. Ibid., 417, n.3. Indi is an alternative spelling of Inti, the Sun.

33. Ibid., 374.

34. See www.amawtaywasi.edu.ec/english/antecedentes.html.

35. Ibid.

36. See Michael Fobes Brown, "Dark Side of the Shaman," *Magic, Witchcraft, and Religion: An Anthropological Study of the Supernatural*, ed. Arthur C. Lehmann and James E. Myers (Mountain View: Mayfield, 2001), 110; Beth A. Conklin, "Shamans versus Pirates in the Amazonian Treasure Chest," *American Anthropologist* 104 (2002): 1050–1061.

37. Rachel Corr, "To Throw the Blessing: Poetics, Prayer, and Performance in the Andes," *Journal of Latin American Anthropology* 9 (fall 2004): 382–408.

38. Orta, *Catechizing Culture*, 205.

39. Ibid., 105.

40. John Burdick, *Blessed Anastacia: Women, Race, and Popular Christianity in Brazil* (New York: Routledge, 1998).

41. Orta, *Catechizing Culture*, 103.

42. Ibid., 109.

43. Orin Starn, "Missing the Revolution: Anthropologists and the War in Peru," *Cultural Anthropology* 6 (1991): 86.

44. Clifford Geertz, *The Interpretation of Cultures* (New York: Basic Books, 1973), 90.

45. Of course, these are not the only functions of these institutions; as I mentioned, the Intercultural University Amawtay Wasi promotes the study of science, technology, and other areas of study.

46. James Peacock, "Religion and Life History: An Exploration in Cultural Psychology," *Text, Play, and Story: The Construction and Reconstruction of Self and Society*, ed. Edward M. Bruner (Prospect Heights: Waveland Press, 1988), 94–116.

47. Orta, *Catechizing Culture*, 122.

48. The importance of hair to indigenous identity is recognized by the Ecuadorian military, which allows Otavalan indigenous men to keep their braids during their obligatory service, while others have their heads shaved.

PART THREE

The Implications
of Conversion

10

Indigenous Conversion to Catholicism

Change of Heart in Chiapas, Mexico

CHRISTINE KOVIC

This chapter focuses on the much-overlooked conversion from Traditionalism to Catholicism among the Mayas of highland Chiapas, their own understandings of the meaning of conversion, and its impact on their lives. This volume points out the complexities of conversion, emphasizing that conversion is not a sudden and dramatic change in belief, but an ongoing process. The editors call for attention to the agency of converts rather than assuming that people passively join and absorb a new religion. In order to emphasize the agency of indigenous Catholics this chapter explores how religion is practiced in acts of everyday life. Mayan Catholics describe conversion as "a change of heart" that takes places over a long period, in some cases years, and brings significant changes to their lives. Above all, Catholicism is understood in terms of actions and behavior such as rejection of alcohol, the reconfiguration of gender roles, and the reassertion of ethnic identity more than belief. These consequences of conversion are commonly unexpected for converts as well as for social scientists. For Mayan Catholics, conversion and faith have meaning within a community where they as indigenous people are engaged in struggles for self-determination and to live a dignified life. As such, it is in acts of reading and interpreting the Bible in groups, visiting and praying with the ill, strengthening family and community ties, and analyzing political and social events that conversion can be understood.

The following descriptions of Mayan Catholic religious events demonstrate two of the many ways that converts celebrate their faith. On February 2, 1995, hundreds of men, women, and children crowded into a small chapel to attend a Catholic Mass honoring the Virgin of Candelaria, patron saint of this highland community of Tzotzils (Mayas) from San Juan Chamula. Bright garlands of flowers hung from the rafters, pine needles covered the floor, the smoke of incense filled the air, and statues of the Virgin of Guadalupe alongside saints, all in traditional Chamulan dress, lined the altar. The ceremony began as six men dressed as nineteenth-century French soldiers (traditionally called *maxetik* in Tzotzil, or "monkey assistants") entered the chapel playing traditional wooden instruments and carrying banners adorned with brightly colored ribbons. Although a priest was present, indigenous deacons ordained by Bishop Samuel Ruiz García of the Diocese of San Cristóbal directed the ceremony. In their native language of Tzotzil, they presented and discussed biblical readings, led prayers, and gave out communion after the priest consecrated it. At the end of Mass, maxetik led a procession from the chapel, followed by women who carried candles and paintings of the Virgin of Candelaria.

During the same month, Catholic celebrations of the "Word of God" were held each Sunday in the indigenous community of Guadalupe, located on the outskirts of the city of San Cristóbal de Las Casas.[1] Dozens of families, Tzotzils from Chamula, gathered in the chapel and began by singing lively songs common to Protestant and Charismatic Catholic celebrations. A man playing an electric guitar accompanied the singing, and amplifiers carried the music to nearby homes and the dirt road in front of the chapel, announcing that the celebration was about the begin. A priest visited the community to celebrate Mass only on special occasions, so each week indigenous catechists read from the Bible, directed discussions of the meaning of the readings, and led prayer, all in Tzoztil. Each ceremony began and ended with the congregation kneeling together in a prayer, at once collective and individual, as each person simultaneously voiced their thanks and wishes to God as a community.

These two religious celebrations with their differing styles and inclusion of Mayan traditions are carried out by indigenous peoples who define themselves as converts to Catholicism, specifically as adherents of the Word of God, or *Palabra de Dios* in Spanish. The term "Word of God" refers to reading the Bible and active participation in the pastoral project of the Diocese of San Cristóbal. These Catholics differentiate themselves from self-defined Traditionalists, *Tradicionalistas* in Spanish, who practice Mayan and Catholic ritual. In the contemporary period "conversion" in Chiapas, and in Latin America more broadly, commonly refers to a change from Catholicism to Protestantism, and indigenous conversion to Catholicism is seldom addressed, perhaps because it is assumed that indigenous peoples of Latin America are already Catholic.[2] Certainly, five hundred years of colonization and missionization have had an impact, and Catholic beliefs are integral to

Traditionalists. Indeed, some Traditionalists describe themselves as "true Catholics." Yet, in Chiapas and other parts of Latin America, Traditionalists and Word of God Catholics define themselves as distinct, and sometimes conflicting, religious groups. The religious practices of the two groups are significantly different, with Word of God Catholics focusing on the Bible as a guide for behavior and Traditionalists focusing on the ways of their ancestors.

This chapter focuses on the practice of religion following the call of scholars such as David Hall and Robert Orsi to study "lived religion," that is, "the everyday thinking and doing of lay men and women."[3] Orsi notes the importance of examining religion in its relationship with multiple aspects of life, recognizing that religion is much more than affiliation, adherence to a set a beliefs, or study of text. "Religion is not only sui generis, distinct from other dimensions of experience called 'profane.' Religion comes into being in an ongoing, dynamic relationship with the realities of everyday life."[4] Anthropologists similarly have pointed to the importance of examining religion as practice or performance rather than as identity or belief. In such analyses, the daily work of living or carrying out religion becomes apparent. While it was important to community members that I attend religious celebrations while conducting fieldwork—and, indeed, over the years I spent dozens of hours at such events—I only began to understand the significance of conversion by observing daily events and speaking with the Catholics about their experiences.[5] It was, for example, in talking with women as they wove woolen skirts and accompanying men on visits to Catholics in nearby communities that I saw religion could not be separated from the building of community, family relations, and understandings of inequality and ethnic relations.

The Context of Conversion: Traditionalists, Catholics, and Transformations in Political Economy

Religion has been described as a conflictive, even explosive, issue for indigenous communities of Mexico's southern state of Chiapas. Indeed, some descriptions of highland Chiapas, a marginalized region with profound poverty, emphasize religious conflict of Mayas against one another as the region's principal crisis. The complex religious arena of the highlands includes Traditionalists, Protestants, Catholics, and a small number of Muslims, among others. According to census data for the year 2000, Chiapas is the state with the lowest percentage of Catholics, 64 percent as compared to 88 percent nationally; the highest percentage of Protestants, 14 percent; and the highest percentage of respondents with "no religion," 13 percent.[6] Indigenous conversion to Protestantism has been described as a major cause of violent conflict in the region. Newspaper headlines decry violent religious conflicts between Protestants and Traditionalists in highland communities, particularly Chamula. In the twenty-five-year period from 1974 to 2000, municipal officials have expelled some twenty-five thousand Tzotzils, forcing them to leave their homes and land and to move elsewhere. Government officials and media accounts commonly present expulsion as a religious conflict between Traditionalists and Protestants and blame Protestant converts for threatening indigenous customs by their refusal to participate in traditional rituals. In turn, Protestant missionaries blame Traditionalists for their religious intolerance. Others focus blame on the Catholic Church, in particular on Samuel Ruiz García, bishop of the Diocese of San Cristóbal from 1960 to 2000. Enemies calling him the "red bishop" accuse him of inciting indigenous uprising against mestizos and the state and of promoting religious conflict.

Not only are these sensationalistic descriptions of Chiapas boldly inaccurate, they fail to address the political context of conflict. Most important is the economic and political marginalization of indigenous peasants struggling to make a livelihood without sufficient land in the context of five hundred years of racism and exclusion. Without any context, indigenous peoples are made out to be irrational fanatics who are intolerant of dissent. Conflicts in highland Chiapas are much more about the distribution of resources and mestizos and state forms of racism than they are about religion. A brief historic overview is necessary to place contemporary religious change in context.

In highland communities, anthropologists have long recognized that religion and politics are closely linked. Historically, state policies consolidated the power of indigenous caciques, or entrenched local leaders who define themselves as Traditionalists, working to support the continuity of their communities and the ways of their ancestors. Jan Rus shows how the state worked from within the indigenous community of Chamula beginning in the 1940s to co-opt native leaders so that "the very community structures previously identified with resistance to outside intervention and exploitation . . . had become institutionalized revolutionary communities" supporting the state.[7]

By the 1950s, the majority of indigenous peoples of the highland region supported the Institutional Revolutionary Party (PRI), Mexico's ruling party of seventy years. Community leaders saw that votes were provided to the PRI-controlled state and federal government in exchange for material resources and a limited form of political autonomy. Although dissent always existed, this corporatist system remained in place as long as the state continued to provide resources. Beginning in the 1970s, Chiapas's agrarian sector entered a period of crisis, which worsened with the national economic crisis of 1982, implementation of neoliberal reforms mandating cuts in credits and subsidies for rural producers, and the dramatic drop in coffee prices, among other factors. With increasing poverty in the 1970s and especially 1980s, indigenous peasants chose one of two paths in their struggle for survival. One group insisted on strengthening their ties to the PRI in order to gain resources, while another searched for new alliances to survive. In this second group, people joined cooperatives, opposition parties, peasant organizations, and new churches. Opposition to political and economic repression, above all to the PRI, increased in the 1980s even as state repression against independent groups escalated.

Particularly important to formation of independent organizations was the work of the Catholic Diocese of San Cristóbal. Influenced by the historic meetings of the Second Vatican Council and the Medellin Latin American Bishops Conference, Bishop Ruiz and pastoral workers formally committed themselves to work with and among the poor in the 1970s. They trained indigenous catechists to take on social and political roles in their communities, supported the formation of regional and statewide networks, shared concrete organizing skills, and provided a language which supported the struggle for liberation. Many indigenous peoples who affiliated with the Catholic diocese began to challenge the power of caciques and organize for social change. At the same time, some joined Protestant churches (with Presbyterian and Pentecostal denominations attracting the largest numbers of converts) and in these new alliances found support for resisting the authority of caciques.

The expulsion of thousands of indigenous peoples from highland communities has been mistakenly described as a religious conflict between Protestants and Traditionalists. Indeed, Protestants, Catholics, and even Traditionalists have been expelled for political and economic reasons, although indigenous authorities commonly describe expulsion in religious terms. The state and federal governments have played an important role in implicitly or explicitly supporting local indigenous leaders responsible for expulsion, justifying expulsion as a way to preserve indigenous tradition in the face of "external" incursions such as Protestantism. In contrast, Jan Rus describes the expelled as social or political dissidents who have challenged entrenched local leaders in a variety of ways.[8] In other words, the case of expulsion is similar to others in which religion masks political and economic struggles.

Hence, profound changes in contemporary Chiapas frame indigenous conversions to Christianity, both to Catholicism and Protestantism. Yet, just as it is a mistake to examine religious change without situating it within its political and economic context, it is a mistake to explain religion exclusively in political and economic terms. While historic context necessarily impacts religious conversion, it explains neither why a particular religion carries meaning for converts nor their own understandings of religion. More importantly, religion cannot be explained away as a purely calculated political-economic response.

Conversion as a Process, Religion as Action: From Hearing the Word of God to Changing One's Heart

Indigenous Catholics of highland Chiapas describe conversion as a long-term process, which can take place over years and unleash a series of changes in their lives, many of them dramatic and unpredictable. The conversion narratives I gathered inevitably began with when and how the converts had first "heard" the Word of God and how, in time, they came to understand and change their hearts. *A'iel*, the Tzotzil verb for "to hear," also means to feel and to understand. Converts describe the process of conversion as a long-term process due to the complexity of religion itself as well as the profound role it plays in their lives.

My own fieldwork with indigenous Catholics was based primarily in the *colonia* (a neighborhood or unregulated urban settlement) of Guadalupe, which is located on the outskirts of the mestizo-dominated city of San Cristóbal de Las Casas. There I conducted research for twelve consecutive months (in 1994 and 1995) and for shorter periods over a decade and attended dozens of religious celebrations, such as the ones described in the introduction of this chapter. Day-to-day participant observation along with listening to life histories revealed the complex reasons for the conversion to Catholicism as well as the ongoing work involved in being Catholic. Many of the residents of Guadalupe were expelled from their native community of Chamula and began a new life on the edge of the city.[9]

Hearing the Word of God

When and how does conversion take place? That is, when and how did people first hear the Word of God? In their conversion narratives, Catholics of Guadalupe commonly began by describing their contact with a Catholic: a neighbor or friend, an indigenous catechist, a priest or nun who visited their community, or a relative such as a sibling, cousin, or uncle. One man, Agustin, explained that he first went to a Catholic church in San Cristóbal because his cousin was a catechist there. Some families came in contact with Catholics while living and working outside Chamula, a common situation give the extreme land scarcity within the municipality, and began to attend religious ceremonies. For example, Yolanda, who moved to Guadalupe in 1994, lived previously for years with her family in the Lacandon jungle, where they were engaged in subsistence production. She explained how her conversion began as a means of joining a new community. "My husband and I heard the Word of God in the municipality of Las Margaritas [in the Lacandon jungle]. We lived in *el Nacional* [federal lands endowed to peasants] for twelve years in an area populated by Catholics. Priests and nuns came to visit. We went to church and met the catechists." Hearing the Word of God in the Lacandon jungle, Chamula, or elsewhere raised awareness of another religious option but did not mean automatic conversion, or even a desire to convert. Many converts spoke of hearing the Word of God several times over a period of months or years before deciding to take up a new faith.

Illness and healing commonly played a role in conversion. Catholics told me that once they heard the Word of God, they were cured of illnesses. Juana, a widow with two daughters, explained, "I started to listen to the Word of God [in Chamula] because I was sick. My body was very weak and I couldn't work. When I understood the Word of God, my illness went away." In her case, the power of religion came in the form of physical healing. Catholics as well as Protestants of highland Chiapas offer regular prayer rituals for those who are ill. Female converts spoke of religion "healing their illnesses," referring to problem drinking, domestic violence, and other issues. Others found healing in the church through pragmatic rather than spiritual means. Traditionalists of Chamula commonly visit *iloletik* (healers), who ask for payment in the form of money, soft drinks, candles, chickens, or other items. Women in Guadalupe told me that they became frustrated with the iloletik, either because of the expense or because these healers did not cure their own and their families' illnesses. Instead, they were cured by praying with Catholics and by use of patented medicines, which they associated with the Catholic Church.

Marcela, for example, explained how she converted following the healing of her son: "[Thirteen years ago] one of my children who was three months old was sick, and I looked for someone to cure him. The *curanderos* are always going to charge. . . . I paid the curandero, but my child wasn't cured. They asked for chickens, alcohol, and candles. But my son wasn't cured; he was going to die. We went to a doctor in Chenalhó, and I looked for medicine. That's how my son was cured. We began going to church in Chenalhó. From our home in Chamula, it is an hour and twenty minute walk downhill and over two hours back up."

Numerous scholars have noted a link between health and conversion. In her work on Word of God Catholics in the highland municipality of Chenalhó, Chiapas, anthropologist Heidi Moksnes describes the importance of illness and frustration with traditional healers as a motive for conversion.[10] She notes that Catholic converts found compelling the religion's focus on other aspects of health, such as the rejection of alcohol. For the case of urban Brazilians, John Burdick and Andrew Chesnut point to the importance of illness and healing in conversion to Pentecostalism.[11] Chesnut describes converts as seeking "immediate solutions to their health problems stemming from poverty" and notes that the success of faith healing commonly led to conversion, especially for women.[12] In addition, Burdick and Chesnut point to Pentecostalism's rejection of vices such as alcohol, tobacco, and gambling as being particularly attractive to women living in poverty as they work to save household money and build a better life. In all of these cases, illness and conversion mix the spiritual (healing through prayer) and material (rejection of earthly vices and at times economic support).

Working and Walking to Change One's Heart

In highland Chiapas, conversion to Catholicism entails a commitment to a new way of life, specifically, a commitment to liberation. This means that Catholics work in community to create a new society with social, economic, and political liberation. Converts described following the Word of God as a difficult process involving ongoing struggle and effort. Many told me that when they first heard the Word of God in Bible readings, they did not really understand. Only with work and an investment of time did understanding come.[13] David Smilde, in this volume, describes the importance of social relationships in networks such as family ties in facilitating conversion. This is very similar to the case of highland Chiapas, although I found that it is community rather than networks which facilitates and strengthens conversion. As described in this section, community is both a physical and symbolic space where religion is practiced and has meaning.

In conducting fieldwork I observed catechists and other Catholics in Guadalupe practice their faith within community in myriad ways. One of the most common events was visiting the ill, praying with them, and providing material and moral support to their families. On many occasions, I accompanied Catholics on such visits, which could last several hours. In one case when an ill child was taken to a local clinic following a prayer session, at least a dozen people from the community, including the child's parents, grandparents, a catechist, and several other church members, traveled together to the clinic. Several children died during the period of my fieldwork, and catechists gave up a day's work and wages in order to be present with the families during and after the burial, and other community members visited grieving families to provide comfort and material support. Joyful events, such as baptisms and weddings, also necessitated community involvement. This began with careful preparation of the parents or couple involved as well as the godparents. Catechists spent hours explaining the meaning of sacraments and sharing relevant readings from the Bible. In addition, catechists and older Catholics regularly visited households to read the Bible together and discuss its meaning.

Religion is an active process, albeit carried out in different ways, for the Traditionalist as well. Traditionalist Mayas of Guatemala and Chiapas put tremendous time, money, and effort into the rituals, which support life and the ways of the ancestors. Writing of Santiago Atitlán, Guatemala, Robert Carlsen distinguishes three religious groups: Protestants, Roman Catholics, and followers of the Old Ways (Traditionalists), whom he labels with their autonym, "the Working People." This term refers to participation in extensive rituals believed to be "absolutely essential for the continuity of the world's vital cycles of existence."[14] In highland Chiapas Traditionalists also describe maintaining the ways of the ancestors as work. "We Mayans Work to Give Thanks to the Gods," a poetic essay by indigenous bilingual writers of the cooperative Sna Jtz'ibajom (House of the Writer), describes the many types of work done by Mayan peoples from the time of the Popol Vuh to the present. They describe housework, work in the fields to cultivate crops, "work carried out for the town so that our community can live in peace," and the "flowery work" of carrying out rituals, fiestas, prayers, and ceremonies. The flowery work is described as the most important because it is carried out "to serve and delight the gods."[15]

Work continues to be a central element of religious life for Word of God Catholics. In her research on the highland community of Santa María Magdalenas, Ruth Chojnacki describes the ways Catholics carry out the "work" of the Word of God in reclaiming (and working) their land, in reflecting on and attempting to understand the Word of God, and in the hours of labor of deacons and catechists in supporting the Catholics of their community in religious celebration, visits, Bible study, and other acts.[16]

For Chenalhó, Moksnes notes that both Traditionalists and Catholics practice their religion through constant effort. In performing complex community and family rituals Traditionalists gain *cuxlejal*, or "the divine protection of life." "The Catholics, instead, describe cuxlejal as something petitioned for through regular attendance and prayers in church meetings and their continuous struggle to understand and implement the Word of God. It is through the converts' continuous effort to comply with this task, in spite of difficulties and pain, that they show their veneration and dedication, and for their sacrifice, will be given life."[17]

In Guadalupe, converts spoke of their ongoing efforts at maintaining a community of faith in which people lived together in respect. This involved meeting in the chapel three or four times a week to read and discuss the Bible. This was necessary, the catechists explained to me, because many in the community had not learned to read and write and could not read the Bible in their homes. In addition, the group worked together discussing the material and attempting to understand it. During religious celebrations, members of the congregation would speak out to ask and address questions as they related the readings to their own lives.

"Walking with one heart" was a common metaphor for efforts of Word of God Catholics to practice their faith. Walking represented physical labor, a task common for peasants who had once walked to the fields, town center, or cities in areas without roads. Although small Volkswagen vans provided transportation to Guadalupe from San Cristóbal's market for less than twenty-five cents, many walked the miles, lacking money for the fare. Catholics constantly walked to visit those who were ill and to share the Word of God. Most important was walking to the municipalities of Chamula, Chenalhó, and Teopisca to worship with small congregations of Catholics. Public transportation carried Guadalupe residents part of the distance, but some walking was necessary to reach the communities. I accompanied a catechist to a community in Chenalhó, which involved an hour and a half uphill walk following an hour's ride. These visits not only involve the effort of walking, but the sacrifice of time—time away from one's work, home, and family— and the expense of bus fare.

Walking with one heart also meant walking united as a community in the path of God. Unity was the most difficult part of the task. Members of the congregation worked to avoid divisions and to counsel men who wanted to leave their wives or who had begun drinking. Countless visits were made to congregants who were ill, depressed, tired, or thinking of leaving the church.

The Tzotzil phrase "of one heart" (*jun ko'ontontic*) refers to those who place the interests of the community before their own individual interests and remain faithful to themselves and their people. In contrast, someone with two hearts is not to be trusted. In this sense walking with one heart meant creating a strong community of faith in which people would have the strength to fight poverty and injustice. As Heidi Moksnes writes for Chenalhó, "The Catholics hold that God wants to see human society immersed in his love and justice."[18]

The work of creating unity, a community with one heart, was described as a work of love, and, as such, a work that expressed God's love and one's love for God. A favorite biblical reading in Guadalupe was the first letter of John 4:7–12, "Beloved, let us love one another, because love is from God; everyone who loves is born of God and knows God. . . . No one has ever seen God; if we love one another, God lives in us, and his love is perfected in us." The Guadalupe Catholics worked to put this love in practice in visiting each other and members of other communities.

Conversion and Changes in Social Life

Conversion to Catholicism for Tzotzils involves numerous changes in social life, all of which require considerable work. This section addresses three significant changes: rejection of alcohol, reconfiguration of gender roles, and development of social and political networks through the San Cristóbal Diocese. Scholars studying conversion to Protestantism in Latin America have noted similar changes, especially those related to gender and alcohol, which suggests that conversion itself may be linked to social change. Yet in Chiapas secular groups, most notably members of the Zapatista Army of National Liberation as well as their civilian supporters, reject all use of alcohol and have demanded changes in gender roles. For this reason, these changes in social life can be seen as part of an indigenous project of self-determination, which resists social and economic oppression.[19] Indigenous Catholics justify these social changes in religious terms, yet the changes are part of a struggle to live a dignified life rather than mere moralistic concerns.

Rejection of Alcohol

Although not all indigenous Catholics reject drinking, powerful movements exist to restrict the use and sale of alcohol in highland communities. The Catholics of Guadalupe strongly rejected all use of alcohol and shared with me painful stories of problem drinking by their fathers or husbands. For Juan, a catechist for over thirty years, alcohol is linked to memories of his father's excessive drinking, which contributed to his early death and left a young Juan and his siblings orphans. When he converted to Catholicism in his early twenties, Juan gave up drinking.

Women shared stories of their spouses drinking and criticized both the expense of alcohol and aggression, including domestic violence, brought on by drinking. In a context of extreme poverty, men and women described the purchase of alcohol as "wasting money." Several women told stories of beatings by their husbands before they converted to Catholicism and gave up drinking. Indeed, women often converted first and, in time, were able to convert their husbands. Some women never succeeded in convincing their husbands to give up alcohol or to convert and wound up leaving them. These women receive material and moral support within the community of Guadalupe.

Converts emphasize the contrast between drinking and thinking, stating that drinking precludes one from thinking clearly. Emiliano, husband and father of seven children, told me that he used to drink before he heard the World of God, but stopped after his conversion. "When we changed our religion we changed our hearts. Now we are happy. With the money we spent on alcohol there wasn't money left for food. When a man is drinking a lot he doesn't like to buy food. With the World of God you know how to think well. If you believe in the Bible, you can't drink. You can't hit. You have to love others. That's what the Bible says." Andrés, husband and father of five, contrasted drinking with the capacity to think and to support one's family.

"The Bible says that one should not drink. If people are drunkards, they are going to lose their ability to think. A man with a good heart does not drink. He knows how to help his wife and children."

Rejection of alcohol is part of a growing movement among indigenous peoples of Chiapas and includes Catholics, Protestants, and secular groups such as the Zapatistas. Anthropologist Christine Eber has detailed women's organizing to limit problem drinking in Chenalhó.[20] In prohibition movements in Chenalhó, Guadalupe, and elsewhere women work to conserve scarce cash and to promote personal respect. As Eber notes, "Through their participation in meetings and rallies, women deepened their capacity to connect their personal troubles, such as problem drinking, to political issues. For example, although they criticized their kinsmen for drinking up precious cash, when they spoke out in public meetings, they also decried the injustice of their children going hungry while mestizo rum sellers strutted around in shiny boots with their fat stomachs leading the way."[21]

Changing Gender Roles

Numerous scholars studying Protestant conversion in Latin America have documented its link to changes in gender roles, primarily its curtailing (or at least critique) of alcohol abuse, domestic violence, and spousal abandonment, as well as an increased value placed on women's roles and authority in the home.[22] Contrary to assumptions about evangelical gender relations in the United States and in spite of evangelical support of patriarchy, the religion can respond to women's needs. For the case of Colombia, Elizabeth Brusco notes that evangelical Protestantism can be an "antidote to machismo" in encouraging men to orient themselves toward church and home rather than toward the public sphere.[23] Although this aspect of conversion has been developed for Protestantism, little is written on conversion to Catholicism and gender roles.[24]

In Chiapas, both male and female converts described their actions to increase respect between women and men. Given that the Catholic Church is a patriarchal institution, it is perhaps ironic that conversion can lead to a positive reconfiguration of gender roles. This renewed respect is linked in great part to the rejection of alcohol, which meant an end to problem drinking, a reduction in domestic violence, and more money for household expenses. Conversion also entailed rejection of males abandoning their families and community support for women who left abusive husbands. Of particular significance to men in respecting their wives was "listening to" and "working with" them. In Guadalupe, this change in respect takes place even as men are in dominant roles in the church as catechists.[25] As stated by Emiliano, "When I came here [to Guadalupe] I began to live in peace with my wife. . . . I respect her and she respects me as well. Here we are united.

Husband and wife must unite to work well together and with their children. When there are problems, we pray to God in our faith."

Gender equality is part of a broader pastoral project of the San Cristóbal Diocese. Following the preferential option for the poor, the diocese focused in the 1970s on "the poor" as an undifferentiated group of people suffering similarly from the structure of inequality. In time, pastoral workers recognized the specific role of ethnicity in structuring the marginality of indigenous peoples of Chiapas. By the early 1990s, the diocese formally took up the issue of gender inequalities by adding a "work area" on women, making gender integral to some diocesan projects. Diocesan-based Fray Bartolomé de Las Casas Human Rights Center workshops held in indigenous communities commonly emphasize the importance of gender equality. For example, in one workshop participants responded to the question, "What does God say of the rights of women?" They noted, "We have the same dignity, men and women. We have to respect men and women because we are all children of God. Men shouldn't mistreat, hit, or beat women, nor women men."

Another initiative is the Diocesan Coordination of Women, CODIMUJ, which consists of hundreds of grassroots women's groups. In local groups women unite to share biblical readings from a women-centered perspective, in their words, "with the eyes, mind, and heart of a woman," using readings and discussion questions put together by pastoral workers. They form local cooperatives where they raise chickens or vegetables, bake bread, or sell artisan products to earn extra cash. Women from rural and urban communities attend regional and diocesan-wide meetings where they discuss their problems, pointing to regional, national, and international structures that constrain them and sharing ideas on how to work to change their lives.[26]

New Networks and New Identities

Affiliation with the San Cristóbal Diocese also provides links to diocesan-wide networks and a broad political project to assist in building the "Kingdom of God," that is, to building a more just world. At the 1974 Indigenous Congress, organized by Bishop Samuel Ruiz at the request of Governor Velasco Suárez, over a thousand indigenous delegates from the state's four largest indigenous groups came together to discuss problems around land, commerce, education, and health. At this historic meeting, participants saw not only that they shared common problems due to structural inequalities but also that they would have much more power if they worked together to find solutions.

Beyond this historic meeting, two powerful changes came through constant discussion among Word of God Catholics with the support of diocesan pastoral workers. First, poverty and its related problems such as illness were linked to structural factors of inequality and racism in Chiapas. As in

liberation theology, the poor are not blamed for their suffering, but institu-
tionalized violence and structural sin are defined as the cause of suffering.
Guadalupe Catholics expressed this daily in reasserting their own dignity as
"children of God;" criticizing a social order in which indigenous and mestizo,
rich and poor were not treated equally; and working through political and
social networks to live a dignified life.

The second change which came through the diocesan structure was that
indigenous Catholics were linked to the distinct ethnic groups within the
diocese as well as to Catholics throughout Mexico and even the world. As
Catholics, they view themselves as being engaged in a common struggle to
create a more just world. In describing the theology of indigenous Catholics
of Chenalhó, Moksnes notes that they see themselves as "part of a global
humanity and a global Catholic congregation."[27] The Catholics of Guadalupe
see themselves as part of a wider community of faith and feel connected to
Catholics around the world because they share in similar beliefs and participate in similar rituals.

The contemporary diocesan structure lays the groundwork for a series of
regional and diocesan-wide networks among indigenous peoples. The diocese
is broken down into seven pastoral teams based on the regions of the diocese, and each team is organized by parishes. Meetings of catechists, health
promoters, human rights promoters, and others are organized at a municipal level, and delegates from each region and pastoral team come together
for larger meetings. In November 1993, I attended a catechist meeting for
the Deaconías (a region including the rural communities surrounding San
Cristóbal). At its opening, representatives were asked to share information
on the problems and successes in their communities as well as their work in
studying the biblical book Acts of the Apostles (a task organized at the previous meeting). Catechists from one community stated that their Bible study
had provided "one more example of the path to find unity by strengthening
our faith." Common problems discussed included political conflicts, the use
of alcohol, poverty, and illness, among others. At this and other meetings,
catechists worked to support one another in finding solutions as they recognized and criticized the structural causes of their problems.

Conversion, Agency, and Colonialism

Throughout Latin America, Catholicism is linked to colonialism, and historically the church has been actively involved in the oppression, exploitation,
death, and destruction of indigenous culture. Through conversion missionaries have attempted to transform, with varied success and failure, some of
"the most intimate and fundamental components of indigenous social life."[28]
In highland Chiapas, Traditionalists accuse Christian converts, both Protestants and Catholics, of threatening indigenous customs and community.

Yet, the contemporary conversion of indigenous peoples to Word of God Catholicism represents, to a certain extent, resistance to colonialism rather than subordination to Western ways. The rejection of alcohol is one powerful example of how Word of God Catholics are agents who craft religion to serve as a tool for liberation. To begin with, official Catholic doctrine does not prohibit drinking. As indigenous Catholics interpret Catholicism as promoting abstention, they demonstrate one of the many ways that they are Catholics on their own terms. Although indigenous people used alcohol in ritual in the pre-Columbian period under rigid controls, alcohol is linked to colonial domination. To give but one example, coffee plantations commonly paid workers in the form of rum or as a way of encouraging indebtedness. Through their own appropriation of Catholicism, indigenous peoples are actively engaged with the religion rather than subordinating themselves to it.

Understanding the Complexities of Conversion

Important works on indigenous conversion such as Sheldon Annis's *God and Production in a Guatemalan Town* point to economic motives, emphasizing the creation of rational Protestants involved in commercial production and lessened expenses on community involvement.[29] While economic factors clearly play a role in conversion, it seems that Annis and other scholars attempt to "explain away" religion in terms of a single factor, be it economics, politics, or benefits to converts. It is in this context that it is useful to examine the costs as well as benefits of conversion.

Indigenous Catholics of highland Chiapas describe the difficulties of following the Word of God and walking with one heart. In the Catholics' own descriptions of changes brought by conversion, benefits are evident. For example, rejecting drinking is beneficial to women and families, and the diocesan-wide networks facilitate moral and economic support as well as political mobilization. Indeed, in great part converts to Catholicism in Guadalupe were marginalized in Chamula: some were orphans, others widows, and most had little more than a tiny parcel of land to cultivate. This group likely saw the chance of having something to gain in conversion.

Yet conversion in highland Chiapas also entails significant costs. Most obvious for Guadalupe Catholics is the cost of expulsion, that is, the cost of losing one's home and land and being forced to make a living elsewhere.[30] Guadalupe Catholics constantly spoke of the difficulties of first leaving Chamula and of struggling to make a life for themselves in the new urban setting. Even those who were clearly better off in Guadalupe, although this improvement took place years after expulsion, continued to lament what had been left behind. Some found the cost of conversion unbearable. Numerous men told me that they had "given up" their new religion in Chamula once or several times before returning to the church.

The costs for conversion are not limited to Chamula. In Chenalhó Word of God Catholics became targets of paramilitary groups who labeled them as political enemies. Indeed, forty-five members of Las Abejas (the Bees), an organization of Catholics dedicated to non-violent resistance, were massacred by paramilitaries on December 22, 1997, and tens of thousands of Tzotzils, many of them Catholic, fled their homes due to paramilitary violence in the region.[31]

The most powerful case from my fieldwork of the cost of conversion is the experience of Don Lucas and Micaela, one of the oldest and poorest Catholic couples of Guadalupe. Although they were far from well-off in Chamula, they were socially and economically established when they first heard the Word of God. Micaela made and sold *pox*, a homemade rum, and Don Lucas was able to hire men to assist in cultivating crops on his land. Don Lucas recalled his loss of social standing after his conversion. Local authorities ridiculed him; they were annoyed that someone so old and therefore presumably wise had left the traditional ways. Don Lucas "gave up his religion" for several weeks as he faced the possibility of losing his land, social standing, and home. In the end he and Micaela continued to "follow the Word of God" and authorities expelled them from Chamula. They eventually wound up living in Guadalupe. A cost/benefit analysis would suggest that the couple had nothing to gain. In Guadalupe, the couple had one of the simplest homes, in contrast to three homes in Chamula. When I spoke to Micaela seven years after her expulsion, she continued to lament the loss of income from selling alcohol, even though she was strongly committed to abstinence.

The costs to conversion evident for Don Lucas and Micaela and others serve as a reminder of the need to value the perspective of converts themselves as much as a reminder of the necessity of examining the myriad roles religion plays in everyday life. Faith carries a profundity, power, and intimacy that cannot be explained away in economic terms. It is, as Robert Orsi states, a lived experience that includes the sacred and the profane of everyday life.[32] The religious practice of highland Catholics involves physical labor in walking to visit the ill and to share the Word of God, a constant struggle to understand biblical readings, and a commitment to new forms of social behavior.

The stories of conversion and changes in life demonstrate the need to examine religion in relation to multiple aspects of life—well beyond worship or affiliation—from illness and healing to family relationships, understandings of suffering and justice, and visits to and networks with indigenous Catholics of the region. Attention to the detail of daily life through fieldwork—conducting in-depth interviews, listening to life histories, and observing day-to-day events—reveals the changes embodied conversion, changes that "may not be immediately discernible at the macro level."[33] Observing the practice of religion demonstrates the complexities of conversion as it reveals the agency of converts working and walking to change their hearts.

NOTES

The author thanks Edward Cleary, Timothy Steigenga, Susan Fitzpatrick Behrens, Christine Eber, Francisco Argüelles, Ruth Chojnacki, and the Catholics of Guadalupe for their comments, insight, and inspiration.

1. The community of Guadalupe, a pseudonym, is described in depth in Christine Kovic, *Mayan Voices for Human Rights: Displaced Catholics in Highland Chiapas* (Austin: University of Texas Press, 2005).

2. A number of works focus on indigenous conversion to Catholicism in Guatemala. See, for example, Kay Warren, *The Symbols of Subordination: Indian Identity in a Guatemalan Town* (Austin: University of Texas Press, 1978); Ricardo Falla, *Quiché Rebelde: Religious Conversion, Politics, and Ethnic Identity in Guatemala* (Austin: University of Texas Press, 2001); and Richard Wilson, *Maya Resurgence in Guatemala: Q'eqchi' Experiences* (Norman: University of Oklahoma Press, 1995).

3. David D. Hall, ed., *Lived Religion in America: Toward a History of Practice* (Princeton: Princeton University Press, 1997), vii. See also Robert Orsi, *Between Heaven and Earth: The Religious Worlds People Make and the Scholars Who Study Them* (Princeton: Princeton University Press, 2004); and Michel de Certeau, *The Practice of Everyday Life* (Berkeley: University of California Press, 1988).

4. Robert Orsi, "Everyday Miracles: The Study of Lived Religion," in *Lived Religion in America*, ed. Hall, 7.

5. I conducted fieldwork with Mayan Catholics in highland Chiapas from 1993 to 1995 and for shorter periods from 1996 to 2004 as part of a larger project on indigenous rights and religion.

6. Data from Mexico's Instituto Nacional de Estadística, Geografía e Informatica (INEGI), www.inegi.gob.mx. The percentage of Protestants for the nation was 5.2 percent in 2000. A large part of the group identifying as having "no religion" is Traditionalists who likely differentiate themselves from Catholics and Protestants with this label and who consider religion as an integral part of life rather than a separate sphere of experience. Many Traditionalists also identify as Catholic for the purposes of the census, distinguishing themselves from Protestants.

7. Jan Rus, "The Comunidad Revolucionaria Institucional: The subversion of Native Government in Highland Chiapas, 1936–1968," in *Everyday Forms of State Formation and the Negotiation of Rule in Modern Mexico*, ed. Gilbert M. Joseph and Daniel Nugent (Durham, NC: Duke University Press, 1994), 265.

8. Jan Rus, "The Struggle against Indigenous Caciques in Highland Chiapas: Dissent, Religion, and Exile in Chamula, 1965–1977," paper presented at the Caciques and Caudillos in Twentieth-Century Mexico Conference, Oxford University, September 19–21, 2002.

9. The focus of this section as well as the chapter is on the reasons for conversion and the changes it embodies rather than on expulsion. For discussion of expulsion in

highland Chiapas see Kovic, *Mayan Voices for Human Rights*; and Gaspar Morquecho Escamilla, "Expulsiones de los Altos de Chiapas," in his *Movimiento campesino en Chiapas* (San Cristóbal de Las Casas, Mexico: DESMI).

10. Heidi Moksnes, "Mayan Suffering, Mayan Rights: Faith and Citizenship among Catholic Tzotziles in Highland Chiapas, Mexico" (PhD diss., Goteborg University, 2003).

11. John Burdick, *Looking for God in Brazil: The Progressive Catholic Church in Urban Brazil's Religious Arena* (Berkeley: University of California Press, 1993); and R. Andrew Chesnut, *Born Again in Brazil: The Pentecostal Boom and the Pathogens of Poverty* (New Brunswick, NJ: Rutgers University Press, 1997).

12. Chesnut, *Born Again in Brazil*, 5.

13. For some, conversion involved learning to read and write in order to study the Bible. Hundreds of indigenous men and women passed through two schools for catechists in San Cristóbal in the 1960s. One man remembers attending the school for four full months, learning to read and write, studying the Bible, and receiving the sacraments of first communion and confirmation. Ruth Chonjacki writes of the importance of literacy for Word of God Catholics in "Indigenous Apostles: Maya Catholics Catechists Working the Word in Highland Chiapas" (PhD diss., University of Chicago, 2004).

14. Robert S. Carlsen, *The War for the Heart and Soul of a Highland Maya Town* (Austin: University of Texas Press, 1997), 171.

15. Sna Jtz'ibajom, "We Mayans Work to Give Thanks to the Gods," mimeo, n.d.

16. Chonjacki, "Indigenous Apostles."

17. Mosknes, "Mayan Suffering, Mayan Rights," 139–140.

18. Ibid., 148.

19. This argument is developed further in Kovic, *Mayan Voices for Human Rights*, chap. 7.

20. See especially Christine Eber, *Women and Alcohol in a Highland Maya Town: Water of Hope, Water of Sorrow* (Austin: University of Texas Press, 1995); and Christine Eber, "'Take My Water': Liberation through Prohibition in San Pedro Chenalhó, Chiapas," *Social Science and Medicine* 53 (2001): 251–262.

21. Christine Eber and Christine Kovic, eds., *Women of Chiapas: Making History in Times of Struggle and Hope* (New York: Routledge, 2003), 7.

22. Works addressing gender roles and Protestant conversion include Burdick, *Looking for God in Brazil*; Linda Green, *Fear as a Way of Life: Mayan Widows in Rural Guatemala* (New York: Columbia University Press, 1999); Elizabeth Brusco, "The Reformation of Machismo: Asceticism and Masculinity among Colombian Evangelicals," in *Rethinking Protestantism in Latin America*, ed. Virginia Garrard-Burnett and David Stoll (Philadelphia: Temple University Press, 1993); and Timothy Steigenga and David Smilde, "Wrapped in the Holy Shawl: The Strange Case of Conservative Christians and Gender Equality in Latin America," in *Latin American Religion in Motion*, ed. Christian Smith and Joshua Prokopy (New York: Routledge, 1999); among others.

23. Brusco, "The Reformation of Machismo," 148.

24. In interviews with conservative Catholics and Protestants, Steigenga and Smilde found that both groups have beliefs supporting greater gender equality, contrary

to common assumptions. See their "Wrapped in the Holy Shawl." John Burdick argues that Catholicism in urban Brazil does not respond to women's needs due to a number of factors including its intensification of gossip and its failure to adequately respond to women's domestic needs. See Burdick, *Looking for God in Brazil.*

25. In other communities, women serve as catechists as well, although they struggle to be recognized and respected for their work. See Moksnes, *Mayan Suffering, Mayan Rights.*

26. On CODIMUJ see Christine Kovic, "Demanding Their Dignity as Daughters of God: Catholic Women and Human Rights"; and Pilar Gil, "Irene: A Catholic Woman in Oxchuc," both in *Women of Chiapas,* ed. Eber and Kovic.

27. Moksnes, *Mayan Suffering, Mayan Rights,* 207.

28. Andrew Orta, *Catechizing Culture: Missionaries, Aymara, and the "New Evanelization"* (New York: Columbia University Press, 2004), 6.

29. Sheldon Annis, *God and Production in a Guatemalan Town* (Austin: University of Texas Press, 1987).

30. Although political factors underlying religious change are the cause of expulsion, indigenous leaders in Chamula commonly emphasize only religious factors as a motive. At times, they accuse political enemies, be they Catholic or even Traditionalist, of being Protestants and demand that they leave the community.

31. The conflict in Chenalhó, like that of expulsion, is a political rather than religious one. However, Catholics are targeted for their links to a broader political project.

32. Orsi, "Everyday Miracles."

33. Steigenga and Smilde, "Wrapped in the Holy Shawl," 184.

11

Stop Suffering?

The Iglesia Universal del Reino de Dios in the United States

VIRGINIA GARRARD-BURNETT

The Universal Church of the Kingdom of God, or, as it is more generally known in the United States, the Iglesia Universal del Reino de Dios (IURD), is one of the most rapidly growing denominations in the early twenty-first century. Like most of the other two hundred fast-growing mega-church denominations in the United States, the IURD is neo-Pentecostal in its beliefs and practice and innovative in its liturgy, utilizing contemporary praise music and highly participatory worship; and it aggressively incorporates modern marketing techniques in evangelization. Like the other emerging mega-churches, the IURD, which was founded during the mid-1970s, is part of the new Protestant movement that emerged not from the Reformation, but from the neo-Pentecostal movement of the 1960s.[1]

But unlike most of its counterparts, the IURD is Brazilian in both its origins and orientation. As such, the church's expansion in the United States and Western Europe might be taken to evince a type of reverse missionary movement, a postcolonial reversal of the spiritual manifest destiny of the nineteenth century. As its rather presumptuous name implies, the IURD is a denomination with vast global aspirations, and it effectively employs a sophisticated mixture of marketing, message, and performance to advance its interests; that is to say, evangelize. Its rapid expansion in one of the most highly developed religious markets in the world, the United States, suggests that the IURD is a nimble competitor in the market sector where it seeks the vast majority of its converts: poor urban immigrants from Latin America.

As such, the IURD espouses what might be called a postmodern version of Christianity, in which a malleable theology can be tailored to local spiritual concerns and social aspirations, and where church planners enjoy some flexibility in modifying and reinterpreting church dogma to coincide as closely as possible to local conditions and expectations. It is one of the fastest-growing Christian denominations in the world. The denomination began its international expansion in 1985 by starting a congregation in neighboring Paraguay; by 2006, the IURD had "planted" churches in every Latin American country except (at this writing) Haiti, in more than half of the countries on the African continent, in the United States and Canada, in the Far East (Japan, the Philippines, India), and in twelve countries in Europe.[2] In 1995, the denomination had established an estimated 221 churches abroad, a number that had more than doubled by 1998 to 500 and doubled again to 1,000 in 2001, an astonishing rate of growth that (presumably) continues to the present day. Moreover, the expansion of the church into virgin mission territory is more than merely symbolic: in at least ten of these countries,[3] the denomination has fifty or more congregations.[4]

From the vantage point of sheer market expansion, the IURD would seem to be an ideal case study with which to test the theories of the "religious market places" as popularized by scholars such as Peter Berger, Rodney Stark, Roger Finke, Anthony Gill, and Andrew Chesnut (this volume and elsewhere).[5] By the standards of the religious marketplace, the IURD is an effective vender of "credence goods."[6] This is precisely because of its ability to gauge the spiritual and physical needs of it target clientele with acuity and to generate a theology that fits a given market niche—so long as the theology still fits within the loose parameters of the IURD's dogma, as articulated by its founder, Edir Bezerra Macedo, who founded the church in Rio de Janeiro in 1977. And, as importantly, each congregation is expected to remain loyal to the church's organizational hierarchy, especially in matters of church finances. Thus, the church might concern itself with the exorcism of the *exús* (African spirits) in Brazil, with tackling mental health issues in Argentina, or with vanquishing witchcraft and AIDS in South Africa.[7] In the United States, however, the primary focus of the IURD is on prosperity, health, and, equally importantly, "the pursuit of happiness."

The IURD in the United States

The IURD has a relatively short but contentious history in the United States. The denomination established its first church in the United States in 1986 in the Bronx, New York, and quickly moved on to open churches in California, now home to the largest U.S. branch of the church, in Los Angeles, then on to Texas, Massachusetts, Rhode Island, Connecticut, New

Jersey, Illinois, Florida, Washington, and Arizona.[8] By 2001, the church had 101 churches spread across United States, or at least in the states with sizeable immigrant populations.[9] As its Spanish-language name indicates, the church evangelizes almost exclusively among Latino immigrants to the United States, many of whom live in the country illegally, beneath the radar of social services, in poor, immigrant barrios of large urban centers. Significantly, the church uses its English name, the Universal Church of the Kingdom of God, in only a few locations in the United States, in congregations in New York and New Jersey and in Atlanta, Georgia; but even in these cases, the congregations are made up of immigrants, primarily African-descended people from the Caribbean.[10] The IURD does not appeal nor does it attempt to appeal to what might, with some inaccuracy, be called a conventionally "American" constituency of white, black, Hispanic, or Asian citizens who are already integrated into long-established social networks of school, church, family, and community, a point to which we shall return later.

Because the IURD is "foreign" in its origin, clergy (pastors in the United States, as in other countries, are almost exclusively Brazilians, although their helpers [obreros, or obreiros in Portuguese] are typically local), and clientele, the church has attracted relatively little attention in the United States as compared to other countries. In England it has been systematically denounced as "a bizarre cult" that preys on the ill and superstitious. In Belgium the Parliament put the church under investigation for its alleged "unlawful practices of a sect."[11] Most notably, in its home country, Brazil, the church is under almost constant attack for its aggressive money-raising techniques, for accusations of church officials' misuse of funds, and for its growing influence in the spheres of media and politics.[12]

By contrast, lack of concern over the IURD's presence in the United States may be due in part to Americans' historic laissez-faire attitude toward extreme religious expression or to the long tradition of what sociologist Nancy Ammerman has called "upstart sects" in this country.[13] Nevertheless, what little attention has been paid to the IURD outside its sphere of influence has been overwhelmingly negative, focused on the church's message of prosperity and its excessive emphasis on the coercion of members to give money to the church in amounts far beyond the biblical tithe. A sample of newspaper headlines about the Universal Church conveys the flavor of this concern: "Saving Souls for Dollars: Brazil's Fastest Growing Pentecostal Church Reaps Billions Selling Salvation to an Empire of Sinners,"[14] "Holy Roller Church Cashes in on the Faithful,"[15] "Prosperity Theology Pulls on the Purse Strings,"[16] "Demons on Broadway: Miracles. Exorcism. Catholic-bashing. Going for Broke in the Universal Church."[17]

Prosperity Theology

Such headlines underscore what is both the most controversial and, conversely (for believers), one of the most compelling doctrinal elements of the IURD, and this is its heavy emphasis on what is often called "prosperity gospel" or "health and wealth theology." This theology, which is perfected by, but is by no means original to, the IURD, is based on a simple but miraculous formula: God rewards his faithful with material blessing, good jobs, and robust good health. As theologian Harvey Cox has described it, "The idea is that through the crucifixion of Christ, Christians have inherited all the promises that God made to Abraham, and these include both spiritual and material well-being. The only problem is that Christians have too little faith to appropriate what is rightly theirs. What they need to do is state that claim loud and clear."[18] As U.S. televangelist Jim Bakker used to exhort his viewers, "When you ask the Lord for a camper, be sure and tell Him what color you want."

Thus, for the believer, much is expected financially, but much can be expected in return; for example, a pastor might urge the faithful to put their entire paycheck into the offering plate in order to reap the blessing of a better-paying job or unexpected wealth in return. Within the IURD, the giving of money to the church is a central tenet of belief; it is, in fact, central to salvation. In the church's thirteen-point statement of belief, the issue of the giving of tithes appears before statements about the Lord's Supper or eternal life made possible through Jesus' sacrifice. In the church's own words, "Tithes and offering are so sacred, as sacred as the Word of God. Tithes and offering signify the loyalty and love that the servant has toward the Lord. One cannot disassociate tithes and offering from the redemptive work of the Lord Jesus; they signify, in truth, the blood of the saved for those who need salvation."[19]

This formula for earthly salvation, which IURD founder Obispo (Bishop) Edir Macedo has referred to as "the miracle of the tithe" (*el milagro del diezmo*) or "putting God to the test," is as much sympathetic magic—essence for essence, money for money—as it is an article of faith.[20] According to the church, the giving of money in larger and larger amounts is both a test of faith and an act of obedience. As Macedo phrases it, "God *orders* us to test Him so that blessing can descend upon us" (emphasis mine).[21]

The Origins of Prosperity Theology

While Latin Americans may associate prosperity theology with neo-Pentecostal churches and with the IURD in particular, it is, in fact, sui generis (at least in its modern manifestation) to the United States. Prosperity theology's long history in this country dates back at least as far the nineteenth century, when preachers who advocated what they called the Gospel of Wealth urged believers to expect God to reward their faith with "acres of diamonds."[22] The simple algebra of "faith plus donation equals the good life" has long been a minority current in American evangelical Protestantism and has been a common denominator in North American televangelism for nearly a century.[23] The subtext of prosperity as an outcome of faith has a long history in American Protestantism that dates from the time of the Puritans, who eventually found alimentary abundance as much as religious freedom in their new land. The modern manifestation of "prosperity theology" dates back to the early twentieth century, having its origins, perhaps not coincidentally, around the time of the Azusa Street Revival (1906), the movement that launched modern Pentecostalism. Prosperity theology's roots are clearly linked to the emergence of religious media, where early preachers such as Charles R. Fuller (the first religious radio host and founder of Fuller Theological Seminary) and Aimee Semple McPherson, in the years prior World War II, crafted ministries based around the idea of God raining down blessings upon his faithful people.[24]

The distinguishing characteristic of contemporary prosperity theology is the miraculous quality of the blessing; material welfare is not merely a Horatio Alger–like byproduct of virtuous living, but it is, ipso facto, God's supernatural gift to the faithful, not unlike other gifts of the Holy Spirit such as glossolalia or faith healing. Although the concept of reliance on and trust in God for physical sustenance has deep biblical roots, the idea that God rewards his faithful with money and material well-being is a distinctly twentieth-century notion that has grown with the advent of radio and television evangelism. Early pioneers of religious media such as Rex Humbard, Kenneth Hagin, and, especially, Oral Roberts exhorted their audiences to send in money to support their technologically expensive ministries. In time, this evolved into a "theology" that demanded money as a proof of faith, which God would then return to the giver tenfold or more.[25] As Daniel Míguez has pointed out, the rhetorical distance between money as the root of all evil and money as the manifestation of God's grace proved to be remarkably short.[26]

By the end of the twentieth century, prosperity theology had become a staple of religious media in the United States and a dominant preoccupation of many of the fastest growing evangelical "non-denominational" churches in the country. The message of prosperity in many new churches surpasses that of holiness, aesthetic behavior, sin and salvation, or other more traditional foci of Protestant theology. To the contrary, prosperity theology exists in what Edin Abumanssur has called an "absence of macro-temporalness." Abumanssur writes, "The neo-Pentecostal discourse encourages the investment of time, money and attention in this life. Emphasizing the life to come, the final judgment, eternal suffering in the way that the [other] Protestants do would be totally out of keeping with this theology of prosperity."[27] At the same time, the image of the greedy con-man "stealing in the name of the Lord" has become an icon of American literature, song, and popular culture, so much so that it may account in part for why the IURD does not proselytize actively among the poor, rural, white and black, English-speaking American Protestants who make up the televangelists' primary, sizeable, and some-times gullible audience.[28] From a religious marketplace perspective, for a newcomer such as the IURD, that market is saturated.

While many Anglo-Americans and African Americans today subscribe to prosperity theology, particularly as developed in North American non-denominational (but almost always evangelical and usually Pentecostal) mega-churches such as Joel Osteen's thirty-thousand-member Lakewood Community Church in Houston[29] or Dallas-based T. D. Jakes Ministries, such congregations, though typically multiethnic and multi-class, are often difficult for non-English-speaking immigrants to penetrate. Although many American mega-churches, Lakewood included, offer worship services in Spanish, such services are often offered at off-hours. The American churches also lack the cultural context that makes a denomination like the IURD so attractive to immigrants.

The IURD's Use of Media

Within Brazil and elsewhere in South America where the IURD has flourished, the denomination has made extensive and effective use of the media to spread its message.[30] The IURD is like many other neo-Pentecostal churches in and from Latin America that spread their message primarily through oral as opposed to written culture, another point that distinguishes them from mainline Protestants, who have long reified the written word, from Scripture to prayer books to printed tracts.[31] Certainly, the denomination's influence in media has expanded far beyond evangelism to the point of being nearly inescapable in Brazilian popular culture. Besides basic religious program-ming, infomercials, and televised worship services, the church owns two television channels (Rede Record de Televisão and Rede Familiar), thirty-nine television stations, two national newspapers (including the widely read *Folha de São Paulo*), thirty radio stations, and also publishes a magazine.[32]

Within Brazil, the IURD, with more than two thousand churches (large and small) located in virtually every medium-sized to large city in the country, has enormous name recognition.[33] Brazilians tend to have strong feelings about the church in one way or another, a passion that was under-scored on October 12, 1995, when a pastor of the church kicked, poked, and mocked a statue of Nossa Senhora de Aparecida, Brazil's Catholic patroness, on national TV.[34] The public profile of the denomination is such that one of Rede Record's competitors, Rede Globo, ran a popular *telenovela* series that was transparently and unflatteringly based on the foibles of IURD's founder, Edir Macedo, and the flawed lives of the faithful.

The IURD's Media and Message in the United States

Outside of Brazil, the IURD is also a media giant, with an extensive network of radio and television broadcasts throughout South America. Even in Mexico, where the denomination has a much smaller footprint and where religious television programming is restricted, the church has bought time on Televisa, the major television outlet. Most of the IURD's television programming in the United States also comes from Televisa, although some also appears on Azteca América, a Mexican-oriented Spanish-language media outlet that is based in Los Angeles. Yet despite this vast global media presence, the IURD does not broadcast in English in the United States, and even most of its Spanish-language programming appears in off-market hours, such as midnight and early morning, at 6:30 and 8:00 a.m. in this country.

Why this apparent relative neglect of the American religious media market? Because the IURD, ever the astute student of the consumer market, does not attempt to capture an already-saturated religious media in the United States. Instead, to spread its message it relies largely on word of mouth and the church's visible and expanding presence in major American cities where there is a sizeable Latino immigrant population. Curiously, although the IURD has an active and highly successful missionary presence in Africa, it does not seem to proselytize aggressively among African immigrants to the United States, perhaps reflecting a limitation to their strategy of a Spanish-dominant ministry in the United States. This also underscores the point that the IURD's work abroad does not exist primarily to serve people who already belong to the church, but to bring new souls to the denomination. As Latin America's most aggressive missionary organization, the IURD largely replicates the model of its North Atlantic predecessors by seeing fields "ripe for the harvest" among both non-Christians and non-practicing Christians and among practicing Christians in other denominations, including other Protestant churches. Adapting the approach that has served them well in Brazil to their efforts in the United States, the IURD has applied an expansion strategy of building a presence first in large cities, then medium-sized cities, and then expanding with satellite churches in smaller communities.[35]

The IURD's "Liberation of Theology"

The meteoric growth of the IURD in the United States suggests that the Brazilianized interpretation of health-and-wealth theology has tapped into a deep vein of physical and metaphysical need for Latino immigrants.[36] What the IURD brings to this body of theology, expressed mainly through the teachings of Macedo and passed down through the careful training of the Brazilian missionary-pastors, is the specific emphasis on the life of abundance, good health, and happiness, cast against the illness, poverty, family problems, crime, and alcoholism that plagued one's life before *membership in the church*.[37]

The emphasis here is placed because within the IURD, the church itself becomes the means of salvation, the conduit to Jesus Christ; salvation is found inside the walls of the church, and all spiritual transactions take place in the building. In a visit to a church in Houston, Texas, the pastor, in heavily Portuguese-inflected Spanish, told the congregation, "Sure, you can pray at home, but this is the place you come to pray. What if you tried to buy beef steak at a pharmacy? Would you try to buy medicine in a shoe store? They'd think you were crazy. So if you want to pray, you should come to a house of prayer (*casa de oración*)."

The denomination places strong emphasis on attendance. Most IURD churches hold services seven days a week, with at least four services per day. Regular attendance at church is an essential part of the IURD's modus operandi; salvation comes only within the sacred precincts of an IURD temple. IURD TV and radio programming strongly emphasizes this point; unlike most U.S. religious television, where viewers are urged to consider themselves part of a virtual congregation as they sit at home in front of their TVs, the IURD demands that its followers attend actual services.[38]

Church services on specific days of the week carry a special intercession: health and curing, peace in the home, relief from addition, help in finding a job, increasing wealth. Members are encouraged to attend church every Sunday and regularly on at least one weekday as well, but additional benefits accrue to those who attend the most services. In addition, the church advocates making a "chain of prayer," that is, praying for the same thing twelve or thirteen Thursdays or Fridays in a row, with the believer having to start all over again if the chain is broken.[39] Perhaps in a nod to the Mexican Catholic origin of so many of its U.S. members, the IURD actually refers to these prayer chains as "novenas" in Texas—a use of Catholic liturgical terminology that would be considered anathema in most Latin Protestant churches. Most popular are the *sesiones de descargo* (acquittal or release sessions), which are exorcisms that occur regularly, sometimes six days per week.

The Miracle of the Tithe

Members are urged to give a donation at every service they attend, although in the services I visited in Houston, the pastor, perhaps influenced by presence of the incongruent *gabacha* in the audience, was careful to state that God's blessing was not dependent on the amount of the money, but the spirit of the giver. Instead, the emphasis of the service was on constant and repeated participation of the congregation in the service, underscored by the pastor's stern admonition and a headcount of who would attend the same service the following week.

In economic parlance, the IURD demands heavy investments not only of economic capital, but also of human capital from its members. This aspect is critical to the growth of the church, and not only in terms of sheer numbers. As Laurence Iannoccone has pointed out, most religious human capital is "context specific" (relevant only to the particular congregations, denominations, or religious tradition in which it arose), enhancing the real or perceived value of the particular religious group that occasioned its accumulation.[40] Thus, in building up consistency and attendance, the IURD carefully interweaves social and physical spaces, habit and repetition, and coercion and voluntarism into what members feel is a seamless spiritual garment.

Conversion and Liminality

The allure of such a garment is obvious, especially considering that the majority of Spanish-speaking immigrants made their way to the United States for economic reasons. Nevertheless, immigrants are, in Victor Turner's works, "liminal *personae*" (threshold people) who slip through the networks that normally position people within a given cultural space.[41] In this regard, the IURDs are perfectly and paradoxically congruent with many immigrants' long-deferred and often modest economic dreams. A series of testimonies from church members living in the United States offers clear evidence of this equation: "From poverty in New York to owner of a bread factory (*fábrica de pan*)," one testimony announces proudly. "New home and American residency," proclaims another. The testimony of a third states, "I am the owner of a new car, through the power of God."[42]

Choosing the IURD

Yet the transparent logic of prosperity theology, one could argue, is not sufficient to explain the allure of the IURD in the United States, even though its message seeks to appeal to both material and religious "economic" interests. To paraphrase the old saying, fools and their money may soon be parted, but most assuredly the church's members are anything but fools; to the contrary, they are generally hard-working, frugal people who have made the arduous and challenging choice to begin a new life in a new country. Most would not willingly give away their hard-earned money unless they felt they were receiving something worthwhile in return. The choice to join or not join a church such as the IURD may indeed be based upon rational choice or at least on rational decision-making. In Rodney Stark's axiom, this exchange can be understood as one in which people find "it is necessary to enter into a long-term exchange relationship with the divine and with divinely inspired institutions, in order to follow the instructions [on how the reward can be achieved over the long term], ... [C]hurches rest upon these underlying exchange relationships."[43] But for those who remain in the church, the decision to stay, perhaps, has more to do with the *spiritual capital*—that is, the social networks and sense of belonging—that members feel they acquire through the church, a point to which we shall return later.

Beyond the investment of human and economic capital that it requires of its members, the church has additional spiritual goods to offer in exchange, and this has to do with the display of charismata in the local services. IURD services are renowned for their fiery, full-throated-style preaching, where the pastor shouts out his message at the top of his lungs and peppers the congregations with questions for which he demands swift and emphatic answers. The trademark style of IURD preaching—part bullying, part paternal, and part cheerleader—is carefully taught to Brazilian pastors and is therefore remarkably uniform in style, if not necessarily content, from one church to another.[44] Consistent, too, is the interaction between the pastor and his *obreros* (workers or assistants, easily identified by their white shirts and navy pants or skirts), who move through the congregation, laying hands on each person present to bless or to cast out demons with a loud and sibilant *¡Sal!* (Out!) It is in this context where local issues are likely to emerge and where the denomination's plastic theology can mold itself to parochial tastes. Not surprisingly, it is in this aspect of practice that the IURD in the United States takes on what is perhaps its most local character.

Spiritual Warfare

In his 1990 work, *Is Latin America Turning Protestant?* anthropologist David Stoll notes, "Evil spirits are the terms in which the poor and not-so-poor understand their difficulties. . . . As for pentecostalism, it is Christianity's main bid to subdue or . . . 'rebuke' the clouds of demons swarming around the planet."[45] Although the tone of Stoll's observation is somewhat droll, it does, in fact, describe precisely the worldview of many Pentecostals, especially those in and from Latin America, who see the world in strictly bifurcated terms: the church and the *mundo* (world), a dangerous domain largely ruled by Satan and his minions. Those who share this worldview also share a firm sense that the modern society's as well as each individual's ills are literally demonic in origin and must be confronted on exactly those terms. The struggle between these two worlds, in which believers are actively engaged as celestial warriors, is known as Spiritual Warfare, a battle which the IURD highlights in its *sesiones de descargo*.

Spiritual Warfare is a highly aggressive theological approach in which Pentecostal "Armies of God" seek quite literally to cast out the demons which plague modern society. Spiritual Warriors engage in what they call "spiritual mapping," in which they purport to identify the dark spirits that have set up a "stronghold" in a given locality. According to Francis Frangipane, a leading proponent (who is not associated with the IURD), "There are satanic strongholds over countries and communities, and there are strongholds which influence churches and individuals. Wherever a stronghold exists, it is a demonically induced pattern of thinking. Specifically, it is a 'house made of thoughts' that has become a dwelling place for satanic activity."[46] These dark forces ("fallen angels, principalities, dominions, and demons") are then forced out of a locality through prayers, fasting, and exorcism.[47] Once exorcised and "redeemed in Jesus' name," Spiritual Warriors claim that the locality is, in the term of art, "transformed" in ways that are measurable even by a secular yardstick, such as improved employment, health, and family relations.

Modernity as the Demonic Parody

As with prosperity theology, Spiritual Warfare did not originate with the IURD (its terms of art make their modern appearance in the writings of C. Peter Wagner, George Otis. Jr., and others of Fuller Theological Seminary during early 1990s), but the Brazilian denomination has become its international proponent par excellence, both because of the deeply supernatural theology's popular appeal and because of its unique adaptability to local conditions. As an organizing principle by which to order one's life, Spiritual Warfare makes particular sense to converts, since the idea that Satan's manifest presence in this world is hardly new in Latin American cosmovision and religious popular thought, dating as far back as Christianity's earliest days in the New World.[48] The belief that the Devil is the quite literally modernity's patron "saint" is also nothing new—in Taussig's quarter-century-old study of Bolivian miners, for example, he points to the statue of the "Tio" (a figure of Satan) as the miners' symbol and icon of "commodity capitalism."[49] The underlying premise of many popular religious practices, such as Mexican curanderismo, Cuban Santería, Brazilian Umbanda, or even the everyday practice of petitioning the Catholic saints, presupposes a universe that is literally vibrating with spirits, holy beings, santos, sacred energies, African gods, living essences, and Amerindian deities, many of whom are in constant competition with one another and whom believers can influence through supplication or opposition.

For converts, part of the great appeal of Spiritual Warfare theology and the IURD in particular is that the church specifically does not negate the existence of these spirit beings, who often loomed large in the existential realities of converts in their former lives. Instead, it dramatically re-orders their place in the cosmos, as still-powerful demons and fallen angels who seek to destroy the harmonious universe over which God presides. Alejandro Frigerio (in this volume, chapter 2) refers to the Brazilian academic preference to speak of conversion as "passage," and the term is, indeed, applicable here. The church and its theology also offer protection for converts during that vulnerable period of transition as they are moving from one world to the next, from the *mundo* to the church—a spiritual journey that in many ways echoes the physical passage across the international border in both its peril and its urgency.

As an adaptive strategy, Spiritual Warfare is highly malleable to local conditions, and its discursive elements often directly reflect the most volatile cultural fault lines within a given society. One of the major preoccupations of the IURD in Brazil is the expulsion of demons and fallen angels, as the many gods of the African diaspora are identified by the church. In South Africa, spirit moves to vanquish witchcraft and to banish the ancestors who are angered by their children's conversion and neglect. But in the United States, the spirits to be exorcised are the very tangible evils that afflict the liminal, urban, "illegal" poor. Often, the expulsion of evil spirits is accompanied by talismanic rituals—small pieces of cloth on which the faithful wipe, then burn away their physical or mental pains. Holy oil is blessed to anoint heads and hearts and footbaths of colored water are laid out through which troubled souls may walk out evil and pain. But the climax of the service is the *descargo*, the casting out of demons and evils spirits.

Cura Divina

In Brazil and in many other parts of Latin America, the healing of physical illness (faith healing, known in Spanish as *sanación* or *cura divina*) predominates these efforts both in neo-Pentecostalism, in general, and in the IURD, in particular.[50] But in the United States, at least at the worship services observed for this study, the focus of exorcism was not so much on the physical body as on afflictions of the mind and spirit: "Sal! Evil spirit of sexual abuse, of depression, of alcoholism! Out! Demons of unemployment, of spouses who are addicted to drugs! Sal, spirit of migraines! Out! Dark angels of envy and curses! Out! Spirit that made my child join a street gang. Out! Devils of diabetes and AIDS! Sal! Evil spirit of cancer. Out! Demons of hopelessness and violence and gunfire!"

In the United States as in Brazil, many of the church's supplicants are women, as are many of those who are temporarily possessed by demons—those evil beings scream and howl their way out of the church. Edir Macedo, the IURD's founder, has written of women's special vulnerability as women of God, especially in the matter of being becoming vessels of evil during exorcism.[51] However, scholar Fernanda da Silva Pimentel has suggested that the act of possession itself provides a woman with "the possibility to liberate her demons, a chance that she would never have in everyday life."[52]

In the IURD, the naming of these demons is not metaphoric, but absolutely real and concrete. Although the church in the United States shies away from the word "exorcism" (*exorcismo*), it nonetheless fully embraces the practice, for the purging of demons and evil spirits from believers lie at the heart of the church's message and its appeal. In the lexicon of the denomination, the church, by the power of Jesus Christ, re-orders a moral universe that is not merely capricious, but innately evil. In casting out spirits, the church seizes power away from evil and returns it to the loving power of God through his people.[53] Again, the testimonies of the faithful—liminal people no longer, but fully participating citizens of the Kingdom and warriors in God's own celestial army—bears witness to the reclamation of God's power through the church.

"My own street gang planned to kill me." "My grave was [already] prepared, but now I am healthy." "My husband was involved in vices, using drugs and drinking alcohol, and he used to beat me." "I [used to] drink a lot, I used drugs—marijuana, cocaine, pills—and I prostituted myself. . . . today I am different, all the suffering has ended. This is why I affirm that the Iglesia Universal is the church of God, living and powerful. I have the proof in my life."[54] While the performance of such testimonies may be formulaic and almost ritualized,[55] the content of believers' testimonies nonetheless provides a catalogue not only of personal anguish but also of perceived resolution. A close reading of such testimonies suggests that if religious belief, as J. Milton Yinger has implied, is grounded in suffering, then the church has been very successful in identifying its function.[56]

The Question of Conversion and the IURD

The IURD's ability, within reason, to mold its theology to local religious "consumer needs" and its dexterity in keeping its finger on the pulse of that market is, we argue here, one of the keys to its success both in Brazil and abroad. But this very flexibility raises some interesting questions as to whether or not the church's new members, whether they come from the Catholic, nominalist, or other Protestant backgrounds, genuinely convert; that is to say, do they experience the kind of radical change of life that sociologist Max Heirich, in a seminal 1977 article, spoke of as "changing a sense of root reality" or providing a "conscious shift of one's sense of grounding."[57] Heirich identifies two forms of conversion. One involves a "dramatic turnout . . . accepting a belief system and behaviors strongly at odds with one's previous cognitive structure and actions." The other involves "returning to a set of beliefs and commitments against one has been strongly in rebellion."[58]

While conversion to the IURD clearly involves a strong element of the first, it explicitly does not demand that the convert *reject* his or her prior religious worldview—in Heirich's phrase, "root reality"—but rather that the convert simply *invert* it. In their study of the sociology of conversion, David Snow and Richard Machalek suggest that conversion, as a radical personal change, necessarily includes a radical transformation in what G. H. Mead has called a "universe of discourse."[59] Snow and Machalek argue that "conversion concerns not only a change in values, beliefs and identities, but more fundamentally and significantly, it entails the displacement of one universe of discourse by another."[60] It is not hard to argue that converts to the IURD may well exhibit the kind of radical change in lifestyle and outlook that define "conversion." But the universe of discourse in which this takes place is not so much replaced as it is upended. By perceiving their previous universe of discourse as a demonic parody, converts need not abandon their root reality, but simply seek to dwell through the church in its mirror image.

Stop Suffering

This brings us, finally, to the logo found at all IURD churches: a heart bisected by a white dove, above which are written the words, "Stop Suffering" (*Pare de sufrir*). While some of the theology and even the name of the IURD may differ from one location and one country to another, the slogan of the church never, ever varies and is instantly identifiable to anyone who has had any familiarity with the group, even in Belgium or Guatemala, where the church entered the country under an assumed name.[61]

It is, frankly, difficult to know with any certainty whether Edir Macedo established the IURD with his eye on God or Mammon. But as the church is starting to grow into its name and become a genuinely universal church, Macedo's original motives are increasingly beside the point. In either case, the IURD is growing because people believe that it is able to make good on this single, simple promise: stop suffering. Through its exorcisms, talismans, and prosperity gospel, the IURD offers its members a new moral framework for contextualizing human suffering and a clear-cut blueprint for relief. In so doing, the church addresses head-on the fundamental conundrum of any religion, the question that Max Weber poses as "theodicy" or the "problem of how the extraordinary power of . . . God may be reconciled with the imperfection of the world that he has created and rules over."[62] For its believers, the church has, by accident or design, uniquely found an answer to this fundamental riddle.

Conclusion

From a religious marketplace perspective, the IURD is successful because of its skillful ability to identify and target its market (poor immigrants) through a transparent formula that makes prosperity the direct result of one's faith and, just as importantly, membership in the church. Yet I would argue that, in fact, it is precisely this equation that points up the limitations of strict economic explanations (here, meant in the sense of economic determinism) for conversion, for the simple reason that joining the IURD does not make actual economic sense in terms of dollars and cents. Members of the IURD do not, quantitatively, appear to do better financially than their neighbors who do not subscribe to prosperity theology. Data from an ongoing quantitative study of wealth/poverty and church affiliation in Rio de Janeiro shows no measurable statistical income differential between IURD members and comparable Catholics.[63]

Members figure this out sooner or later, but many continue to attend services and, indeed, demonstrate their loyalty by continuing to give money to the church. On the other hand, the IURD tends to have a high congregational turnover rate in many parts of the world; this is presumably also true in the United States as well. Among those who do stay, this suggests one of two things: (1) that people are willing to retain unrealistic hope for a supernatural cure for their financial woes or (2) that they believe the church provides them with spiritual benefits or spiritual capital that extends beyond the art of the deal.

In support of this latter argument, I return to Pierre Bourdieu's notion of social capital, the collective value of social networks and mutual community responsibility that have benefits at both the individual and community levels.[64] As David Smilde points out in chapter 5, the issue of social networking has to do not only with the influence of the group and conformity, but also with meaning. As Smilde notes, "events and contingencies can reevaluate existing discourses, determine what direction they take, the symbolic elements that dominate." This can create a symbolic reordering that both echoes and helps to regularize the many changes inherent in immigration to a new country.

This concept has been recently refined by Robert Putnam, who suggests that religion is a major factor in the formation of social networks and trust; as such, "spiritual capital" is a critical subset of social capital. In a most basic sense, spiritual capital is the notion that religious beliefs can provide benefit on their own terms, building on the kind of self-referential internal logic described by Clifford Geertz.[65] In more specific terms, religion offers those who believe in it specific kinds of resources that they have not obtained or cannot obtain as effectively from other sources: knowledge, belief, emotion, experience, motivation, meaning, community, power, purposefulness, satisfaction, a sense of peace and well-being, and even love.

If we may expand the narrow definition of spiritual capital to include all of these elements, the IURD would seem to offer spiritual capital at a high rate of return. It does so by not only by providing relief from everyday ills and the various pathogens of poverty, but also by reordering a universe in which a benevolent God desires lots of good things, quite literally, for his beloved. At the most basic level, as Brazilian psychologist Mary Ruta Gomes Esperandio has noted, "Salvation, in this form of religion, is synonymous with prosperity and a sense of well being."[66] Far less concerned than traditional Christianity with fundamental ideas of sin and grace, the IURD instead is preoccupied with the empowerment and temporal success of its members, so long as they remain part of the church and continue to contribute money to it. As such, the IURD provides its members with the means to slip the bonds of liminality to become part of an extensive network of self-affirming fellow believers, and, of course, it claims to provide a methodology for achieving financial success.

In theoretical terms, then, this expanded concept of spiritual capital may, I believe, help us to clarify why transnational immigrants convert to a church that separates them both from the religious culture of their homelands (whether Catholic or Protestant) and from the very hard-earned money that they have come to the United States to earn. Allan Deck has argued that Latinos join new churches to "free themselves from the hierarchical, strongly communal, rural, traditional social and family structure, a system that seems more and more dysfunctional in the new circumstances of immigrant life in the United States."[67] Yet by the same token, a church such as the IURD, which has a very clear idea of the needs and aspirations of its target membership, is uniquely adept at producing a new set of relationships, social networks, fictive kinships (made up of *hermanas/hermanos*), and tightly prescribed patterns for living that build social capital and help develop both the individual and the church community at large. To put it another way, members of the IURD stop suffering. In short, the IURD may not make its members rich, but it can, indeed, provide them with spiritual capital—that is, a set of beliefs, social networks, a renewed sense of self-worth and purpose—that helps immigrant converts, empowered celestial warriors all, to successfully navigate the rugged terrain of urban America.

NOTES

1. For an early account of the emergence of the modern Pentecostal movement, see Walter Hollenweger, *The Pentecostals* (Peabody, MA: Hendrickson Publishers, 1968).

2. See www.universalchurch.com; Ricardo Mariano, "Expansão Pentecostal no Brasil: O caso da Igreja Universal," *Estudos Avansados* 18, no. 52 (2004): 140.

3. This data is from 2004, so it is somewhat dated. At that time, the countries (outside of Brazil) where there IURD had ten or more churches were the United States, Argentina, Venezuela, Portugal, the United Kingdom, Ivory Coast, Mozambique, and South Africa (Mariano, "Expansão Pentecostal no Brasil," 141).

4. Mariano, "Expansão Pentecostal no Brasil," 137–146.

5. See Peter Berger, *The Sacred Canopy* (Garden City, NY: Anchor Books, 1969); Anthony Gill, *Render unto Caesar* (Chicago: University of Chicago Press, 1998); Rodney Stark and Roger Finke, *The Churching of America, 1776–1990* (New Brunswick, NJ: Rutgers University Press, 1992); and Andrew Chesnut, *Competitive Spirits: Latin America's New Religious Economy* (New York: Oxford University Press, 2003).

6. "Credence goods" are defined as goods "for which 'quality' is not easily determined before or after purchase. Reputation of the supplier is the primary assurance of quality." Ekelund et al., as cited in Anthony Gill, "The Struggle to Be Soul Provider," in *Latin American Religion in Motion*, ed. Christian Smith and Joshua Prokopy (New York: Routledge, 1999), 39.

7. For some specific case studies, see Pablo Semán, "A Igreja Universal na Argentina," in *Igreja Universal do Reino de Deus: Os novos conquistadores da fé*, ed. Ari Pedro Oro, André Corten, and Jean-Pierre Dozon (São Paulo: Paulinas Livros, 2003), 69–78; and André Corten, "A Igreja Universal no Africa do Sul," in ibid., 137–146; see also "Yisha Sathane, Yisha Tokoloshe," *Johannesburg Mail and Guardian*, April 2, 1999.

8. These locations are noted on the IURD's Web site at http://noticias.arcauniversal. com.br/ arcanews/integra. According to the Web site, there were main churches (as opposed to satellite churches) in New York City and environs (16), Florida (3), Texas (10), Washington, D.C. (1), Illinois (Chicago area) (1), Nevada (Las Vegas) (1), Massachusetts (1), Rhode Island (1), and California (28). The site is clearly not regularly updated, however, as evinced by the fact that it listed only one church in Texas, at a location in Houston that is no longer used by the church. The IURD has congregations in at least six other Texas cities: Dallas, San Antonio, El Paso, Laredo, McAllen (both the Laredo and McAllen churches are located where they can be seen from the Mexican side of the border), and, as of spring 2006, Austin.

9. The 1986 date comes from Brazilian sociologist Ricardo Mariano and is probably accurate, corresponding to when Edir Macedo moved to the United States to escape legal and political problems in Brazil. However, the official history on the church's Web site places the date of the first U.S. congregation in 1994. See Ricardo Mariano, "A Igreja Universal no Brazil," in *Igreja Universal*, ed. Ari, Corten, and Dozon, 53–67.

10. A. Seymour Jr., "Church Raises Eyebrows on Peachtree Street: Brazilian Sect Has Faced Past Investigations," *Atlanta Journal-Constitution*, June 19, 2001.

11. See, for example: "'Bizarre' Sect Seeks Street Collections," *Birmingham Post*, July 17, 2001; Mary Braid, "The Church that 'Drives Evil from the Possessed,'" *London Independent*, January 2001; Jonathan Petre, Chris Hastings, and Adam Lusher, "Purging of 'Demons' Nets Millions," *Telegraph*, U.K. online newspaper, January 14, 2001; "Church Provokes Unholy Row," *BBC News*, February 28, 2000. The Belgium report was delivered on April 28, 1997, but was inconclusive. See Deinst Algermen Zaken-Kramer, Quaesttuur@deKamer.be.

12. The IURD's influence is not limited to media. During the 2002 presidential elections, according to religious anthropologist Ari Pedro Oro, the church's unlikely political alliance with the Partido dos Trabalhadores and the Partido Liberal provided a bloc of evangelical votes that contributed to the election of Luis Inácio Lula da Silva (Lula) to the presidency. It also signaled the church's formal entry into the political field. Oro, Corten, and Dozon, *Igreja Universal*, 281; see also Alexandre Brasil Fonseca, "Igreja Universal: Um império midiático," in *Igreja*

Universal, ed, Oro, Corten, and Dozon, 259–280; and Ken Serbin, "Brazilian Church Builds an International Empire—The Universal Church of the Kingdom of God, *Christian Century*, April 10, 1996.

13. Nancy T. Ammerman, "Religious Choice and Religious Vitality: The Market and Beyond," in *Rational Choice Theory and Religion*, ed. Lawrence A. Young (London: Routledge, 1997), 121.

14. *Time*, March 11, 1996.

15. *New York Post*, July 23, 2000.

16. *Washington Post*, February, 13, 2001.

17. *Los Angeles Weekly*, July 5, 2001.

18. Harvey Cox, *Fire from Heaven: The Rise of Pentecostal Spirituality and the Reshaping of Religion in the Twenty-First Century* (Reading, MA: Addison-Wesley Publishing Company, 1995), 271–272.

19. See http://iglesiauniversal.com.ar/iurd/fundam.htm.

20. See IURD, *Vida en Abundancia* (Colección Reino de Dios), capitulo VI. This is a devotional manual published by the church (no city or date of publication).

21. IURD, *Vida y Abundancia*, 62.

22. This is the title of a speech that is considered by many to be the opening salvo of modern prosperity theology. It comes from Russell H. Conwell, a successful businessman cum popular preacher and inspirational speaker in the late nineteenth and early twentieth centuries. In his speaking career, which ran from 1870 until his death in 1925, Conwell gave the "Acres of Diamonds" speech more than six thousand times. Conwell, who was also the founder of Temple University, did not see the speech as having to do with wealth, but rather to him it signified this: "Your diamonds are not in far-away mountains or in distant seas; they are in your own back yard if you will but dig for the them." See http://www.temple.edu/about/temples_founder.html.

23. See Joel A. Carpenter, *Revive Us Again: The Reawakening of American Fundamentalism* (New York: Oxford, 1997).

24. See Mark A. Noll, *The Work We Have to Do: A History of Protestants in America* (New York: Oxford, 2000), 100–104.

25. It bears mentioning that the first true televangelist, Billy Graham, who was the first to combine old-time tent revival techniques with large-capacity venues such as football stadiums and television in the early 1950s, has never been a proponent of prosperity theology per se.

26. I have flagrantly mistranslated and paraphrased Míguez here, while retaining, I hope, the flavor of his meaning. His actual phrase is "del capitalismo del demonio al capitalismo del Espiritu Santo." See Daniel Míguez, "Pentecostalism and Modernization in a Latin American Key: Rethinking the Cultural Effects of Structural Change in Argentina," paper presented to the Latin American Studies Association, Washington, D.C., 2001, 4.

27. Edin Sued Abumanssur, "Crisis as Opportunity: Church Structure in Times of Global Transformations. Religion within a Context of Globalisation: The Case of Brazil," *Revista de Estudos da Religião* (REVER) 3, no. 2 (2002): http://www.pucsp.br/rever.

28. For examples, see Sinclair Lewis's scathing novel, *Elmer Gantry* (1924), about an unscrupulous evangelist or the 1950s movie based on that book. In recent years,

the ministries of Jim Bakker, Robert Tilton, and Jimmy Swaggart were all felled in part by revelations of misuse of donated funds to support the extravagant lifestyles of these televangelists. The line from the song quoted above is from "Papa Was a Rolling Stone," by the Temptations, circa 1972. See Jeffrey K. Hadden and Anson Shupe, *Televangelism: Power and Politics on God's Frontier* (New York: Holt, 1988).

29. "Lakewood Church Set to Open Doors: The Nation's Largest Church," http://www. htexas.com/feature.cfm?Story=451.

30. See Leonildo Silveira Campos, *Teatro, templo e Mercado: Organização e marketing dum empreendimento neopentecostal* (Petrópolis: Voces e São Paulo, Umesp e Simpósio, 1997).

31. See Leonildo Silveira Campos, "O marketing e as estratégias de comunicação da Igreja Universal do Reino de Deus," http://www.intercom.org.br/papers/1999/gt17/17c08.PDF; see also Quentin Schultz, "Orality and Power in Latin American Pentecostalism," in *Coming of Age: Protestantism in Contemporary Latin America*, ed. Daniel R. Miller (Laham: University Press of America, 1994).

32. Campos, "O marketing."

33. Ricardo Mariano, "Expansão Pentecostal no Brasil," 121–155.

34. See Paul C. Johnson, "Kicking, Stripping, and Re-Dressing a Saint in Black: Visions of Public Space in Brazil's Recent Holy War," *History of Religion* 37, no. 2 (November 1997): 122–140.

35. Mariano, "A Igreja Universal," 125.

36. "Liberation of Theology" is the title of one of Edir Macedo's well-known works. It is an obvious and negative reference to Catholic Liberation Theology. Obispo Macedo, *La liberación de la teología* (Barcelona: Editorial Intercontinental, 1996).

37. See IURD, *Vida y Abundancia*.

38. See Karina Medeiros de Lima, "Propaganda e fé: Como a Igreja Universal do Reino de Deus utiliza as técnicas de propaganda e marketing para sua expansão-exemplo de caso sul-mato-grossense," paper presented at Sociedade Brasileiro de Ciências de Comunicação, Campo Grande, http://www.intercom.org.br/papers/xxiv-ci/np03/NP3LIMA.pdf.

39. "Uneasy feeling by a concerned member," February 10, 2001, http://www.rickross. com/references/universal/18html.

40. Laurence R. Iannoccone, "Framework for the Scientific Study of Religion," in *Rational Choice Theory and Religion*, ed. Young, 32–33.

41. See Victor Turner, "Liminality and Communitatas," in his *The Ritual Process: Structure and Anti-Structure* (Chicago: Aldine Publishing, 1969), 94–113, 125–130.

42. See http://www.universalchurch.org/testimonios.htm.

43. Stark and Finke, *The Churching of America*, 7.

44. IURD pastors are not strictly required to have any formal theological training per se, but all receive training in the IURD's trademarked "função pastoral"—prayer, preaching, exorcism, how to ask for offerings and tithes, singing, and counseling (Mariano, "A Igreja Universal," 56).

45. David Stoll, *Is Latin America Turning Protestant? The Politics of Evangelical Growth* (Berkeley: University of California Press, 1990), 112.

46. Francis Frangipane, *The Three Battlegrounds: An In-Depth View of the Three Arenas of Spiritual Warfare, The Mind, the Church, and the Heavenly Places* (Cedar Rapids, IA: Arrow Publications, 2002), 29.

47. Harold Caballeros, *Guerra espiritual, intercesión y mapeo espiritual: Especial para todos aquellos que tienen una carga de oración por su nación* (Guatemala: Iglesia El Shaddai, Centro de Adiestramiento Cristiano, n.d.).

48. Examples of this perspective are legion, but see especially Fernando Cervantes, *The Devil in the New World: The Impact of Diabolism in New Spain* (New Haven: Yale University Press, 1994).

49. See Michael Taussig, *The Devil and Commodity Fetishism in South America* (Chapel Hill: University of North Carolina, 1980).

50. For more on faith healing and Pentecostalism, see Miriam Cristina Rabelo, "Religião e cura: Algumas reflexões sobre e experiência religiosa das classes populares urbanas," *Cadernos de Saúde Pública* 9, no. 3 (July–September 1993), http://www.scielo. br; see also Manuela Cantón Delgado, *Bautizados en fuego: Protestantes, discursos de conversión y política en Guatemala (1989–1993)* (Antigua, Guatemala: CIRMA, 1998).

51. Edir Macedo, *O Perfil da Mulher de Deus* (Rio de Janeiro: Editora Gráfia Universal, 2002).

52. Fernanda da Silva Pimentel, "Psiquê nos Domínios do Demônio-um olhar sobre a relação entre exorcismo e cura num grupo de mulheres fiéis da Igreja Universal do Reino de Deus," *Revista de Estudos da Religião* 2, no. 5 (2005), http://www.puscp. br/rever.

53. See Obispo Edir Macedo, *La Liberación de la Teología* (Barcelona: Colección Reino de Dios, 1996).

54. See http://www.universalchurch.org/testimonios.htm.

55. Many studies have demonstrated that convert testimonies (not only in Protestant churches but even in groups such as AA or Zen practitioners) "tend to be constructed in accordance with group-specific guidelines for interpreting certain experiences as religious conversion." David A. Snow and Richard Machalek, "The Sociology of Conversion," *Annual Review of Sociology* 10 (1984): 175.

56. See J. Milton Yinger. *The Scientific Study of Religion* (New York: Macmillan Press, 1970), 228.

57. Max Heirich, "Change of Heart: A Test of Some Widely Held Theories about Religious Conversion," *American Journal of Sociology* 83, no. 3 (1977): 674.

58. Ibid., 654.

59. Snow and Machalek, "The Sociology of Conversion," 170; G. H. Mead, *Mind, Self, and Society* (Chicago: University of Chicago Press, 1962), 88–90.

60. Snow and Machalek, "The Sociology of Conversion," 170.

61. In Guatemala, the church goes by the name Comunidad de Dios. In Belgium, where the church has a large following among African immigrants in Antwerp and Brussels, it is known as Communauté chrétienne du saint-esprit.

62. Max Weber, as cited in "Social Class, Religion, and Power: A Classic Field of Inquiry," in *Sociology of Religion, Contemporary Developments*, ed. Kevin J. Christiano, William H. Swatos Jr., and Peter Kivisto (New York: Altamira Press, 2002), 129.

63. See Joseph Potter, Sarah McKinnon, and Virginia Garrard-Burnett, "Protestantism and Adolescent Fertility in Rio de Janeiro: Recent Data Based on the 2000 National Census," forthcoming, 2007.

64. See Pierre Bourdieu, "The Forms of Capital," in *Handbook of Theory and Research for the Sociology of Education*, ed. John G. Richardson (New York: Greenwood Press, 1986).

65. See Robert Putman, *Bowling Alone: The Collapse and Revival of American Community* (New York: Simon and Schuster, 2000); Clifford Geertz, *The Interpretation of Cultures* (New York: Basic Books, 1973.)

66. Mary Ruta Gomes Esperandio, "A (est)ética do cuidado e religiosidade contemporânea: A Igreja Universal do Reino de Deus em perspectiva," http://www.est.com.br/nepp/numero_07/Mary.htm.

67. Allan Deck, "The Challenge of Evangelical/Pentecostal Christianity to Hispanic Catholicism," in *Religion and American Culture*, ed. David G. Hackett (New York: Routledge, 1995), 471, as cited in *Christianity, Social Change, and Globalization in the America*, ed. Anna Peterson, Manuel Vásquez, and Philip Williams (New Brunswick, NJ: Rutgers University Press, 2001), 7.

The research for this chapter was sponsored in part by a grant from the Metanexus/Templeton Foundation.

12

Healing the Nation

Pentecostal Identity and Social Change in Bolivia

JILL M. WIGHTMAN

In the past twenty years, Bolivia has undergone a drastic shift away from the type of society it had become after the 1952 National Revolution. Beginning in the mid-1980s a series of economic and political reforms, generally classified under the rubric of neoliberal reform, were enacted. These reforms are popularly conceived of as having triggered an economic crisis that still plagues the nation and having caused immense suffering among Bolivia's impoverished majority and increasingly volatile middle-class as they struggle to provide for themselves and their families. In light of recent widespread public protest in Bolivia against these neoliberal policies (culminating in the election of Evo Morales to the presidency),[1] it is clear that ordinary men and women are rejecting policies and relations advocated or enforced by the neoliberal state. The new situation has called for new identities and new types of coalitions through which the marginalized can define themselves against the state, the elite, and the forces of global capitalism. In the face of this drastic reshaping of Bolivian society, I am interested in examining the ways in which Bolivians are creating new subjectivities for themselves through discourses of "born-again" conversion as well as the ways in which Pentecostals as a group are harnessing these new identities to a project of social change and the promise of a new Bolivia.

Pentecostals in Latin America have often been saddled with a reputation for being otherworldly and averse to participation in the social and political affairs of their nations. But in Bolivia and elsewhere in Latin America they can be seen actively engaging in the public life of their cities and states and heard actively critiquing the political status quo and calling for change. During my ethnographic research in Pentecostal congregations in Cochabamba, Bolivia, I often heard pastors and lay persons alike use the pulpit to discuss political matters, to criticize Bolivian and world leaders, and to offer an alternative vision for a "new Bolivia." And I saw them mobilizing as Pentecostals to "take the streets" in a show of their social power in the annual March for Jesus. My ethnographic research suggests that many Pentecostals and other *evangélicos* see themselves as forces of positive change in society. They see themselves as working to win "Bolivia for Christ" and to "heal the nation," changing Bolivia into a more moral and prosperous society one soul at a time through the promotion of Christian values and a personal relationship with Christ.

In this chapter I attempt to understand Pentecostal identity politics in the context of recent neoliberal reforms, and I explore how the Bolivian Pentecostal project of social change is related to their understanding of conversion. I argue that social engagement on the part of Bolivian Pentecostals can be understood by looking at the ways in which Pentecostals conceive of conversion—not only as being "born again," but as being healed. Talk of healing permeates the discourses of personal change that accompany conversion and the concept of healing is also often extended to the ways in which Pentecostals talk about and conceive of their relationship to society as well.

Neoliberal Reform and Pentecostal Growth

My research is set in the city of Cochabamba, Bolivia's third-largest city. The city of Cochabamba has a population of just over five hundred thousand, according to the 2001 census, an increase of almost 250 percent since the mid-1970s.[2] The population of Cochabamba's peri-urban area has more than doubled in the last decade, creating a metro area of almost eight hundred thousand people. This growth is due largely to the influx of migrants to Cochabamba and the steadily expanding squatter settlements that have grown up around it. Many of these newcomers to Cochabamba are not stereotypical rural-to-urban migrants, but are displaced laborers from the mining towns that were shut down in the mid-1980s. However, migrants from nearly every part of the country and a variety of circumstances—highlands and lowlands, displaced miners, coca growers, and peasants—now inhabit the city's peripheral neighborhoods.

This explosive urban growth has largely corresponded with similarly explosive growth in Pentecostalism in Cochabamba and Bolivia more generally. There are an ever-increasing number of Pentecostal churches in the city of Cochabamba, spreading from the city center out through the sprawling squatter settlements that ring the city. Cochabamba also boasts no fewer than six evangelical Protestant radio stations and two local evangelical television channels. Although reliable numbers can be hard to come by, it is clear that the 1980s and 1990s were a time of tremendous Protestant growth in Bolivia. In the mid-1980s a conservatively estimated 4 percent of the Bolivian population identified as *evangélico*. By the 1992 census, the number of evangélicos had climbed to just over 10 percent. Although religious affiliation was omitted from the 2001 census (and this is a topic of much conspiracy theorizing among evangelicals), a subsequent survey by the National Institute of Statistics shows that roughly 16 percent of the Bolivian population consider themselves to be evangélico.[3] This represents roughly a quadrupling of the number of evangelical Christians in Bolivia in the last twenty years, and by all accounts Pentecostal churches comprise the majority of this recent growth.

As noted above, this Pentecostal growth has been occurring during a time of dramatic social, political, and economic change in Bolivia. In 1952 Bolivia underwent what is known as the National Revolution, which brought about sweeping land reform, the nationalization of most major industries (most significantly the mining sector, long the centerpiece of Bolivia's economy), and the establishment of a highly centralized social welfare state. During this time labor unions and peasant syndicates became very powerful players in Bolivian political and civil society. Beginning in 1985 (under pressure from the International Monetary Fund) the Bolivian government implemented a series of neoliberal economic reforms that included a severe program of economic austerity and the privatization of most state industry and many social services. These reforms achieved the desired effect of reining in Bolivia's bloated public sector and the devastating hyper-inflation of the early 1980s, but they also resulted in the almost complete dismantling of the mining sector and the unemployment and dislocation of tens of thousands of miners and their families. These changes have led to a withdrawal of the state from its role as a provider of employment and social services, widespread unemployment and underemployment, and the rapid growth and overcrowding of urban peripheries.

In the mid-1990s a second generation of neoliberal reforms were enacted, generally referred to as the "Plan de Todos" (Plan for Everyone). These reforms broke with Bolivia's nationalist model, in place since the National Revolution, which sought to incorporate and assimilate diverse populations as modern, national citizens. According to Kevin Healy and Susan Paulson, the reforms "dramatically reversed the nation's cultural integrationist stance by linking market-oriented economic policies with a new kind of political project including decentralization, popular participation, educational reform, and constitutional recognition of plural cultures and multiple ethnic and gender identities."[4] The reforms refocused the problems of social and economic inequalities in Bolivia, which had been exacerbated by the earlier economic reforms, by prioritizing issues of cultural identity.[5] The reforms included amending the Constitution to define Bolivia as a multiethnic and multicultural society; sweeping educational reform, including bilingual education; a reallocation of political power and money to the municipalities; the establishment of a Secretariat of Ethnic, Gender, and Generational Affairs; social security reform; and the "capitalization" of the hydrocarbon industry and other state-run enterprises. All of these reforms were promoted as creating the conditions and institutions necessary to give voice and power to new and diverse social actors.[6]

The neoliberal reforms of the 1980s and 1990s thus set in motion large-scale unemployment, massive urban growth, the loss of political power of labor and syndicate-based organizations, and increasing political spaces for new groups and interests to be heard in the public sphere. Old forms of working-class consciousness and affiliation have dissolved into a vast array of interest groups formed around neighborhood organizations, small associations of vendors, and other groups, including religious organizations.[7] I contend that Pentecostalism is one way in which marginalized Bolivians are building coalitions in the face of a changing social order and a diminished relationship with the state.

But just because new spaces for public participation had been opened up, it was not a given that Pentecostals would step into that space. Much of the early research on the growth of evangelical and Pentecostal churches in Latin America was strongly critical of evangelical Protestant churches for what was perceived by the researchers to be an aversion to politics based on an escapist, otherworldly ideology and, in some cases, an explicit prohibition on entering politics.[8] Although more recent studies of evangélicos in Latin America have increasingly taken into account their growing participation in politics, particularly in Brazil and Central America,[9] the image of evangélicos as apolitical and preaching submissiveness to authority has largely remained in place in the popular perception of these groups. To understand why Bolivian Pentecostals have increasingly entered the public sphere, I think it is important to look at how they conceive of this participation in relation to Pentecostal conceptions of conversion.

Healing, Personal Transformation, and Pentecostal Identity

Discourses of healing are prevalent in nearly all aspects of Pentecostal practice, including sermons, *testimonios*, and prayer meetings, and my research suggests that the promise of a framework for understanding and overcoming suffering is one of the main appeals of Pentecostalism among the urban Pentecostal congregations I studied and a crucial element of Bolivian Pentecostal subjectivity. I found that divine healing is the central point in most conversion narratives; petitions for the healing of friends and family members dominate prayer meetings, and the quest for personal healing draws many of the large number of people who turn out for mass Pentecostal revival meetings. The language of healing is not only applied to physical ailments and other afflictions that are generally medicalized, such as addictions and mental problems. The trope of healing is also often used when discussing a broad array of difficulties including financial situations, homelessness, unemployment, marital difficulties, and other familial discord.[10] Believers often speak broadly of how Jesus has healed their lives (*sanó mi vida*).

In Bolivia, Pentecostal discourse on suffering and illness is not generally that of rewards in the afterlife, but rather emphasizes healing. It provides a framework for thinking about the suffering and lack of opportunity that come with poverty and living in the third world and that have been exacerbated for many by the economic crisis of recent years in Bolivia. It gives meaning and value to the lives led by those who are struggling to maintain themselves and their families under conditions of social and economic strain but does not tell them to suffer quietly and piously and await their eternal salvation. Suffering is only valued as a past state, what happened before the act of conversion and being "born again." Suffering is something to be overcome through faith, the gifts of the Holy Spirit, the grace of God, and also through "right" living—the last of these is particularly significant in that it gives the individual sufferer a mode of action for overcoming his or her personal grief or affliction. It is the triumph over suffering which is glorified in Pentecostal discourse and which constitutes its primary appeal to many potential converts. (See also Virginia Garrard-Burnett's chapter in this volume for further discussion of the centrality of overcoming suffering in Pentecostal conversion.) While certainly not everyone who seeks healing through Pentecostalism will ultimately have a conversion experience or consider himself or herself successful in the quest for healing, my point is that continued earthly suffering with a glorious reward in heaven is not a major trope in Bolivian Pentecostal discourse. Instead, Pentecostalism offers a project of personal transformation.

The importance of suffering and healing to the Pentecostal experience can be particularly evident in testimonios. Testimonios are personal stories told by parishioners during services and prayer meetings and to potential converts—what U.S. born-again Christians call "testifying" or "witnessing." Testimonios often take the form of inspiring and even miraculous conversion narratives. These conversion narratives recount the teller's life in a before-and-after framework with conversion—generally glossed as "knowing the Lord" (*conocer al Señor*)—providing the fulcrum on which the story turns. Testimonios can also be small inspirational stories, generally told in church or prayer meetings to fellow believers, that tell of how faith in God helped the teller (or someone the teller knows) get through a difficult time. These can be stories of fortitude inspired by faith, of small miracles, or of the "tests" (*pruebas*) of faith that God puts before believers and which ultimately make their faith stronger. These testimonios generally tell of suffering (whether illness, grief, addiction, violence, poverty, or the smaller-scale injustices of everyday life in Bolivia or as an immigrant). And what makes these stories testimonios is that they are stories of how this suffering has been overcome.

Narrating one's conversion experience through specific Pentecostal genres (such as testimonios) and tropes (such as being "born again" and healing) is not merely a reflection of one's changing identity as a *cristiano*, but an integral part of forming a new Pentecostal identity. The telling of one's life and conversion as interpreted through the framework of Pentecostalism is a central practice of Pentecostalism and one that allows the individual to perceive himself or herself as existing as part of a community of believers as well as in a personal relationship with God.[11] The bodily experiences inherent to Pentecostalism are also important to the development of a Pentecostal identity. Feeling the presence of the Holy Spirit and witnessing its visible manifestations is very important in convincing potential believers of the truth of Pentecostalism and is important in defining membership in the in-group of Pentecostal believers. Both the discursive practices and the bodily experiences of Pentecostalism play a key role in assimilating converts into the group and creating for them a new identity as Pentecostals. Conversion creates an "inter-subjectivity" with other believers which is manifested in a shared language, practice, ethic, community, and identity.[12]

While most Pentecostals do not seek to isolate themselves from the larger society, they do tend to emphasize their common identity with other cristianos or evangélicos and use it to their benefit whenever possible.[13] Employment opportunities are often arranged through church networks, and Pentecostals tend to patronize the businesses of other evangélicos. This is often justified by reference to a Protestant work ethic. Evangélicos hold themselves to be honest and hard-working—an opinion of them which is shared by a number of non-Protestants I have spoken with as well. This Protestant work ethic provides a strong marker of identity in a country that is renowned for its acceptance of corruption as business-as-usual.

Through these and other discourses and practices Bolivian Pentecostals define themselves in relation to an "other"—variously defined as the non-Christian, the unsaved, the pagan, the corrupt. While these categories of other do include other marginalized members of Bolivian society (particularly as concerns so-called pagan religiosity and its associated alcohol consumption), this is also quite explicitly employed in critique of the elite classes who control the dominant discourses of the nation-state—not only political discourses, but also discourses of tradition, nationality, education, and morality. Pentecostal affiliation provides an identity within the community or the nation, and Pentecostals also see themselves as part of a global social movement. Through these connections with a global movement, Pentecostals in Cochabamba can tap into a discourse that offers an alternative vision of globalization to the secular, capitalist one that has restructured their lives and increased their marginalization and alienation from the state.

"Heal the Nation": Pentecostal Identity and Social Critique

Healing as a central metaphor for Bolivian Pentecostalism extends to Pentecostals' understanding of society as well. Pentecostals perceive themselves as having a Christian mandate to "heal the nation" (*sanar la nación*). Because the personal relationship with Jesus Christ is the core of Pentecostal faith and practice, the primary focus in healing the nation is proselytizing—carrying the Word of God to (and sharing their personal experiences with) as many people as possible so that those people might also "come to know God" (*conocer al Señor*). Even though the emphasis of Pentecostalism is on changing individual lives, many Pentecostals see this as a form of promoting social change and changing the society in which they live. Their own personal transformation through being born again puts them in a position to change society—by example, through sharing their testimonios, and by working for justice in their own lives. This duty to reshape Bolivian society in their own Christian image becomes part of their Pentecostal subjectivity.

In the literature portraying evangélicos as unconcerned with worldly oppression, it has been noted—to the point of becoming a stereotype—that they tend to preach submissiveness to political authorities, most notably by emphasizing a verse from the New Testament, Romans 13:1, which reads: "Let every person be subject to the governing authorities. For there is no authority except from God, and those that exist have been instituted by God." I found in my field research that Bolivian Pentecostals do preach on this much-cited Bible verse that directs them to be subject to the authority of their leaders, but this does not mean that they believe that all politicians merit the unreflexive submission of the citizenry. The Pentecostals with whom I have been involved in my research have a more nuanced understanding of the meaning of "authority" and fairly rigorous moral standards for determining who is deserving of being invested with such authority. I have even heard this biblical dictum employed in denouncing certain political leaders as

illegitimate and calling for their replacement with others who better represent "Christian" values. I have also found in my ethnographic research that
many Pentecostals see themselves as forces of change in society. They see
themselves as working to win Bolivia for Christ and heal the nation. They see
their mission as changing Bolivia into a more moral and prosperous society
one soul at a time through the promotion of Christian values and a personal
relationship with Jesus Christ.

Pentecostals are concerned about not becoming too focused on "worldly"
solutions to personal and societal problems, but that is not to say that they
are unconcerned with worldly problems. Pastors at times argue that it is
not laws or human rights that are important for making a better world,
but rather that individuals have Jesus in their hearts. Or they note that the
problems of the world will not be solved by men, but by the second coming
of Christ. But these same pastors lead their congregations in praying for the
political leaders of the country and for the well-being of its citizenry. Praying
for the nation's leaders plays an important part in the worship portion of the
March for Jesus, the major public display of faith for the county's evangélicos
each year. I attended the Cochabamba March for Jesus in 2001 and 2003, and
both years there were local public officials present and various pastors were
asked to lead the crowd in praying that God grant these leaders wisdom and
guidance and that they be upright and perform their duties morally. Also,
on Corpus Cristi, a Catholic feast day which is not recognized by evangelical
churches but which is a national holiday in Bolivia, one large Assemblies of
God congregation held a special afternoon prayer session with the explicit
purpose of praying for the nation's leaders.[14]

These pastors also use the metaphoric language of healing the nation
and of waging battle against the unholy and the worldly, and in this way they
encourage believers to go out into the world, winning Bolivia for Christ one
soul at a time. In practice this has the potential to translate into actions
of social change and justice as individuals do daily battle with immorality,
suffering, and injustice. In Pentecostal discourse there is a tension between
the inward and the outward: between the primacy given to the individual-
Jesus relationship (if this relationship is absent there can be no salvation
and there is little or no expectation that an individual could change for the
better) and the need and desire that Pentecostals work to shape their society
into the "kingdom of God on earth." These discourses of personal salvation
can be effectively harnessed to a project of social transformation, however,
and this part of cristiano identity also can become an important part of an
individual's testimonio.

Below is an example of a woman who has come to see her own story
of fighting "the system" as a classic Christian battle of good and evil. Her
story shows a willingness to critique political authorities from an explicitly

Christian position as well as how personal Christian identity can become grounded in fighting for social change.

Hermana Maria's Testimonio

"Hermana Maria," a woman of approximately fifty years of age, is an elder (*anciana*) and a lay leader in a small Pentecostal church. She is also a schoolteacher and, previously, was the principal of a public elementary school in Cochabamba. The Bolivian government has recently put into place a series of new laws and institutions collectively referred to as Educational Reform. In an effort to institutionalize and professionalize administrative positions, all public school principals were required to pass an examination in order to retain their positions. Maria sat for and passed the required exam, but was nevertheless removed from her position. Maria contends that this action was illegal and that she was replaced because she was not a member of the one of the ruling political parties. She believes that in spite of the new rules, the same old corrupt games are being played in the Ministry of Education: school directorships are handed out as *pegas*, rewards for members of whichever party currently controls the ministry.

Maria, with the counsel of an attorney who is also a member of her church, has filed a lawsuit in the matter, which is currently winding its way through the courts, seeking reappointment to her post and recognition that she was removed in violation of the law. She has been very frustrated with her experiences in the courts, which she describes as just as corrupt and partisan as the educational system. At one point she was offered some sort of compromise by the Ministry of Education, short of the reappointment and admission of wrongdoing that she is seeking. She rejected this offer because she felt that this compromise was corrupt and did "not serve justice." Pentecostals often speak of *pruebas de fe*—situations where God puts their faith to the test—and Maria often described her situation in these terms.

As these events were unfolding, Maria repeatedly discussed them with the members of her congregation, and as it developed over time it became her testimonio, and as such became integral to her own vision of herself as a Pentecostal Christian. By Maria's own description, she sees herself as pitted in a battle of good versus evil, and she sees it as her duty as a Christian to fight the injustice and corruption that is so prevalent in Bolivia, to do her part to make her society a more moral and Christian environment. Maria sees herself as taking a stand for social change and justice, and she sees this stand as an essential part of her identity as an evangelical Christian. For Maria, winning this one legal battle in the name of justice is part of healing the nation. Even though the emphasis of Pentecostalism is on changing individual lives and creating personal relationships with Jesus Christ, many Pentecostals see this as a form of promoting social change and changing the society in which they live. Maria's identity as a cristiana has led her to work to change her society—both by fighting corruption in her own life and through sharing her testimonio.

An Evangelist's Call to Action

The critique of corrupt or illegitimate political authority from a position of Christian moral authority is widely present in Bolivian Pentecostal discourse. As but one example, I provide below a short excerpt from a sermon by arguably Bolivia's most influential Pentecostal evangelist, Julio Cesar Ruibal. Ruibal, who was killed in Cali, Colombia, in 1995, was one of the founders of Ekklesía, a large independent church with branches in eight of Bolivia's nine departments. Starting at age nineteen, he led a series of revival meetings around Bolivia in the early 1970s in which thousands of people were inspired to conversion and hundreds of people claimed to have been miraculously healed. His ministry was mentioned to me by members of all the congregations with which I worked as being the seminal event in Pentecostal growth in Bolivia, what in the language of Pentecostals is referred to as the *gran avivamiento* (great revival or awakening). He subsequently moved to Colombia, preaching and founding churches there until his death. The following excerpt is from a sermon by Ruibal, which was presented to a large crowd at a revival meeting in Cochabamba in 1995 and was also broadcast on one of the Christian radio stations. In the sermon Ruibal asks those listening to ponder the lack of development in Bolivia, and he tells them that Bolivia is not more developed because its people, particularly its leaders, are sinful.

> What a great country we have. What a beautiful country God has given us. And it is also a country of hard-working people, of accommodating people, of humble people, people that want and can do many things. But I ask tonight why Bolivia isn't greater? Why doesn't Bolivia have more highways? Why doesn't Bolivia have better education? Why isn't Bolivia more advanced? Why are entire cities, like Cochabamba, still suffering, when here the people are not asking for gold, silver, or riches, but merely asking and crying out for a little drinking water? This is beginning to sound like a political campaign, isn't it? (Laughs) . . . Bolivia is backwards because of the sins of its people. Bolivia is backwards because the Bolivians who govern this country, because the Bolivians who have managed the destiny of this country, because Bolivians in general serve neither God nor justice. They serve themselves and they serve sin. This is why Bolivia isn't what it could be today. . . . That is why Bolivia suffers. Because there are not more Bolivians that love God and serve justice. . . . If God continues changing Bolivians, like he is changing them now, in the [near future] this

country will be a totally different country because it will be run by men who serve God and justice and therefore become servants of the people, not thieves of the people, not oppressors of the people, but servants of the Bolivian people.[15]

The overarching theme of this sermon is that Bolivia is an underdeveloped nation because the Bolivian people have resigned themselves to a political and social system in which corruption, lying, and deception are the norm. It will be through the forging of relationships with Jesus Christ by an ever-expanding number of individual Bolivians that Bolivia will become a more moral society and, therefore, a more prosperous and progressive society. There is a very explicit critique of the nation's contemporary political leadership and an implicit call for them to be replaced by people who have accepted Jesus Christ and will, therefore, be more upright and just leaders. Ruibal then shifts the focus from those in power to the listeners, calling on each of them to break with the status quo of corruption and unrepentant sinfulness.

The preceding passage is an illustration of the argument that I am making in this chapter, that the Pentecostal discourses about personal salvation and the primacy of the individual relationship with Jesus Christ, which are central to Pentecostalism, can be effectively harnessed to a project of social transformation. Ruibal makes it clear that only Jesus Christ has the power to change Bolivia's dismal political and economic situation, but in order to do so he must first forge relationships with individuals who will go out into society and work to change it. Christians must take up the charge to change the status quo that keeps Bolivia from being the great nation that it should be. Born-again Christians should no longer allow unrepentant sinners to serve in positions of authority but rather should take up the charge themselves.

Marching for Jesus: Performing Pentecostal Identity in the Public Square

During my fieldwork in Cochabamba I also became attuned to the ways in which Bolivian Pentecostals are social actors in the nation-state and insert themselves in the public sphere as cristianos. In presenting themselves as a group of people who identify and act as cristianos, they establish themselves as having a specific Pentecostal identity and as being distinct from mainstream society. One of the ways they are performing their Pentecostal identity to the larger society is through the annual March for Jesus.

Every year in Cochabamba (and other major cities in Bolivia) hundreds, and some years thousands, of Bolivians participate in the International March for Jesus. There is a vast cross-section of Cochabamba's urban population represented in the March for Jesus. There are people from a broad array of ethnic categories and from a variety of economic classes—from the poor migrants of the city's peripheral barrios to SUV-driving elites. The marchers are organized by congregations and come from all over the city. Some carry signs with slogans such as "Jesus loves you," "Christ lives," "Only Jesus saves and heals," and "Bolivia for Christ." Many of the signs are decorated in Bolivia's national colors (red, yellow, and green), and some people carry Bolivian flags. There are marching bands, and some groups sing or chant slogans. They are not like the usual political chants and songs one hears on a protest march, but are praise songs (*alabanzas*) and chants about Jesus' love. Some people decorate cars and buses and drive these along the parade route. Most of the marchers are dressed in their regular clothes, some in Western clothes and some in typical Andean dress, long full skirts and bowler hats for the migrant women from the highlands, short full skirts and straw hats for the women from the Cochabamba Valley. There are also groups of young women in matching dresses waving ribbons and flags or shaking tambourines. A few people are dressed up as characters from Bible stories. And there is large group of youth dressed up as clowns, carrying signs declaring, "Christianity is not boring." The March for Jesus has a very festive air, and though they are walking several kilometers in the hot sun, the marchers all seem happy and in high spirits. The marchers follow a route through the center of the city that is similar to those used in other sorts of processions and marches. They start at a secondary plaza in the southern part of the downtown area and pass through downtown on major avenues and through important public and commercial spaces in the city. Unlike a religious procession or a political march, they do not end in the city's main plaza, which fronts both the cathedral and the city's main government buildings. Instead, the March for Jesus ends at the municipal stadium, generally the site of athletic contests, concerts, and other secular entertainments and civic events. Once the crowd is gathered in the stadium, what occurs is a mixture of pep rally and church service. Several bands play, ranging from small electronic pop groups to mariachis to the large brass and drum bands common at Andean festivals, all playing alabanzas in styles and rhythms ranging from traditional Andean to modern rock. The crowd sings along to many of the songs, as the same or similar songs are sung in most of the churches. In front of the stage there are groups of young women in matching dresses performing choreographed moves with ribbons, flags, and tambourines. In between the songs, a number of pastors take the stage. Most lead the crowd in a prayer and then say a few words to raise the crowd's enthusiasm, often calling for cheers and applause for the Lord. Several local and regional political officials are present, and the pastors welcome them and tell the crowd that they are pleased to have them here on this occasion. The pastors lead a prayer thanking God for these authorities and asking him to guide them in their work so that Bolivia will be a better, more Christian country. The politicians, in turn, say a few words praising the Lord and noting that evangélicos are an important part of Cochabamba and Bolivia.

The Cochabamba March for Jesus is part of an internationally coordinated effort to encourage evangelical Christians around the globe to take to the streets on a given day in the name of Jesus, and the Cochabamba March for Jesus certainly draws on international models for the event. But ultimately it takes on, as it must, distinctly Bolivian forms and meanings. While it has no overt policy agenda, the March for Jesus is political in its very existence. Evangelical Protestants have been, and in many ways remain, a marginal group in Bolivia. The Catholic Church has used its centuries-old social and political hegemony to downplay (and at times to outright demonize) their presence in Bolivia. Through the March for Jesus Bolivian evangelical Protestants are inserting themselves in the public square and claiming a space and a voice in Bolivia's national dialogue. As they march, they are self-consciously presenting an image of themselves to the larger society. They are presenting themselves as patriotic Bolivian citizens, as we can see through the flags and other national symbols as well as through slogans such as "Bolivia for Christ." I argue that in incorporating these national symbols (as well as Bolivian folkloric symbols) they are making an overt attempt to portray their religious movement as wholly Bolivian, to dispel the perception that it is an import from the North.

Through the clowns, the festive music, the pep rally atmosphere, and the more obvious "Christians are not boring" signs, they are presenting themselves as fun. This is significant in that they are often perceived as social "wet blankets" because of their criticism of carnival and other festivals and the ubiquitous drinking that occurs during these festivals. As demonstrated by the cars, trucks, buses, and taxis, they are showing that they are economically powerful. In Bolivia a vehicle, and particularly one with commercial potential, is a significant capital investment.[16] By convincing political authorities to attend and incorporating them into the event, they are asserting their political relevance and defining themselves as a political constituency. And, perhaps most significantly, by occupying public spaces, such as the streets and the stadium, they are presenting themselves both as a normal part of Cochabamba's social and civil landscape and as a legitimate social group.

The March for Jesus is not overtly political, but in Bolivia "taking the streets" is widely understood as a display of political and social power.[17] Labor unions, syndicates, and other social sectors frequently take Bolivia's streets to demands rights and services from the state. Certain groups involved in staging folkloric parades have notoriously used these events to exert their social, economic, and political power in the city.[18] Regarding folkloric

festivals, Nelson Martinez has argued that through the public presentation
of themselves in the middle of the city, marginal social sectors "produce a
series of discourses that construct their identity for themselves and for the
rest of the city."[19] Similarly, Daniel Goldstein has argued that spectacular
performance "provides a form of vivid political protest for groups of people
ordinarily excluded from the mainstream of urban public life."[20] And, he
notes, spectacular performance is interesting not merely because identities
and newly imagined social orders are "performed in public, but because
spectacular events enable groups of people to establish themselves as a
public."[21] Through the March for Jesus Bolivian Pentecostals are consciously
participating in a similar process of public representation.

By "taking" the city, Bolivian Pentecostals are showing the power in their
numbers and that they, like other social sectors, deserve and are capable
of claiming a voice in Bolivian society. They are presenting themselves as a
constituency, a block of people with a common identity and interests who
should be recognized and taken seriously not only by the population at
large, but by those in power. And through the ways in which they choose to
represent themselves, individually and collectively, during their moment in
the streets, they are actively constructing their social identity vis-à-vis the
nation. Through representing themselves as better, more patriotic Bolivians
than those who bring the nation to ruin through corruption, greed, etc., they
lay claim to moral authority over the nation as they wage their criticisms of
Bolivian society and its leaders as immoral and therefore illegitimate. Their
ultimate concern may be the eternal salvation of souls, but this does not pre-
clude a concern with changing the society in which they live. Using the Bible
and, specifically, the teachings of Jesus as a blueprint for a moral, just, and
compassionate society, Bolivian Pentecostals believe in working to remake
Bolivian society in their own image.

Conclusion

The growth in recent decades of evangelical Protestantism in Bolivia and
across Latin America (long considered the "Catholic continent") has been
met with consternation from many sides, not only from the Catholic Church,
but also from leftists and in academia and the popular press. One of the concerns and critiques often used to devalue the notion of these new religious
groups as potentially significant social actors is that they are apolitical and
individualistic. Latin American evangelicals have been written off as otherworldly: concerned solely with individual spiritual salvation and content
with rewards in the next life rather than working to make this world a better
place. As more thorough study has been done on Latin American Protestants
(the majority of whom are now Pentecostals), these characterizations have

been called into question. My work builds on previous work in interrogating these assumptions through an ethnographically grounded study of Pentecostalism in Cochabamba, Bolivia.

I have found that the individual Pentecostal identity that is formed through born-again conversion is often tied to a Pentecostal group identity and mobilized in a project of social transformation. Pentecostalism draws upon the opening up of new forms of social and political participation that have been occurring in recent decades in Bolivia, allowing for the creation of new associations and identities through which Bolivians can define themselves and call for social change. Bolivian Pentecostals are mobilizing to present themselves as having a distinct identity and specific demands within the nation-state, including a strong critique of political corruption and abuses of economic and political power.

To understand contemporary Pentecostalism in Latin America it is imperative that we examine the phenomenon of Pentecostalism at both the individual and the group level. We need to explore the level of personal transformation and the ways in which individuals come to believe the message of Pentecostalism through identifying themselves within broader church discourses and new Pentecostal subjectivities. And it is equally essential that we look at the ways in which these individual experiences and new identities can be harnessed to a project of social critique and change. These Pentecostal projects of personal and social transformation are connected through the key metaphor of healing. The broad personal transformations that are attributed to conversion in the testimonios of Bolivian Pentecostals are frequently conceived of and talked about within a framework of healing. This trope of healing is present in the discourse surrounding Pentecostal calls for social change as well. By and large, Bolivian Pentecostals see themselves as being called to heal the nation, leading them to critique what they see as corrupt and immoral in society and to seek to replace the status quo with an alternative that conforms to their Christian vision of the world.

NOTES

1. Since 2000 there have been numerous and widespread protests against policies of privatization, free trade, transnational exploitation of natural resources, and IMF-backed economic policy. These protests led to the forced resignations of President Gonzalo Sánchez de Lozada in 2003 and President Carlos Mesa Gisbert in 2005.

2. The 1976 census reported a population of 207,000; the 1992 census reported a population of 408,000. Instituto Nacional de Estadísticas (INE), *Cochabamba: Resultados Departamentales. Serie II: Resultados Departamentales*, vol. 3, *Censo Nacional de Población y Vivienda 2001* (La Paz: INE, 2002).

3. Instituto Nacional de Estadística, Nota de Prensa No. 65, La Paz, Bolivia, May 3, 2002, http://www.ine.gov.bo/pdf/boletin/NP_2002_65.pdf. This figure does not include

"cultos de origin cristiano," such as Mormons, Jehovah's Witnesses, and Adventists, which comprise an additional 3.24 percent.

4. Kevin Healy and Susan Paulson, "Political Economies of Identity in Bolivia, 1952–1998," *Journal of Latin American Anthropology* 5, no. 2 (2000):5.

5. Ibid., 11.

6. Ibid., 5.

7. See Lesley Gill, *Teetering on the Rim: Global Restructuring, Daily Life, and the Armed Retreat of the Bolivian State* (New York: Columbia University Press, 2000).

8. Christian Lalive d'Epinay, *Haven of the Masses: A Study of the Pentecostal Movement in Chile* (London: Lutterworth Press, 1969); David Stoll, *Is Latin America Turning Protestant? The Politics of Evangelical Growth* (Berkeley: University of California Press, 1990); Enrique Dominguez and Deborah Huntington, "The Salvation Brokers: Conservative Evangelicals in Central America," *NACLA Report on the Americas* 18, no. 1 (1984): 2–36; Lesley Gill, "Like a Veil to Cover Them: Women and the Pentecostal Movement in La Paz," *American Ethnologist* 17 (1990): 709–721.

9. Edward L. Cleary and Hannah W. Stewart-Gambino, eds, *Power, Politics, and Pentecostals in Latin America* (Boulder: Westview Press, 1997); Harvey Gallagher Cox, *Fire from Heaven: The Rise of Pentecostal Spirituality and the Reshaping of Religion in the Twenty-first Century* (Reading, MA: Addison-Wesley, 1995); Paul Freston, *Evangelicals and Politics in Asia, Africa, and Latin America* (Cambridge: Cambridge University Press, 2001); Virginia Garrard-Burnett and David Stoll, eds., *Rethinking Protestantism in Latin America* (Philadelphia: Temple University Press, 1993); Frans Kamsteeg, *Prophetic Pentecostalism in Chile: A Case Study on Religion and Development Policy* (Lanham, MD: Scarecrow Press, 1998).

10. See Garrard-Burnett in this volume for a discussion of the importance of exorcism in curing these types of affliction among immigrants in the United States. While exorcism of this sort was practiced in some of the churches I attended, these afflictions were not directly associated with the presence of demons in most of the churches in which I did research. In terms of discourses of healing, I did not find that a clear distinction was made between afflictions of the physical body and those which Garrard-Burnett discusses as being of the mind and spirit.

11. See Susan Harding, *The Book of Jerry Falwell: Fundamentalist Language and Politics* (Princeton: Princeton University Press, 2000).

12. See Victor Hugo Calisaya, Alberto Lizarraga, and Natalia Camacho, *Los Angeles Mueren de Pie: Pobreza Urbana y Religiosidad Protestante en la Ciudad de Cochabamba* (Cochabamba: PIEB, 2000). The authors associate the growth of evangelical Protestantism with the emergence of new actors and social practices in the political, economic, and social scene; an increase in the indices of poverty; the construction of new urban spaces; the emergence of new individual and social subjectivities; and the constitution of new logics, realities, and survival strategies.

13. In Bolivia, the term *evangélico* is used generally to refer to all Protestants and other non-Catholics, including Mormons and Jehovah's Witnesses. The term *cristiano* is used more frequently for self-identification among Pentecostals and is important for defining their Pentecostal subjectivity. Catholics are quite explicitly excluded from the term *cristianos* as it is used by most Pentecostals, as they have not been born again and are therefore not seen as true Christians. Catholics are also denounced for their participation in the religious fiestas which combine Catholic

practices with indigenous religious traditions and which are viewed as pagan and idolatrous by Pentecostals.

14. I would argue that an implicit but no less important purpose of holding prayer meetings on holidays is to distract parishioners from the heavy consumption of alcohol and public displays of Catholic and Andean religiosity prevalent on these days.

15. The tape of this sermon, recorded from the radio broadcast, was given to me by a parishioner of one of the churches I regularly attended during my research. She did not know the exact date of the revival meeting or its radio broadcast, but she told me that she remembered that he preached this particular sermon on his last visit to Bolivia shortly before his death. News accounts place him in Cochabamba in May 1995. All translations from the original Spanish are mine.

16. There is also a local tradition of bringing vehicles out to be blessed by the priests during festivals.

17. Nelson Martinez Espinoza, "La Ciudad Tomada," paper presented at the II Congreso de Patrimonio Histórico e Identidad Cultural, Cochabamba, Bolivia, 2001.

18. After the death of former President Victor Paz Estenssoro in June 2001 the organizers of the fiesta of El Señor del Gran Poder refused the request of city officials to postpone the folkloric *entrada* in mourning for his passing. This was widely perceived as a public demonstration of who really controlled the city: the powerful urban Aymara confraternities rather than the white elites of the municipal government.

19. Nelson Martinez, "La Ciudad Tomada," 9, translation mine.

20. Daniel Goldstein, *The Spectacular City: Violence and Performance in Urban Bolivia* (Durham: Duke University Press, 2004), 19.

21. Ibid., 19.

13

The Politics of
Pentecostalized Religion

Conversion as Pentecostalization in Guatemala

TIMOTHY J. STEIGENGA

As we have argued throughout this volume, the definition and processes of conversion have been underspecified in much of the literature on religious change in Latin America. Given this shortcoming, it should come as no surprise that the political effects of conversion have also been frequently over-generalized. After all, if conversion is to be understood as a continuum and/or career taking place in an increasingly fluid and competitive religious market, we should automatically be skeptical about sweeping claims that attempt to reify the links between simple religious affiliation and various forms of democratic or anti-democratic politics in the region. Based on survey data and qualitative interviews conducted in Guatemala, this chapter provides evidence that conversion to "pentecostalized" forms of religious practice is associated with political tendencies that cannot be neatly characterized as "democratic" or "authoritarian." Specifically, I argue that the political tendencies that can be significantly connected to religious variables are complex and variant and have more to do with the "pentecostalization" of religious practice in Latin America than with conversion to particular religious or denominational affiliations. As utilized throughout this volume, pentecostalization refers to the acceptance of certain religious beliefs (such as a dramatic personal conversion, millennialism, and, to some degree, biblical literalism) and the experience of particular pneumatic religious practices (such as speaking in tongues, divine healing, and other charismatic practices).[1] Although Latin Americans have experienced conversions to many different religions over the past thirty years, the majority these of conversions have been to some form of pentecostalized religion.

In terms of politics, the Guatemalan case is particularly illustrative as it has one of the highest rates of Pentecostal adherence in Latin America,[2] has experienced a recent and as of yet unconsolidated transition to democracy, and has drawn significant scholarly attention on religion and politics, primarily due to the role of two evangelical presidents: Efrain Rios Montt in the 1980s and Jorge Serrano Elias in the 1990s. With a population that is close to 50 percent indigenous, the relationships between religion and politics in Guatemala may also hold important insights for understanding these connections in the Andean region, where the recent resurgence of indigenous participation in national politics has caught many observers by surprise.

The fault lines of the debate among those who study religion and politics in Latin America generally fall between those who view conversion to Pentecostal Protestantism as a potential boon for democracy[3] and those who interpret it as primarily corporatist or authoritarian.[4] In part, this scholarly debate and disagreement over the political effects of Pentecostal growth is a function of the size and scope of the answers being sought. As Carol Ann Drogus has noted, researchers have approached the topic of religion and politics with very different conceptions of the role of civil society in democratization, the role of religious identity in carrying values, and the role of religious organizations as a source of political mobilization.[5] It is these differences in perspective, more than the evidence provided through myriad case studies, which have contributed to the creation of a false dilemma in the study of the effects of conversion to Latin American Pentecostalism. A clearer definition of terms combined with measurable and comparable results brings us significantly closer to unlocking the political complexity of the pentecostalization of religion in Latin America.

While authors such as Paul Freston and Rowan Ireland have laid the foundation for a potential bridge across this debate through their excellent studies documenting and analyzing the political diversity within Protestantism in Latin America, the specific causal mechanisms for this diversity remain under-specified.[6] My findings from Guatemala suggest that political differences between religious groups are more attributable to pentecostalized beliefs and practices than to religious affiliation. Thus, studies that focus on comparing political attitudes or affiliations between religious groups at the macro-level are likely to miss the key religious variables driving political attitudes and practices. In particular, some of the conservative religious beliefs associated with conversion to pentecostalized religion provide a powerful rationale for a diverse set of policy positions that cross the political spectrum (from campaigns for public morality to principles of gender equality). Furthermore, those who convert to pentecostalized religion are not averse to political participation. While they may eschew highly conflictive activist politics, they generally view their political participation as a right and a duty to be expressed primarily at the community level through self-help and volunteerism.

The first section of this chapter provides a brief overview of survey data on religious beliefs and practices collected in Guatemala. The overwhelming finding from this data is the degree to which religious beliefs and practices across religious groups in Guatemala have become pentecostalized. More importantly, the political effects of these religious beliefs and activities appear to be much more complex than the conventional wisdom might suggest. While there is a correlation between pentecostalization and political quiescence and political conservatism on some issues (such as evaluating the poor), the findings in terms of other political issues (such as gender equality) suggest new and counterintuitive Pentecostal political trajectories.

The second section examines the specific mechanisms that have been posited as the "democracy-enhancing" elements of evangelical religion with reference to qualitative interviews collected in Guatemala. I argue for more explicit and well-defined claims about the relationship between religion and democracy, claims that focus on community building, civic duties, and equal rights. While these connections certainly may be prerequisites to functioning democracy, the political context in which they take place is likely to be the deciding factor in whether or not they may be called democracy-enhancing. In the context of Guatemala, where the state is largely absent in many rural areas and vigilante justice is common, there is also a potential risk that certain elements of pentecostalized religion can contribute to "uncivil society." The final section concludes with some predictions about the future political trajectory of pentecostalized religion in Guatemala and elsewhere in Latin America.

Conversion and the Pentecostalization
of Religious Practice in Guatemala

During the summer of 1993, a survey on religion and politics with a sample of 404 respondents was conducted in Guatemala City, Antigua, and the surrounding rural villages in the Department of Sacatepequez.[7] Survey respondents were coded as Catholics, Mainstream Protestants, Pentecostals, neo-Pentecostals, others (including Mormons, Jehovah's Witnesses, and Seventh-Day Adventists), and the religiously non-affiliated.

In table I, we can see that the experience of a personal conversion is widespread across religious affiliations in Guatemala. At first glance, these figures appear extraordinarily high (particularly for Catholics and the religiously non-affiliated). However, as we have argued throughout this volume, if we conceptualize conversion as a career or a continuum of religious commitment, we should expect to find high rates of reporting "conversion experiences" across religious groups. In a country like Guatemala, where the rapid expansion of the religious market provides multiple options and degrees of religious commitment to potential converts, the rate of conversion may be particularly high.[8]

Reports of conversion rates among Catholics (over 71 percent) and the religiously non-affiliated (25 percent) are the most likely to shock many observers. For Catholics, we can assume that a significant portion of these conversion experiences are related to the growth of Charismatic Catholicism, while others may be individuals who convert to social Catholicism. Still others may simply represent former non-practicing Catholics who re-entered the church after a conversion experience (as described in Christine Kovic's analysis of indigenous conversion in Mexico, in chapter 10). For the non-affiliated, there is clear evidence that there are a significant number of Guatemalans who have joined and left organized religious groups, or at least have attended religious services or events sufficiently to characterize themselves as having experienced a personal conversion. As part of the definition of pentecostalized religion, a dramatic personal conversion is certainly prevalent among all religious affiliations polled in Guatemala.

TABLE 13.1

Percent Experiencing Personal Conversion

Religious affiliation	Percent responding that they had experienced a personal conversion	n
Catholic	71.6	85
Mainstream	84.2	38
Pentecostal	90.3	200
Neo-Pentecostal	87.9	33
Other	69.6	23
Non-affiliated	25.0	25
Significance	$x^2=66.0$	
	P=.00000	

Pentecostalized Religious Experiences

Beyond the experience of conversion, the respondents we polled also reported high levels of the other key elements of pentecostalized religion (charismatic practices, millennialist beliefs, and biblical literalism). As we see in table 2, one of the most striking findings in this study is the high number of individuals across religious affiliations who report having experienced a miraculous cure of illness or injury.

Although Pentecostals (at an astonishing 88 percent) claim to have this experience more often than other groups, it is clear that a large portion of the Guatemalan population places great faith in religious healing of one form or another. As many as 64 percent of the religiously non-affiliated and more than 70 percent of Catholics reported having experienced miraculous cures. As Andrew Chesnut has noted in the Brazilian case, the importance of healing for understanding recruitment and conversion should not be underestimated.[9]

The pentecostalization of religion was also apparent in the high numbers of respondents who reported the experience of speaking in tongues. While it is not surprising that Pentecostals would report the experience of speaking in tongues at much higher levels than other groups, I found that 50 percent of Mainstream Protestants and nearly 20 percent of Catholics and the non-affiliated also reported the experience of glossolalia. These findings suggest that religious practice among mainstream denominations and even within a significant number of Catholic congregations has taken

TABLE 13.2

Religious Experiences by Religious Affiliation

	Miracle cure (%)	Tempted by the Devil (%)	Speak in tongues (%)	n
Catholic	70.6	63.4	19.8	85
Mainstream	84.2	76.3	50.0	38
Pentecostal	88.4	85.7	43.8	200
Neo-Pentecostal	78.8	78.1	51.5	33
Other	65.2	77.3	18.2	23
Non-affiliated	64.0	80.0	20.8	25
Significance	x^2=21.4	x^2=17.4	x^2=25.4	
	p=.00068	p=.00382	P=.00009	

on a distinctly Pentecostal flavor. A considerable subgroup of Catholics has clearly embraced one of the most defining characteristics of Pentecostalism. These Catholics appear to have more in common with their Protestant counterparts in terms of their religious practices and experiences than they do with other Catholics. I also found that Catholics who speak in tongues attend church more frequently than do other Catholics. Furthermore, Catholics who speak in tongues claim to have had the religious experiences of a miraculous cure (93 percent), of being tempted by the Devil (71 percent), and of a personal conversion to their present religion (94 percent) more often than other Catholics.[10]

Pentecostalized Religious Beliefs

The pentecostalization of religious practice in Guatemala is also evident in terms of religious beliefs. I found high numbers of Catholics and even the religiously non-affiliated (between 60 and 70 percent) to be biblical literalists who hold millennialist beliefs. On measures of millennialism, Pentecostals were the most millennialist with 78 percent agreeing or strongly agreeing that "Christians should not be concerned about this world because Christ will return soon to establish his kingdom." Eighty-seven percent of Pentecostals agreed or strongly agreed that "there are many 'signs of the end times' that signify that Christ will return soon"; 88 percent of neo-Pentecostals agreed or strongly agreed with this statement as well. Catholics and members of the "other" category had the lowest scores on these measures of millennialism, although roughly half of each group also concurred with such statements.[11]

Pentecostals and neo-Pentecostals also tended to hold more judgmental images of God than other religious groups. More than 90 percent of Pentecostals and neo-Pentecostals agreed or strongly agreed that "God judges all those who do wrong"; 85 percent of Pentecostals and 76 percent of neo-Pentecostals also agreed that "those who violate God's laws must be punished by God." Mainstream Protestants and members of the "other" category held the least judgmental images of God. Catholics exhibited an intermediate posture, but in all cases over 60 percent fell into the "judgmental image" category.[12]

In terms of doctrinal orthodoxy, Pentecostals and neo-Pentecostals again had the highest scores. Over 90 percent of these individuals agreed that "the Bible is inspired by God and must be accepted literally word for word" and over 95 percent agreed that "for my salvation I must believe that Christ died for our sins." Almost 80 percent of Pentecostals and neo-Pentecostals agreed that "God created the world in six days of twenty-four hours," but that percentage was never below 52 percent among other groups and reached 75 percent among the religiously non-affiliated. Once again, the most astonishing findings had to do with the high scores for Catholics and the religiously non-affiliated on all measures of pentecostalized religious beliefs. More than 60 percent of Catholics and the religiously non-affiliated agreed with six of the seven statements designed to measure the conservative religious beliefs that are generally associated with Pentecostal religion.[13]

Measuring Religious Intensity

As expected, Protestants in Guatemala also scored higher on measures of religious intensity than Catholics. More than 90 percent of Mainstream Protestants, Pentecostals, and neo-Pentecostals claimed to know the name of their pastor and nearly as many reported contributing money to their churches (see table 3). Interestingly, neo-Pentecostals scored lower than other Protestants on working for the church and being visited by their pastor. These latter findings are most likely a consequence of the size of the neo-Pentecostals churches, which tend to be much larger than most Protestant churches (the Fraternidad Cristiana is currently finishing construction on a massive new "Mega-Frater" building which is estimated to hold more than twenty thousand in the sanctuary alone). With churches of this size, it is not surprising that a relatively small percentage of the congregation gets visits from their pastor. This same principle applies to larger Catholic churches, accounting for lower scores on these measures of intensity among the Catholic population as well. In general, however, Mainstream and Pentecostal Protestants as well as sect members reported higher levels of religious intensity than Catholics.

As Henri Gooren argues in chapter 3, measures of religious intensity may cut both ways in terms of an individual's conversion career. On the one hand, closer contact with church representatives and holding a position within the church can be critical factors influencing the movement from affiliation to conversion and to confession. On the other hand, as Kurt Bowen has argued, the high demands associated with pentecostalized churches may be one factor that eventually leads to recidivism among converts.[14] In either case, this data provides substantial evidence to suggest a broad trend of pentecostalization in religious practice, beliefs, and intensity across religious affiliations in Guatemala.

Religious Affiliation, Pentecostalization, and Politics

Until recently, the conventional wisdom held that evangelicals (particularly Pentecostals) in Latin America are either politically conservative (based on conservative religious beliefs and ties to the North American religious right) or politically quiescent (due to otherworldly beliefs and the notion that politics is "tainted" and thus to be avoided). For the most part, Mainstream Protestants have been considered to be an exception to these rules.

TABLE 13.3

Measures of Religious Intensity by Religious Affiliation

	Catholic (%)	Mainstream (%)	Pentecostal (%)	Neo-Pentecostal (%)	Other (%)	Significance
Know the name of pastor/priest	43.5	94.7	90.0	97.0	78.3	x^2=94.1
						p=.0000
Have been visited by pastor/priest	14.1	52.6	56.5	18.2	65.2	x^2=54.3
						p=.0000
Do work for church	22.4	63.2	55.0	30.3	65.2	x^2=36.6
						p=.0000
Contribute $ to church	76.5	91.9	86.9	93.9	91.3	x^2=9.9
						p=.0430
n=	85	38	200	33	23	

Pentecostalization and Political Participation

The data I collected on religious affiliation in Guatemala substantiate the notion that Pentecostals are more likely than Catholics or the non-affiliated to find certain political activities (such as working for a political party, criticizing public officials, and running for public office) morally incorrect.[15] These negative attitudes toward certain political activities also translated into lower frequencies of engaging in those political activities among Pentecostal Protestants. A clear pattern emerged with Catholics the most willing to engage in political activities such as working for a political party and contacting public officials, while Pentecostals and members of other groups engaged less frequently in these relatively "hard" political acts. Comparing voting rates, however, differences between all Protestants and Catholics were not significant, with Mainstream and Pentecostal Protestants actually voting slightly more frequently than Catholics.[16]

At first glance, measures of political quiescence also appear to confirm the conventional wisdom about religious affiliation. Pentecostals were significantly more likely than Catholics or the non-affiliated to agree that political discussions serve no good purpose. In addition, Pentecostals and Mainstream Protestants were significantly more likely than Catholics to agree that the government should be obeyed in all circumstances.[17] Thus, it appears as though the *apolitical* tendencies ascribed to Protestants in the literature on Latin America have some merit. However, a more nuanced picture emerges when we take other relevant factors into account. Religious affiliation dropped out as a significant predictor of quiescent attitudes when other religious, political, and economic variables were added in multivariate analysis. Specifically, measures of pentecostalized religious beliefs and practices such as millennialism and the charismatic act of speaking in tongues emerged as better predictors of political quiescence across religious affiliations.[18] I will return to this important distinction below.

Pentecostalization and Political Attitudes

In terms of explicitly political attitudes, the conventional wisdom that links Protestantism to political conservatism is also apparently overstated. Pentecostals in Guatemala held political views about women and the poor that were not significantly different from Catholics. Differences in party affiliation, ideological position, and approval of political figures and organizations were minimal as well.[19] Within Protestantism, neo-Pentecostals were distinguishable for their higher rates of adherence to the "health and wealth" gospel, for less favorable evaluations of the poor, and for a correlation with placement on the right in an ideological scale.

While religious affiliation generally faded as a predictor of political conservatism and quiescence in my analysis of political variables, measures and markers for pentecostalized religious belief and practice emerged as important explanatory variables. In other words, the pentecostalized religious beliefs and charismatic experiences that are widespread across religious affiliations in Guatemala appear to be the most important religious factors driving political attitudes and actions.

Three prominent findings emerged from my study regarding the relationship between conservative religious beliefs and political variables. First, the most consistent effect of religious conservatism is in terms of political quiescence, with religious conservatives less likely to challenge political authority. In Guatemala, a scale of religious conservatism (created by combining responses measuring millennialism and theological orthodoxy) was positively related to agreement that the government should be obeyed in all circumstances, agreement that political discussions generally serve no good purpose, and placement on the right of an ideological scale. Individuals who are more millennialist and doctrinally orthodox may also be more likely to hold literal interpretations of biblical passages (such as Romans 13) that may discourage challenges to political authority. Despite this aversion to authority-challenging behavior, religious conservatism does not uniformly translate into significantly less political activity. As noted above, I found that religious conservatism actually has a positive influence on voting frequency in Guatemala.[20]

Second, there is a link between religious and political conservatism on the issue of attitudes toward the poor. Measures of religious conservatism are significantly related to agreement with the statement that the poor lack the impulse and ambition to get ahead. Again, this finding crosses religious affiliations and suggests that religious beliefs, rather than religious affiliations, serve as the most important religious explanatory variables for more conservative political attitudes.

Finally, on the issue of equal political rights for women, there is an interesting and counterintuitive relationship between religious conservatism and support for women's rights. As I have noted elsewhere, doctrinal orthodoxy is positively associated with agreement that women deserve all of the political rights and opportunities that men have.[21] This finding both corroborates and extends findings from earlier studies linking Pentecostalism and greater gender equality in Latin America. Elizabeth Brusco, David Smilde, Carol Ann Drogus, and others have argued that certain beliefs and practices within Latin American Pentecostalism may undermine machismo by providing a base for female authority in the home and for female associational participation within churches and other religious organizations.[22] My data suggests that these opportunities within the home and church may translate into a political ideal of gender equality among doctrinally orthodox Christians, extending into the public realm. In other words, doctrinally orthodox Christians may utilize biblical norms on equality (the priesthood of all believers and the creation of all people in the image of god) and obedience to political authority (the duty to obey legal norms on gender equality) to reinforce an ethic of equal rights for men and women in the public sphere. Doctrinally orthodox Guatemalan Christians (a group frequently assumed to be the most patriarchal and conservative in terms of Latin American gender relations) actually hold more favorable attitudes toward gender equality than other respondents. Combined with the changes in domestic relations and a culture of associational participation for women in Pentecostal churches, this counterintuitive finding provides powerful evidence that the pentecostalization of religion may be fundamentally altering gender relations in Guatemala and, by extension, elsewhere in Latin America.

Charismatic Christianity and Politics

Since the experience of speaking in tongues represents the clearest marker of religious charismaticism in Guatemala, it provides us with a simple classification scheme for Charismatics.[23] While the experience of speaking in tongues was not significantly related to measures of political orientations, it was related to both the frequency of engaging in political activities and measures of political quiescence. Glossolalia was negatively related to the scale of the perceived moral correctness of political acts, the frequency of voting, criticism of politicians, and community volunteer work. On measures of political quiescence, glossolalia was positively related to agreement that the government should be obeyed in all circumstances and that good citizens mind their own business.[24]

These findings suggest that religious charismaticism in Guatemala is related to political quiescence and a tendency to avoid political participation. In separate regression analyses with only Catholics in the sample, the relationships are the same, suggesting that it is religious charismaticism, and not religious affiliation, that is the crucial factor determining this outcome. It is important to note, however, that charismaticism is not necessarily associated with political conservatism. While Charismatics may be less likely to engage in political activity and may be more likely to support existing authorities, they are not more politically conservative than non-Charismatics.[25]

Interpreting the Complexities of Pentecostalized Politics

How can we interpret these results? First, the tendency among religiously conservative Charismatics (the pentecostalized) to respect and obey political authority is extremely strong. As noted earlier, practitioners of

pentecostalized religion in Latin America take a literal approach to biblical passages such as Romans 13 and Titus 3 that preach submission to
political authority. While these passages also include criteria for evaluating the legitimacy of political authorities, those passages tend to receive
less emphasis. One explanation for this selective literalism is rooted in the
history of Protestantism as a missionary religion in Latin America. Hoping
to avoid conflicts with political authorities that might jeopardize their missions, Protestant missionaries emphasized submission, with less attention
to the complexities of the political legitimacy of any specific regime. It is
no surprise that Guatemalan Pentecostals have adopted part of this message as part of the "package" of beliefs associated with religious conversion.
The Guatemalan case may even be an extreme version of this trend, given
its context of thirty years of civil war and a still tenuous human rights
situation.

The most significant implication of this trend, however, is that pentecostalized religious practitioners in Latin America could represent a solid
base of electoral support for any government or candidate for political office
(of the left or the right) as long as the government or candidate is considered to be representative of a duly constituted political authority. On the
other hand, politicians who blatantly violate the norms of pentecostalized
religion through involvement in corruption, personal immorality, or explicit
rejection of Pentecostal moral discourse may be considered illegitimate
and therefore lose their status as duly constituted authorities worthy of
support.

Second, this research does not support some of the more pessimistic
interpretations of the political effects of the growth of Pentecostalism in
Latin America. I found little evidence to suggest that evangelicals or even
the most pentecostalized religious practitioners in Guatemala hold views
that are necessarily authoritarian or antithetical to the values associated
with liberal democracy as Jean-Pierre Bastian has argued.[26] On the other
hand, the links between pentecostalization, quiescence, and some measures
of political conservatism call into question the more optimistic visions of
the relationship between Protestantism and democracy put forth by authors
such as David Martin and Amy Sherman.[27] Simply put, the political tendencies associated with conversion to Pentecostalism do not fit neatly into the
categories of "authoritarian" or "democratic." We are therefore better served
by characterizing the political outcomes of conversion to Pentecostalism as
a function of the interactions between pentecostalized beliefs and variant
democratic or authoritarian political contexts rather than as a direct result
of those practices and beliefs.[28]

So what are we to make of these mixed findings for understanding the
political impact of pentecostalized conversion both within and between

religious affiliations in Latin America? As we have argued throughout this volume, we must begin by understanding that conversion itself is a complex process with multiple levels and changes over time. The political implications of such a complex and long-term process are bound to defy simple generalizations. When we do attempt to generalize from religious variables to political outcomes and processes, we must take great care to carefully define the religious and political concepts and variables being used. As I have argued here, the high degree of pentecostalization across religious groups in Guatemala serves as a clear message that specific beliefs and practices must be disaggregated if we wish to understand their political impact as independent variables. As for the dependent variables, interpreting the intricate relationship between pentecostalization and democracy in Latin America requires further inquiry into the specific mechanisms that have been posited as the democracy-enhancing elements of pentecostalized religion. The concepts of civil society, citizenship, and community lay at the core of any such endeavor.

Community, Citizenship, and Democracy

As Carol Ann Drogus has noted, the debate surrounding religion and democratization in Latin America is hampered by multiple interpretations of the concept of civil society.[29] If civil society is understood simply as the growth of autonomous, voluntary organizations, there is little doubt that increasing religious pluralism enriches civil society in Guatemala and elsewhere in Latin America. However, more demanding definitions of civil society require a clearer articulation of the links between associational participation and democratic deepening. After all, thriving voluntary organizations that encourage racism, intolerance, or even violence may do little to enhance the quality of democracy. Studies by Newton J. Gaskill and Andrew Chesnut, for example, have argued that Protestantism may meet a minimalist definition of civil society in Latin America, but the broader political implications of Pentecostalism do more to reinforce patronage and clientalism than to deepen democracy.[30]

In the Guatemalan case, the absence of state authorities in rural communities combined with widespread vigilantism has led to a particularly heinous form of what John Booth and Patricia Richard have called uncivil society.[31] During 2005, nearly three thousand *linchamientos* (mob lynchings) took place in the country. In at least one instance, in the lakeside village of San Lucas Tolíman, the lynching was instigated and carried out by a group of evangelicals.[32] While Pentecostal participation in this sort of "social cleansing" appears to be the exception rather than the rule in Guatemala, the case of San Lucas suggests one particularly disturbing trajectory for pentecostalization in other areas suffering from a similar disintegration of civil society.[33] In the absence of a functioning judicial system, radicalized Pentecostals may vie for the role of self-appointed moral enforcers with traditional Mayan systems of authority and punishment, leading to greater extra-judicial violence in the countryside. Though I would not estimate that connection between Pentecostalism and vigilante justice is widespread in Guatemala, this particular convergence of religion and mob violence merits further study.

On the other hand, some of the more dire predictions about the political implications of Pentecostalism are not universally accepted by analysts who also adopt a more demanding definition of civil society. Paul Freston, Michael Dodson, Rowan Ireland, Phillip J. Williams, Christian Smith, and Carol Ann Drogus all explicitly or implicitly seek to apply some version of Alexis de Tocqueville's arguments concerning popular religion and democratization to Pentecostalism in Latin America.[34] According to these authors, Pentecostalism may foster egalitarianism, civility, initiative, and community engagement among religious participants, thereby increasing civic engagement and possibly strengthening democracy. The extent to which democracy is strengthened, however, may vary in relation to the political opportunity structure and to evolving conceptions of civil and social citizenship rights.[35] Links between religion and democracy are mediated by regime type and the degree to which democratizing potential may be circumscribed by local national or international factors that inhibit the transformational potential of social movements in general.

Phillip Williams and Manuel Vásquez also pay special attention to the concept of civil and uncivil society in Latin America, but in this case arguing that Pentecostalism may ameliorate the widespread culture of violence in war-torn contexts such as El Salvador and Peru. According to Vásquez, "Maybe what is involved here is a deeper, simultaneously more foundational and more encompassing definition of democratic politics. Perhaps it involves not just the institutions and procedures of formal democracy but the formation of a 'culture of citizenship' as Elizabeth Jelin puts it, in which individuals learn responsibility and care toward self and others."[36]

Vásquez cites evidence from studies in El Salvador, Peru, and Brazil that demonstrate the community-level actions of evangelical communities. In El Salvador, Ileana Gómez details the role of evangelical churches in dealing with the pressing issues of crime and youth gangs in Morazán.[37] In her 1999 study of neighborhood politics in Huaycán, Peru, Hortensia Muñoz concludes that evangelical churches, like Catholic Base Christian Communities, may provide participants with the basic skills and motivations necessary for community-level political action.[38] In the case of Venezuela, David Smilde shows how Pentecostal plaza services provide members of Caracas's politically marginalized lower classes with a space for public discussion of national life through the alterative rationality provided by evangelical meanings.[39] Common to these studies is the notion that while religious factors may not lead directly to the formation of political parties or mass-based political action, the effects of pentecostalized religion are no less "political" in that they provide resources, generate grievances, provide citizenship identities, and mobilize opinions around issues that impact the day-to-day lives of participants. Whether or not these processes lead to more macro-level democratic politics in Latin America has more to do with the contexts in which they take place than with the processes themselves.

Evidence from the Guatemalan Case

The evidence I have collected from Guatemala provides clear support for the kind of careful and well-defined claims about religion and democracy that characterize much of this recent literature on Pentecostalism and politics. While I found political activity among many Pentecostal Protestants and Charismatic Catholics to be circumscribed by literal interpretations of Romans 13 (on submission to political authorities), most individuals I spoke with did not interpret this as a permanent barrier to political action. One theme that arose multiple times during interviews with pastors and church workers was the idea that Christians should participate in politics because it is both their right and their duty to do so. In other words, evangelicals and Charismatic Catholics appeared to take their duties as citizens quite seriously. A number of those I interviewed referred to participation in terms of the right to vote, with most evangelicals emphasizing that they are "equal" to other groups and that religion should not be an obstacle to voting. As one young Pentecostal explained, "Evangelicals should participate, because we are all equal; the only difference is religion, and this is not an obstacle because we have the right to vote."

These qualitative insights provide keys for interpreting trends in the survey data. I found that Pentecostals and Mainstream Protestants were more likely than Catholics and the religiously non-affiliated to see voting as morally correct. Pentecostals and members of sects were also significantly more likely than Catholics and Mainstream Protestants to rate as morally incorrect other political activities such as running for public office, criticizing public officials, working for a political party, or working for a political campaign.[40] These findings may be understood in light of the attitudes expressed by many of the evangelicals I interviewed. Pentecostals in Guatemala tend to perceive their political involvement as a duty and a right. They express this right primarily through the act of voting or through taking on other political "duties."

A recent interview with an indigenous Pentecostal pastor in a small village near Quetzaltenango was particularly illuminating. When asked about the relationship between Pentecostalism and politics, he replied:

> You have to understand that God is everywhere: in church, work, school, sports, everywhere. That is what most people don't understand about us. . . . We are not of the world, but we live in the world. . . . In the church, we use a completely different language [than what] is used in the political realm, but we have to respect the importance of politics and their way of speaking. I served as mayor when I was called upon to do so. My dream, for the long-term, is to create a clinic and a private school here on the land we have purchased. That is the only way that we can bring development to this community, to provide our children with a moral foundation and provide them with the skills to move ahead.

The central themes that emerged in my interviews with Pentecostals and Charismatic Catholics had to do with civic duties and rights, fighting corruption, and the need for community-level participation. These themes resonate with the well-defined claims about civil (and uncivil) society made by many of the authors discussed above. In Guatemala, the trend is that pentecostalized religion generally contributes to civil society by encouraging volunteerism, self-help, space for public dialogue, and an ethic of equality before the law. It should come as no surprise that the ongoing political effects of pentecostalized religion in Guatemala will be less visible at the level of party organization and protest activity and more pronounced in terms of community building, self-help, and local resource mobilization. The degree to which these activities translate into a stronger civil society or facilitate a political culture of clientalism depends upon the larger institutional and political context of Guatemalan democracy. The economic and political impediments to democratic deepening in Guatemala remain strong, circumscribing many of the potential positive contributions of pentecostalized religion and accentuating the tendency toward quiescence, clientalism, and, in the worst cases, religiously organized intolerance and violence.

Looking to the Future: The Politics of Pentecostalized Religion in Latin America

Given that evangelicals and Charismatic Catholics are not averse to political participation, what sort of political agenda might we expect from these groups in the future? Analysis of my data suggests a more complex perspective on politics and political participation among these groups than has often been assumed. Like John Burdick, Carol Ann Drogus, and Rowand

Ireland in their studies of Brazil, I found evidence of a complex set of political views among pentecostalized converts in the Guatemalan case, making them difficult to characterize.[41] My research does suggest, however, that there are certain touchstones around which the pentecostalized may become mobilized.

Mayanization and Pentecostalization

The evolution of Mayan Protestantism in Guatemala, particularly as it relates to conversion, merits further scholarly inquiry and attention. As Virginia Garrard-Burnett has argued, it is precisely the "binary" worldview of converts, dividing their lives into the time before and after they experienced their conversion, that stands as the greatest obstacle to the widespread adoption of an evangelical inculturation theology: a religious worldview that incorporates both a Mayan cosmovision and a set of pentecostalized religious beliefs and practices.[42] However, there appears to be a growing number of Pentecostals who are finding their own ways to mediate this tension. Garrard Burnett explains:

> Yet the pull of Mayan cultural and spiritual identity remains strong, even for Pentecostals. This seems particularly true for Mayan evangélicos who are long established in their conversions or who have been brought up in a Protestant church. With more distance from the conversion experience, some Mayan evangélicos are seeking ways to bridge whatever cognitive dissonance they may feel between their religion and their culture. For them, the accommodation of the full spectrum of Mayan beliefs—cosmovision, Catholicism, and Pentecostalism—becomes more a matter of spiritual discernment than of theological or political debate.[43]

My recent experience in Guatemala suggests that this process may be accelerating and spreading among many indigenous Pentecostals. In a day-long workshop, "Mayanization of Daily Life," sponsored and attended by Mayan activists and academics, I observed a fascinating exchange between some of the participants.[44] The workshop included commentaries based on sixteen ethnographies of Mayan communities throughout the country. After one presenter outlined the role of religion across these communities, a Mayan activist in the audience gave a scathing critique of the role of Pentecostal churches in Mayan communities, calling them "dividers of our people and destroyers of our culture." Afterwards, a number of the individuals who had conducted the fieldwork expressed their clear disagreement with his position. As one young student explained, "In the community where I did my fieldwork, the very same people you see in the evangelical churches also participate in Mayan rituals. I have seen it with my own eyes. While there may be some divisions, to consider them as an enemy to the Mayan movement is probably wrong. They are just as 'Mayan' as they were before they converted." His perspective was echoed by the others who had conducted fieldwork in other locations.

The process of inculturation theology (or to put it another way, the "Mayanization" of Pentecostalism) is important because, though incipient, it could open the door to greater inclusiveness and effectiveness for the Mayan movement in Guatemala. On the other hand, ethnic, ideological, and other divisions within the Mayan movement as well as theological and political differences within the higher ranks of evangelical churches are likely to limit national-level cooperation. Ironically, it is the very dualism (good/evil, past/present) within the Pentecostal conversion narrative and practice that maintains indigenous cultural and religious elements perpetually within the mind frame of indigenous Pentecostals. As Jorge Casanova has argued about Pentecostalism in a global context, "It is in their very struggle against local culture that they prove how locally rooted they are."[45]

When I asked the same Pentecostal pastor (and former mayor) of the small town near Quetzaltenango about the role of the multiple evangelical churches and the Catholic Church in his town, he told me that, for the most part, the people who attend the churches cooperate and get along quite well. The problem, he said, is with leadership: "We have a great spirit of community here and there is really no need for divisions. The big problem is that sometimes church leaders are poorly trained both theologically and in terms of development. How are we going to promote development if we can't cooperate with each other?" When I asked him how he conceptualized his identity as both a Mayan and an evangelical, he took out a piece of paper and drew me a figure with two columns with the headings "God" and "Mayan culture." Down the left column he wrote *traje* (the traditional Mayan dress), "language" (*Caq'chikel*), *costumbre* (locally proscribed religious beliefs and life ways), and "religion." For each word, he drew an arrow across to the right-hand column and provided me with an explanation:

> With the traje, we have no problem. My wife and my daughters all wear the traje with pride. Language? Caq'chikel is my mother tongue. Although I learned Spanish in school, I still speak with my family and friends in Caq'chikel. Costumbre? Well, there are some elements that are acceptable. For the most part I have no problem with practicing costumbre. But religion, that is the big problem. You see the ones who truly practice Mayan religion have many minor gods, and we have only one true god. That we cannot reconcile.

This particular Pentecostal pastor's description of his "way of being Mayan" holds elements of both the potential and the limits of Mayan

pentecostalization for incorporation into a larger pan-Mayan political movement. As was abundantly clear at the Mayanization workshop, there are
strong differences of opinion as to the role that Mayan religion should play
in the Mayan movement in Guatemala. Given the high rate of pentecostalization among the indigenous population of Guatemala, the strategic move for
Mayan leaders might be to take a more inclusive tone with relation to both
the Catholic Church and evangelical churches. On the other hand, there are
clear limits to how far Pentecostals will go in defining their Mayan identity beside and within their identity as Pentecostals. If a minimal common
agenda can be established between these groups, the potential for a significantly more potent local and national Mayan movement in Guatemala exists.
Given that the pentecostalized are not averse to local political involvement,
vote in high numbers, and are not necessarily politically conservative, they
represent a major untapped resource in the campaign for indigenous rights
and local development in Guatemala.

A Pentecostalized Religious Right?

The second major potential political trajectory of pentecostalization in
Guatemala cuts in a completely different direction. Not surprisingly, most
of the evangelical pastors with whom I spoke in Guatemala cited the traditional evangelical issues of abortion, drugs, and homosexuality among the
concerns for Christians in their countries. Interestingly, the Catholic bishops
in Central America have expressed similar concerns.[46] Given this convergence in political interest and the high number of pentecostalized Catholics
in Central America, it appears as though the groundwork for a conservative ecumenical political movement may also be in place. However, a final
critical issue for Pentecostals makes such a coalition unlikely: the hotly con-
tested question of the relationship between church and state. In Guatemala,
as elsewhere in Latin America, the issue of the legal status and privileges of
the Catholic Church are primary issues for Protestants. Although Catholicism has no status as the state religion in Guatemala, the Catholic Church
is automatically recognized as a distinct legal personality in the Guatemalan
constitution, making it exempt from the bureaucratic processes required of
other religious organizations who seek to rent or purchase property or gain
tax-exempt status. The political sparring between the Catholic bishops and
Guatemala's two Protestant presidents has left a bitter taste in the mouths
of many evangelicals and Catholics. The issue is unlikely to fade anytime in
the near future.

In sum, the process of conversion to pentecostalized religious practice
and beliefs in Guatemala is not likely to lead to a single political trajectory among evangelicals and Charismatic Catholics. While the basis for
agreement on some issues of public morality is latent, disagreements over

questions of church and state are likely to curb the propensity for ecumenical movements of the religious right. Furthermore, the complexity of political opinions among the Pentecostals and Charismatic Catholics I polled and interviewed should give pause to those who would characterize them as monolithically politically conservative. The pentecostalized may vote for candidates who appeal to certain widely held values, but they will likely be divided in terms of both their political agenda and the actions they are willing to take in the political arena.[47] The pentecostalized may be good citizens who respect authority and tend to abide by the laws, but this does not mean that they will embrace authoritarianism or hold ultra-conservative views.

Moving beyond Guatemala

There is recent evidence to suggest that those who experience a conversion to pentecostalized forms of religious practice are also available as potential political supporters for populist, anti-neoliberal, or even leftist candidates or governments in Latin America. In a 1999 random sample poll following the election of Hugo Chavez in Venezuela, 60 percent of evangelical respondents reported that they voted for Chavez. In the same poll, the questions I used in Guatemala to measure pentecostalization were inserted, with strikingly similar results. In other words, as in Guatemala, the Venezuelan population is highly pentecostalized across religious affiliations. Thus, it appears as though pentecostalized religious beliefs and practices did not significantly reduce support for Chavez. I would not be surprised to find similar results in electoral data for recent elections in Ecuador, Bolivia, or Peru.

The potential convergence of pentecostalization with indigenous identity politics also remains a fertile field for further study. Although there are core elements of the Pentecostal conversion process that fundamentally conflict with many of the religious aspects of indigenous identity, the Guatemalan case suggests that the everyday practice of lived religion among the pentecostalized may be far more flexible than church leaders or indigenous activists would admit. This finding underscores a wider theme within the worldwide study of Pentecostalism; the recognition of Pentecostalism's somewhat unique ability to simultaneously maintain elements of both the global and the local. As Joel Robbins has recently argued, Pentecostalism is not really undergoing a process of "syncretic melding" with "primal forms" of indigenous religion worldwide. To the contrary, Pentecostalism maintains an ongoing dialogue with local religion and culture precisely because of the sharp division Pentecostals place on life pre- and post-conversion, keeping the world of local spirits and practices alive at the forefront of the Pentecostal worldview.[48] Constant reminders from the pulpit and fellow congregants about the potential power and seduction of local deities and practices may serve as both an attractant and a repellent for indigenous Pentecostals, explaining the discrepancy between official religious and cultural discourse and findings from ethnographers studying the everyday practice of religion.

Without question, some of the most interesting and substantial political effects of the pentecostalization of religion in Latin America are those that defy broad generalizations and thus tend to remain under the radar of many social science analyses. Religion often serves to motivate social and political changes that are difficult to discern and interpret because they are not immediately recognizable at the level of national politics. While Protestant political parties, evangelical presidents, and right-wing televangelists provide tangible and familiar subjects for analysis, the household politics of gender, church-related community volunteerism, changes in public discourse, and religiously motivated attitudes toward citizenship can be more difficult to measure and evaluate.

Some of the conservative religious beliefs associated with pentecostalized religion in Latin America have been utilized to turn traditional power relations on their head in terms of gender.[49] Biblical passages and a worldview which pits good against evil, God against the devil, and the righteous against the sinful may be used to formulate justifications for what might be considered progressive or even subversive political opinions, such as calls for economic or gender equality. Indeed, as David Smilde has pointed out, a political candidate (such as Hugo Chavez in Venezuela) who explicitly appeals to a Pentecostal discourse may gain the support of pentecostalized voters even if the candidate does not share a religious affiliation with these voters.[50]

The pentecostalization of religion in Latin America represents neither a new reformation, with myriad implications for democracy and development, nor a simple continuation of clientalist traditions, with absolutely no transformational potential. As a relatively young religious movement in Latin America, Pentecostalism has already done much to reshape the religious, the social, and, to some degree, the political landscape of the region. It is likely that the most durable and consequential effects of conversion to pentecostalized religion will be those that have taken place quietly in the homes, plazas, and churches of Latin America, changes in beliefs, motivations, volunteerism, and confidence. The long-term political impact of these changes will depend primarily upon the political opportunity structure in which they take place.

NOTES

1. The degree to which Charismatic Catholics adhere to biblical literalism has varied across time and national context. See chapter 8 of this volume for a more complete history of the Catholic Charismatic Renewal within the Catholic Church.

2. As noted in the introduction, the generally agreed upon figure in academic circles for non-Catholics in Guatemala is between 25 and 30 percent.

3. See David Martin, *Tongues of Fire: The Explosion of Protestantism in Latin America* (Oxford: Basil Blackwell, 1990); and Amy Sherman, *The Soul of Development: Biblical Christianity and Economic Transformation in Guatemala* (Oxford: Oxford University Press, 1997).

4. See Jean Pierre Bastian, "The Metamorphosis of Latin American Protestant Groups: A Sociohistorical Perspective," *Latin American Research Review* 28 (1993): 33–62; and Steve Brouwer, Paul Gifford, and Susan Rose, *Exporting the American Gospel: Global Christian Fundamentalism* (New York: Routledge, 1996).

5. Carol Ann Drogus, "Religious Pluralism and Social Change: Coming to Terms with Complexity and Convergence," *Latin American Research Review* 35 (2000): 263–265.

6. See Paul Freston, *Evangelicals and Politics in Asia, Africa, and Latin America* (New York: Cambridge University Press, 2001). Also see Paul Freston, "Charismatic Evangelicals in Latin America: Mission and Politics on the Frontiers of Protestant Growth," in *Charismatic Christianity: Sociological Perspectives*, ed. S. Hunt, M. Hamilton, and T. Walker (New York: St. Martin's Press, 1997), 184–204. Also see Rowan Ireland, *Kingdoms Come: Religion and Politics in Brazil* (Pittsburgh: University of Pittsburgh Press, 1991).

7. For a complete description of the sample and methods, see Timothy Steigenga, *The Politics of the Spirit: The Political Implications of the Growth of Pentecostalized Religion in Central America* (Baltimore: Lexington Press, 2001).

8. Indeed, in the Costa Rican context the conversion rate for Catholics was significantly lower, at only 52 percent. Steigenga, *The Politics of the Spirit*, 113.

9. Andrew Chesnut, *Born Again in Brazil: The Pentecostal Boom and the Pathogens of Poverty* (New Brunswick, NJ: Rutgers University Press, 1997).

10. See Steigenga, *The Politics of the Spirit*.

11. See Timothy Steigenga, "Democracia y el crecimiento del protestantismo evangélico en Guatemala: Entendiendo la complejidad política de la religión pentecostalizada," *América Latina Hoy* 41 (2005): 99–119.

12. Ibid.

13. Ibid.

14. See Kurt Bowen, *Evangelism and Apostasy: The Evolution and Impact of Evangelicals in Modern Mexico* (Montreal: McGill-Queen's University Press, 1996).

15. Steigenga, *The Politics of the Spirit*, 167.

16. Ibid., 85–86.

17. See Steigenga, "Democracia y el crecimiento," 108.

18. Ibid., 94–96.

19. Ibid., 87–91.

20. Of course, voting may be understood as yet another form of support for the current political system rather than an authority-challenging political behavior.

21. Timothy Steigenga and David Smilde, "Wrapped in the Holy Shawl: The Strange Case of Conservative Christians and Gender Equality in Latin America," in *Latin American Religion in Motion*, ed. Christian Smith and Joshua Prokopy (New York: Routledge, 1999), 147–173; and Steigenga, *The Politics of the Spirit*.

22. Elizabeth Brusco, "The Reformation of Machismo: Asceticism and Masculinity among Colombian Evangelicals," in *Rethinking Protestantism in Latin America*, ed. Virginia Garrard-Burnett and David Stoll (Philadelphia: Temple University Press, 1993), 143–158; David Smilde, "Gender Relations and Social Change in Latin American Evangelicalism," in *Coming of Age: Protestantism in Contemporary Latin America*, ed. Daniel R. Miller (New York: University Press of America, 1994), 39–64; David Smilde, "The Fundamental Unity of the Conservative and Revolutionary Tendencies in Venezuelan Religion: The Case of Conjugal Relations," *Religion* 27 (1997): 343–359; Carol Ann Drogus, "Private Power and Public Power: Pentecostalism, Base Communities, and Gender," in *Power, Politics, and Pentecostals in Latin America*, ed. Edward L. Cleary, O. P. Stewart-Gambino, and Hannah Stewart-Gambino (Boulder, CO: Westview Press, 1997), 55–75.

23. This is with the caveat that those who have not had the experience of speaking in tongues may also be Charismatic, since not all Charismatics actually have this religious experience. See chapter 8 for a more complete description of the evolution of the Catholic Charismatic Renewal.

24. See Steigenga, *The Politics of the Spirit*, 169.

25. Ibid. 169.

26. Bastian, "The Metamorphosis of Latin American Protestant Groups," and Jean Pierre Bastian, "Protestantism in Latin America," in *The Church in Latin America: 1492–1992*, ed. Enrique Dussell (Maryknoll, NY: Orbis, 1992).

27. David Martin, *Tongues of Fire: The Explosion of Protestantism in Latin America* (Oxford: Basil Blackwell, 1990); Sherman, *The Soul of Development*.

28. For a more complete elaboration of this argument see Steigenga, *The Politics of the Spirit*. Also see David Smilde, "Contradiction without Paradox: Evangelical Political Culture in the 1998 Venezuelan Elections," *Latin American Politics and Society* 46 (1999): 75–102.

29. Drogus, "Religious Pluralism and Social Change."

30. Newton J. Gaskill, "Rethinking Protestantism and Democratic Consolidation in Latin America," *Sociology of Religion* 58 (1997): 69–91; Chesnut, *Born Again in Brazil*.

31. John Booth and Patricia Richard, "Civil Society, Political Capital, and Democratization in Central America," *Journal of Politics* 60 (1998): 780–801.

32. See Virginia Garrard-Burnett's transcript of talk given on "Christianity and Conflict in Latin America," Thursday, April 6, 2006, National Defense University, Washington, D.C., posted on the Web site of the Pew Forum on Religion and Public Life, http://pewforum.org/events/index.php?EventID=102.

33. Garrard-Burnett, "Christianity and Conflict."

34. Freston, *Evangelicals and Politics*; Michael Dodson, "Pentecostals, Politics, and Public Space in Latin America," in *Conflict and Competition*, ed. Cleary, Stewart-Gambino, and Stewart-Gambino, 25–40; Edward Rowan Ireland, "Popular Religions and the Building of Democracy in Latin America: Saving the Tocquevillian Parallel," *Journal of Interamerican Studies and World Affairs* 41 (1999): 111–136; Phillip J. Williams, "Religious Pluralism, Citizenship, and Democracy in Latin America," paper presented at the Latin American Studies Association Meeting, Miami, 2000; Christian Smith, "The Spirit and Democracy: Base Communities, Protestantism, and Democratization in Latin America," *Sociology of Religion* 55 (1994): 119–142; Drogus, "Religious Pluralism and Social Change."

35. See Williams, "Religious Pluralism," 10.

36. Manuel Vásquez, "Toward a New Agenda for the Study of Religion in the Americas," *Journal of Interamerican Studies and World Affairs* 41, no. 6 (1999): 1–20.

37. Ileana Gómez, "Religious and Social Participation in War-Torn Areas of El Salvador," *Journal of Interamerican Studies and World Affairs* 41 (1999): 53–72.

38. Hortensia Muñoz, "Believers and Neighbors: Huaycán Is One and No One Shall Divide It," *Journal of Interamerican Studies and World Affairs* 41, no. 8 (1999): 73–92.

39. See David Smilde, "Popular Publics: Street Protest and Plaza Preachers in Caracas," *International Review of Social History* 49, Supplement (2004): 179–195. Also see Smilde in chapter 5 of this volume.

40. Steigenga, *The Politics of the Spirit.*

41. John Burdick, *Looking for God in Brazil: The Progressive Catholic Church in Urban Brazil's Religious Arena* (Berkeley: University of California Press, 1993); Carol Ann Drogus, "No Land of Milk and Honey: Women CEB Activists in Post-transition Brazil," *Journal of Interamerican Studies and World Affairs* 41 (1999): 21–34; Ireland, "Popular Religions and the Building of Democracy in Latin America."

42. See Virginia Garrard-Burnett, "God Was Already Here When Columbus Arrived: Inculturation Theology and the Mayan Movement in Guatemala," in *Resurgent Voices in Latin America: Indigenous Peoples, Political Mobilization, and Religious Change*, ed. Edward L. Cleary and Timothy J. Steigenga (New Brunswick, NJ: Rutgers University Press, 2004), 125–153.

43. Garrard-Burnett, "God Was Already Here," 114.

44. "Mayanización y vida cotidiana: La ideología y el discurso multicultural en la sociedad guatemalteca," 6ª Encuentro de Discusión, jueves, May 4, 2006, Centro de Formación de la Cooperación Española en La Antigua Guatemala.

45. Jorge Casanova, "Religion, the New Millennium, and Globalization," *Sociology of Religion* 62, no. 4 (winter 2001): 415–441, 438.

46. Brian H. Smith, *Religious Politics in Latin America: Pentecostal vs. Catholic* (Notre Dame, IN: Notre Dame Press, 1997), 97.

47. See Smilde, "Contradiction without Paradox," 75–102.

48. Joel Robbins, "The Globalization of Charismatic and Pentecostal Christianity," *Annual Review of Anthropology* 33 (2004): 117–143, 129, 130.

49. Steigenga and Smilde, "Wrapped in the Holy Shawl."

50. Smilde, "Contradiction without Paradox."

CONTRIBUTORS

PATRICIA BIRMAN obtained her PhD in anthropology from the Federal University of Rio de Janeiro. She did post-doctoral studies at the Ecole des Hautes Etudes en Sciences Sociales (EHESS), France. She is full professor of anthropology at the State University of Rio de Janeiro. She has published more than forty-five articles in journals and twenty-three chapters in books in France, the United States, and Brazil.

MARÍA JULIA CAROZZI is a tenured research fellow of the National Council for Scientific Research in Argentina. She received her PhD degree in anthropology from the University of California, Los Angeles, in 1988 and since then has conducted research on religious conversion processes, the construction of religious movement frames through discourse and interaction, and the sacralization of bodies in popular religion. Her most recent books are *A Nova Era no Mercosul* (1999) and *Nueva Era y Terapias Alternativas. Construyendo significados en el Discurso y la Interacción* (2000). She is currently researching the social mechanisms of knowledge transmission in popular religion.

ANDREW CHESNUT is a professor of history at the University of Houston. His research focuses on religion in twentieth-century Brazilian and Latin American history. His first book, *Born Again in Brazil: The Pentecostal Boom and the Pathogens of Poverty* (1997), examines the meteoric growth of Pentecostalism among the popular classes of Brazil. His second book, *Competitive Spirits: Latin America's New Religious Economy* (2003), considers the three religious groups that have prospered the most in the region's new pluralist landscape.

EDWARD L. CLEARY is a professor of political science and the director of Latin American Studies at Providence College. He lived and worked in Latin America for many years and edited *Estudios Andinos*, a periodical dedicated to the Andean region and its indigenous population, for six of those years. His publications include seven books and numerous articles and chapters on themes ranging from indigenous spirituality to human rights, religious competition, and popular religion in Latin America.

RACHEL CORR is associate professor of anthropology at Harriet L. Wilkes Honors College, Florida Atlantic University. She has been undertaking research in Ecuador since 1990 and has published several articles on South American cultural systems. Her research focuses on historical and cosmological concepts of space, religious experience, and ethnic diversity.

ALEJANDRO FRIGERIO lives, teaches, and carries on research in Buenos Aires at the Universidad Católica Argentina. He has studied the expansion of Afro-Brazilian religions in the Southern Cone for the past twenty years, focusing especially on the construction of personal, social, and collective identities and on the increasing social problematization these religions have undergone. His most recent interests include the role of folk religious beliefs in the development of occult economies and the relations between religion, space, and race. He has edited four volumes on the study of new religious movements in Argentina and the Southern Cone and has published numerous articles in books and journals in Latin America, Europe, and the United States.

VIRGINIA GARRARD-BURNETT is an associate professor in history and Latin American studies and interim director of Religious Studies at the University of Texas in Austin. She is author or editor of three books and numerous articles on religion in Latin America.

HENRI GOOREN is a post-doctoral researcher with the Faculty of Theology at Utrecht University in the Netherlands. He has done fieldwork on religion in Costa Rica, Guatemala, and Nicaragua and published articles on Catholicism, Protestantism, and Mormonism in all of these countries. His dissertation, "Rich among the Poor: Church, Firm, and Household among Small-Scale Entrepreneurs in Guatemala City" (1999), analyzes the relationship between church membership and running a microenterprise. Gooren is currently working on a book to be entitled "Conversion Careers: Why People Become and Remain Religiously Active."

CHRISTINE KOVIC is an associate professor of anthropology at the University of Houston, Clear Lake. She has spent long periods living and researching in Chiapas, Mexico. Since 1993, she has conducted research on the issues of indigenous rights and the Catholic Church in highland Chiapas. She has recently published two books based on this research: *Women in Chiapas* (2003) and *Mayan Voices for Human Rights* (2005). Her recent research focuses on the human rights of Central Americans crossing southern Mexico en route to the United States.

DAVID SMILDE is associate professor of sociology at the University of Georgia and is currently serving as a Fulbright scholar to Venezuela. He is author of *Reason to Believe: Cultural Agency in Latin American Evangelicalism* (2007).

TIMOTHY J. STEIGENGA is an associate professor of political science and Latin American studies at the Harriet L. Wilkes Honors College of Florida Atlantic University. He has published multiple articles and chapters on religion and politics in Latin America as well as two recent books: *The Politics of the Spirit: The Political Effects of the Pentecostalization of Religion in Guatemala and Costa Rica* (2001) and *Resurgent Voices in Latin America: Indigenous Peoples, Political Mobilization, and Religious Change* (2004). His current research focuses on issues of transnationalism, migration, and religion.

JILL M. WIGHTMAN is a visiting instructor at Knox College and a PhD candidate in anthropology at the University of Illinois at Urbana-Champaign. Her research interests include religious conversion, neoliberalism and globalization, and medical anthropology.

INDEX